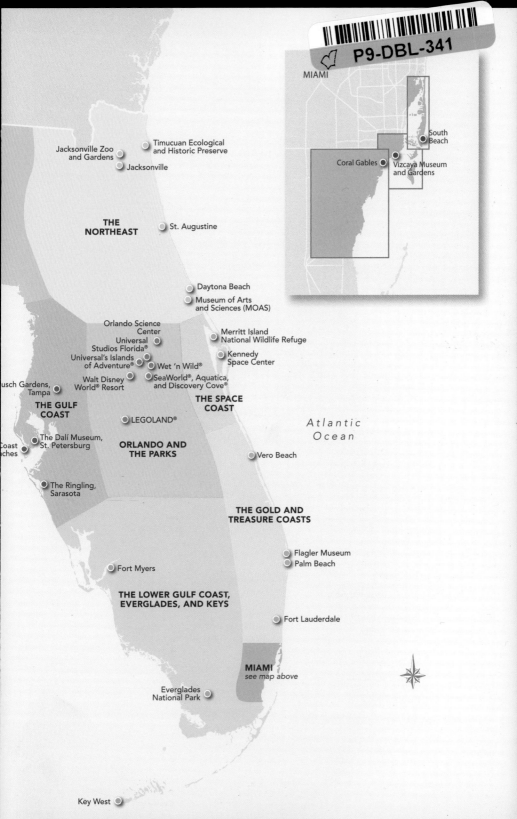

P9-DBL-341

MIAMI

South Beach

Coral Gables

Vizcaya Museum and Gardens

Jacksonville Zoo and Gardens

Timucuan Ecological and Historic Preserve

Jacksonville

THE NORTHEAST

St. Augustine

Daytona Beach

Museum of Arts and Sciences (MOAS)

Orlando Science Center

Universal Studios Florida®

Universal's Islands of Adventure®

Wet 'n Wild®

Walt Disney World® Resort

SeaWorld®, Aquatica, and Discovery Cove®

Merritt Island National Wildlife Refuge

Kennedy Space Center

...usch Gardens, Tampa

THE GULF COAST

THE SPACE COAST

Atlantic Ocean

LEGOLAND®

The Dalí Museum, St. Petersburg

...Coast ...ches

ORLANDO AND THE PARKS

Vero Beach

The Ringling, Sarasota

THE GOLD AND TREASURE COASTS

Flagler Museum

Palm Beach

Fort Myers

THE LOWER GULF COAST, EVERGLADES, AND KEYS

Fort Lauderdale

MIAMI
see map above

Everglades National Park

Key West

EYEWITNESS TRAVEL

FAMILY GUIDE

FLORIDA

EYEWITNESS TRAVEL

FAMILY GUIDE

FLORIDA

Penguin
Random
House

MANAGING EDITOR
MadhuMadhavi Singh

EDITORIAL MANAGER
Sheeba Bhatnagar

DESIGN MANAGER Mathew Kurien

PROJECT EDITOR Shreya Sarkar

EDITORS Shobhna Iyer,
Sushmita Ghosh

PROJECT DESIGNER Vinita
Venugopal

DESIGNER Meghna Baruah

PICTURE RESEARCH MANAGER
Taiyaba Khatoon

SENIOR PICTURE RESEARCHER
Sumita Khatwani

SENIOR DTP DESIGNER
Azeem Siddiqui

SENIOR CARTOGRAPHIC MANAGER
Uma Bhattacharya

ASSISTANT CARTOGRAPHIC MANAGER
Suresh Kumar

CARTOGRAPHER Zafar-ul-Islam Khan

PHOTOGRAPHY Steven Greaves

CARTOONS Julian Mosedale

OTHER ILLUSTRATORS Arun Pottirayil,
Richard Bonson, Richard Draper,
Chris Orr & Assocs, Pat Thorne,
John Woodcock

DESIGN CONCEPT Keith Hagan at
www.greenwich-design.co.uk

Printed and bound in China

First published in the UK in 2013 by
Dorling Kindersley Limited, 80 Strand,
London WC2R 0RL. A Penguin Random
House Company

19 20 21 10 9 8 7 6 5 4 3 2 1

Reprinted with revisions 2019

**Copyright © 2013, 2019 Dorling
Kindersley Limited, London**

A CIP catalogue record is available
from the Library of Congress.

ISBN 978-0-2413-6558-8

MIX
Paper from
responsible sources
FSC™ C018179

Contents

Alligators in a swamp in Florida

Kids playing in the sand on the beach at Sand Key Park, Clearwater

Art Deco facade of a landmark hotel on Ocean Drive, Miami

How to Use this Guide

This guide is designed to help families get the most from a visit to Florida, providing expert recommendations for sightseeing with kids along with detailed practical information. The opening section contains an introduction to Florida and its highlights, as well as all the essentials required to plan a family vacation (including how to get there, getting around, health, insurance, money, restaurants, accommodations, shopping, and communications), a guide to family-friendly festivals, and a brief historical overview.

The main sightseeing section is divided into areas. A "best of" feature for every chapter is followed by the key sights and other attractions in the area, as well as options for where to eat, drink, play, and have more fun. At the back of the book are detailed maps of Florida and Miami.

INTRODUCING THE AREA
Each area chapter opens with a double-page spread setting it in context, with a short introduction, a locator map, and a selection of highlights.

Locator map locates the area in the region.

Brief highlights give a flavor of what to see in the area.

THE BEST OF...
This planner shows at a glance the best things for families to see and do in each area, with themed suggestions ranging from history, art, and culture to gardens and games.

Themed suggestions for the best things to see and do with kids.

REGIONAL MAP

Introductory text describes the key characteristics and geography of the area, and gives information on the transportation infrastructure.

The map shows the area covered and all the sights in that chapter.

The Lowdown gives all the practical information you need to visit the area. The key to the symbols is on the back jacket flap.

SIGHTSEEING IN FLORIDA

Each area features a number of "hub" destinations (see below): pragmatic and enjoyable plans for a morning, afternoon, or day's visit. These give adults and children a real insight into the destination, focusing on the key sights and what makes them interesting to kids. The sights are balanced by places to let off steam, take cover options for rainy days, suggestions for where to eat, drink, and shop with kids, ideas for where to continue sightseeing, and all the practicalities, including transportation.

The "hub" destinations are the best places to visit in each area, and use lively and informative text to engage and entertain both adults and children.

Key Features uses illustrated artworks to show the most interesting features of each sight, highlighting elements likely to appeal to children.

Letting off steam suggests a place to take children to play freely following a cultural visit.

Eat and drink lists recommendations for family-friendly places to eat and drink, from picnic options and snacks to proper meals and gourmet dining.

Kids' Corner is featured on all sightseeing pages (see below).

The Lowdown provides comprehensive practical information, including transportation, opening times, costs, activities, age range suitability, and how long to allow for a visit.

Find out more gives suggestions for downloads, games, apps, or movies to enthuse children about a place and help them to learn more about it.

Next stop... suggests other places to visit, either near the key destination, thematically linked to the sight or a complete change of pace for the rest of the day.

Further sights around each hub destination, selected to appeal to both adults and children, are suggested on the following pages.

Places of interest are recommended, with an emphasis on the aspects most likely to attract children, and incorporating quirky stories and unusual facts. Each one includes a suggestion for letting off steam or taking cover.

Kids' Corner is designed to involve children with the sight, with things to look out for, games to play, cartoons, and fun facts. Answers to quizzes are given at the bottom of the panel.

The Lowdown provides comprehensive practical and transportation information for each sight.

Where to Stay section has a wide range of recommendations for places to stay with families, from hotels and B&Bs that welcome children to resorts and self-catering apartments.

Easy-to-use symbols show the key family-friendly features of places to stay.

The Price Guide box gives details of the price categories for a family of four.

The Colony Hotel and other classic Art Deco establishments, lit up in colorful hues, on Ocean Drive Miami Beach

Introducing
FLORIDA

The Best of Florida

Famously known as the "Sunshine State," Florida is one of the most popular travel destinations in the world, drawing more than 100 million visitors a year, including many families. With over 600 miles (965 km) of world-class beaches, and numerous waterways, Florida offers dozens of activities, from yachting and kayaking, to fishing and snorkeling. Nature-lovers can discover exotic flora and fauna in a host of nature preserves, or explore glorious scenery on the many biking and hiking trails. In addition, there is an array of world-famous theme parks, plus excellent museums that hold a special appeal for kids.

Beach bonanzas

The first decision is: which coast? Families can choose between the exciting Atlantic Ocean waves on the east coast or the soft sand and calm waters of the Gulf of Mexico on the west coast and in the northern Panhandle. **Miami Beach** *(see pp66–70)*, **St. Pete Beach** *(see p212)*, or **Fort Lauderdale** *(see pp80–81)*, with miles of accommodations on the sand, are very convenient for families. For a beach with plenty of room to toss a beach ball or build a sand castle without competing for space, head to **Anna Maria Island** *(see p212)* on the Gulf Coast, or the secluded **Virginia Key Beach Park** *(see p64)* on Key Biscayne in Miami. **Bradenton Beach** *(see p212)*, on the Gulf Coast, offers several restaurants and shops, and mini-golf a short stroll away, but those who prefer beaches that are quiet, undeveloped, and ringed with scenic dunes or sea pines will be happy on the **Gulf Islands National Seashore** *(see p194)* or the **Canaveral**

National Seashore *(see p148)* on the east coast. **Sanibel Island** *(see p238)* is a good place for kids to hunt for cockles, conchs, clams, and other prize shells, but even better beachcombing may be found at **Venice Beach** *(see p213)*, or by taking a boat to **Caladesi Island State Park** *(see p212)* near Clearwater, or **Shell Island** *(see p193)* off the Panhandle.

Right The Kilimanjaro Safari in Disney's Animal Kingdom®
Below Kids playing on Venice Beach, on the Gulf Coast

Above The high-speed thrill ride Kumba at Busch Gardens, Tampa **Right** *Visitors viewing sharks and other sea life at Shark Encounter®, SeaWorld®*

Scream machines

"Roller Coasters 'R' Us" could be the motto of central Florida, and for many families, theme parks are Florida's biggest lure. If you have only a day for a park, consider **Busch Gardens** *(see pp214–15)* in Tampa, which has a choice of half a dozen world-class thrill rides such as Kumba.

Most kids would love to spend days in Orlando's theme parks. Harry Potter™ fans will not want to miss the Wizarding World of Harry Potter™, split between **Universal's Islands of Adventure®** *(see pp120–21)* and **Universal Studios Florida®** *(see pp118–19)*; the two parks are connected by the Hogwarts™ Express. The Hollywood Rip Ride Rockit® in Universal Studios Florida® is billed as one of the most high-tech coasters in the world.

The biggest theme park, **Walt Disney World® Resort** *(see pp106–117)*, excites with attractions such as the Rock 'n' Roller Coaster® Starring Aerosmith at **Disney's Hollywood Studios®** *(see pp114–15)*, and Space Mountain® in **Magic Kingdom®** *(see pp108–9)*, which does its swoops and swings in the dark. Avatar Flight of Passage at **Disney's Animal Kingdom®** *(see pp112–13)* offers a breathtaking 3D adventure. Don't forget Orlando's **SeaWorld®** *(see pp122–3)*, where the Kraken® coaster dives underground three times, and Manta®, the flying roller coaster, lets riders spin, glide, skim, and fly like a giant ray. At **LEGOLAND® Florida Resort** *(see pp132–5)*, Coastersaurus is a wooden coaster that curves and dips through a prehistoric jungle of animated and life-size dinosaurs made of LEGO® blocks.

Be warned, however, that the lines for major rides at all the theme parks can be long. See individual entries for tips on cutting the line.

The great indoors

Family fun is weatherproof in Florida, even for children who do not usually enjoy museums. The **Ringling** *(see pp224–5)*, in Sarasota, is the place to see the world's largest miniature circus. Children of all ages will enjoy the collection of wacky art by Salvador Dalí in **The Dalí Museum** *(see pp220–21)* in St. Petersburg, which is devoted to the Surrealist. The **Morse Museum** *(see p130)* in Orlando's Winter Park features one of the world's most comprehensive collections of amazing glass creations by Louis Comfort Tiffany, including a chapel of glimmering glass tiles. At the **Cummer Museum of Art and Gardens** *(see p160)* in Jacksonville, Art Connections introduces kids to art by inviting them to "walk" through a painting, "listen" to a sculpture, or "paint" with a virtual paintbrush.

Miami, St. Petersburg, Orlando, and Tampa are among several cities with terrific museums designed specifically for younger kids. Others, including the **Museum of Arts and Sciences** *(see pp176–7)* in Daytona Beach and the **Museum of Science and History** *(see p160)* in Jacksonville have separate museum wings filled with a variety of hands-on science activities geared to kids.

Butterfly, bird, and flora gardens

Florida's tropical climate fosters fabulous exotic plants, and the state's exceptional gardens allow kids to work off energy while their parents savor the scenery. Children will enjoy Miami's **Fairchild Tropical Garden** (see p56), which is the largest of its kind, with rare plants and 11 lakes, as well as a colorful butterfly garden. At the **Marie Selby Botanical Gardens** (see p226) in Sarasota, home to over 6,000 orchids, kids can run on the lawn and feed fish in the koi pond. The **Morikami Museum and Japanese Gardens** (see p87), in Delray Beach, is a Japanese cultural center, with six gardens inspired by the most famous gardens of Japan. Visitors can stroll the zigzag bridges and picnic at the Lake Biwa and Saki Pavilion. The **Harry P. Leu Gardens** (see p130) in Orlando are known for their camellias and the best rose gardens in Florida. The **Alfred B. Maclay Gardens State Park** (see p201) in Tallahassee is also famous for its camellias, which begin blooming as early as January, while early spring is peak time for the prize azaleas here. The lush grounds of **Bok Tower Gardens** (see p135), south of Orlando, are beautiful year-round.

Something fishy

Florida's waters are filled with fantastic and colorful sea life. At Tampa's **The Florida Aquarium** (see p216), the showstopping Coral Reef Gallery is a colossal coral grotto in which more than 2,000 fish can be seen. Other favorite exhibits are the sea horses and the Penguin Promenade, where black-footed African penguins waddle their way through the lobby in daily parades. If kids get restless, **The Splash Pad** (see p216), a rainforest-themed outdoor water play area, lets them have fun with dump buckets and in spray zones while parents relax in the shade. **The Aquarium at Mote Marine Laboratory** (see p226), in Sarasota, is the place to see sharks, manatees, and tropical fish, and to peep into the labs to see scientists doing research on sea life. Kids can see dolphins in their natural habitat near the **Cumberland Island National Seashore** (see p167), or at the Treasure Coast, off the shores of **Fort Pierce** (see p96). Snorkeling opportunities are plentiful, but the best place to see colorful fish in the wild is at **John Pennekamp Coral Reef State Park** (see p251) in Key Largo, the country's first underwater preserve. You can also go underwater without getting wet at the floating underwater observatory at **Homosassa Springs Wildlife State Park** (see p219), where visitors can look at the resident manatees and hundreds of fish.

Right Snorkelers at John Pennekamp Coral Reef State Park
Below Visitors enjoying nature at Fairchild Tropical Garden

Above *Traditional buildings on the extensive, picturesque grounds of Mission San Luis, Tallahassee*

Arresting architecture

Florida's architecture can help bring to life different phases of the state's history for kids. Tallahassee's **Mission San Luis** *(see p200)* has a reconstructed thatch-roofed council house, used by the Apalachee Indians, plus small thatched houses built by the early Spanish settlers in the 1600s. The **Oldest House** *(see p168)* in St. Augustine is the state's oldest surviving Spanish Colonial home, dating to the early 1700s. Florida's vernacular style is exemplified by Cracker houses, built by the early pioneers. Although few survive, they have influenced local building styles for centuries *(see p86)*.

The Gilded Age brought lavish mansions such as Henry Flagler's 1902 Beaux Arts-style Whitehall, now the **Flagler Museum** *(see pp90–91)*, in Palm Beach, and James Deering's Italian Renaissance **Vizcaya** in Miami *(see pp60–61)*, along with grand hotels such as the **Loews® Don CeSar Hotel** *(see p228)* on St. Pete Beach. During this same period, Art Deco hotels were setting the style in

Miami's **South Beach** *(see pp68–9)*, while lavish Spanish Revival homes were being built in other parts of southern Florida. Find examples of these in Addison Mizner's homes in **Palm Beach** *(see pp88–9)* and in George Merrick's brilliant designs in **Coral Gables** *(see pp52–3)*.

On the road

Pleasant day trips from a base can be more fun for families than long drives that try the patience of young kids, and smaller roads may often offer more accessible pleasures than the super-highways. The Everglades Parkway (I-75), also called Alligator Alley, is the expressway through the **Everglades** *(see pp242–3)*, but the route following US 41 west from **Miami** *(see pp44–73)* to **Naples** *(see p240)* allows for more interesting stops along the way, and offers stunning views.

Head west on Route 40 from **Daytona Beach** *(see pp174–5)* to Ocala, driving through the green **Ocala National Forest** *(see p178)* and the mysterious, mossy oaks that inspired Marjorie Kinnan Rawlings' book *The Yearling* (1938).

To appreciate the variety of Florida's beaches, spend a day following Highway 789 from **Sarasota** *(see pp224–7)* through posh **Longboat Key** *(see p212)* to lively **Bradenton Beach** and the more secluded **Anna Maria Island**. On the east coast, Route A1A hugs the shoreline of the barrier beaches all the way from **Miami Beach** to **Fernandina Beach** *(see p166)*, near the Georgia border. This allows for either a short outing or a multiday tour of the state taking in **The Gold and Treasure Coasts** *(see pp74–99)*, **The Space Coast** *(see pp138–53)*, and **The Northeast** *(see pp154–83)*.

Left *The Flagler Kenan Pavilion with Henry Flagler's personal Railcar No. 91 at the Flagler Museum in Palm Beach*

Florida through the Year

With its subtropical temperatures, southern Florida is most popular in the winter high season, from mid-December to mid-April, while northern Florida's beaches draw larger crowds in spring and summer. Avoid heading to the Panhandle or Daytona Beach in March, when colleges are on spring break and hordes of young people visit the beaches. Each season brings its own share of fun and festivals that add excitement to a visit anywhere in Florida.

Spring

Spring celebrations salute everything from shells and strawberries to tall ships and motorcycles, while sports go into high gear with baseball spring training and traditional Scottish Highland Games.

MARCH

The **Bay Area Renaissance Festival** in Tampa features armor-clad knights sword-fighting on horseback. Another era of history comes to life as the 1668 **Sack of St. Augustine** is re-enacted.

Baseball brings cheering fans to spring training games all over the state, while motorcycle enthusiasts head for the annual **Bike Week** at Daytona Beach. The **Carnaval & Calle Ocho Festival** is a lively series of Latin-infused events in Little Havana, with food, Cuban music, and colorful costumes.

More March favorites include the treasures of the **Sanibel Shell Festival**, the **Florida Strawberry Festival** *(see p211)* in Plant City, near Tampa, and **Springtime Tallahassee**, a weekend festival that includes a parade of costumed floats.

APRIL

Kids will love the **Zoo Miami's Great Egg Safari**, where besides hunting for eggs, the fun includes face painting, rock climbing, bouncy castles, and visits from the Easter Bunny. The amazing underwater **Easter Egg Hunt** in Tavernier is open to divers and snorkelers of all ages.

Military musters are part of the festivities at the annual **Conch Republic Independence Celebration** *(see p234)* in Key West, while the **Dunedin Highland Games** on the Gulf Coast feature competitions between colorful kilted bands, Highland dancers, and athletes having a go at throwing the hefty Dunedin Stone.

MAY

SunFest *(see p78)*, in West Palm Beach, calls itself "Florida's largest waterfront music and art festival," with more than 100 artist booths, food stands, and three stages of entertainment on the tree-lined walkways along the Intracoastal Waterway. A Family Activities Tent offers games and fun for little ones. Folk songs, crafts, and the chance to feast on gumbo and barbecue have drawn families to the **Florida Folk Festival** at Stephen Foster Folk Culture State Park, about an hour's drive west of Jacksonville, for more than 60 years. Jacksonville is the place to be on **Memorial Day**

Below left Kids at Fort Walton Beach's annual Billy Bowlegs Pirate Festival, which pays tribute to a local pirate legend
Below right Costumed participants at the Bay Area Renaissance Festival, Tampa

weekend, when musicians perform downtown for the **Jacksonville Jazz Festival** *(see p158)*. Kids will love watching ships and boats sail past at nearby Jacksonville Landing on the St. Johns River.

Summer

The fun carries on with festivals featuring great food and beach activities. July 4 brings fireworks, the rodeo promises Old West excitement, and the Blue Angels aerobatics fill the skies with thrills.

JUNE

The **Monticello Watermelon Festival**, near Tallahassee, offers arts and crafts, a bed race, and cool, juicy watermelon for $1 a slice. More sweet treats await at the **Panhandle Watermelon Festival** *(see p188)* in Chipley, which includes live music, a parade, an antique car show, a street fair, and dancing. Not far away, in Fort Walton Beach, pirate gangs skirmish at the **Billy Bowlegs Pirate Festival**, which has a whole bunch of activities for young buccaneers.

For a change of pace, the **Silver Spurs Rodeo** in Kissimmee, 4½ miles (7 km) south of Gatorland, offers a chance to watch some bareback riding, bronco riding, and barrel races. The event pays tribute to the four-century-long history of cattle ranching and cowboy culture in Florida.

JULY

Independence Day on July 4 is celebrated all over the state, but Miami has the biggest events of all. The festivities begin at 11am in Key Biscayne, and feature a parade with marching bands, stilt dancers, floats, and bagpipers. Head to Bayfront Park to participate in **America's Birthday Bash**, a full day of fun and food that includes an afternoon Kids' Zone as well as fireworks starting at 9pm. Miami Beach offers free blues and jazz concerts and nighttime fireworks.

More than 100 stocky, bearded Ernest Hemingways show up in Key West for the Papa Hemingway Look-Alike Contest, a highlight of the **Hemingway Days Festival**. Don't miss the mock "running of the bulls," in which bulls on wheels are pushed around with Hemingway look-alikes perched on top.

All eyes are on the sky when the Blue Angels, the US Navy Flight Demonstration squadron, perform their famous aerial stunts. The **Blue Angels Air Show** *(see p188)* is held in Pensacola. Arrive early to get a seat in the bleachers at the National Naval Aviation Museum viewing area.

AUGUST

In Key West, the end of summer means the opening of the lobster season and cause for a party, **Lobsterfest**, with free concerts, a street fair, and lots of lobster to eat. A 45-minute drive north of Panama City, in Wausau, an all-American small-town parade, arts and crafts vendors, and great food make the **Wausau Possum Festival** *(see p188)* a much-loved tradition.

Fall

More seafood feasting, medieval jousting on horseback, lavish Latin parades, Halloween, and the American Sandsculpting Festival add flavor and fun to a fall visit. Late summer and early fall are the least crowded times in the theme parks.

SEPTEMBER

The oldest city in the US, dating from 1565, celebrates the **St. Augustine Founding Anniversary** with a re-enactment of the Spanish landing near the spot where it took place. More historic hi-jinks take place on **British Garrison Day**, at the Castillo de San Marcos, when Colonial re-enactors portray the British troops who occupied St. Augustine in the late 18th century.

Below left *A diver in rabbit costume hunting for underwater Easter eggs at the Easter Egg Hunt, Tavernier*
Below right *Ernest Hemingway look-alikes on fake bulls at the Hemingway Days Festival, Key West*

OCTOBER

In Zellwood, just a few miles away from Orlando, guests are challenged to "get lost" in **Scott's Maze Adventure**, a 7-acre (28,328 sq m) cornfield maze. Visitors can also navigate a number of other mazes and games.

Fort Lauderdale International Boat Show is one of the world's largest displays of boats, from skiffs and canoes to super-yachts. Shuttles, water taxis, and riverboats take visitors to the show's various venues. Hook the Future fishing clinics for kids teach young anglers how to catch the big ones.

NOVEMBER

The entries in the **American Sandsculpting Festival** at Fort Myers Beach boggle the imagination with sand sculptures ranging from statues of Venus to giant butterflies. The **Florida Seafood Festival** in Apalachicola has oyster-shucking and eating contests, blue-crab races, and the chance to explore a charming historic nautical town.

The **Medieval Fair** *(see p211)* in Sarasota takes visitors back to 11th-century England as jousters in armor tilt at each other on horseback. The **North Florida Fair** in Tallahassee has more

contemporary lures, such as livestock contests, rides, pig racing, and magic shows, plus lots of food and music.

Winter

Boats brighten the harbors with holiday lights, art shows abound, pirates parade, and the circus and state fairs delight in the busy winter season. Note that Christmas and New Year vacation weeks are the most crowded at theme parks; plan to arrive early to avoid crowds.

DECEMBER

Holiday parades on the water dazzle, as boats compete for best displays. The biggest and brightest parades are the **Winterfest Boat Parade** in Fort Lauderdale, with over 100 boats competing for the best decorated, and the **Jacksonville Light Parade**, which ends in a blaze of fireworks.

Millions of tiny lights create a magical scene during **Nights of Lights** *(see p169)* in St. Augustine, a two-month-long celebration. Night tours led by storytellers in period garb, train and trolley tours, and art walks through the narrow brick streets add to the festive feel.

Fort Taylor's Pyrate Invasion, in Key West, includes sailing trips with the "pirates."

JANUARY

The New Year means football championships in Florida, with the **Orange Bowl** in Miami, the **TaxSlayer Bowl** in Jacksonville, and the **Outback Bowl** in Tampa hosting top college teams and attracting fans from near and far.

Epiphany, also known as Three Kings' Day or Twelfth Night, brings a gala **Three Kings Parade**, featuring the costumed Three Wise Men, in Miami's Little Havana. All ages will enjoy a stroll along Las Olas Boulevard, in Fort Lauderdale, to see life-size sculptures, colorful paintings, jewelry, and photography at the **Las Olas Art Fair**.

Pirates invade Tampa in late January or early February, tossing beads to the spectators from lighted floats at the elaborately costumed **Gasparilla Pirate Festival** *(see p211)*, which is followed by a lively street fair. Meanwhile, the Alachua County Fairgrounds are transformed into a medieval marketplace, with another chance to see knights in armor jousting on horseback, for the **Hoggetowne Medieval Faire** *(see p158)*, on weekends at the end of January and into February.

*Below left Stunning sand sculpture at the American Sandsculpting Festival, Fort Myers
Below right Jousting tournament at the Medieval Fair, Sarasota*

FEBRUARY

A favorite with children, **Circus Sarasota** (see p37) pitches its tent for most of the month of February each year, bringing world-class international circus talent to thrill the crowds. In Daytona Beach, engines roar for the fabled **Daytona 500** (see p158) race.

The 12-day **Florida State Fair** in Tampa is a chance for the state's farmers to show off their best animals – from sheep and cows to pygmy goats, exotic pigeons, and rabbits. The fairgrounds overflow with rides, music, food booths, a colorful horse show, a dog show, and plenty of free country-western entertainment.

The **Swamp Cabbage Festival** in La Belle, east of Fort Myers, has some unique entertainment on its agenda, including an armadillo race. The festival also features a parade, a rodeo, food stalls, arts and crafts, and the crowning of Miss Swamp Cabbage Festival.

The **Coconut Grove Arts Festival** (see p51) in Miami is one of the best and most colorful outdoor fine arts shows, a place where people get the chance to meet and talk to artists and enjoy good food and music. Children can have a go at creating their own works of art.

The Lowdown

Spring

Bay Area Renaissance Festival
www.bayarearenfest.com
Bike Week www.officialbikeweek.com
Carnaval & Calle Ocho Festival
www.carnavalmiami.com
Dunedin Highland Games
www.dunedinhighlandgames.com
Easter Egg Hunt www.captainslate.com
Florida Folk Festival
www.floridastateparks.org/folkfest
Sack of St. Augustine
www.visitstaugustine.com
Sanibel Shell Festival
www.fortmyers-sanibel.com
Springtime Tallahassee www.visit
tallahassee.com/events
SunFest www.sunfest.com
Zoo Miami's Great Egg Safari
www.zoomiami.org

Summer

America's Birthday Bash
www.bayfrontparkmiami.com
Billy Bowlegs Pirate Festival
www.billybowlegspiratefestival.com
Hemingway Days Festival
www.hemingwaydays.org
Lobsterfest www.keywest
lobsterfest.com
Monticello Watermelon Festival
www.monticellojeffersonfl.com
Silver Spurs Rodeo
www.silverspursrodeo.com

Fall

American Sandsculpting Festival
www.fmbsandsculpting.com
British Garrison Day
www.staugustineinfo.com

Florida Seafood Festival
www.floridaseafoodfestival.com
Fort Lauderdale International Boat Show www.showmanagement.com
Scott's Maze Adventures
www.longandscottfarms.com
Medieval Fair
www.sarasotamedievalfair.com
North Florida Fair
www.northfloridafair.com
St. Augustine Founding Anniversary
www.staugustineinfo.com

Winter

Coconut Grove Arts Festival
www.cgaf.com
Florida State Fair floridastatefair.com
Jacksonville Light Boat Parade
www.jacksonvillelanding.com
Las Olas Art Fair www.artfestival.com
Orange Bowl www.orangebowl.org
Outback Bowl www.outbackbowl.com
Swamp Cabbage Festival
www.swampcabbagefestival.org
TaxSlayer Bowl www.taxslayer
bowl.com
Winterfest Boat Parade
www.winterfestparade.com

Public Holidays

New Year's Day Jan 1
Martin Luther King, Jr.'s Birthday
3rd Mon in Jan
President's Day 3rd Mon in Feb
Memorial Day last Mon in May
Independence Day July 4
Labor Day 1st Mon in Sep
Election Day 1st Tue in Nov
Veterans Day Nov 11
Thanksgiving 4th Thu in Nov
Christmas Day Dec 25

Below left Participants showcasing their animals at the Florida State Fair, Tampa
Below right Race cars on the track during the Daytona 500, a famous NASCAR event

Sports and Outdoor Activities

Florida's sunny climate means that families can enjoy outdoor activities and sports year-round. The state's excellent nature parks and preserves attract hikers and cyclists, while its numerous beaches and rivers offer opportunities for boating, fishing, sailing, surfing, snorkeling, and swimming. There are also tennis courts and the well-developed golf courses that Florida is so famous for. Fans of all ages can enjoy cheering on some of America's top sports teams.

Biking

Cyclists will find bike paths in nature preserves, parks, state forests, and on beaches. **Rails-to-Trails**, former railroad routes that are now paved for bikers and hikers, are ideal for family outings. The 14-mile (23-km) Jacksonville–Baldwin Trail near Jacksonville (see pp160–61) winds beneath a leafy canopy. The Myakka River State Park (see p227) offers miles of bike trails through scenic landscapes. The state's official **bike trails guide** can be found online.

Above Cyclists exploring a picturesque trail in the Myakka River State Park

Hiking

Florida's many state and national parks offer excellent hiking. The **Florida Trail**, stretching over 1,500 miles (2,500 km) across the state, has options for short hikes. In Ocala National Forest (see p178), trails take hikers through pine and hardwood forests, and prairies. The 10-mile (16-km) trail from Clearwater Lake Recreation Area to Alexander Springs includes one of the region's largest natural springs. Park websites have maps and suggestions for hikes.

City trails

The path through Sarasota's Bayfront Park (see p227) borders Sarasota Bay, while Tampa's (see pp214–19) 4.½-mile (7-km) Bayshore Boulevard is called "the world's longest continuous sidewalk." Jacksonville's Arlington Lions Club Park offers a path and boardwalks along the St. Johns River (see pp60–63), and Miami's mile-long Riverwalk through Bayfront Park (see p62) has shops, cafés, and art galleries. The trail in Matheson Hammock County Park (see p52) offers a taste of wilderness in the city.

Kayaking and canoeing

Most parks, nature centers, and wildlife refuges on the coast or on rivers offer paddling; John Pennekamp Coral Reef State Park (see p251), and Everglades National Park (see pp242–3) are both scenic. The **Suwannee River Wilderness Trail** has multiday paddling trips, and the Wekiva River, near Orlando, offers kayak and canoe rentals.

Fishing

Islamorada (see p250) in the Florida Keys is the state's sport-fishing capital, while the Panhandle's Destin has its largest charter boat fleet. The **Destin Fishing Rodeo** has big money prizes, and categories for kids and teens too. Lake Okeechobee, inland from the Treasure Coast, is the choice spot for freshwater fishing.

The Lowdown

Biking guides www.dep.state.fl.us/gwt
Destin Fishing Rodeo www.destinfishingrodeo.org
Florida Panthers panthers.nhl.com
Florida Trail www.floridatrail.org
Golf www.doralresort.com; www.golfstpete.com/mangrovebay/index.html; www.lpgainternational.com
Hiking www.floridastateparks.org; www.floridahikes.com
IMG Bollettieri Tennis Academy www.imgacademy.com
Jacksonville Jaguars jaguars.com
Miami Heat www.nba.com/heat
Miniature golf www.golflink.com/miniature-golf/state.aspx?state=FL
National Parks www.nps.gov
Parasailing cocoabeachparasail.com; daytonaparasail.com
Rails-to-Trails www.railstotrails.org
Ron Jon Surf School www.ronjonsurfschool.com
Sailing schools windwardsailing.com; www.offshoresailing.com
Shipwreck Snorkel Trail www.floridadiveconnection.com
Suwannee River Wilderness Trail floridastateparks.org/wilderness
Tampa Bay Rays tampabayrays.mlb.com

Above Spectacular view of the TPC Blue Monster golf course at the Doral Resort, Miami Left Surfing in Sebastian Inlet State Park, Vero Beach

Snorkeling and diving

The Keys are the site of America's largest living coral reef, and Biscayne National Park *(see p244)* is rich with colorful coral. The Keys Shipwreck Heritage Trail features nine sites to explore. The **Shipwreck Snorkel Trail**, near Fort Lauderdale *(see pp80–81)*, is an artificial "shipwreck," and shallow-water snorkeling can be enjoyed on Siesta Key's Crescent Beach, or around the rock jetty at St. Andrews State Park *(see pp192–3)* on the Panhandle.

Watersports

The calmer waters off the Gulf Coast, and the Intracoastal Waterway, are ideal for sailing. The Fort Lauderdale area offers 300 miles (480 km) of inland waterways and Sebastian Inlet State Park *(see p94)* offers great surfing opportunities. Short sailing courses are available at **Windward Sailing** at Fernandina Beach *(see p166)* or at the **Offshore Sailing School®** at Fort Myers *(see pp236–41)*. Cocoa Beach *(see p150)* is the state's undisputed surfing and parasailing center, and the **Ron Jon Surf School** offers lessons.

Golf and tennis

The golf courses at the **Doral Resort** in Miami and the **Mangrove Bay Golf Course** in St. Petersburg are well known. There are miniature golf courses in almost every Florida town, and no experience is required. Tennis enthusiasts will find public courts in most towns, many offering lessons, and tennis programs at most resorts. In Bradenton, the **IMG Bollettieri Tennis Academy**, where top pros train, offers teen programs.

Spectator sports

In the fall, the Miami Dolphins, Tampa Bay Buccaneers, and **Jacksonville Jaguars** provide football action. Late fall and winter are best to catch the **Miami Heat** and Orlando Magic basketball teams, and ice hockey competition gets fierce for Miami's **Florida Panthers** and the Tampa Bay Lightning. March brings the Grapefruit League, the chance to see 15 baseball teams prepare for the season. The **Tampa Bay Rays** and Miami Marlins are in action from April through October.

Above left Snorkeler near coral reefs in Key Largo Left An ice hockey match in progress between the Florida Panthers and the Tampa Bay Lightning

Going Wild

Florida is a paradise for spotting wildlife, from alligators, dolphins, and manatees to pelicans, egrets, and great blue herons, and there are plenty of preserves where sightings are almost guaranteed. In addition, guided walks to see sea turtles are offered by nature centers all along the Atlantic coast in June and July. Be still so as not to frighten the birds and animals away, and maintain a safe distance from the alligators.

Everglades National Park

The only subtropical preserve in North America, the Everglades (see pp242–3) teems with wildlife, from tiny frogs to full-grown alligators. Covering 1,562 sq miles (4,046 sq km), and accessible from both east and west coasts, the park is home to birds such as the roseate spoonbill, wood stork, and great blue heron, and is the only place in the world where alligators and Florida crocodiles coexist. National Park Service rangers offer tours from the park's many visitor centers.

Myakka River State Park

This park (see p227) is home to 57 sq miles (148 sq km) of untouched wetlands, prairies, and woodlands. Stroll along a canopy walkway in the tree tops, or spot alligators, turtles, and birds on hiking trails, on airboat rides that skim over the water, or by canoeing or kayaking in the Myakka River.

Lion Country Safari

A 4-mile (6-km) drive-through safari in this extensive preserve (see p92) in West Palm Beach offers the chance to see more than 900 animals from around the world living freely in the open. They are divided into seven home regions, from the pampas of South America to the forests of India and the Serengeti of Africa. Spot lions, tapirs, tortoises, llamas, zebras, giraffes, chimpanzees, and hippos, to name just a few. The safari is sure to be a hit with kids, and tickets include an amusement park with rides and a water "sprayground."

J. N. "Ding" Darling National Wildlife Refuge

Named for a conservationist who was instrumental in preserving the area, this Sanibel Island preserve (see p239) boasts an enormous bird population. Endangered manatees, sea turtles, and Florida

The Lowdown

Crystal River National Wildlife Refuge
www.fws.gov/refuge/crystal_river
Everglades National Park
www.nps.gov/ever
Homosassa Springs Wildlife State Park www.floridastateparks.org
J. N. "Ding" Darling National Wildlife Refuge www.fws.gov/dingdarling

Lion Country Safari
www.lioncountrysafari.com
Merritt Island National Wildlife Refuge www.fws.gov/merrittisland
Myakka River State Park www.florida stateparks.org/park/Myakka-River
Wakulla Springs State Park
www.floridastateparks.org

Below left Alligator in the Everglades National Park Below center Impala deer at Lion Country Safari Below right Birdwalk in Myakka River State Park

Above Tour boat through Wakulla Springs State Park **Center left** Flamingos at Homosassa Springs Park **Below left** Manatee feeding at Homosassa Springs

crocodiles shelter here as well. See the refuge on a 5-mile (8-km) self-guided driving trail, on a guided tram tour, or by hiking, biking, or canoeing.

Wakulla Springs State Park

Turtles, alligators, deer, and many birds are just a few of the wild animals at home in these environs *(see p202)* near Tallahassee. Riverboat tours are offered daily, while glass-bottom boat tours over the springs, in late winter and early spring, give a chance to spot the fossilized remains of mastodons at the bottom. Well known as the location of three Tarzan movies with Johnny Weissmuller, the park's wooded area has nature trails, and a playground.

Crystal River National Wildlife Refuge

The Crystal River is one of the state's largest manatee wintering grounds, home to about 200 of these unusual creatures. The refuge, established in 1983 to protect the endangered manatee, is accessible only by boat. Several operators at the marina in the town of Crystal River offer glass-bottom boat tours, and snorkeling tours that offer great fun for the whole family.

Merritt Island National Wildlife Refuge

This vast refuge *(see pp148–9)* has coastal dunes, and saltwater and freshwater marshland, with habitats for over 1,500 species. Explore the area on a 6-mile (10-km) drive, nature trails, a manatee observation deck and boardwalk, or canoe waterways.

Homosassa Springs Wildlife State Park

Watch manatees swim in the upper Gulf Coast's Homosassa Springs *(see p219)* and see fish up close from the Fish Bowl, a floating underwater observatory – only in this case people are inside and the fish are outside the bowl!

Getting to Florida

Among the most popular destinations in the US, Florida attracts millions of visitors each year. The state is served by two major international airports and several important secondary airports. It is a good idea to read up on entry requirements and be ready with all necessary credentials, including passports for children, to ensure a hassle-free entry. Advance planning will also help to get the best fares.

US entry requirements

Nationals of 40 countries, including most European nations, do not need a visa to travel to the US for stays of less than 90 days, but travelers must apply in advance for authorization to travel via the **Electronic System for Travel Authorization**. Note the authorization number and keep a print-out for reference. Citizens of all other countries need a valid visa. The **Transportation Security Administration** provides information on security regulations for travelers. Visitors arriving by air or sea no longer need to complete the **US Customs and Border Protection** agency I-94/I-94W form, because all information is now collected by the agency through electronic travel records. The agency will issue an I-94 form at border ports of entry.

Arriving by air

The airports at **Miami (MIA)** and **Orlando (MCO)** serve most international flights and have frequent connections from other US cities. Major airlines, including **Air Canada**, **Air France**, **British Airways**, and **Virgin Atlantic**, arrive at both airports. **Aer Lingus** flies to Orlando, and Miami is serviced by many South American airlines. British Airways also has flights to **Fort Lauderdale (FLL)** and **Tampa (TPA)**. Tampa is the major airport for the Gulf Coast destinations, while **Jacksonville (JAX)** is the main gateway to northern Florida. Several domestic airlines, such as **American Airlines**, **Delta**, **JetBlue** and **United**, offer frequent services to Florida.

Air fares are lowest between April and mid-November, except for holiday periods. For those traveling with children, direct flights are more convenient, although expensive.

Airport transfers

All major airports have counters that arrange onward transport, but do check with your hotel in advance about an airport shuttle service. Car rental companies (see pp24–5) have booths at all airports.

The **Airport Flyer** express bus costs $2.35 from MIA to downtown Miami or Miami Beach. A taxi fare for one to five people averages $22 to downtown and a $32 flat fee to Miami Beach. Shared rides such as the **Super Shuttle** average $26 for the first person to downtown or the beach, and $11 for each extra person.

MCO is about 16 miles (25 km) from Walt Disney World® Resort, and the 30–45-min taxi ride costs $40–60.

Below left *Travelers in a departure lounge of Orlando International Airport*
Below right *The busy skyline of downtown Miami*

Shuttle buses charge $21 per person, $34 for a round trip. The local bus is slow but affordable at $4 per person.

Arriving by rail

Amtrak is the national rail system in the US, with stops in Jacksonville, Orlando, Tampa, and Miami. These are not high-speed trains, may require a night on board, and are pricier than airplanes. Check the Amtrak website for family rates and frequent specials.

Arriving by bus

Greyhound is the largest intercity US bus line. Its newer buses have ample leg room, and electrical outlets. Book tickets online in advance and check for family discounts and other offers.

Arriving by car

Florida has a great road system and welcome centers offering information along the main highways. I-95 serves the east coast and I-75 covers central Florida, with connecting roads to the west coast. The main west coast artery, Route 41, is not an expressway and is slow, so it is better to use I-75 and consult a map. The expressways from east to west include I-10 across northern Florida and I-4 connecting Orlando to Tampa. In the south, I-75

goes through the Everglades. The Beach Line Expressway, between Orlando and the Space Coast, and the Florida Turnpike, from Orlando to south of Miami, are toll roads. I-95 becomes congested between Fort Lauderdale and Miami and is best avoided during the morning and evening rush hours.

Arriving by sea

Florida has America's most popular cruise ports, with excellent facilities, porters to help with baggage, and plentiful taxis. Several cruises from South America, the Caribbean, and Europe sail to Florida ports. **Seaborn, Holland America,** and **Royal Caribbean** are well-known cruise lines. Most cruises come into Fort Lauderdale, the largest and busiest port, and also the most convenient for air connections to other cities. The **Disney Cruise Line** ships arrive at Cape Canaveral. The two other major ports, Miami and Tampa, have connections from the cruise docks by taxi or shuttle to downtown or the airport.

The Lowdown

US entry requirements
Transportation Security Administration www.tsa.gov
US Customs and Border Protection, ESTA www.cbp.gov

Arriving by air
Airports
FLL www.fll.net
JAX www.airport-jacksonville.com
MIA www.miami-airport.com
MCO www.orlandoairports.net
TPA www.tampaairport.com
Airlines
Aer Lingus www.aerlingus.com
Air Canada www.aircanada.com
Air France www.airfrance.com
American Airlines www.aa.com
British Airways www.britishairways.com
Delta www.delta.com

JetBlue www.jetblue.com
United www.united.com
Virgin Atlantic www.virgin-atlantic.com

Airport transfers
Airport Flyer www.miami-airport.com/bus_and_rail_info.asp
Super Shuttle www.supershuttle.com

Arriving by rail and bus
Amtrak www.amtrak.com
Greyhound www.greyhound.com

Arriving by sea
Disney Cruise Line disneycruise.disney.go.com
Holland America www.hollandamerica.com
Norwegian Cruise Line www.ncl.com
Royal Caribbean www.royalcaribbean.com
Seabourn www.seabourn.com

Below left A typical dark-blue Greyhound bus
Below right The Royal Caribbean cruise ship Enchantment of the Seas *docked at the Key West cruise terminal*

Getting around Florida

While train and bus connections are available between major cities, it is more economical and convenient for a family to rent a car. Florida is an easy state to navigate, with excellent roads and good signage. Larger cities have public transportation and many towns offer sightseeing trolleys, but the routes are limited and having a car will allow you to be flexible. RVs are also a good way to travel, especially since campsites blanket the state.

In-state connections

Miami, Fort Lauderdale, Orlando, and Tampa airports (see p22) offer connections to smaller cities around the state, usually on small commuter planes. Amtrak trains connect Jacksonville, Orlando, Tampa, and Miami, while Greyhound buses (see p23) serve smaller destinations, with an express service between Fort Lauderdale, Tampa, and Jacksonville. Red Coach, Megabus, and The Florida Express Bus offer services between cities, airports, and cruise terminals. However, fares can be costly for a family, making it more economical, and quicker, to travel by car. Most of the popular destinations are within a 4- or 5-hour drive of each other. Distances that may be worth the cost of a flight are from south to north, from Miami to destinations such as Tallahassee (466 miles/750 km), or Panama City (558 miles/898 km).

By car or RV

Car rental agencies, including **Avis**, **Budget**, and **Thrifty**, are found at all airports and in larger cities around the state. Rates vary with the seasons, but are generally less than $200 for a week's rental of a small car. Agencies require the driver to be over 21 (or 25 in some cases), with a valid driver's license and a major credit card. All US and most foreign licenses are accepted, but getting an international license is a good idea if your license is not in English. If your home auto insurance does not cover travel, consider buying insurance when renting. Note that state and local taxes can add up to 20 percent to the bill. Reserving in advance saves money. Travel sites such as **Expedia** also give a good overview of the car rental rates in an area. Gas stations are plentiful, but many are closed at night. Florida's population centers have heavy traffic from 7 to 9am and 3:30 to 6pm, so avoid these times if possible.

DRIVING REGULATIONS

All US traffic travels on the right-hand side of the road. Speed limits are 20–30 mph (32–48 km/h) in commercial and residential areas, and 55 mph (88 km/h) on highways except Interstate expressways, where the limit goes up to 70 mph (112 km/h) per hour. Most road signs are clear and easy to understand. Right turns are allowed at a red stoplight, unless signs indicate otherwise. Florida law requires all occupants to wear seat belts, and a federally approved infant carrier or car seat must be used for kids of 5 and under. The **Florida Highway Safety and Motor Vehicles** website is the best source for driving regulations.

Below left Cars cruising past Art Deco hotels on Ocean Drive in South Beach, Miami
Below right The Walt Disney World® Resort Monorail plying between Disney parks and resorts

RV TRAVEL

Recreational vehicles (RVs), or mobile homes, can be great for families, providing comfortable living quarters as well as efficient transportation. Companies such as **Cruise America** and **USA RV Rentals** offer rentals in a variety of sizes to fit all budgets. Many RV campgrounds in Florida are mini-resorts, with plenty of amenities (see p31).

Public transportation

Most of Florida's cities have bus services, but the need is small and the time between buses can be an hour or more. Miami Beach is well served by two routes of the **South Beach Local** bus, and **Walt Disney World® Resort** (see pp106–17) is also served by buses, trams, boats, and a monorail. Two passenger train services that have commenced operations are **Brightline**, which serves coastal cities and towns from Miami to West Palm, and **SunRail**, which serves four Central Florida counties. Beach towns such as Bradenton and Sarasota have tourist trolleys connecting town and beach, and the **Suncoast Beach Trolley** connects all the beaches from Clearwater to St. Petersburg.

By bike

Florida is very bicycle-friendly and cycling families will find lanes almost everywhere to help them get around town, though pedaling on busy thoroughfares may be a bit intimidating. Those keen on longer tours can sample the Pinellas Trail, which stretches from Tarpon Springs to St. Petersburg, passing through pretty towns and scenic coastal areas for 43 miles (69 km). Check out **Bike Florida** for more information and ideas.

By boat

The Intracoastal Waterway parallels the Atlantic coastline of Florida for 380 miles (611 km), and offers calm water for sailing or motorboats. Boat rentals are available in many towns, particularly in Fort Lauderdale and Miami. Boats with a crew can also be chartered. **Fort Lauderdale Water Taxi** and **Delray Beach Cruises** offer sightseeing cruises.

Great Rivers of Florida, a 7-day cruise offered by **American Cruise Lines** on the American Glory riverboat from Jacksonville, takes passengers along the St. Johns and Tolomato rivers, passing through Ocala National Forest and with stops at St. Augustine and Amelia Island. Houseboating offers the chance to explore the islands of southwestern Florida around Sanibel, cruise the Keys, or discover the beauty of the St. Johns or Suwannee rivers. Operators such as **Suwannee Houseboats** offer rentals by the day, the weekend, or the week.

The Lowdown

By car or RV
Avis www.avis.com
Budget www.budget.com
Cruise America www.cruiseamerica.com
Expedia www.expedia.com
Florida Highway Safety and Motor Vehicles 840 617 2000; flhsmv.gov
Thrifty www.thrifty.com
USA RV Rentals www.usarvrentals.com

By bike
Bike Florida www.bikeflorida.org

Public transportation
Brightline www.gobrightline.com
South Beach Local www.miamidade.gov/transit
Suncoast Beach Trolley www.psta.net/beachtrolley.php
SunRail www.sunrail.com

By boat
American Cruise Lines www.americancruiselines.com
Delray Beach Cruises www.delraybeachcruises.com
Fort Lauderdale Water Taxi www.watertaxi.com
Suwannee Houseboats www.suwanneehouseboats.com

Below left A bike route signboard in Sanibel Island
Below right A trolley driving up Fifth Avenue in Naples

Practical Information

Florida is well prepared with all the practical facilities and services visitors might need, from health care to Wi-Fi connections and ATMs. Advance planning will help to keep things running smoothly and avoid any travel hassles, which can be magnified when holidaying with kids. Travel insurance is always a wise investment for visitors arriving from other countries.

Insurance

The high cost of medical care for non-US residents in America, and the difficulties of lost luggage or flight delays, mean that travel insurance is essential. Policies should cover emergency medical and dental care, trip cancellation, and both baggage and travel document loss. Transportation back home in case of emergency is another option to consider. Your travel agent or insurance company can recommend a suitable policy.

Health

Prescription medications should always be carried in hand baggage, along with general medications for headache, allergies, or stomach upset. Keep prescriptions in their original containers with pharmacy labels so they will pass easily through airport security. Notify security officials if carrying any special items, such as supplies for diabetics. Bring sunscreen for protection from the strong Florida sun, and carry bottled water to avoid dehydration.

MEDICAL EMERGENCIES

Your hotel can recommend a nearby doctor or walk-in facility. While physicians and dentists usually accept credit cards, some may want payment in cash. The locations of hospital emergency rooms can be found online, or ask the concierge or hotel manager for directions. Pharmacies are listed on the map pages in this book. Dial 911 for an **ambulance**.

Personal safety

It pays to be alert, especially to pickpockets, in cities or crowded amusement parks. Keep wallets safe in an inside pocket and carry bags in the crook of the elbow, close to the body. Bags with shoulder straps should go over the head and across the body, and all bags should be kept in the lap in restaurants. Do not flash smartphones or tablets about, and avoid bringing expensive jewelry. Cash must not be left unattended at the beach; waterproof containers that hang around the neck can be purchased from travel stores.

Use the hotel safe to hold passports, a credit card, and some cash; laptops or tablets can fit into many safes. Bringing a photocopy of your passport and credit cards will help with quick replacements in case they are lost. At night, ask the hotel concierge if a neighborhood is safe before venturing out.

Keep your hotel room locked when inside, and don't put out the "make up the room" sign when you go out for the day. Make sure that luggage is only given to a member of the hotel staff, and that a receipt

Below left A crowded amusement park, where visitors should be careful of pickpockets
Below right A City National Bank of Florida ATM, which can be used by most major card holders

is issued for stored luggage. Never leave luggage unattended at airports, at taxi stands, or in hotel lobbies.

Calling 911 is the quickest way to reach the **police** to report a crime, in case of a **fire**, or to summon help if you are hurt. If valuables are lost or stolen, make sure you get a copy of the police report for your insurance claim at home. Contact the embassy of your home country if your passport is lost. The **US Department of State** website has contact information for all foreign embassies in the US.

When visiting crowded theme parks or beaches, decide in advance on a meeting place in case you are separated. Advise kids to look for someone in an official uniform for help if they are lost.

DRIVING SAFETY

Most visitors to Florida get around by car, and while crime is rare, car safety is prudent. Have keys out and ready in order to get into your car quickly, and keep the tank filled to avoid having to search for a service station in an unfamiliar area. It is safer to keep the doors locked and the windows up, using the air-conditioning if necessary. Program an emergency breakdown number into your cell phone and, if an accident occurs, dial 911 to call for police and medical help. If

arriving at an airport late at night, it may be best to stay at an airport hotel and pick up a car in the morning, rather than try to reach an unfamiliar destination on dark roads.

Money

BANKS AND BUREAUX DE CHANGE

Foreign currency can be changed into dollars at banks and bureaux de change such as **Travelex**, which are found at major airports, except at Orlando International Airport, which uses **Interchange**. However, ATMs offer the best exchange rates and the fee is usually lower than at a bureau. Most bank ATMS are part of the worldwide Plus or Cirrus network. ATMs, and almost all businesses and restaurants, accept popular debit and credit cards, though cash advances with credit cards carry interest fees. Check the fees with your own bank or credit card provider before traveling. To guard against crime in towns, use an ATM inside the bank rather than those accessed from the street.

CURRENCY

The basic unit is the dollar, which equals 100 cents. Coins come in one cent (penny), five cent (nickel), ten cent (dime), and 25 cent (quarter) denominations. Each is of a different

size, so it is easy to tell them apart. There is a $1 coin but it is rarely used. The most common bills are $1, $5, $10, and $20, though $50, $100, and larger denominations are available. ATMs give out mostly $20 bills.

CREDIT CARDS, TRAVELER'S CHECKS, AND CASH CARDS

Major credit cards, such as Visa, MasterCard, and American Express, and debit cards are widely accepted throughout the US. Large purchases are best paid for by credit card.

Traveler's checks are still accepted, but have become less common due to ATMs, and are slowly being replaced by cash cards. As with traveler's checks, these cards are paid for in advance, and funds are drawn on as the card is used. Cash cards are issued by card companies such as Visa or MasterCard, and are as easy to use as a credit card, but exchange rates are fixed in advance and security is greater as they have a limited value. They are protected by use of a PIN and/or signature. Fees apply to some services, including reloading the cards.

Visitor information

Visit Florida is the state's official tourism bureau and it can provide contact details for local tourist offices.

Below left Sunbathing near a lifeguard tower at South Beach, Miami
Below right Motorbike policeman patrolling a busy street in Daytona Beach during Bike Week

Communications

Florida has a number of area codes. Toll-free calls are prefixed by 800, 866, 877, or 888. To call outside the area, dial 1 before the area code, even on toll-free calls.To call overseas directly, dial 011, plus the country code, city area code, and number. For operator-assisted calls, dial 01, country code, city code, and number.

CELL PHONES

The prevalence of cell phones has limited public telephones to airports and rail terminals. Hotels often add a hefty charge for phone calls, making cell phones a convenient and economical option. Most modern phones will be compatible with US services, though they may run up high roaming charges; check with your service provider at home. Prepaid phone cards are available at chain stores, such as **WalMart** and Target, as well as convenience stores, such as **7-Eleven**. The phone cards offer lower per-minute rates than most phones.

INTERNET AND EMAIL

Most hotels offer Internet access and/or Wi-Fi, some for free. Free Wi-Fi is also available at many city libraries, and at many branches of Starbucks and McDonald's.

POSTAL SERVICE

Many hotels sell stamps and will mail postcards for guests, or they can direct you to the nearest post office. Delivery of mail abroad usually takes 5 to 10 working days.

Media

NEWSPAPERS AND MAGAZINES

Every large Florida city has its own daily newspaper. Among the most widely read are the *Miami Herald* and *Tampa Bay Times*. National publications such as *USA Today* and *The New York Times* can often be found in street dispensers, along with local papers. For foreign newspapers and other publications, a bookstore is the best bet.

TELEVISION AND RADIO

The major national TV networks are CBS, NBC, ABC, and PBS. Several channels, including CNN, Fox, and ESPN, are available on cable. Kids will enjoy Nickelodeon, Disney, and Cartoon Network, while MTV will appeal to teens. Hotels may also offer pay-per-view movie channels.

Every area has its own radio stations. AM consists mostly of pop music, rock, and talk shows, and some religious stations. In southern Florida, Spanish talk shows and music are popular. Classical music stations are found on the FM band. National Public Radio is popular, with news, talk, and classical music.

Disabled access

Most public transportation, public buildings, hotels, theme parks, restaurants, and attractions are accessible to people with disabilities. **State parks** offer many accessible trails, and many beaches provide wheelchairs that can navigate over sand. Check **Visit Florida**, or the sites you plan to visit, for specific local information.

Restrooms

Most attractions, museums, department stores, and shopping malls have restrooms, complete with baby-changing facilities.

What to pack

Florida life is informal, and dressy clothing is rarely needed, even at upscale restaurants. The air-conditioning in restaurants and theaters can be frigid, so taking a sweater along is advisable.

Hats, insect repellent, sunglasses, and sunscreen are a must for everyone. Bathing suits need time to dry, so a few changes are useful.

Below left *Street dispensers for newspapers and magazines on Sanibel Island*
Below right *Free Internet access for guests advertised at The Radisson Hotel in Buena Vista, Orlando*

Florida does have cool spells in winter, so if you are visiting then, pack a jacket. Do bring rain gear too, as there can be showers year-round.

Stores carrying diapers and formula for infants are plentiful, but carry an emergency supply. Pack a favorite game or book, pajamas, a sweater, water, and a snack in a separate small wheeled suitcase or backpack for each child to carry for quick access en route.

Involving the kids

Children are more excited about travel when they share in the planning. Look at this book with them in advance, and let them choose and look forward to some of the activities ahead. The Internet also has many resources for planning. An inexpensive camera for each child keeps kids interested and provides wonderful souvenirs of the trip.

Opening hours

Business hours are usually 9am to 5pm. Stores open at around 9 or 10am and close at 5 or 6pm, Monday through Saturday, though some may stay open later. Sunday hours vary: some stores open at noon, others do not open at all. Banking hours are traditionally 9am to 3pm Monday to Thursday, and to 6pm on Friday, though several larger banks now remain open until 5 or 6pm during the week. Banks with Saturday hours usually open from 9am to noon. Most museums are open daily, 10am to 5:30pm, but check individual listings.

Electricity

The standard US electric current is 110 volts. An adapter is necessary for European appliances, which run on 220–240 volts.

Florida time

Most of Florida is on Eastern Standard Time, 5 hours behind Greenwich Mean Time (GMT). The exception is the western Panhandle, which is in the Central Standard Time zone, 1 hour behind EST.

Etiquette and tipping

Florida is a favorite family destination and everyone from hotel clerks to bus drivers usually has a friendly smile for young visitors. However, parents should encourage children to be polite and respectful, and if noisy squabbles or loud crying occur in public places, it is best to take kids outside until they calm down.

Visitors should remember that tips are expected for service personnel in the US. The usual amounts are 15–20 percent for waiters or taxi drivers, as well as barbers or hair stylists. Room service tips are often added to the bill. Hotel bellhops should receive around $1 per bag, hotel maids $1–2 per day, and coat checks $1 per garment. While not mandatory, when waiters or others are especially helpful with children, a small extra tip is always appreciated.

The Lowdown

Health and safety
Police, ambulance, fire 911
US Department of State
www.usembassy.gov

Money
Currency exchange locations
www.us.travelex.com
Interchange
www.interchange.eu

Visitor information
Visit Florida 2540 West Executive Center Circle, Suite 200, Tallahassee, 32301; 866 972 5280;
www.visitflorida.com

Communications
7-Eleven
www.7-eleven.com
WalMart
www.walmart.com

Disabled access
State parks floridastateparks.org
Visit Florida www.visitflorida.com/articles/florid-able

Below left *Travelers by the arrival and departure schedule at Orlando International Airport*
Below right *Disability access on the Miami-Dade transit Metrobus*

Where to Stay

With numerous lavish resorts, condos for rent, and campgrounds attracting millions of visitors every year, Florida truly can accommodate every taste and budget. There is a spectrum of accommodations for families – from exclusive resorts to basic motels, which usually have a pool where kids can splash around. Listings of suggested lodgings appear at the end of each chapter in this book, with price categories reflecting the cost for a family of four.

Getting the best deals

The winter months, especially holiday periods, are the most popular and the most expensive. Generally, the closer to the beach, the higher the price, so staying in a basic highway motel and driving to the beach means saving, with rooms lodging four for as little as $150 per night, even in high season. Most places let kids stay free in their parents' room; but some specify that sharers must be under age 12. Bargains can be found in the off-seasons, spring and fall. **Hotels.com**, **Travelocity**, and **Expedia** are good sources to find the lowest rates, while **Kayak** compares many discount hotel sites.

Hidden extras

The state's 6 percent sales tax, plus tourism taxes, can bring the total up a hefty 12 percent.

Remember that tipping (see p29) is not discretionary in the US. Many hotels also add on a daily resort fee. Ask before you book, or you might be presented with an unexpectedly large bill at the end of your stay.

Resorts

Florida boasts resorts with golf, spas, tennis, beaches, and a variety of dining options. **Sandestin Golf and Beach Resort** (see p204) is one that offers a range of accommodations, kids' programs, and its own shops and restaurants. If budget allows, **Ritz-Carlton** resorts and hotels are among the top facilities in the state.

Hotels and motels

Space and cooking facilities are two important pluses for families choosing a hotel or motel. All-suite properties offer extra space, kitchens, and sometimes two TVs. Many modest hotels and motels provide microwaves and small refrigerators. Check whether cots or cribs are available and if they are free, if kids' menus are offered in hotel restaurants, and if the hotel will help with recommended babysitters.

Condos and apartments

Florida is filled with condominiums and efficiency or studio apartments whose owners rent out their quarters when not in residence. Condo units provide comfortable space plus kitchens. Many condo buildings are conveniently located, some right on the beach, and usually have a pool. One-, two-, and three-bedroom units are available, and prices are competitive with hotels. However, there is usually no maid service.

Below left Tents pitched in Little Talbot Island State Park
Below right Kitchen, dining, and living area in Hawks Cay Resort, Duck Key

Condo listings are found in the accommodations guides published by local tourist offices, and also on websites such as **HomeAway**.

House-swapping

Many families report success with house swaps. If you live in Europe, for example, a Florida family might be happy to swap their home for yours, saving each of you a considerable amount of money. Swaps are arranged through specialized agencies such as **Home Exchange** and **Home Link**. For a small monthly fee, prospective swappers sign up and list their homes. Members can scan listings for the places they want to go, select properties, and send privacy-protected emails directly to the owners. It is always a good idea to exchange emails, talk on the phone, and trade recent home photos before signing an agreement.

Campgrounds

Many of the campgrounds for RVs across the state offer playgrounds and pools, as well as table tennis, volleyball, and basketball courts. All offer picnic grounds and convenient laundry facilities. **Camp Florida** has a complete RV Park

directory, with hundreds of listings across the state. There are several RV rental agencies (see p25). Some campgrounds also provide rustic cabins for those without RVs. Guests staying in the cabins at **Disney's Fort Wilderness Resort & Campgrounds** (see p137) are offered complimentary coach transfers from the airport, and transportation to all Walt Disney World® attractions is available from the resort's campground.

State parks

Most of Florida's state parks have campgrounds for tents, and 19 of them also have cabins for rent at rates below most motels, with access to all park facilities. Lodgings range from well-equipped modern cottages such as those at **Grayton Beach State Park** (see p205) to simple log cabins at **Myakka River State Park** (see p229). Bookings are essential and can be made 11 months in advance; check the **Florida State Parks** website for more information.

Bed & breakfast

B&B inns are listed in local tourism directories and can be found through several booking services. These lodgings may be private

homes or small inns. While often charming, not all offer the privacy or noise tolerance that families appreciate. Be sure to ask about specifics and family policies before booking.

The Lowdown

Getting the best deals
Expedia www.expedia.com
Hotels.com www.hotels.com
Kayak www.kayak.com
Travelocity www.travelocity.com

Resorts
Ritz-Carlton www.ritzcarlton.com

Condos and apartments
HomeAway www.homeaway.com

House-swapping
Home Exchange
www.homeexchange.com
Home Link usa.homelink.org

Campgrounds
Camp Florida www.campflorida.com

State parks
Florida State Parks
www.floridastateparks.org

Bed & breakfast
B&B agencies
www.bedandbreakfast.com
www.florida-bed-and-breakfasts.net
www.florida-inns.com

Below left Loungers near the swimming pool at The Biltmore Hotel, Miami
Below right Lavishly decorated lounge at the Hilton Hotel, St. Augustine

Where to Eat

Florida dining offers something to please every palate. Bountiful waters and a benign climate produce superb seafood and tropical fruits. A wide variety of cuisines is available, including simple food for those who prefer it. Because families make up such a large share of the state's visitors, there are plenty of kid-friendly informal restaurants. The price categories in this guide allow for a two-course lunch with a family of four, excluding wine but including soft drinks.

Eating out

Formal restaurants usually open from 7 to 10am for breakfast, from 11:30am to 2pm for lunch, and from 5:30 to 10pm for dinner, but many places serve food all day. "Earlybird specials," for dinner served before 6pm, are economical for families with kids.

A reservation is usually not needed for lunch or at budget restaurants, but dinner at a popular spot usually requires one, especially during the busy seasons. Most restaurants can accommodate strollers and will offer booster seats, but ask in advance at upscale places. A smoking ban is enforced in all restaurants, cafés, and even bars. Tipping is considered mandatory at any non self-service eatery. The minimum acceptable tip is 15 percent, and the standard tip for good service is 20 percent.

Catch of the day

Firm and tender fish such as grouper, mahi mahi, amberjack, pompano, snapper, tuna, and wahoo are staples on the menu, both as entrées and in tasty sandwiches. Large, sweet Gulf shrimp are legendary, and may be served cold with cocktail sauce or used as an ingredient in many dishes. Stone-crab claws are another Florida delicacy, especially prized as they are only available from mid-October to mid-May. Head to Miami's **Joe's Stone Crab** (see p69), where these sweet, meaty claws are served chilled, with a melted butter and mustard sauce.

Tropical treats

Florida is blessed with a bounty of tropical fruits such as oranges, mangoes, melons, and papayas. Weekly farmers' markets are good places for sampling them. Stands offering fresh orange-strawberry juice should not be missed.

Southern comfort

Northern Florida shows its Southern heritage at stops such as **Fish House** (see p195) in Pensacola, which serves a delicious Southern specialty made with grits, a savory porridge made of fine-ground corn, similar to polenta. Shrimp and grits has become a staple around the state. Farther south, the Latin American influence can be seen on menus featuring *ceviche* (a first course of raw seafood usually with a citrus sauce), beans and rice, and plantains.

Choice Cuban

Tampa and Miami, with their large Cuban populations, have

Below left *Elegantly decorated Patio Dining Room of the Columbia Restaurant, Ybor City*
Below center *Fresh tropical fruit at the Lincoln Road Farmers' Market, South Beach*

restaurants serving Spanish dishes such as roast pork, *arroz con pollo* (chicken with spiced rice), and paella. Cuban sandwiches of ham, roast pork, cheese, and pickles served on crunchy bread are a mainstay. **Versailles Restaurant** *(see p62)* is the best-known Little Havana stop on Miami's Calle Ocho, and Tampa's **Columbia Restaurant** *(see p218)* in Ybor City, founded in 1905 and the oldest restaurant in the state, is a must for its flamenco dancers, traditional decor, and great food. It has branches in Sarasota, Orlando, Clearwater, and St. Augustine.

Family favorites

Well-behaved kids will be welcome anywhere, but Florida's many informal outdoor dining choices, especially those on the water, are good for families with young children. Watching the boats at **The Old Salty Dog** *(see p226)* in Sarasota will help to keep youngsters happily occupied. The **Five Guys Burgers and Fries** and **Johnny Rockets** *(see p83)* chains found in many cities offer burgers that are sure to please. For more formal restaurants, dining early is a good idea with kids. To be certain whether better restaurants encourage families, ask if they offer

a kids' menu. If children want more than the usual burgers, chicken fingers, or hot dogs, consider having them split an adult portion.

Sweet treats

The most typical dessert found on menus is Key lime pie, truly authentic only when the tangy filling is made with the small, round, yellow-green limes grown in southern Florida. Flan, a typical Spanish custard, will appeal to youngsters. Many towns have locally owned ice cream parlors that offer specialties such as home-made cones or real Italian-style ices. Miami's **Dolce Vita Gelato Cafe** *(see p55)* is famous for its gelato, while St. Augustine's **Hyppo** *(see p168)* serves gourmet popsicles in unusual flavors.

Allergies and diets

Wheat, milk, and shellfish are mainstays of Florida cooking, so tell your waiter about any special food needs. Most restaurants are good about substitutions, including vegetarian dishes and gluten-free foods. Be sure to mention any nut allergies and carry emergency medications for the whole family.

Below left The Old Salty Dog, a waterfront restaurant that serves hearty food, Sarasota
Below right Diners enjoying a meal at Johnny Rockets, Fort Lauderdale

Shopping

Whether bargain buys, high fashion, toys, books, arts, or handicrafts are on the most-wanted list, Florida does not disappoint shoppers. Children will find irresistible souvenirs across the state, from spacemen and rockets to clown noses and Mickey Mouse ears.

Opening hours

All shops are open from at least 10am to 5pm Monday to Saturday. Sunday hours are generally noon to 5 or 6pm. Call ahead to check if you want to visit a specific shop or mall.

Bargain bonanzas

The state's big outlet malls, with stores from major manufacturers, sometimes called factory stores, promise savings. The biggest outlet is **Sawgrass Mills** in Sunrise, with more than 350 shops including Polo Ralph Lauren for Children, Tommy Hilfiger Kids, and the Children's Place Factory Store. Patient kids can be rewarded with stops at the Build-a-Bear Workshop, LEGO® store, and the Game Works arcade.

The **Dolphin Mall** in Miami offers well-known brands and factory outlets for popular stores such as Coach Leather and Banana Republic. Toys"R"Us will please

kids, Gymboree has clothes for newborns to age 12, and Justice and Journeys are stores aimed at tweens and teens.

Premium is a major outlet operator with malls around the state, including in Orlando and St. Augustine. **Silver Sands Premium Outlets** in Sandestin (see p191) offers GapKids, Gucci Kids, and The Children's Place outlets. The customer service offices at the malls usually have a free coupon book with extra savings at selected stores.

Markets

Most communities have weekly markets where local farmers display fresh produce and stalls sell cooked savories and desserts. The **Saturday Morning Market** on St. Petersburg's waterfront (see p211) is one of the biggest and best of these events, as is the colorful **Daytona Flea and Farmers' Market**, where flea

market finds add to the fun every Friday, Saturday, and Sunday.

Arty adventures

Artists and artisans seem to thrive in the Florida sun, and galleries abound in every town. The **Quayside Art Gallery** (see p195) in Pensacola is owned and run by local artists, and the **Florida CraftArt Gallery** in St. Petersburg shows the best of jewelry and other creative crafts.

The many colorful outdoor fairs that take place around the state are fun for the family, and often offer a chance to talk to the artists. The **Florida Folk Festival** (see p14) is one where artisans show and sell traditional folk crafts.

Disney delights

The World of Disney® store in the **Disney Springs® Marketplace** (see p117) has everything any kid could want, from a Mickey Mouse watch

Below left Fresh produce for sale at one of the many farmers' markets across Florida
Below right Prints and gifts inspired by Salvador Dalí at the store in The Dalí Museum, St. Petersburg

to a princess tiara. Once Upon a Toy, a delightful toy store with a miniature train running on suspended tracks overhead, stocks some classic games redesigned with Disney themes and lets kids play with toys at the build-your-own light saber and Mr. Potato Head areas. The LEGO® Imagination Store here is sure to inspire young builders with its fun LEGO® display sculptures. Star Wars fans of all ages will find everything from T-shirts and costumes to action figures from all the Star Wars films, along with plushy Yodas and BB-8s.

Museum shops

Museum shops stock items to interest all ages, especially the ones in the **Ringling** (see p225), which has all kinds of circus paraphernalia, including juggling balls and puzzles, and **The Dalí Museum** (see p221) with its melted watches and other souvenirs.

Pocket-money toys

Learning Express stores, located across Florida, will please parents and kids alike with their stock of toys that are educational as well as fun. Stores such as **Dollar General** and **Family Dollar**, where many

things, including toys and snacks, cost just $1, are a shopper's delight. Almost every town has a dollar store and the variety of offerings is surprising.

Books

The big stores, such as **Barnes & Noble**, are almost everywhere, and have extensive kids' departments, but book-loving Florida still has many independent stores. The enormous **Vero Beach Book Center** includes a separate store dedicated to kids. In St. Petersburg is Florida's largest

book store, **Haslam's Book Store**, packed with some 350,000 new and used books.

Many Florida communities hold outdoor book fairs that are fun for the entire family. Author signings and children's events are part of the festivities. The biggest, the **Miami Book Fair International**, held in November, draws as many as 350 authors and includes a Children's Alley with storytelling, puppets, and games. The **Festival of Reading** in St. Petersburg features a Children's Storyland with costumed characters, games, and activities.

The Lowdown

Bargain bonanzas
Dolphin Mall www.shopdolphinmall.com
Premium www.premiumoutlets.com
Sawgrass Mills www.simon.com/mall/?id=1262

Markets
Daytona Flea and Farmers' Market 1425 Tomoka Farms Rd, 32124; 386 253 3330; www.daytonafleamarket.com

Arty adventures
Crafts Fairs www.artfestival.com
Florida CraftArt Gallery 501 Central Ave, St. Petersburg, 33701; 727 821 7391; www.floridacraftart.org

Pocket-money toys
Dollar General www.dollargeneral.com

Family Dollar www.familydollar.com
Learning Express www.learningexpress.com

Books
Barnes & Noble www.barnesandnoble.com
Festival of Reading University of South Florida, St. Petersburg; www.tampabay.com/expos/festival-of-reading
Haslam's Book Store, 2025 Central Ave, St. Petersburg, 727 822 8616; www.haslams.com
Miami Book Fair International, Miami-Dade College, 305 237 3258; www.miamibookfair.com
Vero Beach Book Center, 392 21st St, Vero Beach; 772 569 2050; www.verobeachbookcenter.com

Below left The food court at Premium, one of the biggest outlet malls in Orlando
Below right A plethora of Disney plush toys and memorabilia at the Disney Springs® Marketplace

Entertainment

Florida's menu of entertainment runs the gamut from Broadway musicals and rock concerts to the ballet, with many performances aimed at kids. A wide range of events is found in southern Florida, especially in Miami and along the Gold Coast. Tampa and Sarasota are major cultural centers on the Gulf Coast, and theme-park haven Orlando has no lack of interesting happenings either. University cities such as Gainesville and Tallahassee also host exciting events.

Sources of information

In most Florida cities, the Friday newspapers usually include a weekend section listing regional events. Convention and Visitors' Bureaus and Chambers of Commerce are good sources for brochures and local information.

Making reservations

It is best to check online for advance sales information and pay by credit card. Buying by phone or online usually involves a service charge anywhere from $2–8 above the ticket price. Some venues handle sales through **Ticketmaster**.

Major venues

The largest venues feature a range of productions that may include appearances by touring Broadway companies and well-known national performers, and local companies. The largest centers on the east coast are the **Adrienne Arsht Center for the Performing Arts** in Miami, **Broward Center for the Performing Arts** in Fort Lauderdale, and the **Raymond F. Kravis Center for the Performing Arts** in West Palm Beach. West coast centers include the **David A. Straz Center for the Performing Arts** in Tampa, and the **Barbara B. Mann Performing Arts Hall** in Fort Myers. Rock stars usually play in stadiums such as the **Hard Rock Stadium** in Miami Gardens, **Florida Citrus Bowl** and **Amway Center** in Orlando, and **EverBank Field** in Jacksonville.

Theater

The **Asolo Repertory Theater** in Sarasota and the **Florida Rep** in Fort Myers present a range of plays, including many musicals that enthrall families. The **Orlando Shakespeare Theater** (see p130) offers modern plays and the Bard's works, along with plays for kids. The **Riverside Theater** (see p94) in Vero Beach and **Actors' Playhouse** (see p52) in Miami also include kids' theater, while the **Miami Children's Theater, Fort Lauderdale Children's Theater,** and Jacksonville's **Theatreworks** are devoted to young audiences. In Delray Beach, the **Puppetry Arts Center** delights with its puppet productions and museum.

Dinner theater

A number of theaters serve dinner along with entertainment, the latter being generally family-friendly works, including Broadway

Below left *The Orlando Shakespeare Theater staging the classic fairy tale* Snow White and the Seven Dwarfs
Below center *Graceful aerialists performing at the Flying High Circus in Tallahassee*

musicals. Theme theaters such as **Medieval Times**, in Kissimmee, have special lures, in this case knights in armor jousting on horseback. The **Murder Mystery Dinner Train** in Fort Myers combines dinner with a train ride and the chance to solve a mystery.

with many international stars, pitches its tent for the month of February. The **Sailor Circus**, featuring young performers, takes place in Sarasota during the last week in December and January and the first week in April. The **Flying High Circus** shows off awe-inspiring aerial and ground

routines in Tallahassee each April. While the popular **Cirque du Soleil** show La Nouba closed in 2017 after a 20 year run at Disney Springs in Orlando, a new show, inspired by Disney's rich history of animation,is slated to open soon under the big white tent.

Music, dance, and film

The **Miami Symphony Orchestra** plays around the region, while a stunning Miami Beach building by architect Frank Gehry, the New World Center, is home to the **New World Symphony**. The **Miami City Ballet** dances in Miami, Palm Beach, Fort Lauderdale, and Naples, and presents free programs for young people in winter. The **Sarasota Orchestra** plays both classical and pop music, as does the **Orlando Philharmonic Orchestra**. The **Florida Film Festival** draws international filmmakers to central Florida, while the **Sarasota Film Festival** devotes a day to "Short Stacks," with pancakes to eat and short films for family viewing.

Circuses

Florida's circus heritage can be seen in shows delighting all ages. **Circus Sarasota**, a one-ring circus

The Lowdown

Making reservations
Ticketmaster *www.ticketmaster.com*

Major venues
Adrienne Arsht Center for the Performing Arts *www.arshtcenter.org*
Amway Center *www.amwaycenter.com*
Barbara B. Mann Performing Arts Hall *bbmannpah.com*
Broward Center for the Performing Arts *browardcenter.org*
David A. Straz Center for the Performing Arts *www.strazcenter.org*
EverBank Field 1 Stadium Blvd, Jacksonville; 904 633 6100
Florida Citrus Bowl *www.fcsports.com*
Hard Rock Stadium *hardrockstadium.com*
Raymond F. Kravis Center for the Performing Arts *www.kravis.org*

Theater
Asolo Repertory Theatre *www.asolorep.org*
Florida Rep *floridarep.org*
Fort Lauderdale Children's Theater *flct.org*
Miami Children's Theater *www.miamichildrenstheater.biz*

Puppetry Arts Center *puppetcenter.org*
Theatreworks *theatreworksjax.com*

Dinner theater
Medieval Times *medievaltimes.com*
Murder Mystery Dinner Train *semgulf.com*

Music, dance, and film
Florida Film Festival *www.florida filmfestival.org*
Miami City Ballet *miamicityballet.org*
Miami Symphony Orchestra *themiso.org*
New World Symphony *www.nws.edu*
Orlando Philharmonic Orchestra *www.orlandophil.org*
Sarasota Film Festival *www.sarasota filmfestival.com*
Sarasota Orchestra *sarasota orchestra.org*

Circuses
Circus Sarasota *www.circusarts.org*
Flying High Circus *circus.fsu.edu*
Sailor Circus *www.circusarts.org*
Cirque du Soleil *www.cirquedu soleil.com*

Below left *An actor mingling with guests aboard the Murder Mystery Dinner Train, Fort Myers*
Below right *Dance performance at Miami City Ballet*

The History of Florida

Beyond its sunny beaches and theme parks, Florida has a rich history to share – from prehistoric times and Native American settlements to Spanish arrival and an eventful couple of hundred years when the area constantly changed hands, before relaxing into a Golden Age. The grand buildings of yesteryear that sit alongside modern architecture are just one example of the fascinating remnants of Florida's past waiting to be discovered.

Early settlers

Florida's history began with the Paleo-Indians – big-game hunters who probably crossed the Bering Strait from Asia (Eurasia) into North America over a land and ice bridge as long as 12,000 years ago. They settled where fresh water was available, sharing the land with massive animals such as mastodons, giant sloths, and mammoths.

Over the centuries, tribes settled down into villages, grew crops, and began customs such as creating burial mounds, which can still be seen today. By the time Europeans arrived in this part of the New World, Florida was inhabited by an estimated 350,000 people from a number of tribes. The Spanish and British recorded the names of nearly 100 groups they came across; the largest among these were the Apalachee and the Timucua.

Timucua Indians killing alligators in northeast Florida, around the mid-16th century

Spanish Florida

Florida's written history began when the Spanish explorer Ponce de León "discovered" the region in 1513, probably landing near St. Augustine. He named his discovery "La Florida" after the Spanish Easter feast known as Pascua Florida. More explorations followed, some led by the conquistador Hernando de Soto (around 1497–1542). The Spanish introduced Christianity, horses, and cattle to Florida, but they also brought new diseases such as smallpox and typhoid fever, and massacred many of the local people in their quest to find gold and treasure. In the 1770s, Florida's Native American tribes became known collectively as Seminoles, a name meaning "wild people" or "untamed."

Hot on the heels of the Spanish came the British, who wanted another kind of treasure – valuable hides and furs. They took control of Florida in 1763 by swapping Cuba for it. After the British lost the Revolutionary War to the US, the Spanish regained Florida with the Second Treaty of Paris of 1783. They remained in charge until 1819, when the region was handed over to the US to settle Spain's debts and

Timeline

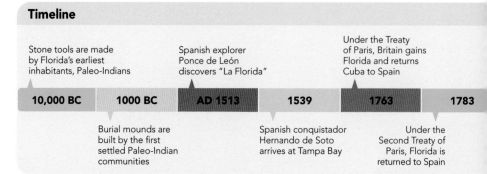

Stone tools are made by Florida's earliest inhabitants, Paleo-Indians	Spanish explorer Ponce de León discovers "La Florida"	Under the Treaty of Paris, Britain gains Florida and returns Cuba to Spain	
10,000 BC	**1000 BC**	**AD 1513**	**1539**	**1763**	**1783**
	Burial mounds are built by the first settled Paleo-Indian communities	Spanish conquistador Hernando de Soto arrives at Tampa Bay	Under the Second Treaty of Paris, Florida is returned to Spain

became a US territory. Spain's lasting influence can be seen in the state's churches, architecture, and food.

The Seminole Wars

In the period before the Civil War, known as the antebellum, runaway slaves taking refuge in Florida found sympathy from the Indian tribes, creating growing conflicts with the US. By 1817, antagonism had escalated into the first of three Seminole wars. Future US president Andrew Jackson invaded the then-Spanish Florida and defeated the Seminoles. Under the US flag, a plantation economy based on slavery, as in other Southern states, began to develop here. Land was at a premium and pressure grew on the US government to remove the Indians from their lands. In 1832, the US signed the Treaty of Payne's Landing with some of the Seminole chiefs, promising them lands west

Seminole Indians preparing to ambush American troops in the First Seminole War

of the Mississippi River if the tribes would leave Florida peacefully. Many agreed, but those who remained were prepared to defend their land. From 1835 to 1842, and again from 1855 to 1858, Seminole warriors defied the far more powerful US Army. In the end, though, it was a lost cause and almost all the Seminoles were forcibly exiled. But a band of some 300 stubbornly remained, hiding in the Everglades wilderness. Their descendants are the Seminole tribes of today.

The State of Florida

Florida became the 27th US state in 1845. Most of the state's population was in the northern area, where the plantation culture flourished. By 1850, the population had grown to 87,445; almost half were African-American slaves. In 1861, to preserve its plantation way of life, the state broke away from the Union and joined the Confederate States of America. Located well south of the fighting, Florida was spared the destruction experienced in other Southern states during the Civil War (1861–5). Its main role was to provide an estimated 15,000 troops, plus cotton, and food supplies, including salt, beef, and pork, to the Confederacy. When the Confederates lost the war and slavery was outlawed, the plantation economy waned. But soon canny developers had their eyes on a new source of wealth – tourism.

HISTORICAL SITES

Cathedral Basilica of St. Augustine
Admire the fine example of Spanish architecture that has influenced many of Florida's buildings *(see p171)*.

Museum of Arts and Sciences (MOAS)
Gaze at the prehistoric giant sloth here, which stands 12 ft (4 m) high *(see pp176–7)*.

Indian Temple Mound Museum
Discover the huge collection of ceramic artifacts at this museum adjacent to one of Florida's largest Indian ceremonial mounds *(see p191)*.

Mission San Luis
Witness a rare example of racial harmony, as costumed interpreters bring to life the site shared by the Spanish and Apalachee Indians *(see p200)*.

Kingsley Plantation
Visit the oldest plantation house in Florida and explore its restored main house, kitchen, and barn, plus the ruins of 25 original slave cabins *(see p165)*.

Ybor City Museum State Park
Trace the story of the city's cigar industry and look at a restored cigar worker's home *(see p218)*.

Andrew Jackson's army enters Florida in First Seminole War

Florida becomes the 27th US state

1818　　**1825**　　**1845**　　**1861**

The village of Talasi is chosen as the state capital and renamed Tallahassee

Florida joins the Confederate States of America

Florida's Golden Age

While most of Florida's early development had been in the northern part of the state, the agreeable climate of the land farther south made it attractive for development. Railroad barons such as Henry Flagler on the east coast and Henry Plant on the west expanded their railroads in the late 1880s and 1890s, and began building the first grand hotels to attract passengers. Tourism boomed, fortunes were made, and fine mansions were built.

The railroads also meant that the Sunshine State's juicy crops of oranges and lemons could reach eager buyers all over the country, and soon Florida was the nation's biggest citrus fruit producer. Immigrants from the nearby Caribbean island of Cuba brought with them the skill of making highly

Portrait of Henry Flagler, founder of the Florida East Coast Railway

prized cigars. Tampa's warm, humid climate suited the rolling of tobacco leaves perfectly, and Ybor City (see p218) was founded there in 1885 by Cuban manufacturer Vicente Martinez Ybor as a home for his factory and workers.

Boom and bust

Henry Ford's Model T began rolling off the assembly lines in 1908, making automobiles affordable for the first time, and nowhere was the effect felt more strongly than in Florida, where "tin can tourists" came streaming in. In 1914, entrepreneur Carl Fisher came up with the idea of building the north–south Dixie Highway, which eventually ran all the way from the Canadian border to southern Florida. At the southern end of the highway, Fisher dreamed up a new resort city, Miami Beach (see pp66–71). During the 1920s, investors of all kinds raced to buy and sell land in South Florida communities such as Miami and Palm Beach (see pp88–9). Prices soared, and con men entered the picture. Some foolish buyers purchased land sight unseen, only to find themselves the owners of worthless swampland. By 1925, prices were astronomical, buyers became scarce, and the real estate boom turned to bust. A devastating hurricane in Miami in 1926 depressed the market even farther. By the time the Great Depression began in the rest of the nation in 1929, residents of Florida had already experienced economic hardship.

Children riding on a flivver car in Coral Gables, a "tin can tourist" tent city

A second boom

Government work programs and the flourishing citrus industry helped Florida ride out the Depression, and many unemployed people arrived from all over the US, looking for work and helping the state's economy grow. World War II brought another boom as Florida's year-round mild climate made it ideal as a major training center for the US army and navy. Highway and airport construction followed, and by the war's end an up-to-date transportation system was ready and waiting for visitors.

Newcomers arrived from other countries too, especially in Miami. Fidel Castro's rise to power in Cuba in 1959 brought an influx of Cubans, and unrest in Haiti in the 1970s led to the founding of the community known as Little Haiti.

The first Daytona 500 roared into action in 1959, making the Daytona International Speedway (see p174) a mecca for auto-racing fans the world over. Space exploration and the arrival of NASA

Timeline

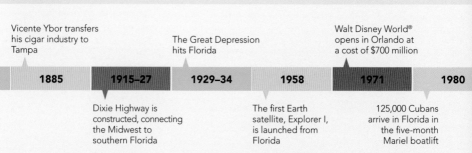

Vicente Ybor transfers his cigar industry to Tampa

The Great Depression hits Florida

Walt Disney World® opens in Orlando at a cost of $700 million

| 1885 | 1915–27 | 1929–34 | 1958 | 1971 | 1980 |

Dixie Highway is constructed, connecting the Midwest to southern Florida

The first Earth satellite, Explorer I, is launched from Florida

125,000 Cubans arrive in Florida in the five-month Mariel boatlift

and the Kennedy Space Center *(see pp144–7)* in 1962 also brought jobs and more visitors. The theme park era began in 1959 when Busch Gardens *(see pp214–5)* opened in Tampa, and 10,000 people were waiting impatiently at the gates when Walt Disney World® *(see pp106–17)* made its debut in 1971.

Florida today

Modern-day Florida is the fourth most populous state in the US, and one of the most popular vacation destinations in the world. Twenty percent of this flourishing state's diverse population consists of retirees aged over 65, who are drawn by its mild climate. Well over 300,000 of the Cubans who fled to South Florida from the 1960s onwards have settled here, raised families, and become influential in business and state politics. Walt Disney World® grows bigger every year and has been joined by Universal Studios

Florida® *(see pp118–19)*, SeaWorld® *(see pp122–3)* and LEGOLAND® Florida Resort *(see pp132–5)* to make Orlando the theme park capital of the world.

Miami Beach's 1930s Art Deco architecture has been rediscovered by the young and hip, who flock to the hotels and nightclubs in town. The state has also become the major US center for the growing cruise industry, with ports in Miami, Fort Lauderdale *(see pp80–81)*, Tampa, and Port Canaveral, near Orlando, serving thousands of cruisers each year. All of this means jobs, and with the citrus industry and tourism joined by more recent industries including electronics, plastics, construction, and international banking, younger job aspirants have added to the rush to Florida. Like most of the world, Florida has felt the cloud of the global economic slowdown that began in 2008, but whatever lies ahead, the sun will continue to shine in Florida.

The Art Deco facade of the Jackie Gleason Theater of the Performing Arts, Miami

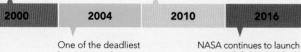

2000	2004	2010	2016

George Bush wins presidential election, with Florida as the decisive state

One of the deadliest hurricanes in history, Hurricane Frances, inflicts damage worth $9 billion

A major oil spill by a BP oil rig slows down tourism. A successful clean-up effort follows

NASA continues to launch spacecraft from Florida, along with private ventures such as Space-X

The beautiful white-sand beach at Fort Zachary Taylor Historic State Park, Key West, with coral rocks and a backdrop of Australian pines

Exploring
FLORIDA

Miami

Exotic, glamorous, colorful, and cosmopolitan: Miami is everything the movies make it out to be. The city took on its multicultural character with the early migrations of New York Jews and Bahamians. Since then, an influx of people of other nationalities, including Cubans, Haitians, Brazilians, and Jamaicans, has influenced Miami's food, arts, and culture. Families will enjoy the city's carnival-like atmosphere.

Highlights

Vizcaya Museum and Gardens
Miami's best-known and most-eccentric landmark, this fantasy palace and its gardens offer a fun, imaginative day out (see pp60–61).

South Beach
Admire this neighborhood, Miami's most-filmed district, with dazzling Art Deco buildings. Kids love it for its great beach (see pp68–9).

Coral Gables
Built out of locally quarried rock in the 1920s, the "City Beautiful" boasts elegant architecture, and offers family-friendly museums and parks (see pp52–3).

Coconut Grove
Shop, dine, and enjoy the festive atmosphere in this fashionable destination, once a Bahamian settlement and then a hippie hangout (see p54).

Downtown Miami
Head to this bustling area that is home to the lively Bayfront Park and Marketplace, as well as the Little Havana Cuban community (see pp58–9).

North Miami Beach
Enjoy the world-class shopping and high-rise resorts in Miami's latest hot spots: Surfside, Sunny Isles, and Bal Harbour (see p70).

Left Classic vintage Cadillac parked outside a hotel in the historic Art Deco District, South Beach
Above right Brightly plumaged macaws in Jungle Island

The Best of
Miami

Though Miami is famous for its nightlife, the city also ranks high as an arty destination, with annual festivals, museums, theaters, and galleries that reflect its rich and varied cultural heritage. The city's coastal location makes it attractive to families interested in watersports and other seaside activities. In addition, there are a variety of parks, zoos, and hands-on attractions that are of great interest and appeal to visitors of all ages.

A weekend at the beach

The best family beaches lie across the causeway from downtown on Virginia Key and Key Biscayne. Get to **Bill Baggs Cape Florida State Park** (see p65) in time for a lighthouse tour, and climb the lighthouse for an overview of Key Biscayne's beaches and beyond. Have lunch at the park's beach restaurant before renting a kayak or hydro-bike to play in the waves. Visit **Crandon Park** (see pp64–5) in the afternoon to relax on the beach, then explore the park's **Marjory Stoneman Douglas Biscayne Nature Center** (see p65) for a break from the sun. Next, go to **Virginia Key Beach Park** (see p64) for some fun in the playground. Visit **South Beach** (see pp68–9) to round off a weekend on the beaches of Miami. Head for **South Pointe Park** (see p68) to get away from the crowds and watch cruise ships chugging in and out of port.

Left Signboard at the entrance to Española Way, South Beach
Below The Stone House in the Deering Estate at Cutler

Above *One of the numerous brightly colored lifeguard stations in South Beach*

Retro ride through the city

For a relatively new city, Miami has lots of history, most of which centers around the 1910s and 1920s. Start with a guided Art Deco District walking tour in **South Beach**, then visit the **Jewish Museum of Florida** (*see p68*), which explores another aspect of the state's past. South of downtown, the **Vizcaya Museum and Gardens** (*see pp60–61*) was built in 1916 to look old and European. In **Coral Gables** (*see pp52–3*), homes dating back to the 1920s populate one of the country's most successful planned developments; learn more at the **Coral Gables Museum** (*see p53*). Built around 1891 in a virgin hardwood forest, **The Barnacle Historic State Park** in **Coconut Grove** (*see p54*) offers a chance to glimpse old Florida. Visit the **Deering Estate at Cutler** (*see p56*), which belonged to Charles Deering, brother of James Deering, who built **Vizcaya**. Another historic structure reveals a man's bizarre dream in the **Coral Castle** (*see p57*) in Homestead.

Animal safari

Families that love animals can see them in the wild and at attractions throughout Miami. Take a boat excursion from **Bayside Marketplace** (*see p61*) to look for dolphins in the sea, then head to **Miami Seaquarium®** (*see p64*) on Key Biscayne to take a closer look at them, along with whales and sea lions. Check out the crocodiles, sharks, manatees, and other sea creatures. Heading south, the **Phillip and Patricia Frost Museum of Science** (*see p63*)

and **Zoo Miami** (*see pp56–7*) both provide opportunities to get up-close with animals. En route to **South Beach**, **Jungle Island** (*see p63*) is home to exotic birds, kangaroos, and big cats.

Culture quest

The clacking of dominoes, the whiff of strong coffee, the strains of Latin salsa, and the thick, heady aroma of cigar smoke are as much a part of Miami as its beaches. Little Havana is the place to start cultural explorations. Walk **Calle Ocho** (*see p62*) and take in Domino Park, the shops, and the food. While in downtown, check out **Perez Art Museum Miami** (*see p62*). In **Coconut Grove**, get a taste of Bahamian architecture in Charles Avenue Historic District. In **South Beach**, a true taste of Haiti is on offer at the **Tap Tap Haitian Restaurant** (*see p69*). Along **Española Way** (*see p68*), Latin is the flavor *du jour*.

Right *Paraphernalia on display at the Cuban settlement of Calle Ocho in Miami*

Miami

The southernmost point in Florida, before the mainland tapers off into the string of islands known as the Florida Keys, Miami consists of a massive metropolitan and suburban area fronted by bustling Miami Beach and quieter Key Biscayne. Biscayne Bay separates the mainland from the two islands; the toll causeway leads to Key Biscayne, and five bridges cross over to Miami Beach. Interstate 95 and Florida's Turnpike (Route 821) dissect the city north to south. Highway 1, also known as Dixie Highway, runs parallel near the bay. The Miami-Dade Transit buses and trains provide public transportation.

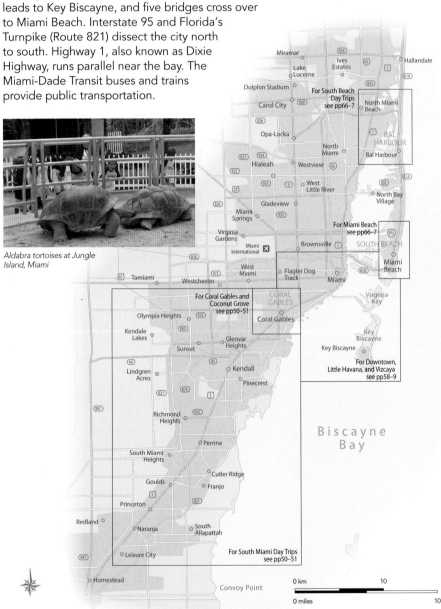

Aldabra tortoises at Jungle Island, Miami

The famous Big Pink restaurant on Collins Avenue, Miami Beach

Bronze statue of founder George Merrick outside the Coral Gables City Hall

Kids learning about the Cruise Ship exhibit at Miami Children's Museum

View from the lighthouse at Bill Baggs Cape Florida State Park, Key Biscayne

The Lowdown

Getting there and around Air Fly into Miami International Airport (*www.miami-airport.com*). Taxis are readily available at the airport, but not on the streets; call ahead on 305 876 7000 for more information. **Bus** and **Train** Miami-Dade Transit (*www.miamidade.gov/transit*) operates Metrobus, Metromover (in downtown), and Metrorail, with airport connections. **Car** Rental services such as Avis (*www.avis.com*) and Hertz (*www.hertz.com*) are available at the airport; all cars, including rentals, need a transponder device to use Florida's Turnpike.

Visitor information Greater Miami Convention and Visitors Bureau, 701 Brickell Ave, St 2700, Miami, 33131; 305 539 3000 & 800 933 8448; *www.miamiand beaches.com*

Supermarkets Publix (*www.publix.com*) and Winn-Dixie (*www.winndixie.com*) have outlets throughout the city. **Markets** Families will find small ethnic food shops in Little Havana, Little Haiti, South Beach, and other cultural enclaves.

Festivals See Coral Gables and Coconut Grove (*pp50–51*), Downtown, Little Havana, and Vizcaya (*pp58–9*), and Miami Beach (*pp66–7*).

Pharmacies Publix, Walgreens (*www.walgreens.com*), and CVS (*www.cvs.com/pharmacy*) pharmacies can be found around the city; some CVS and Walgreens branches are open 24 hours.

Restrooms Almost all major attractions, restaurants, malls, and most gas stations have public restrooms.

Coral Gables, Coconut Grove, and around

South Miami has some of the metropolitan area's oldest, most interesting, and most family-friendly neighborhoods. Lush tropical greenery shades winding streets where beautiful mansions and well-manicured parks can be found. Coral Gables and Coconut Grove are the two most popular districts in this part of the city, but visitors should not miss historic Cutler Bay, nor Homestead, an agricultural town at the edge of the Everglades National Park and the Florida Keys. Farther afield, families will find plenty to see and do at the Fruit & Spice Park, Coral Castle, and Zoo Miami (see p57).

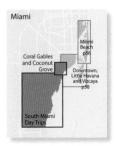

Elegantly decorated interior of the house in Barnacle Historic State Park, Coconut Grove

Places of interest

SIGHTS

1. Coral Gables
2. Coconut Grove
3. The Barnacle Historic State Park
4. Peacock Park
5. Fairchild Tropical Garden
6. Deering Estate at Cutler
7. Zoo Miami
8. Coral Castle

● EAT AND DRINK

1. Publix Supermarket and Deli
2. Al's Coffee Shop
3. The Cascade
4. Ortanique on the Mile
5. The Cheesecake Factory
6. Le Bouchon du Grove
7. Rincón Argentino
8. LuLu
9. Dolce Vita Gelato Cafe
10. Peacock Garden Cafe

● SHOPPING

1. Miracle Mile

● WHERE TO STAY

1. The Biltmore Hotel
2. Sonesta Bayfront Hotel

The Lowdown

🚗 **Getting around** Hiring a car is the best way to get around Coral Gables and Coconut Grove, though traffic gets quite heavy. The Florida Turnpike (see inset map) is quickest when traveling to the southwest quadrant. Metrorail from downtown travels to both neighborhoods and beyond, but not as far as Homestead. However, bus 34 connects the Metrorail terminus with Homestead.

ℹ️ **Visitor information** Coral Gables Chamber of Commerce, 224 Catalonia Ave, Coral Gables 33134; 305 446 1657; coralgables chamber.org. Coconut Grove Chamber of Commerce, 3059 Grand Ave, Suite 210, 33133; 305 444 7270; www.coconutgrove chamber.com.Tropical Everglades Visitor Center, 160 US 1, Florida City, 33034; 305 245 9180; www. tropicaleverglades.com

🛒 **Supermarkets** Publix,14601, S Dixie Hwy, 33176; 305 255 8005 & 2270 SW 27th Ave, 33145; 305 445 9661; www.publix.com
Markets Saturday Farmers' Market, 405 Biltmore Way, Coral Gables, 33134; also at 3300 Grand Ave at the intersection of Margaret St, Coconut Grove, 33133; every Sat

🎪 **Festivals** Redland Festivals at the Fruit & Spice Park (year-round).

Coconut Grove Arts Festival, www.cgaf.com (Feb). Washington's Birthday Regatta (Feb). Deering Seafood Festival (Mar). The Barnacle Old Fashioned 4th of July Picnic (Jul). International Mango Festival (Jul). Zoo Boo at Zoo Miami (Oct)

➕ **Pharmacy** Walgreens, 3595 Coral Way, Coral Gables, 33145; 305 444 8427; www.walgreens.com; open 24 hours

🛝 **Nearest playgrounds** Salvador Park, 1120 Andalusia Ave, 33134; 305 460 5333 (see p53). Peacock Park, 2820 McFarlane Rd, 33133; 305 442 0375; daily (see p55)

Children playing in a tidal pool in Matheson Hammock County Park, Coral Gables

① Coral Gables
City of fantasy

A city out of a storybook, Coral Gables was built by real estate developer George Merrick, who envisioned one of the first and most successfully planned suburbs in the US. Known as the "City Beautiful," it earns its moniker from oak-shaded streets lined with homes of international lineage. The city boasts one of the most beautiful public swimming pools in the world – the Venetian Pool, formerly a limestone quarry. Families will enjoy the area's green spaces and its splendid architecture.

Exterior of The Biltmore Hotel

Key Sights

① **Miracle Mile** Graceful stone fountains bookend this 1950s strip of shops and restaurants decorated down the middle with pretty pineapple-shaped date palms.

② **Actors' Playhouse** Housed within the vintage Miracle Theatre, with an old-fashioned marquee, it stages plays by and for kids, as well as adult programs.

③ **City Hall** Built in Mediterranean Revival style, to match the homes and commercial buildings of the Coral Gables community, this circa-1927 beauty sits on Miracle Mile.

④ **Venetian Pool** Stone bridges, caves, waterfalls, and lush vegetation surround this fantasy swimming pool carved from a former coral limestone quarry – the source of building materials in Coral Gables.

⑤ **The Biltmore Hotel** Favored by the rich and famous since its opening in 1926, this historic hotel looks like a castle out of a fairy tale.

⑥ **Lowe Art Museum** This museum at the University of Miami has American, Native American, Renaissance, European, and Asian art in its permanent collection, and also hosts traveling exhibitions.

⑦ **French Country Village** One of Coral Gables' international villages, this residential village still has several examples of its original architecture. Ivy, wood-slat accents and cottage styling give the homes a French provincial feel.

⑧ **Matheson Hammock County Park** A major draw for families, the Atoll Pool Beach here is entirely enclosed and ringed by palm trees, and is safe for small kids. Playgrounds, shaded picnic areas, bike paths, nature trails, and a sailing school make the park fun for all ages.

Prices given are for a family of four

The Lowdown

🌐 **Map reference** 11 C4
Address Actors' Playhouse: 280 Miracle Mile, 33134; *www.actorsplayhouse.org*. City Hall: 405 Biltmore Way, 33134; *www.coralgables.com*. Venetian Pool: 2701 DeSoto Blvd, 33134; *www.coralgables.com*. The Biltmore Hotel: 1200 Anastasia Ave, 33134; *www.biltmorehotel.com*. Lowe Art Museum: 1301 Stanford Dr, 33124; *www.lowemuseum.org*. Matheson Hammock County Park: 9610 Old Cutler Rd, 33156; *www.miamidade.gov*

🚗 **Metro** Metrorail to Douglas Road station, then bus 37

ℹ️ **Visitor information** Coral Gables Chamber of Commerce, 224 Catalonia Ave, 33134; *coralgableschamber.org*

🕐 **Open** Actors' Playhouse: box office 10am–6pm Mon–Sat & noon–6pm Sun. City Hall: 8am–5pm Mon–Fri. Venetian Pool: 11am–5:30pm Mon–Fri & 10am–4:30pm Sat–Sun; closed Dec–Jan. Lowe Art Museum: 10am–4pm Tue–Sat & noon–4pm Sun. Matheson Hammock County Park: sunrise–sunset daily

💲 **Price** Actors' Playhouse: ticket prices vary. City Hall & The Biltmore Hotel: free. Venetian Pool: $50–70. Lowe Art Museum: $25–40; under 12s free. Matheson Hammock County Park: $5–7 per vehicle

Letting off steam
Salvador Park (1120 Andalusia Ave, 33134) has open spaces shaded by tropical trees, plus playgrounds and picnic shelters. A short distance east, **Whip 'n Dip** (1407 Sunset Dr, 33143) is renowned for homemade ice cream.

Snacks and coffee at the popular Al's Coffee Shop, Coral Gables

Eat and drink
Picnic: under $25; Snacks: $25–50; Real meal: $50–80; Family treat: over $80 (based on a family of four)

PICNIC Publix Supermarket and Deli (2270 SW 27th Ave, 33145; 305 445 9661; www.publix.com) sells take-out subs, salads, chicken wings, beverages, and other snacks. Zip to Salvador Park for a picnic.
SNACKS Al's Coffee Shop (2121 Ponce de Leon Blvd, 33134; 305 461 5919; www.alscoffeeshop.com) is the place to find sandwiches, salads, burgers, and good coffee.
REAL MEAL The Cascade (in The Biltmore Hotel; 305 445 8066; www.biltmorehotel.com), overlooking the

hotel's famed swimming pool, serves contemporary French and Caribbean cuisine. It also offers a kids' menu.
FAMILY TREAT Ortanique on the Mile (278 Miracle Mile, 33134; 305 446 7710; www.ortanique restaurants.com) has a Caribbean-style decor and cuisine. Adults can enjoy a curry crab cake melt or corn fritters, while kids can ask for chicken fingers or pasta.

Shopping
Shop for electronics, books, antiques, and more in **Miracle Mile** (shop coralgables.com). Most shops and restaurants here are independently owned and known for their quality and variety. Many shops are devoted to weddings and children's apparel.

Take cover
The **Coral Gables Museum** (285 Aragon Ave, 33134; 305 603 8067; www.coralgablesmuseum.org) reveals the heritage of the Coral Gables community through permanent and traveling exhibits devoted to the city's history and Spanish roots, architecture, and art.

Miracle Mile, the shopping strip in Coral Gables

Next stop...
CAULEY SQUARE SHOPS Head 14 miles (22 km) southwest of Coral Gables to shop at Cauley Square Shops (www.cauleysquare.com). This is where the old railroad made its last stop in Miami before heading down to the Florida Keys. Check out the Aviary Birdshop with live birds, dine in restaurants housed in vintage cottages, and admire Spanish-style buildings along cobbled streets.

The shaded patio of CocoWalk, an upscale shopping mall in Coconut Grove

② Coconut Grove

Groovy in "the Grove"

Luxurious mansions, and the sight of sailboats racing in the wind or anchored in Biscayne Bay, define Coconut Grove as an affluent community where dining at a sidewalk café is a quintessential experience. The area has come a long way since its countercultural hippie days of the 1960s. Today it

The Lowdown

- 🌐 **Map reference** 12 G5
- 🚌 **Bus** 37 from Coral Gables. **Metro** Metrorail from Coral Gables
- ℹ️ **Visitor information** Coconut Grove Chamber of Commerce, 3059 Grand Ave, Suite 210, 33133; 305 444 7270; *www. coconutgrovechamber.com*
- 👫 **Cutting the line** Visit on a weekday if possible, as the town gets crowded on weekends.
- 👆 **Guided tours** Ghost Tours Miami *(786 236 9979; www.ghostgrove. com)* offers family-friendly historic tours of Coconut Grove. Reserve a month in advance.
- 👫 **Age range** 5 plus
- ⏲️ **Allow** Half a day to a full day
- ☕ **Eat and drink** SNACKS The Cheesecake Factory *(CocoWalk, 3015 Grand Ave, 33133; 305 447 9898; www.thecheesecakefactory. com)* serves flatbreads and starters, such as crab balls and chicken lettuce wraps. FAMILY TREAT Le Bouchon du Grove *(3430 Main Hwy, 33133; 305 448 6060; lebouchondugrove.com)* serves sandwiches, salads, soups, and entrées with a French influence.
- 🎊 **Festival** The Coconut Grove Arts Festival celebrates the arts, music, and food. There is a special area for families with kids (Feb).

Yachts and small boats moored at the marina, Dinner Key

appeals to families with its Peacock Park *(see p55)*, a lively street scene, art galleries, and CocoWalk, an outdoor mall. Surrounding the area's main hub, at the intersections of Grand Avenue, McFarlane Avenue, and Miami Highway, are neighborhoods of Mediterranean-style mansions that stand in contrast to the simple Bahamian clapboard "conch" homes.

Letting off steam

Head 2 miles (3 km) northeast of Coconut Grove's outskirts to **Dinner Key** *(www.miamigov.com)*, a mega yacht basin. This was a seaplane base for Pan American Airways in the 1930s. Take a walk around the marina to look at the historic "PanAm" buildings – one of which now houses Miami's City Hall – and the shiny modern yachts.

③ The Barnacle Historic State Park

A slice of old Miami

Like many Florida pioneers and modern-day residents, Commodore Ralph Munroe moved to Coconut

The Lowdown

- 🌐 **Map reference** 12 G5
- 📍 **Address** 3485 Main Hwy, Coconut Grove, 33133; 305 442 6866; *www.floridastateparks.org/ thebarnacle*
- 🚌 **Bus** 37 from Coral Gables. **Metro** Metrorail from Coral Gables
- ℹ️ **Visitor information** Coconut Grove Chamber of Commerce, 3059 Grand Ave, Suite 210, 33133; 305 444 7270; *www. coconutgrovechamber.com*
- 🕐 **Open** 9am–5pm Wed–Mon
- 💲 **Price** $4–8
- 👆 **Guided tours** There are guided tours ($6–12; under 5s free) of The Barnacle house at 10am, 11:30am, 1pm & 2:30pm Wed–Mon.
- 👫 **Age range** 5 plus
- ⏲️ **Allow** 1 hour
- ☕ **Eat and drink** REAL MEAL Rincón Argentino *(2345 SW 37th Ave, 33145; 305 444 2494; www. rinconargentino.com)* serves soups, salads, steaks, seafood, and scrumptious home-made pasta. FAMILY TREAT Lulu *(3105 Commodore Plaza, 33133; 305 447 5858; www.luluinthe grove.com)* has alfresco seating with views of Coconut Grove's festive street scene. Try their grilled octopus.

Grove from the north of the state. In the late 1800s, he established this extensive homesite and built a house called The Barnacle, named for its octagonal central room. Families can visit this narrow strip of parkland, which runs from Main Highway to Biscayne Bay, and see how Coconut Grove looked more than 100 years ago. Part of the once-vast Miami Hammock, the old-growth forest here harbors secret spots, such as a cemetery with unmarked graves and benches shaded by trees.

The red-roofed Barnacle house in The Barnacle Historic State Park

Letting off steam

The Barnacle has lots of wide-open spaces, but if kids still need some outdoor action, head to **Kampong Botanical Garden** *(4013 Douglas Rd, 33133; 305 442 7169; ntbg.org)*, which offers guided and self-guided tours of its lush grounds – reserve in advance. Check out the massive 80-year-old baobab tree, and see the home and collection of Dr. David Fairchild, who is renowned for **Fairchild Tropical Garden** *(see p56)*.

Banyan trees lining a path in Kampong Botanical Garden

④ Peacock Park

Hoops, balls, and gumbo limbos

Named not for the bird, but for a Coconut Grove pioneer family, the Peacocks, whose daughter married Coral Gables founder George Merrick, this park spreads like a green blanket down to Biscayne Bay. Kids can play baseball, basketball, tennis, and soccer.

View of Biscayne Bay from the boardwalk in Peacock Park

The Lowdown

🌐 **Map reference** 12 G5
Address 2820 McFarlane Rd, 33133; 305 442 0375

🚌 **Bus** 37 from Coral Gables. **Metro** Metrorail from Coral Gables

ℹ️ **Visitor information** Coconut Grove Chamber of Commerce, 3059 Grand Ave, Suite 210, 33133; 305 444 7270; www.coconutgrovechamber.com

🕐 **Open** daily

👫 **Age range** All ages

⏱️ **Allow** 1 hour

🍽️ **Eat and drink** PICNIC Dolce Vita Gelato Café *(3462 Main Hwy, 33133; 305 461 1322; www.dolcevitagelato.com)* offers gelato and other sweet treats for a bayside picnic in Peacock Park. FAMILY TREAT Peacock Garden Cafe *(2889 McFarlane Rd, 33133; 305 774 3332; www.jaguarhg.com/peacockspot)* serves tasty home-made soups, pasta, sandwiches, seafood, and steaks in a pleasant setting.

Gracious old oaks and gumbo limbo trees shade a playground and outdoor tables, where families can stop for great views or a picnic.

Take cover

Head to **CocoWalk** *(3015 Grand Ave, 33133; 305 444 0777; cocowalk.net)*, a collection of shops and cafes with live music and a 14-screen movie theater, located in the heart of Coconut Grove. Shady walkways provide shelter from sun or rain, and CocoWalk also offers family fun days – with child-centric activities, a petting zoo, and a bouncy castle.

KIDS' CORNER

Do the gumbo limbo at Peacock Park

1 The gumbo limbo's botanical name is *Bursera simaruba*.

2 Because it has red, papery bark, locals often jokingly call the tree the "tourist tree," after the visitors who forget to use sunscreen when enjoying the Florida sunshine!

3 In some places, the trees are known as "living fences," because when people stick their branches into the ground in a row, they begin to grow leaves in a short time.

4 Gumbo limbo wood was traditionally used to carve horses for fairground carousels.

DRAWING ROOMS

Commodore Munroe named his home for its eight-sided central room, which he thought resembled a barnacle – a crustacean that clings to mangrove roots, boats, and other wooden hosts. Think of other sea creatures, such as an octopus or a jellyfish. Can you draw room designs to match their shapes?

Choco loco

Coconut Grove's Dolce Vita Gelato Cafe is known for being a little *loco* (Spanish for crazy) with its chocolate flavors. These use local ingredients, as in the chocolate-chili pepper and chocolate-orange flavors. Can you think of other Florida fruits, spices, or vegetables you could mix into chocolate ice cream for a new taste treat?

Picnic under $25; **Snacks** $25–50; **Real meal** $50–80; **Family treat** over $80 (based on a family of four)

⑤ Fairchild Tropical Garden

Butterflies, cactuses, and mango mania

At the start of the 20th century, Dr. David Fairchild began a 37-year quest to collect plant specimens from all over the world. The collection continues to grow, and is now one of the most respected of its kind in the world. Brilliant blossoms scent the lakeside botanical gardens, known for their orchids, mangoes, palm trees, and other tropical flora. The gardens include the only outdoor tropical rain forest plantings in the US. Children will enjoy the colorful butterfly garden, the cactus collection, and the edible garden. The gardens also showcase exhibits by noted artists, offer birding opportunities, and organize family programs such as afternoon teas.

The Lowdown

🌐 **Address** 10901 Old Cutler Rd, Miami, 33156; 305 667 1651; www.fairchildgarden.org

🚌 **Bus** Route 136 (weekdays only). **Car** From Coral Gables follow LeJeune Rd to Old Cutler Rd.

🕐 **Open** 9:30am–4:30pm daily

💲 **Price** $50–74; under 6s free

Cutting the line Check the events calendar online to avoid parking and admission lines when the gardens host art events and family programs.

Guided tours Narrated open-air tram tours depart on the hour 10am–3pm Mon–Fri, 10am–4pm Sat–Sun.

👫 **Age range** 3 plus

Activities For identifying plants and wildlife, ask about activity sheets at the information desk.

⏱ **Allow** 2 hours

☕ **Eat and drink** SNACKS Lakeside Café (on site) serves kids' meals, made-to-order sandwiches and salads, desserts, and ice cream. FAMILY TREAT Red Fish Grill (9610 Old Cutler Rd, Miami, 33156; 305 668 8788; redfishgrill.net; dinner only), in Matheson Hammock County Park (see p52), next door to Fairchild Tropical Garden, offers a fine-dining experience by the waterside.

Festival The International Mango Festival features mango treats, a fruit market, mango experts, and kids' activities (mid-Jul).

Take cover

The air-conditioned **Dadeland Mall** (7535 N Kendall Dr, Miami, 33156; 305 665 6226; www.simon.com/mall), 3 miles (5 km) west of the garden, has toy and kids' clothing stores, and is a perfect place to chill on a hot day, or stay dry on a wet one.

⑥ Deering Estate at Cutler

Can you keep a secret?

Once hunting grounds for the Seminole tribe, and then the settlement of Cutler in the late 19th century, this site has a rich history. Today, the property holds two houses. Richmond Cottage, the older one, built in Cutler's early days, was bought in 1915 by Charles Deering, a businessman and art collector. He built a sturdy Stone House here to contain his vast art collection, which resulted from years of travel abroad. His secret Prohibition-era wine vault adds a dimension of mystery to the house. Richmond Cottage holds historic exhibits, including pictures of the devastating damage from Hurricane Andrew in 1992, from which it took the estate seven years to recover. The estate also offers guided canoeing and biking tours, storytelling, and a tour of its Artist Village; check website for timings.

Letting off steam

The estate's extensive grounds provide plenty of space to run around and explore nature.

Lions unwinding in the lush outdoors at Zoo Miami

Elegant Richmond Cottage on the Deering Estate at Cutler

The Lowdown

🌐 **Address** 16701 SW 72nd Ave, Miami, 33157; 305 235 1668; www.deeringestate.org

🚗 **Car** Rent a car from Coral Gables.

🕐 **Open** 10am–4pm daily

💲 **Price** $31–38; under 4s free

Cutting the line Avoid visiting when school or other groups might be touring.

Guided tours Guides tour the homes 10am & 3pm daily, also Jun–Sep: 12:30pm daily.

👫 **Age range** 6 plus

Activities Special canoe tours for kids 9 plus and other kids' events.

⏱ **Allow** 1–2 hours

☕ **Eat and drink** PICNIC Panera Bread (13617 S Dixie Hwy, Miami, 33176; www.panerabread.com) stocks baked goodies for a picnic in the estate's grounds. SNACKS Offerdahl's Off The Grill (14685 S Dixie Hwy, Miami, 33176; www. offerdahls.com) offers family meals, and half-portions for kids.

⑦ Zoo Miami

Into the Wacky Barn

Formerly known as Miami MetroZoo, Zoo Miami has lots of open space and natural barriers instead of cages and fences. Besides the joy of seeing and even petting animals from around the world, kids can enjoy special attractions designed specifically for them. In the Children's Zoo, they can ride a camel, feed giraffes and parrots, wonder at the Butterfly Garden, ride a carousel depicting 30 endangered animals, or chill out in the Wacky Barn, where small animals live. The zoo also has a state-of-the-art playground with water features.

The Lowdown

- 🌐 **Address** 12400 SW 152nd St, Miami, 33177; 305 251 0400; www.zoomiami.org
- 🚆 **Train** Metrorail to Dadeland South, then bus 252
- 🕐 **Open** 10am–5pm daily
- 💲 **Price** $65–85; under 2s free
- 👥 **Cutting the line** The zoo is busiest on weekends.
- 🎫 **Guided tours** Various tours and programs including guided tram or walking tours and an elevated air-conditioned monorail tour
- 🚶 **Age range** 2 plus
- 🎨 **Activities** Family-friendly activities include giraffe and parrot feeding stations and meet-the-zookeeper talks.
- 🕐 **Allow** 2–3 hours
- 🍴 **Eat and drink** PICNIC Nourish 305 (on site) offers casual fare with a view of the Florida: Mission Everglades exhibit.
  SNACKS Carousel Café (on site) has burgers, pizza, sandwiches, and chicken tenders.

Take cover
A short walk southwest of the zoo is the **Gold Coast Railroad Museum** (www.gcrm.org), which entertains families with train rides on weekends, model train set-ups, and a collection of vintage railroad cars including the presidential *Ferdinand Magellan*.

⑧ Coral Castle
Thousands of pounds of stone and a 100-pound weakling
Latvian immigrant Edward Leedskalnin was motivated by unrequited love and a broken heart, and created an engineering feat. This 100-lb (45-kg) man built a castle out of local coral rock as a monument to his lost love, and the three children he fantasized. A National Register of Historic Places site, its highlights include a Polaris telescope for spotting the North Star, a 5,000-lb (2,268-kg) heart-shaped table featured in *Ripley's Believe It or Not!*, the "Grotto of the Three Bears" playground, and a working sundial.

Letting off steam
In Homestead's historic agricultural district, known as Redland, **Fruit & Spice Park** (www.redlandfruitand spice.com) offers a see-hear-taste tour that takes in 70-plus varieties of banana and avocado, and 160 types of mango, plus gardens representing Asia and other warm climes.

The Lowdown

- 🌐 **Address** 28655 S Dixie Hwy, Miami, 33033; 305 248 6345; www.coralcastle.com
- 🚆 **Train** Metrorail to Dadeland South, then bus 34 or 35
- ℹ️ **Visitor information** Tropical Everglades Visitor Center, 160 US 1, Florida City, 33034; 305 245 9180; www.tropical everglades.com
- 🕐 **Open** 8am–6pm Sun–Thu (till 8pm Fri–Sat)
- 💲 **Price** $50–60; under 7s free
- 🚶 **Age range** 4 plus
- 🕐 **Allow** 1 hour
- 🍴 **Eat and drink** PICNIC Rosita's Restaurante (199 W Palm Dr, Florida City, 33034; 305 246 3114) offers authentic Mexican food to pack and take to the Homestead Bayfront Park nearby. SNACKS Mango Café (24801 SW 187th Ave, 33031; 305 247 5727), in Fruit & Spice Park, uses the park's produce to complement its sandwiches, pizzas, and salads.

Outer walls of the unique Coral Castle, Homestead

KIDS' CORNER

What tree am I?
Learn the names of the trees you see in parks, and at natural attractions such as the Deering Estate, then see if you can guess the names of these trees:
1 I'm an okra stew doing a Caribbean dance.
2 Mix together red and yellow to get my name.
3 I'm a guy with a gang of trees.
4 I wear my hair pulled back with a rubber band.

Answers at the bottom of the page

MONUMENTAL LOVE
Edward Leedskalnin became engaged to Agnes Scuffs when she was 16, but she jilted him one day before the wedding. Singer Billy Joel, inspired by this story, wrote the song *Sweet Sixteen* and the video was filmed in Coral Castle.

Architect-in-training
Richmond Cottage on the Deering Estate was built with steeply pitched shingle roofs and overhanging eaves in the late 19th century. The Stone House was built in 1922 and features terracotta-tiled roofs, balconies, and turrets. Can you spot the differences in architectural styles between the two homes? In which would you prefer to live?

Answers: 1 Gumbo limbo **2** Orange tree. **3** Mangrove. **4** Ponytail.

Picnic under $25; **Snacks** $25–50; **Real meal** $50–80; **Family treat** over $80 (based on a family of four)

Downtown, Little Havana, Vizcaya, and around

Although prettiest at night, when its city lights reflect on the bay, downtown Miami exudes aesthetic appeal in the daytime too. Dotted with skyscrapers, the district is also home to numerous charming old-fashioned buildings. Families will enjoy exploring the beautiful gardens at Vizcaya to the south of downtown. Across the bay, Key Biscayne offers beachy bliss to visitors who want to escape the bustle of the Cuban neighborhood of Little Havana.

Ligers – a lion/tiger cross – lounging in Jungle Island, an interactive zoo

Places of interest

SIGHTS

1. Vizcaya Museum and Gardens
2. Calle Ocho – Little Havana
3. Pérez Art Museum Miami
4. Miami Children's Museum
5. Jungle Island
6. Miami Seaquarium®
7. Virginia Key Beach Park
8. Crandon Park
9. Bill Baggs Cape Florida State Park

EAT AND DRINK

1. Cacique's Corner Restaurant
2. Vizcaya Café
3. Tradewinds
4. Seasons 52
5. Tinta y Café
6. Versailles Restaurant & Bakery
7. La Sandwicherie Brickell
8. Rigatti's Café
9. The Food Court
10. La Moon
11. Lakeside Café
12. Batch Gastropub
13. Pink's Hollywood Hot Dogs
14. Donut Gallery Diner
15. Winn-Dixie
16. The Rusty Pelican
17. La Boulangerie Boul' Mich
18. Cantina Beach
19. Lighthouse Café
20. Boater's Grill

SHOPPING

1. Miracle Mile
2. CocoWalk
3. Bayside Marketplace

WHERE TO STAY

1. Hyatt Regency Miami
2. Mandarin Oriental
3. The Ritz-Carlton Key Biscayne
4. Silver Sands Beach Resort

Sculpture on the facade of an ice cream shop across Domino Park, Calle Ocho

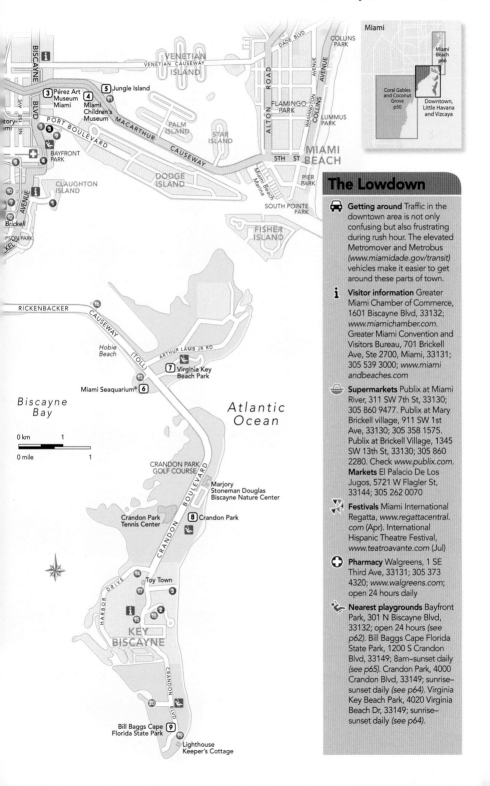

Miami

Miami Beach p66

Coral Gables and Coconut Grove p50

Downtown, Little Havana and Vizcaya

VENETIAN CAUSEWAY

VENETIAN ISLAND

3 Pérez Art Museum Miami

4 Miami Children's Museum

5 Jungle Island

MACARTHUR CAUSEWAY

PALM ISLAND

STAR ISLAND

PORT BOULEVARD

9

Bayfront Park

DODGE ISLAND

CLAUGHTON ISLAND

10

Brickell

DADE BLVD

COLLINS PARK

FLAMINGO PARK

LUMMUS PARK

5TH ST

MIAMI BEACH

PIER PARK

SOUTH POINTE PARK

FISHER ISLAND

RICKENBACKER CAUSEWAY (TOLL)

14

Hobie Beach

ARTHUR LAMB JR RD

Miami Seaquarium® **6**

7 Virginia Key Beach Park

Biscayne Bay

0 km 1
0 mile 1

Atlantic Ocean

CRANDON PARK GOLF COURSE

CRANDON BOULEVARD

Marjory Stoneman Douglas Biscayne Nature Center

Crandon Park Tennis Center

8 Crandon Park

HARBOR DRIVE

14

17

Toy Town

3

15 **18** **2**

KEY BISCAYNE

CRANDON BLVD

Bill Baggs Cape Florida State Park **9**

Lighthouse Keeper's Cottage

The Lowdown

🚗 **Getting around** Traffic in the downtown area is not only confusing but also frustrating during rush hour. The elevated Metromover and Metrobus (*www.miamidade.gov/transit*) vehicles make it easier to get around these parts of town.

ℹ️ **Visitor information** Greater Miami Chamber of Commerce, 1601 Biscayne Blvd, 33132; *www.miamichamber.com*. Greater Miami Convention and Visitors Bureau, 701 Brickell Ave, Ste 2700, Miami, 33131; 305 539 3000; *www.miami andbeaches.com*

🛒 **Supermarkets** Publix at Miami River, 311 SW 7th St, 33130; 305 860 9477. Publix at Mary Brickell village, 911 SW 1st Ave, 33130; 305 358 1575. Publix at Brickell Village, 1345 SW 13th St, 33130; 305 860 2280. Check *www.publix.com*. **Markets** El Palacio De Los Jugos, 5721 W Flagler St, 33144; 305 262 0070

🎉 **Festivals** Miami International Regatta, *www.regattacentral. com* (Apr). International Hispanic Theatre Festival, *www.teatroavante.com* (Jul)

➕ **Pharmacy** Walgreens, 1 SE Third Ave, 33131; 305 373 4320; *www.walgreens.com*; open 24 hours daily

🛝 **Nearest playgrounds** Bayfront Park, 301 N Biscayne Blvd, 33132; open 24 hours *(see p62)*. Bill Baggs Cape Florida State Park, 1200 S Crandon Blvd, 33149; 8am–sunset daily *(see p65)*. Crandon Park, 4000 Crandon Blvd, 33149; sunrise–sunset daily *(see p64)*. Virginia Key Beach Park, 4020 Virginia Beach Dr, 33149; sunrise–sunset daily *(see p64)*.

① Vizcaya Museum and Gardens
Sea horses and frogs in an architectural gem

Miami's iconic sight on Biscayne Bay, the palatial Vizcaya is a monument to early 20th-century opulence and one man's admiration for all things European. Millionaire industrialist James Deering commissioned the 30-plus-room mansion to be built in the style of an Italian palazzo, and filled it with fine furnishings and art. For families, the greatest interest lies outdoors, on the waterfront and in the gardens, where carved dragons, mermaids, and frogs spitting water into basins await.

Carved light fixture

Key Features

Courtyard A glass dome was added in the 1980s to protect the museum's art collection. The leaded glass doors offer views of the bay and gardens.

Entrance

Dining Room This sumptuous room was used mainly for entertaining. Its ornate ceiling is decorated with carved motifs of snakes and sea horses.

East Terrace An outdoor paved space overlooking the bay and a barge built to buffer the shoreline from waves. The barge is decorated with mermaids and dolphins.

Deering Suite The master bedroom overlooks the bay. In the bathroom, the gold-plated swan-shaped faucets dispensed both fresh and salt water.

Swimming Pool The pool, complete with a diving platform, is partially covered. The doors at the back of the pool lead to a café and shop.

Maze Garden South of the East Terrace are the Secret Garden, the Theater Garden, and the Maze Garden, a favourite with families.

Garden Mound and Casino Steps lead to the elevated mound, with its gazebo-like house or "Casino." The ceiling has paintings of angels and minstrels that seem to look down on visitors.

The Lowdown

🌐 **Map reference** 13 D6
Address 3251 S Miami Ave, 33129; 305 250 9133; *www.vizcaya.org*

🚗 **Metro** Metrorail to Vizcaya station. **Bus** Metrobus 48

🕙 **Open** 9:30am–4:30pm daily, closed Tue, Thanksgiving Day & Dec 25. Gardens: till 5:30pm

💲 **Price** $36–48; under 6s free

👪 **Cutting the line** Arrive early to explore the site by audio tour or to join a guided tour.

🏳 **Guided tours** Vizcaya runs guided tours in English daily (schedule varies, call for timings) and in Spanish at 2pm Sat–Sun. Self-guided audio tours are available in five languages, but sell out quickly when the museum is crowded.

👫 **Age range** 6 plus; not suitable for younger kids as the interior of the house is strictly hands-off.

🎨 **Activities** Special maps and guide sheets are available for young visitors.

⏱ **Allow** 2 hours
♿ **Wheelchair access** Yes
🍴 **Café** Vizcaya Café (see p61)
🛍 **Shop** Vizcaya Shop (see p61)
🚻 **Restrooms** Near Vizcaya Café and Vizcaya Shop, south of the house entrance, and southwest of the gardens

Good family value?
Reasonable prices and impressive gardens and mansion interiors make this great value for money.

CocoWalk, an open-air shopping mall in nearby Coconut Grove

Letting off steam

Hit **Bayside Marketplace** *(401 Biscayne Blvd, 33132; 305 577 3344; www.baysidemarketplace.com)* for a half-day or so of shopping and dining, catch a boat excursion, or rent jet skis. Some of the shops here specialize in kids' toys and clothing.

Eat and drink

Picnic: under $25; Snacks: $25–50; Real meal: $50–80; Family treat: over $80 (based on a family of four)

PICNIC Cacique's Corner Restaurant *(100 W Flagler St, 33130; 305 371 8317)* is one of a number of downtown eateries selling quick Cuban take-out items that can be enjoyed on the waterfront at Bayside Park.
SNACKS Vizcaya Café *(ground floor, north wing of Vizcaya; 305 856 8189)* serves sandwiches, burgers, and snacks. Seating is indoors in a library setting and outdoors near the pool. Kids' meals come with French fries and applesauce. Top them off with a dark-chocolate-dipped Key lime popsicle.
REAL MEAL Tradewinds Waterfront Bar & Grill *(401 Biscayne Blvd; 305 416 6944; www.tradewindsbarandgrill.com)* offers pierside dining. There are inexpensive lunch specials, plus seafood, ribs, steaks, and hot fudge sundaes.
FAMILY TREAT Seasons 52 *(321 Miracle Mile, Coral Gables, 33134; 305 442 8552; www. seasons52.com)* is part of a small, Florida-born chain, with a healthy menu that is great for families concerned about their eating habits. Everything is fresh, seasonal, and under 475 calories.

Shopping

The **Vizcaya Shop**, in the museum's north wing, has a vast range of gifts, including postcards, books, and jewelry. The museum is also close to the shopping districts of **Miracle Mile** *(see p53)*, **CocoWalk** *(see p54)*, and **Bayside Marketplace**.

Footwear and other merchandise in the plush Vizcaya Shop

Find out more

DIGITAL For more information about the Vizcaya Museum and Gardens, download worksheets from the Vizcaya website, www. vizcayamuseum.com.

Next stop...

CHARLES DEERING ESTATE
James Deering decided to build a winter home in Miami because his father had moved there, and his half-brother, Charles, had also built a splendid home. The Charles Deering Estate *(see p56)*, 14 miles (23 km) to the south of Vizcaya, makes for a fitting family reunion of historic sites.

A game of dominoes in Domino Park, Calle Ocho

② Calle Ocho – Little Havana

Cubanos, café leche, and dominoes

Cuban refugees settled around Calle Ocho, meaning Eighth Street in Spanish, in the mid-20th century; another major influx occurred during the Mariel boatlift of 1980. Today, the Cuban population constitutes a majority on the streets of Miami. Stroll along Calle Ocho to experience Cuban culture and food. Stars inset along the sidewalk

The Lowdown

🌐 **Map reference** 13 D3

🚗 **Metro** Metromover from downtown. **Bus** Metrobus 6 from downtown.

ℹ️ **Visitor information** Greater Miami Chamber of Commerce, 1601 Biscayne Blvd, 33132; 305 350 7700; www.miamichamber.com

🚩 **Guided tours** Little Havana Tours (www.littlehavanatours.com) offers themed guided tours on the arts, music, and local secrets.

👫 **Age range** 6 plus

⏱️ **Allow** Half a day

🍴 **Eat and drink** SNACKS Tinta y Café (268 SW 8th St, 33130; 305 285 0101), a typical Cuban café, offers sandwiches in full and half portions. Do try the papaya or mango juice. REAL MEAL Versailles Restaurant & Bakery (3555 SW 8th St, 33135; 305 444 0240; www.versaillesrestaurant.com) serves American and Cuban dishes.

🎭 **Festival** Carnaval Miami celebrates Latino culture (Feb or Mar).

remember Latino celebrities such as baseball player Sammy Sosa and singer Celia Cruz. Windows open onto restaurants and bakeries where locals order Cuban sandwiches and papaya shakes. Cigar-makers roll fragrant leaves and stores sell pleated guayabera shirts and tables made for slapping dominoes. In Domino Park, the games go on all day and well into the night.

Take cover

To get an overview of downtown Miami, board the **Metromover** (www.miamidade.gov/transit), an automated, elevated transportation system that goes round in a 2-mile (4-km) loop. The ride is fun and free, and the closest boarding station is at 59 SE 8th Street.

③ Pérez Art Museum Miami

A palette of cultures

Located in bayside Museum Park, the PAMM focuses on modern and contemporary international art. The works – displayed in six galleries spread over three stories – highlight Miami's position as a cross-cultural hub. The artists represented hail from both North and South America, as well as the Caribbean, reflecting the cosmopolitan make-up of the city.

Letting off steam

The lush and lovely **Bayfront Park** (301 N Biscayne Blvd, 33132; 305 358 7550; www.bayfrontpark miami.com) may have one of the coolest playgrounds ever. It features a pirate ship, trampolines, and a play sculpture depicting a life-size wave with a dolphin, a sea turtle, and a manatee surfing it.

The Lowdown

🌐 **Map reference** 14 G1
Address 1103 Biscayne Blvd, 33130; 305 375 3000; www.pamm.org

🚌 **Bus** Metromover and Metrobus route 103/C are best for getting around downtown. **Trolley** Biscayne.

ℹ️ **Visitor information** Greater Miami Chamber of Commerce, 1601 Biscayne Blvd, 33132; 305 350 7700; www.miamichamber.com

🕐 **Open** 10am–6pm Thu–Tue (to 9pm Thu)

💲 **Price** $44–56; under 6s free (free on 1st Thu & 2nd Sat each month)

🚩 **Guided tours** Available Thu–Tue year-round; check website for details.

👫 **Age range** 5 plus

Activities Special hands-on art activities for kids; check website for details.

⏱️ **Allow** 1–2 hours

♿ **Wheelchair access** Yes

🍴 **Eat and drink** SNACKS La Sandwicherie Brickell (34 W 8th St, 33130; www.lasandwicherie.com) offers French-style sandwiches, juices, and tasty smoothies. REAL MEAL Rigatti's Café (100 S Miami Ave, 33130; 305 377 1672) is an Italian restaurant that serves pasta, soups, salads, and sandwiches.

④ Miami Children's Museum

Kids playing grown-up

This museum immerses families in the worlds of finance, business, health, art, and Miami's tropical beat. Become a rock star in the music recording studio, dress up as a policeman and hop on a motorcycle, operate an ATM machine, and cook in a Miccosukee

Kids playing with the giant Pink Snail outside Miami Children's Museum

Indian *chickee* (hut). Try to limbo dance aboard a cruise ship, then shop in a replica Publix supermarket. Do not miss the Castle of Dreams exhibit – possibly the biggest sand castle ever built. Children can climb into it, slide out of it, and feel the texture of sand from around the world.

Letting off steam
Kids can play in the **Peace Playground** *(on site)* and enjoy a picnic at the tables on the plaza.

The Lowdown

🌐 **Map reference** 15 A3
Address 980 MacArthur Causeway, 33132; 305 373 5437; *www.miamichildrensmuseum.org*

🚗 **Bus** Metrobus 113/M or 119/S from downtown

ℹ️ **Visitor information** Greater Miami Convention and Visitors Bureau, 701 Brickell Ave, Ste 2700, 33131; 305 539 3094

🕐 **Open** 10am–6pm daily

💲 **Price** $72; under 1s free

👥 **Cutting the line** Call ahead to check if schools or groups will be visiting.

👫 **Age range** 2 plus

🎨 **Activities** Download kids' activity sheets from the website.

⏱️ **Allow** 2 hours

☕ **Eat and drink** PICNIC The Food Court *(401 Biscayne Blvd, 33132; 305 577 3344; www.bayside marketplace.com)* has lots of take-out food counters. Take the picnic to the adjacent Bayfront Park. SNACKS La Moon *(97 SW 8th St, 33130; 305 860 6209; www.lamoon restaurant.com)* serves authentic Colombian food, although kids will love the *arepas* (corn cakes) and hot dog toppings.

A colorful parrot at Jungle Island, home to a variety of birds from all over the world

⑤ Jungle Island
Parrots and monkeys and a liger? Oh, my!

Begun as a parrot attraction in Coral Gables in 1936, Jungle Island has grown over the years, and now houses animals native to Florida and from around the world. Parrots and macaws remain a major focus, and families can feed and have their pictures taken with the brightly plumaged birds. There are also a lorikeet house, a petting farm, wallabies, penguins, kangaroos, and a liger – a cross between a lion and a tiger. The park hosts shows and keeper talks throughout the day.

Take cover
At the **Patricia and Phillip Frost Museum of Science** *(1101 Biscayne Blvd, 33132; 305 434 9600; www. frostscience.org)*, formerly the Miami Science Museum, indoor adventures include the stunning Frost Planetarium, the three-level aquarium, and various permanent exhibits such as *River of Grass*, which explores the ecosystem of the Everglades.

The Lowdown

🌐 **Map reference** 15 A3
Address 111 Parrot Jungle Trail, 33132; 305 400 7000; *www.jungleisland.com*

🚗 **Bus** Metrobus 113/M or 119/S from downtown

ℹ️ **Visitor information** Greater Miami Convention and Visitors Bureau, 701 Brickell Ave, Ste 2700, 33131; 305 539 3094; *www.miamiand beaches.com*

🕐 **Open** 10am–5pm Mon–Fri & 10am–6pm Sat–Sun

💲 **Price** $146–60; under 3s free

👥 **Cutting the line** Book tickets online and save time.

🔫 **Guided tours** The park offers special tours, including Jungle Encounter, Lemur Experience, VIP Safari tours, and guided audio tours in English and Spanish.

👫 **Age range** 2 plus

⏱️ **Allow** 2 hours

☕ **Eat and drink** SNACKS Lakeside Café *(on site)* offers pizza, wraps, and burgers. REAL MEAL Batch Gastropub *(30 SW 12th St, 33130; 305 808 5555; www.batchmiami. com)* has a reasonably priced menu of light, fun pub fare.

⑥ Miami Seaquarium®

Huge water-critters for little squirts

The world's longest-operating aquarium, the Miami Seaquarium® is the place where episodes of the 1960s TV show *Flipper* were filmed. You can find a variety

A child observing an exhibit at the Miami Seaquarium®

of marine life at this aquarium, including sea lions, manatees, sea turtles, stingrays, and sharks, as well as crocodiles. See them in the exhibits that re-create their habitats and during the 10–20-minute feeding period. Special events such as feeding sea lions bring kids up close to the animals. An elevated ropes course with 18 challenges, a playground, fish aquariums, as well as remote-controlled boats and trucks provide further entertainment for the family.

Letting off steam

Kick up sand on **Hobie Beach** (*Rickenbacker Causeway, 33149; 305 361 2833*) – also known as Windsurfer Beach because of its relatively dependable winds. The beach is good for fishing, taking in the views, running off excess energy, or simply relaxing on the sand. There is also free beachside parking.

⑦ Virginia Key Beach Park

A park with a history

This beach park was developed in the 1940s, before desegre-gation. In those days, it was inaccessible by car. Some of the old structures, such as the covered Dance Floor, can still be seen at the main entrance, where there are also picnic areas, a playground, and a soccer field. The western entrance to the park has more of a family feel, with thatched *chickee* umbrellas and another playground. Like all of the Virginia

Key–Key Biscayne area, the park is extremely popular with cyclists.

Take cover

Drop in at **Toy Town** (*260 Crandon Blvd #43, 33149; 305 361 5501; www. toytownonline.com*) for a shopping break. The store stocks educational and other toys and baby equipment. It also has a teen fashion section.

⑧ Crandon Park

Fun for all the family

Most tennis fans will probably recognize Crandon Park as the host of the Miami Open, an annual tennis tournament. This expansive park takes up a third of Key Biscayne and offers an 18-hole golf course, a marina, cycle paths, a carousel and amusement area, a playground, 3 miles (5 km) of gorgeous beach, a garden, nature trails, a nature preserve, and a nature center. It also hosts a number of recreational and environmental programs.

Touch tank at the Marjory Stoneman Douglas Biscayne Nature Center

The Lowdown

- 🌐 **Address** 4400 Rickenbacker Causeway, 33149; 305 361 5705; *www.miamiseaquarium.com*
- 🚗 **Car** Route 102/B from downtown. Bridge toll $1.75 round-trip
- ℹ️ **Visitor information** Key Biscayne Chamber of Commerce and Visitor Center, 88 W. McIntyre St Ste. 100, 33149; 305 361 5207; *www.keybiscaynechamber.org*
- 🕐 **Open** 9:30am–6pm daily
- 💲 **Price** $140–60; ask about family rates; under 3s free ($10 parking)
- 🎫 **Cutting the line** Order tickets online and save $2 per ticket.
- 🚶 **Guided tours** Sea Trek Reef Encounter lets visitors walk through an underwater tropical reef wearing a special breathing helmet, while the staff feed the fish.
- 👫 **Age range** 2 plus
- ⏱️ **Allow** 4 hours
- 🍴 **Eat and drink** SNACKS Pink's Hollywood Hot Dogs (*on site*) offers a choice of tasty toppings with their hot dogs. REAL MEAL Donut Gallery Diner (*83 Harbor Dr, 33149; 305 361 9985; www. donutgallerydiner.com*) serves breakfast, and sandwiches and entrées for lunch, as well as a good selection of salads, but no donuts.
- 🎪 **Festival** Bunny Palooza has Easter egg hunts and rides (Mar–Apr).

The Lowdown

- 🌐 **Address** 4020 Virginia Beach Dr, 33149; 305 960 4600; *www.virginia keybeachpark.net*
- 🚗 **Car** Route 102/B from downtown Miami. Bridge toll $1.75 round-trip
- ℹ️ **Visitor information** Key Biscayne Chamber of Commerce and Visitor Center, 88 W. McIntyre St Ste. 100, 33149; 305 361 5207; *www.keybiscaynechamber.org*
- 🕐 **Open** Sunrise–sunset daily
- 💲 **Price** $5–8 per vehicle
- 👫 **Age range** All ages
- ⏱️ **Allow** Half a day

- 🍴 **Eat and drink** PICNIC Winn-Dixie (*604 Crandon Blvd, Key Biscayne, 33149; 305 361 8261; www.winn dixie.com*) has a deli and bakery. Pick up ready-made sandwiches and dessert for a beach picnic. FAMILY TREAT The Rusty Pelican (*3201 Rickenbacker Causeway, 33149; 305 361 3818; www.therustypelican.com*) gives diners a choice of sushi, small plates, sandwiches, and grilled seafood and steaks, along with views of Biscayne Bay.

The Lowdown

- **Address** 6747 Crandon Blvd, 33149; 305 361 5421; www.miami-dade.gov/parks
- **Car** Route 102/B from downtown Miami. Bridge toll $1.75 round-trip
- **Visitor information** Key Biscayne Chamber of Commerce and Visitor Center, 88 W. McIntyre St Ste. 100, 33149; 305 361 5207; www.keybiscaynechamber.org
- **Open** 8am–5pm daily
- **Price** $5–6 per vehicle; $7 parking fee on weekends
- **Cutting the line** Arrive early, especially on weekends. Avoid visiting during the Miami Open in March.
- **Guided tours** Eco Adventures (www.miamiecoadventures.org) leads biking, canoeing, and kayak-snorkeling tours.
- **Age range** All ages
- **Activities** The nature center hosts various programs. Check website for details and "Kids Only" page.
- **Allow** Half a day to a full day
- **Eat and drink** PICNIC La Nouvelle Boulangerie (328 Crandon Blvd, 33149; 305 365 5260; www.laboulangerieusa.com) offers fresh pastries and sandwiches for a picnic in Crandon Park. FAMILY TREAT Cantina Beach (455 Grand Bay Dr, 33149; 305 365 4500; www.ritzcarlton.com/keybiscayne), in The Ritz-Carlton Key Biscayne, has Mexican and American choices, plus fruit smoothies, on its kids' menu.

Take cover

Named for the hero who helped save the Everglades, the **Marjory Stoneman Douglas Biscayne Nature Center** (www.biscaynenaturecenter.org) occupies Crandon Park's north end. It displays exhibits that introduce the park's ecology along its trails. Kids will enjoy the touch tank and shell exhibit.

⑨ Bill Baggs Cape Florida State Park

Come one, come all

Often listed among America's top beaches, the park's beach remains relatively uncrowded because of the causeway toll and park entrance fee. There is plenty to do here: renting bikes and kayaks, eating at the two restaurants, hiking the nature trail, running around in the playground, and climbing the 109 steps to the top of its Cape Florida Lighthouse, which was built in 1825. The park has been designated part of the National Underground Railway Network to Freedom due to its role in helping slaves escape to the Bahamas.

Take cover

Explore the little brick **Lighthouse Keeper's Cottage** nearby. There are exhibits on the life of the keeper's family, period-furnished rooms, and kids' toys from the past. An orientation video is screened in the old cookhouse.

Inside the Cape Florida Lighthouse, Bill Baggs Cape Florida State Park

The Lowdown

- **Address** 1200 S Crandon Blvd, 33149; 305 361 5811; www.floridastateparks.org/capeflorida
- **Car** Route 102/B from downtown. Bridge toll $1.75 round-trip
- **Visitor information** Key Biscayne Chamber of Commerce and Visitor Center, 88 W. McIntyre St Ste. 100, 33149; 305 361 5207; www.keybiscaynechamber.org
- **Open** Park: 8am–sunset daily. Lighthouse grounds: 9am–5pm Thu–Mon
- **Price** $8 per vehicle
- **Cutting the line** Arrive early on weekends and during the winter and spring seasons.
- **Guided tours** There are guided tours of the lighthouse 10am & 1pm Thu–Mon.
- **Age range** All ages
- **Allow** Half a day
- **Eat and drink** REAL MEAL Lighthouse Café (on site; 305 361 8487; www.lighthouserestaurants.com) offers breakfast dishes, sandwiches, and Cuban entrées. FAMILY TREAT Boater's Grill (on site; 305 361 0080) serves burgers, pasta, and fancy seafood dinners.

Picnic under $25; **Snacks** $25–50; **Real meal** $50–80; **Family treat** over $80 (based on a family of four)

Miami Beach and around

A long barrier island, Miami Beach stretches from hip South Beach to high-rise communities at the north end. Locals refer to the central part of the island as Middle Beach. Visitors will find a contrast to the mainland's big-city vibe in the wide white sands that carpet Miami Beach's waterfront. Still, the various island communities offer plenty of shopping and dining options that have all the sophistication of the mainland. Haulover Park in North Miami Beach offers a wide variety of watersports. Lummus Park, located in bustling South Beach, is also a popular destination, while to its south, South Pointe Park, with an ocean-themed playground, is quieter.

Boats anchored at the Bill Bird Marina in Bal Harbour

Places of interest

SIGHTS

1. South Beach
2. Middle Beach, Bal Harbour, North Miami Beach
3. Enchanted Forest Elaine Gordon Park
4. Oleta River State Park
5. Ancient Spanish Monastery

EAT AND DRINK

1. La Sandwicherie
2. Tap Tap Haitian Restaurant
3. Big Pink
4. Joe's Stone Crab
5. Café Vert
6. Timó Restaurant & Bar
7. Backyard BBQ and Brew
8. Flanigan's Seafood Bar and Grill
9. Paquitos Mexican Restaurant
10. Carpaccio at Bal Harbour Shops
11. La Granja
12. Area Code 55

SHOPPING

1. Alvin's Island

WHERE TO STAY

1. Acqualina Resort & Spa on the Beach
2. Beacon South Beach Hotel
3. Eden Roc Miami Beach
4. Fontainebleau Miami Beach
5. Kimpton Angler's Hotel
6. Loews Miami Beach Hotel
7. Miami Beach Resort & Spa
8. Nassau Suite Hotel
9. Newport Beachside Hotel & Resort
10. Oleta River State Park
11. Ritz-Carlton Bal Harbour
12. Sea View Hotel

Daniyyel by Boaz Vaadia in the Bass Museum, South Beach

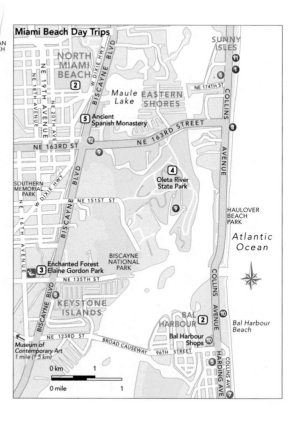

Miami Beach Day Trips

NORTH MIAMI BEACH

Maule Lake

EASTERN SHORES

SUNNY ISLES

5 Ancient Spanish Monastery

4 Oleta River State Park

HAULOVER BEACH PARK

Atlantic Ocean

SOUTHERN MEMORIAL PARK

3 Enchanted Forest Elaine Gordon Park
NE 135TH ST

BISCAYNE NATIONAL PARK

KEYSTONE ISLANDS

NE 123RD ST

Museum of Contemporary Art
1 mile (1.5 km)

BROAD CAUSEWAY

BAL HARBOUR **2**

Bal Harbour Shops

Bal Harbour Beach

96TH STREET

0 km 1
0 mile 1

Pelican Harbor Marina
5 miles (8 km)
LAKEVIEW DRIVE

INDIAN BEACH PARK

MIDDLE BEACH

ARTHUR GODFREY ROAD

BAYSHORE MUNICIPAL GOLF COURSE
Lake Pancoast

MIAMI BEACH GOLF CLUB

Bass Museum of Art
COLLINS PARK

Atlantic Ocean

LUMMUS PARK

Wolfsonian Museum

SOUTH BEACH

Jewish Museum of Florida

MARJORIE STONEMAN DOUGLAS BEACH PARK

PIER PARK

STH POINTE PARK

0 meters 800
0 yards 800

The Lowdown

🚗 **Getting around** Traffic can get heavy along Collins Avenue and South Beach's Ocean Drive, especially at night. Miami-Dade buses (www.miamidade.gov) run the length of the beach regularly.

ℹ️ **Visitor information** Miami Beach Chamber of Commerce, 1920 Meridian Ave, Miami Beach, 33139; 305 674 1300; www.miamibeachchamber.com

Supermarkets Publix on the Bay, 1920 West Ave, 33139; 305 535 4268 & Publix Super Market, 1045 Dade Blvd, 33139; 305 534 4621; www.publix.com.
Markets Lincoln Road Farmers' Market, South Beach, 33139; Sun

Festivals Art Deco Weekend, www.mdpl.org/events (Jan). South Beach Wine & Food Festival, sobefest.com (Feb).

Miami Beach Festival of Arts, web.miamibeachfl.gov (Apr). Art Basel, www.artbasel.com (Dec)

➕ **Pharmacy** Walgreens, 100 Lincoln Rd, 33139; 305 532 7909 & 2300 Collins Ave, 33139; 305 604 8722; open 24 hours daily

Nearest playgrounds Enchanted Forest Elaine Gordon Park, 1725 NE 135th St, 33167; sunrise–sunset (see p70). Indian Beach Park Tot Lot, Collins Ave and 46th St, 33140. Lummus Park, Ocean Dr at 13th St, 33139; 24 hours daily. Marjory Stoneman Douglas Ocean Beach Park, Ocean Dr at 3rd St, 33139; sunrise–sunset. South Pointe Park, 1 Washington Ave, 33109; 24 hours daily (see p68).

① South Beach
SoBe it

Boom and bust best describes the history of South Beach, nicknamed SoBe. A well-developed neighborhood before the Great Depression of the 1930s, it was later resurrected as a showcase of Art Deco architecture. In the 1980s, when developers wanted to raze decrepit buildings, activists began a campaign that turned South Beach into America's Riviera. Besides admiring its preserved Art Deco buildings, families can enjoy relaxing on sandy beaches and great shopping.

Detail of an Art Deco building, South Beach

Key Sights

② Lincoln Road South Beach's main shopping stretch is a pedestrian mall that contains elements of its past and present, including galleries and historic theaters.

③ Española Way This pretty little tree-shaded lane is lively, and lined with Spanish-style buildings housing restaurants, shops, and bars, several of them Latino.

④ Ocean Drive South Beach's fabled runway for aspiring models, this street extends over 15 blocks of Art Deco hotels, with cafés and bars spilling onto sidewalks.

⑤ Wolfsonian Museum Devoted to the decorative arts from 1885 to 1945, this museum's retro vibe fits in well with South Beach's Art Deco orientation. Displays range from sculptures to household items.

⑥ Jewish Museum of Florida While some museums of this nature can be overwhelming, this one focuses on the upbeat history of Jews in Florida.

① Bass Museum of Art Although it mainly hosts temporary exhibitions of modern art, the museum also has a permanent collection of ancient Egyptian artifacts – including mummies and sarcophagi – that will fascinate kids.

⑦ South Pointe Park Families looking for a break from the bustle of South Beach can relax at this park while watching cruise ships sail by. There is a playground for kids.

The Lowdown

🌐 **Map reference** 16 G4
Address Bass Museum of Art: 2100 Collins Ave, 33139; 305 673 7530; www.thebass.org. Wolfsonian Museum: 1001 Washington Ave, 33139; 305 531 1001; www.wolfsonian.org. Jewish Museum of Florida: 301 Washington Ave, 33139; 305 672 5044; www.jmof.fiu.edu. South Pointe Park: 1 Washington Ave, 33139; 305 673 7006; www.miamibeachfl.gov

🚌 **Bus** Miami-Dade buses to South Beach and bus 123 within the city

🕐 **Open** Bass Museum of Art: 10am–5pm Wed–Sun. Wolfsonian Museum noon–6pm daily (till 9pm Fri); closed Wed. Jewish Museum of Florida: 10am–5pm Tue–Sun; closed Jewish hols. South Pointe Park: sunrise–10pm

💲 **Prices** Bass Museum of Art: $25–30; under 12s free. Wolfsonian Museum: $32–40; under 6s free. Jewish Museum of Florida: under 18s free (free on Sat)

👥 **Cutting the line** Avoid traffic around South Beach's eastern side anytime after noon.

🏴 **Guided tours** Daily Art Deco District guided walking tours (1001 Ocean Dr, 33139; 305 531 3484; www.mdpl.org) take in more than 100 historic structures in 90 mins and 20 stops. Cell phone and iPod self-guided tours are also available. Call ahead to make reservations.

👫 **Age range** 7 plus

👥 **Activities** The Bass Museum of Art hosts kids' activities on the last Sun of the month. The Jewish Museum of Florida has a scavenger hunt, and kids who

Letting off steam
Head to **Lummus Park** (5th–15th St and Ocean Dr, 33139), which has paved pathways for biking and walking, as well as playgrounds that will engage the little ones.

Eat and drink
Picnic: under $25; Snacks: $25–50; Real meal: $50–80; Family treat: over $80 (based on a family of four)

PICNIC La Sandwicherie (229 14th St, 33139; 305 532 8934; www.lasandwicherie.com) offers salads, juices, smoothies, and large shareable sandwiches. Enjoy your takeaway at Lummus Park.

SNACKS Tap Tap Haitian Restaurant (819 Fifth St, 33139; 305 672 2898; www.taptapres taurant.com) serves wholesome, West Indian-inspired cuisine.

REAL MEAL Big Pink (157 Collins Ave, 33139; 305 531 0888; www. mylesrestaurantgroup.com) is like an old-fashioned diner, but huge,

Lunchtime at Big Pink, a family-friendly diner in South Beach

complete it get a booklet with puzzles, games, and recipes.

⏱ **Allow** 1–2 days

☕ **Café** In Jewish Museum of Florida (closed for Sabbath Sat)

🚻 **Restrooms** At most attractions and restaurants, and at South Pointe Park

Good family value?
The bustle along Ocean Drive and the parks and museums in this area make boredom impossible.

and with TVs everywhere. Families can order the day's TV dinner or food from the regular or kids' menu.

FAMILY TREAT Joe's Stone Crab (11 Washington Ave, 33139; 305 673 0365; www.joesstonecrab.com; closed for lunch in summer), in business since 1913, claims to have discovered stone crab as a food source in the 1920s. The crabs, and most other seafood items, are high-priced, but the menu does contain some more affordable meals.

Moss-covered fountain in the courtyard of Joe's Stone Crab

Shopping
South Beach is all about shopping, particularly along Lincoln Road and Collins Avenue. Families can find souvenirs and beach buys at **Alvin's Island** (200 Lincoln Rd, 33139; 305 531 9766; www.alvinsisland.com).

Find out more
FILM Miami appears in dozens of major movies, and South Beach stars in most of them. Disney® movies *Old Dogs* (2009) and *Snow Dogs* (2002) were filmed in this area, as was *Marley and Me* (2008).

Next stop…
AMELIA EARHART PARK Families that prefer greenery to city streets might like the Amelia Earhart Park (401 E 65th St, 33014; 305 685 8389; www.miamidade.gov/parks/ amelia_earhart), located 14 miles (23 km) northwest of South Beach. The park's farm has cows, goats, sheep, and geese that younger children adore. Kids will also love the rope bridge that takes them to Tom Sawyer Island's playground. The park's five lakes are stocked with fish, and one is set up with a water-skiing and wakeboarding tow cable. Also on offer are lessons in wakeboarding and wake surfing. For those interested in mountain biking, rentals are available.

② Middle Beach, Bal Harbour, North Miami Beach

Beachfront communities

North of SoBe, the pace changes a bit, as Collins Avenue passes through quieter neighborhoods. Beginning at around 23rd Street is Middle Beach, with its quaint restaurants and shops. North of Middle Beach, the cozy community of Surfside, with a charming shop-and-dine strip, starts at 87th Street. Bal Harbour, a fashionable enclave dotted with soaring hotels and a plush mall, neighbors Surfside. Farther north is Sunny Isles, the last of the beachfront communities. A bridge from here crosses over to North Miami Beach, an older mainland neighborhood with a family feel and some worthwhile stops. Beaches and parks are the biggest draw to the area.

Letting off steam

Located north of Bal Harbour, **Haulover Beach Park** (10800 Collins Ave, 33128; www.miamidade.gov/parks/haulover.asp) contains a 1-mile- (2-km-) long beach with picnic tables. On the bay side, a marina complex houses boat rentals, a kite shop, and a restaurant. Part of the beach is a clothing-optional zone.

High-end shops lining a street in Bal Harbour

③ Enchanted Forest Elaine Gordon Park

Trees with beards

This old-fashioned park is overgrown with tall, gnarled trees wearing Spanish moss beards. The trees shade lovely, spacious picnic grounds and trails that follow and cross over a gurgling creek in the middle of the city. Two playgrounds and pony-riding cinch the deal for kids.

Take cover

The nearby **Museum of Contemporary Art** (770 NE 125th St, 33161; 305 893 6211; www.mocaomomi.org) houses a collection of works by emerging and well-known artists. School-aged kids' art classes are held on the first Saturday of the month. The museum hosts a Family Day as well, which includes workshops, dance lessons, tours, and food for the kids.

Ponies in the lush Enchanted Forest Elaine Gordon Park

④ Oleta River State Park

A little country in the big city

Florida's largest urban park has it all – from a cross-country bike course and a sandy beach to a fishing pier and cabins. The river and the bay afford budding fishermen the opportunity to hook both saltwater and freshwater fish. Rent a kayak, a paddleboard, or a bicycle to explore the park's trails, the river, and the bay front. Bicycling on the park's 10 miles (16 km) of challenging mountain bike trails is one of the most popular activities, but families can also ride the paved trail.

The Lowdown

🌐 **Address** 3400 NE 163rd St, North Miami Beach, 33160; 305 919 1844; www.floridastateparks.org/oletariver

🚌 **Bus** Metrobus105/E and 108/H from Miami Beach

ℹ️ **Visitor information** The Greater North Miami Beach Chamber of Commerce, 16901 NE 19th Ave, 33162; www.nmbchamber.com

🕐 **Open** 8am–sunset daily

💲 **Price** $6 per vehicle

Cutting the line Avoid weekends as they are the busiest days.

⏱️ **Allow** Half a day to a full day

Eat and drink PICNIC Paquitos Restaurant (16265 Biscayne Blvd, 33160; 305 947 5027) offers tacos, burritos and more. Picnic by the bay. REAL MEAL Carpaccio at Bal Harbour Shops (9700 Collins Ave 139, 33154; 305 867 7777; www.carpaccioatbalharbour.com) serves pizza, pasta, and other Italian specialties.

Take cover

Bal Harbour Shops (9700 Collins Ave, 33154; 305 866 0311; www.balharbourshops.com), an upscale shopping mall, also has shops for kids. Check out Young Versace, which even has a merry-go-round. Books & Books features weekly story times for children.

5 Ancient Spanish Monastery

A saintly puzzle

Newspaper publisher William Randolph Hearst purchased the cloisters and outbuildings of a 12th-century Spanish monastery and had them dismantled and shipped to North Miami in 1925. A few years later, the pieces were reassembled like a puzzle, a process that lasted 19 months and cost $1.5 million. The monastery is famed as the oldest building in the western hemisphere. Set amid gardens, the chapel, which serves as a parish church, has arched arcades surrounding a courtyard. Carvings, paintings, and shrines lie along the square walkway. The museum and gift shop hold an old Spanish hearse and other artifacts, and tell the story of the structure's travels from Sacramenia in Spain to Florida.

Letting off steam

Catch a water taxi from **Pelican Harbor Marina** (1275 NE 79th St, 33138; 305 754 9330; www.miamidade.gov/parks) to Pelican Island nature preserve and bird sanctuary. Only 400 yards (365 m) off-shore, the island is equipped with picnic tables, chickee, barbecue grills, and has room to roam.

Dining bell at the entrance to the chapel of the Ancient Spanish Monastery

The Lowdown

🌐 **Address** 16711 W. Dixie Hwy, North Miami Beach, 33160; 305 945 1461; www.spanishmonastery.com

🚌 **Bus** Metrobus 108/H from Miami Beach

ℹ️ **Visitor information** The Greater North Miami Beach Chamber of Commerce, 16901 NE 19th Ave, 33162; www.nmbchamber.com

🕐 **Open** 10am–4pm Mon–Sat, 11am–4pm Sun

💲 **Price** $30–40; under 6s free

Cutting the line Call ahead to avoid visiting during church services (the chapel will be closed) or when special events are taking place (the monastery may be closed).

Guided tours The monastery offers tours in English, Spanish, French, Italian, and German; call ahead to book.

👫 **Age range** 5 plus

⏱️ **Allow** 1 hour

Eat and drink SNACKS La Granja (1901 NE 163rd St, 33162; 305 949 0407; www.lagranjarestaurants.com) serves great Peruvian-style chicken and some excellent Latin specialties. FAMILY TREAT At Area Code 55 Churrascaria (16375 Biscayne Blvd, 33160; 305 947 6202; www.areacode55.com) a gaucho in full costume serves grilled meats on a skewer.

Where to Stay in Miami

Accommodations in Miami come in all shapes and sizes. The most iconic are the small hotels and larger resorts that occupy Miami Beach's historic Art Deco buildings, but the city is also known for its family-friendly luxury resorts, which offer kids' programs. Families will find many modest rental condos and homes.

AGENCIES
Airbnb
www.airbnb.com
Apartments, single rooms in private homes, condos, and a whole house can be rented for a night or longer.

HomeAway
www.homeaway.com
This website lists nearly 1,000 short-term condo and home rentals in Greater Miami. Some can be rented only by the week.

Vacation Rentals
www.vacationrentals.com
Find apartments, penthouses, and homes in all sizes, locations, and price ranges on this website.

Airport   Map 10 H2
HOTEL
Shula's Hotel and Golf Club
6842 Main St, Miami Lakes, 33014; 305 821 1150 or 800 24 SHULA; www.donshulahotel.com
Named for former Miami Dolphins coach Don Shula, this hotel, located close to the Dolphins' home stadium, appeals to golfers, spa-lovers, as well as families.
$$

Bal Harbour   Map 10 H2
HOTELS
Ritz-Carlton Bal Harbour
10295 Collins Ave, 33154; 305 455 5400; www.ritzcarlton.com
Surrounded by water, this luxury resort offers amenities for all members of the family. The Ritz Kids program is entertaining and educational.
$$$

Sea View Hotel
9909 Collins Ave, 33154; 305 866 4441; seaview-hotel.com
Located in a forest of high-rises, this hotel's reasonable rates and friendly waterfront location make

it popular with families. It also has a charming pool and deck, for guests who like to make the most of their time outside.
$$$

Coconut Grove   Map 12 G4
HOTEL
Sonesta Coconut Grove
2889 McFarlane Rd, 33133; 305 529 2828; www.sonesta.com
Right across the street from Peacock Park (*see p55*), and within easy walking distance of the area's shops and restaurants, the Sonesta offers gorgeous views of the bay from its 22 floors. Among the 210 units are double rooms and one- or two-bedroom suites with full kitchens.
$$$

Coral Gables   Map 11 B2
HOTEL
The Biltmore Hotel
1200 Anastasia Ave, 33134; 855 311 6903; www.biltmorehotel.com
A stay at The Biltmore Hotel will make kids and grown-ups feel as if they are guests in a castle straight out of a storybook. Kids can sign up for cooking and golf, as well

as tennis classes, and also spa treatments designed especially for them, or swim in the famous pool.
$$$

Downtown   Map 14 G3
HOTEL
Mandarin Oriental, Miami
500 Brickell Key Dr, 33131; 305 913 8288; www.mandarinoriental.com
Though expensive, the family suites in this hotel are an excellent option; guests receive welcome cocktails and free domestic phone calls. Double-bedded rooms are less expensive. Babysitting, kids' yoga, teen spa treatments, and a private beach club are available.
$$$

Key Biscayne   Map 10 H3
RESORT
Silver Sands Beach Resort
301 Ocean Dr, 33149; 305 361 5441; www.silversandsbeachresort.net
With its homey charm and relatively affordable rates, this resort is great for families. Set on the beach, it has a playground, and complimentary cribs are available in its brightly

The magnificent ballroom in The Biltmore Hotel, Coral Gables

decorated rooms and cottages. While the rooms have kitchenettes, the cottages come with full kitchens.

🌐 🛏 🛇 🐾 ⚓ $$

HOTEL
The Ritz-Carlton Key Biscayne
455 Grand Bay Dr, 33149; 305 365 4500; www.ritzcarlton.com
The beachfront Ritz-Carlton provides a number of family-friendly amenities, and has a thoughtful children's program about culture and conservationism. The rooms are absolutely high-end, as is expected, and the hotel property is beautiful.

🌐 🍽 🛇 $$$

Middle Beach   Map 10 H2

RESORTS
Eden Roc Renaissance Miami Beach
4525 Collins Ave, 33140; 305 531 0000 or 800 319 5354; www.edenrocmiami.com
Families can take advantage of separate adults' and kids' pools, or just go across the street for the full Miami Beach experience. Also on offer are a family infinity pool, jet-skiing, sailing, and water-skiing.

🌐 🍽 🛇 $$$

Fontainebleau Miami Beach
4441 Collins Ave, 33140; 305 538 2000; www.fontainebleau.com
Perhaps Miami Beach's most famous resort, the Fontainebleau is also one of its most family friendly. This Art Deco gem and its two newer towers hold more than 1,500 rooms and suites, eight dining venues, a spa, several bars, and water features – all on the beachfront. The FB Kids program has day sessions and nighttime ones over the weekend.

🌐 🍽 🛇 🌙 $$$

Miami Beach Resort
4833 Collins Ave, 33140; 866 765 9090; www.miamibeachresortand spa.com
A good option for active families, the resort offers extensive watersports opportunities, including jet-skiing and parasailing. Rooms and suites are well equipped and family packages are available.

🌐 🍽 🛇 🌙 $$$

North Miami Beach

CAMPING
Oleta River State Park   Map 10 H2
3400 NE 163rd St, 33160; 305 919 1846; www.floridastateparks.org
The 14 barn-like cabins here make camping comfortable for families; most have a double bed and bunk beds. The cabins have no TV, kitchen, bathroom, or phone and guests must bring their own linen. Families will like the park's beach, trails, and watersports.

🍽 🦀 $

A rustic log cabin at Oleta River State Park campground

South Beach

HOTELS
The Angler's Hotel   Map 16 G5
660 Washington Ave, Miami Beach, 33139; 305 534 9600; www.anglershotelmiami.com
This eco-friendly accommodation, part of the Kimpton chain, is located near the quieter area of South Beach. A comfortable option for families, the hotel offers its guests a pool as well as bikes to explore the surrounding beach paths.

🌐 🍽 🛇 $$

Nassau Suite Hotel   Map 16 G3
1414 Collins Ave, Miami Beach, 33139; 305 532 0043; www.nassausuite.com
Classic Art Deco, this hotel's studio and one-bedroom suites are modern and convenient for families, and the kitchens offer a great way to save on meal costs. Continental breakfast is included in the rates. The beach is a short walk away.

🌐 🦀 🛏 $$

Beacon Hotel   Map 16 G4
720 Ocean Dr, Miami Beach, 33139; 305 674 8200; www.mybeaconhotel.com
Across the street from the beach, in the heart of the Art Deco district,

this 1930s hotel offers complimentary Continental breakfast and beach chairs. The hotel has a restaurant and room service, but is also close to the cafés along Ocean Drive.

🌐 🍽 🛇 $$$

Sunny Isles   Map 10 H2

RESORTS
Newport Beachside Hotel & Resort
16701 Collins Ave, 33160; 305 949 1300 or 800 327 5476; www. newportbeachsideresort.com
A playground on the beach, a children's pool, and loads of family-friendly activities ensure those with kids of all ages are happy here. Many rooms have fold-down wall beds. The on-site restaurant, Kitchen 305, serves only dinner, but guests can have breakfast and lunch at the poolside café.

🌐 🍽 🛇 🌙 $$

Acqualina Resort & Spa
17875 Collins Ave, 33160; 305 918 8000 or 877 312 9742; www.acqualina resort.com
Though pricey, the suites are the best option for families here, as the resort does not offer two-bed rooms. A Children's Center, movie nights, arts and crafts, and private swimming and sports lessons also make it a hit with families. Its award-winning marine biology-focused children's program is free for guests.

🌐 🍽 🦀 🛇 🌙 $$$

Trump International Beach Resort
18001 Collins Ave, 33160; 305 692 5612 or 866 628 1197; www.trump miami.com
This luxurious resort towers over the beach, where a grotto-style pool, watersports rentals, and cabana rentals make it even more fun. The resort's Planet Kids children's club offers exciting half- and full-day programs, featuring an "Enviro-Adventures" themed curriculum.

🌐 🍽 🛇 🌙 $$$

> ### Price Guide
> The following price ranges are based on one night's accommodation in high season for a family of four, inclusive of service charges and additional taxes.
>
> **$** Under $150 **$$** $150–300 **$$$** over $300

Key to symbols *see back cover flap*

The Gold and
Treasure Coasts

North of Miami, Florida's sun-drenched Atlantic shoreline is blessed with miles of fine beaches as well as parks and family-friendly attractions. The Gold Coast has a huge variety of theme parks, zoos, and museums. By contrast, the Treasure Coast, north of Palm Beach, is all about nature, with wild, unspoiled beaches and pine-covered barrier islands set in pristine waters that attract sea turtles, dolphins, and manatees.

The Gold and Treasure Coasts

Highlights

Museum of Discovery and Science
See dinosaur fossils, visit a storm center, feel space simulations, and watch IMAX® movies at this absorbing museum (see p80).

John U. Lloyd Beach State Park
Discover one of the best stretches of unspoiled sand on the Gold Coast, follow a hiking trail, or rent a kayak to explore a creek favored by manatees (see p82).

Butterfly World
Admire tropical greenhouses brimming with butterflies, and then go see the colorful parrots and scary spiders (see p85).

Flagler Museum
Check out the "palace on wheels," tycoon Henry Flagler's private railcar, at this fascinating museum (see pp90–91).

Juno Beach: Loggerhead Marinelife Center
Watch turtle shows, take part in a turtle walk, or see how injured amphibians are treated in the Sea Turtle Hospital (see p93).

Florida Oceanographic Coastal Center
Learn all about Florida's marine life, stroke a stingray, and take a walk through the mangroves of the Indian River Lagoon (see p97).

Left Spectacular drawing room at the Flagler Museum, Palm Beach
Above right Migratory pelicans on a perch near the beach in Fort Pierce, Hutchinson Island

The Best of
The Gold and Treasure Coasts

This part of Florida has something to suit every taste. Fort Lauderdale is a fun, full-scale resort, while the state parks provide opportunities for hiking and kayaking, and reserves such as Hobe Sound National Wildlife Refuge offer pristine strips of sand. Inland, there is plenty to do – wildlife parks, zoos, and marine life centers provide a window into Florida's rich natural habitats, and historic sites and art galleries dish up a slice of culture.

In a week

Start with **Fort Lauderdale** (see pp80–81), taking in a museum or two before sunbathing on the beach or enjoying a cruise on the *Jungle Queen*. Spend day two on the **Big Cypress Seminole Indian Reservation** (see p81), then return to **Fort Lauderdale beach** for an evening dip. Hit the road on day three, stopping at **Butterfly World** (see p85) before sampling the varied delights of **Boca Raton** (see p86). Take a trip to Japan on day four, courtesy of the **Morikami Museum and Japanese Gardens** (see p87), and end the day with a swim at **Palm Beach** (see pp88–9). Stay in town for another day to explore the **Flagler Museum** (see pp90–91), **Palm Beach Zoo** (see p92), and **Lion Country Safari** (see p92). Spend the last two days trawling the Treasure Coast, traveling via **Juno Beach** (see p93) and **Hutchinson Island** (see pp96–7) to an overnight stay at **Fort Pierce** (see p96), then finishing off at the seaside town of **Vero Beach** (see pp94–5).

Left Great Gravity Clock in the grand atrium of the Museum of Discovery and Science, Fort Lauderdale
Below Galleries at the Vero Beach Museum of Art, Vero Beach
Below right A sea turtle on the shore at Juno Beach

Above *Families enjoying a sunny day out on the beach in J. D. MacArthur State Park, Palm Beach*

On the manatee and turtle trail

On Florida's Atlantic coast, summer is turtle nesting time, and hundreds of them crawl up to the beach to lay their eggs. The best place to see them is the **Hobe Sound National Wildlife Refuge** (see p97), where there are guided turtle walks through June and July. The **Florida Oceanographic Coastal Center** (see p97) on **Hutchinson Island** runs a sea turtle program, while the **Loggerhead Marinelife Center** (see p93) is a hospital for sick or injured sea turtles.

Winter is the best time to see manatees in these parts: try the **John U. Lloyd Beach State Park** (see p82), or the **Manatee Observation & Education Center** in **Fort Pierce** (see p96).

Art versus science

Florida's east coast is best known for its beaches, but the region also offers plenty to stimulate young minds. Bright avant-garde works and

Impressionism reign at the **NSU Art Museum** (see p80) in **Fort Lauderdale**, while kids with an inclination for science will find heaps to explore at the nearby **Museum of Discovery and Science** (see p80). Try to catch a concert (and if not, get a bit of shopping done) at the **Seminole Hard Rock Hotel and Casino** (see p83). Younger ones will enjoy the **Young at Art Children's Museum** (see p84) in **Davie** (see p84, and aspiring astronomers can gaze at the stars at the nearby **Buehler Planetarium & Observatory** (see p84). **Boca Raton Children's Museum** (see p86) provides a hands-on, absorbing introduction to Florida's history. Older kids will appreciate the colorful works of US glass sculptor Dale Chihuly on display at the **Norton Museum of Art** (see p88) in **Palm Beach**.

The great outdoors

Nothing quite beats a day lounging or playing on the beach, but active families will find plenty to do off the sands. Tranquil **Hugh Taylor Birch State Park** (see p82), just minutes from downtown **Fort Lauderdale**, offers canoeing, hiking, and biking, while the **John U. Lloyd Beach State Park** features a hammock forest hiking trail and a creek perfect for kayaking. Marvel at the exotic wildlife on show at the **Lion Country Safari, Palm Beach Zoo, Butterfly World,** or **Flamingo Gardens** (see p84). Rent bikes and circle **Palm Beach** on the 3-mile (5-km) **Lake Trail** (see p88), explore the Wakodahatchee Wetlands in **Delray Beach** (see p86), or head inland to **Jonathan Dickinson State Park** (see p97) near Stuart, where intrepid families can explore the pine flatwoods, mangroves, and river swamps along the Loxahatchee River.

The Gold and Treasure Coasts

Running along Florida's Atlantic seaboard, the Gold and Treasure Coasts extend for some 200 miles (322 km) from Miami to the Space Coast. The area is battered by tropical storms in summer, but the weather is subtropical, balmy, and sunny most of the year. The beaches are superb. The coastline is heavily built up as far as Palm Beach, trailing off into sparsely populated barrier islands, swamp, and pine forest farther north. Separated from the barrier islands and beaches by the Intracoastal Waterway, the mainland is dotted with mansions and is rich in marine and bird life. Roads are great in this region, but public transportation is limited north of West Palm Beach.

Birds in the Flamingo Gardens, Davie

Sand castle at a public beach, Palm Beach

Spanish moss and lily pond in the lush McKee Botanical Gardens, Vero Beach

The Lowdown

🚌 **Getting there and around**
Air Flights connect almost every major city in the US with Fort Lauderdale (www.broward.org/airport). Taxis ($15–20) and the Go Airport Shuttle (www.floridalimo.com) provide shared shuttle van rides from the airport to Fort Lauderdale. Flights connect Palm Beach Airport (www.pbia.org) with all the major east coast hubs. Southeastern Florida Transportation Group (www.yellowcabflorida.com) provides taxis and shared rides.
Train Amtrak (www.amtrak.com) connects West Palm Beach and Fort Lauderdale with Miami, Tampa, Jacksonville, Orlando, and places north along the east coast to New York. Tri-Rail (www.tri-rail.com) and Brightline make local stops between West Palm Beach and Miami. **Bus** Greyhound (www.greyhound.com) connects Fort Pierce, Fort Lauderdale, and West Palm Beach with Miami and points north. Local buses are limited. **Car** Much of the region is best explored by car. Avis (www.avis.com) and Hertz (www.hertz.com) have rental offices at airports.

ℹ️ **Visitor information** See individual entries.

🛒 **Supermarkets** Publix (www.publix.com) is the major supermarket chain with outlets throughout this region.

🎪 **Festivals** Sea Food Festival, Fort Pierce: 772 466 3880; www.mainstreetfortpierce.org (Mar).

Easter Egg Hunt, Flagler Museum: kids are invited to hunt for 8,000 eggs on the museum's lawns; www.flaglermuseum.us (Mar–Apr). SunFest, West Palm Beach: live music, a Youth Park area with activities for kids, and a huge fireworks show; sunfest.com (Apr–May). Pineapple Festival, Jensen Beach: 772 334 3444; www.pineapplefestival.info (Nov).

➕ **Pharmacies** Check the Publix chain of supermarkets (www.publix.com), CVS (www.cvs.com), or Walgreens (www.walgreens.com) to find an all-night pharmacy.

🚻 **Restrooms** All major shopping malls, attractions, and most gas stations have public restrooms.

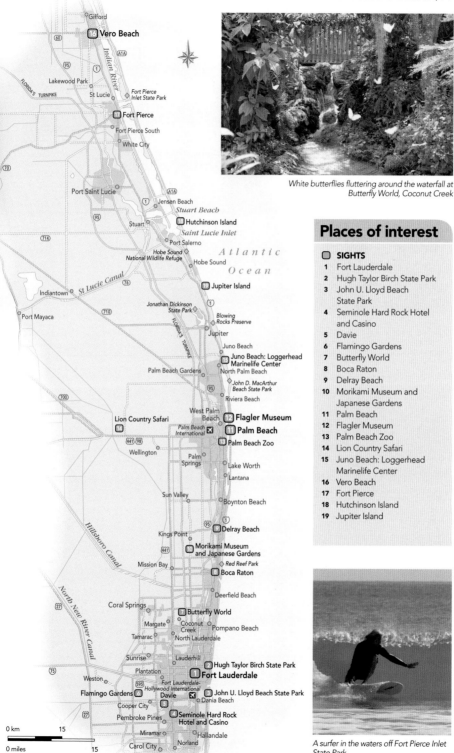

White butterflies fluttering around the waterfall at
Butterfly World, Coconut Creek

Places of interest

🔲 **SIGHTS**

1. Fort Lauderdale
2. Hugh Taylor Birch State Park
3. John U. Lloyd Beach State Park
4. Seminole Hard Rock Hotel and Casino
5. Davie
6. Flamingo Gardens
7. Butterfly World
8. Boca Raton
9. Delray Beach
10. Morikami Museum and Japanese Gardens
11. Palm Beach
12. Flagler Museum
13. Palm Beach Zoo
14. Lion Country Safari
15. Juno Beach: Loggerhead Marinelife Center
16. Vero Beach
17. Fort Pierce
18. Hutchinson Island
19. Jupiter Island

A surfer in the waters off Fort Pierce Inlet
State Park

① Fort Lauderdale

Beaches, vintage cars, and a rocket into space

Little more than a riverside trading camp in 1900, Fort Lauderdale became known as "the Venice of America" when its mangrove swamps were transformed into canals during the 1920s. Today, water taxis and an old-fashioned riverboat, the *Jungle Queen*, glide along these mansion-lined waterways, connecting downtown with a stunning beach. The city is crammed with creaky old houses to explore, hands-on art galleries, and an excellent science museum.

Intricately carved door at Bonnet House

Key Sights

① Museum of Discovery and Science Become an astronaut and travel to Mars, dig for fossils alongside a megalodon shark, or watch a 3-D IMAX® movie at this entertaining museum.

② Riverwalk Park Running along the banks of the New River, this shaded waterside park has winding walkways that take in all sorts of shops and cafés.

③ NSU Art Museum Core exhibits here include the vivid Impressionism of American artist William Glackens, contemporary Cuban art, and the amazing Indigo Room installation by Haitian artist Edouard Duval-Carrié, with themes of voodoo and migration.

④ Stranahan House Built in 1901, this creaky pinewood home served as a trading post where pioneer Frank Stranahan would buy goods such as egret plumes and alligator hides from the local Seminole Indians.

⑤ Fort Lauderdale Antique Car Museum The 22 vintage cars at this museum, which date from 1909 to the 1940s, keep alive the spirit of the Packard automobiles that were once made in Detroit, Michigan.

⑥ Bonnet House Museum and Gardens Explore the lush gardens of this Caribbean-style plantation house, designed by painter Frederic Clay Bartlett in 1920.

⑦ International Swimming Hall of Fame This museum is packed with swimming memorabilia, including exhibits relating to Olympic legend Mark Spitz, and the history of water polo.

The Lowdown

Map reference 10 H1
Address Museum of Discovery and Science: 401 SW 2nd St, 33312; www.mods.org. Riverwalk Park: 20 N New River Dr, 33312; www.goriverwalk.com. NSU Art Museum: 1 E Las Olas Blvd, 33301; www.nsuartmuseum.org. Stranahan House: 335 SE 6th Ave, 33301; stranahanhouse.org. Fort Lauderdale Antique Car Museum: 1527 SW 1st Ave, 33315; antiquecarmuseum.org. Bonnet House Museum and Gardens: 900 N Birch Rd, 33304; www.bonnethouse.org. International Swimming Hall of Fame: 1 Hall of Fame Dr, 33316; www.ishof.org

Train Tri-Rail (www.tri-rail.com) and Brightline (www.gobrightline.com) from Miami and West Palm Beach, or Amtrak (www.amtrak.com) from Orlando or Miami.
Bus 22 links the railroad station to the city center.

Visitor information 101 NE 3rd Ave, Suite 100, 33301; 954 765 4466; www.sunny.org

Open Museum of Discovery and Science: 10am–5pm Mon–Sat & noon–6pm Sun. Riverwalk Park: 24 hours. NSU Art Museum: 11am–5pm Tue–Sat (till 8pm Thu), noon–5pm Sun. Stranahan House: tours at 1pm, 2pm

and 3pm daily. Fort Lauderdale Antique Car Museum: 10am–4pm Mon–Fri. Bonnet House Museum and Gardens: 9am–4pm Tue–Sun. International Swimming Hall of Fame: 9am–5pm Mon–Fri, 9am–2pm Sat

Prices Museum of Discovery and Science: $45–58. NSU Art Museum: $29–34; under 12s free. Stranahan House: $38–48. Fort Lauderdale Antique Car Museum: $16–32; under 12s free. Bonnet House Museum: $56–72; under 6s free. International Swimming Hall of Fame: $20–24

Fort Lauderdale beach, fringed with coconut palm trees

Letting off steam

Just 3 miles (5 km) east of downtown is a sandy beach 7 miles (11 km) long. Backed by an attractive promenade and fringed with palms, it is perfect for swimming.

Eat and drink

Picnic: under $25; Snacks: $25–50; Real meal: $50–80; Family treat: over $80 (based on a family of four)

PICNIC Publix at Las Olas (601 S Andrews Ave, 33301; 954 728 8330; www.publix.com), the closest major supermarket to downtown Fort Lauderdale, offers sandwiches, breads, and deli products that can be enjoyed on the beach.

SNACKS Hot Dog Heaven (101 E Sunrise Blvd, 33304; 954 523 7100; hotdogheaven.infinology.net/home. htm; till 4:30pm Mon–Sat) is a small place with bar stools inside and two tables outside. A local favorite, it serves superb beef Chicago hotdogs with mustard, relish, and a salad.

🚲 **Guided tours** M. Cruz Rentals (www.mcruzrentals.com) runs Segway tours of Fort Lauderdale beach district.

👫 **Age range** All ages

🤸 **Activities** Explore the waterways aboard the *Jungle Queen* riverboat (www.junglequeen.com) or a water taxi shuttle (www.water taxi.com).

⏱ **Allow** At least 2 days

Good family value?
Educative and entertaining sights, as well as a delightful beach, make the city a superb family destination.

REAL MEAL Coconuts (429 Seabreeze Blvd, 33316; 954 525 2421; www.coconutsfort lauderdale.com) offers outdoor seating on the water's edge next to the International Swimming Hall of Fame, with views of the local pelicans and a daily fish feeding. Feast on stone crab, fish tacos, and fresh local seafood.

FAMILY TREAT 3030 Ocean (Harbor Beach Resort Marriott, 3030 Holiday Dr, 33316; 954 765 3030; www.3030ocean.com; dinner only) serves innovative, contemporary American seafood, most of which has been sourced locally.

Shopping

Las Olas Boulevard (www.lasolas boulevard.com) is the city's upscale shopping strip, with plenty of fashion stores and boutiques that will appeal to teenagers. **Galleria** (2414 E Sunrise Blvd, 33304; 954 564 1015; www.galleriamall-fl.com) is one of the best malls.

Find out more

FILM The dog-friendly tear-jerker *Marley & Me* (2008) was set in Fort Lauderdale.

Guided airboat ride in Big Cypress Seminole Indian Reservation, Clewiston

Next stop...

BIG CYPRESS SEMINOLE INDIAN RESERVATION Visit Big Cypress Seminole Indian Reservation, a Native American outpost 78 miles (125 km) northwest of the city, for its fun "swamp safaris" (www.billieswamp. com) and the enlightening Ah-Tah-Thi-Ki Museum (www.ahtahthiki.com).

② Hugh Taylor Birch State Park

Canoes, hikes, and bikes

This rustic park, just minutes away from downtown Fort Lauderdale, preserves a pristine slice of Florida's wilderness, thanks to Chicago attorney Hugh Taylor Birch, who donated his estate as a public park in 1941. The park provides access to an especially inviting section of Fort Lauderdale Beach, but to paddle up and down the park's mile-long (1.6-km) freshwater lagoon, Lake Helen, with younger children, it's best to rent canoes that hold 3–4 people. Older kids might prefer their own kayak. Look out for turtles, ducks, herons, gray squirrels, wading birds, raccoons, and the occasional marsh rabbit.

Back on dry land, the Coastal Hammock Trail is an easy 20–30-minute walk through a tropical hardwood hammock (forest). There are interpretive signs along the way that provide information about native fauna – try spotting one of the park's rare gopher tortoises or gray foxes.

Canoes for hire at Lake Helen in Hugh Taylor Birch State Park

Another fun thing to do is to rent bikes and cycle through the park on the 2-mile (3-km) park road.

Letting off steam

If kids don't get wet enough kayaking, then go 2 miles (3 km) south to splash in the outdoor pools at the **Fort Lauderdale Aquatic Complex** (www.fortlauderdale.gov).

③ John U. Lloyd Beach State Park

A day at the beach

The main attraction at this park is the beach – a wonderful 2-mile (4-km) stretch of unspoiled sand that is evocative of old Florida and perfect for swimming. Just inland is the 45-minute Barrier Island Nature Trail through hammock forest, where squirrels and raccoons sometimes scamper into the brush. Whiskey Creek, which divides the park along its length, has lots of manatees, especially in winter, and there is plenty of bird life to see in the mangroves. The whole family will enjoy watching Port Everglades cruise ships coming and going at the northern end of the park.

Take cover

Head 2 miles (3 km) southwest to watch a game of jai-alai at the **Dania Jai-Alai Stadium** (301 E Dania Beach Blvd, 33004; 954 920 1511; www.betdania.com). Jai-alai is an ancient game from northern Spain – a bit like squash, but much faster.

The Lowdown

- 🌐 **Map reference** 10 H1
  Address 3109 E Sunrise Blvd (off Hwy-A1A), 33304; 954 564 4521; www.floridastateparks.org/park/Hugh-Taylor-Birch
- 🚌 **Bus** Broward County Transit bus 11 from downtown Fort Lauderdale to the park entrance
- 🕐 **Open** 8am–sunset daily
- 💲 **Price** $6 per vehicle; $2 per pedestrian or cyclist
- 🔫 **Guided tours** Ranger-guided walks at 10:30am Fri
- 👫 **Age range** All ages
- 🏃 **Activities** The park offers canoe and kayak rentals ($20 for 1 hour) and bike rentals ($12.50 for 1 hour, $25 for 4 hours, and $35 for 24 hours).
- ⏱ **Allow** Half a day to a full day
- 🍴 **Eat and drink** SNACKS Park & Ocean (on site) offers a varied menu and oceanfront seating with spectacular views. REAL MEAL Franco & Vinny's Pizza Shack (2884 E Sunrise Blvd, 33304; 954 564 9522; francoandvinnys.com; 4–11pm daily) serves excellent pizza and pasta dishes, as well as children's specials including spaghetti with meatballs.

The Lowdown

- 🌐 **Map reference** 10 H2
  Address 6503 N Ocean Dr, Dania Beach, 33004; 954 923 2833; www.floridastateparks.org/park/Lloyd-Beach
- 🚗 **Car** Rent a car from Fort Lauderdale Airport.
- ℹ️ **Visitor information** Dania Beach Chamber of Commerce, 102 W Dania Beach Blvd, Dania Beach, 33004; 954 926 2323; www.daniabeachchamber.org
- 🕐 **Open** 8am–sunset daily
- 💲 **Price** $6 per vehicle; $2 per pedestrian or cyclist
- 👫 **Age range** All ages
- 🏃 **Activities** There are 45-min self-guided nature walks at the south end of the park.
- ⏱ **Allow** Half a day to a full day
- 🍴 **Eat and drink** SNACKS Dania Beach Bar & Grill (65 N Beach Rd, 33004; 954 923 4148; www.daniabeachgrill.com; 11am–6pm daily), just outside the park, has a full range of salads, sandwiches, and burgers. REAL MEAL Islamorada Fish Company (220 Gulf Stream Way, Dania Beach, 33004; 954 927 7737; restaurants.basspro.com/fishcompany/DaniaBeach) offers fresh seafood dishes.

Sunbathing at the beach in John U. Lloyd Beach State Park

Having fun at the T. Y. (Topeekeegee Yugnee) Park

④ Seminole Hard Rock Hotel and Casino

Florida's Native Americans and a Hard Rock Cafe

For a different perspective on Florida's history and culture, visit the Seminole Hard Rock Hotel and Casino near Hollywood. In 1979, the Seminole became the first Native American tribe to develop gaming as a form of income and in 2004 the tribe purchased the Hard Rock Cafe franchise. Today, the millions earned as revenue from the complex finance health care, education, full senior care, and modern community centers.

Older kids may prefer the restaurants and shops in the hotel complex. These include the **Hard Rock Cafe** itself, the authentic Mexican standards (and guacamole prepared tableside) at Tequila Ranch, and Wetzel's Pretzels. Hip kids' clothing store Brats and the Seminole Store are among the shops on site.

If there is time, take in one of the wide range of concerts and shows at the Hard Rock Live, or enjoy a dip in the lagoon-style pool.

Letting off steam

A short drive south from the complex, the **T. Y. (Topeekeegee Yugnee) Park** (*3300 N Park Rd, 33021*) has picnic areas, basketball courts, playgrounds, and a 2-mile (3-km) loop of paved pathways for walking, jogging, skating, and biking. In summer, visit the Castaway Island Water Park, located within the park.

The Lowdown

🌐 **Map reference** 10 H2
Address 1 Seminole Way, 33314; 866 502 7529; *www.seminole hardrockhollywood.com*

🚗 **Car** Rent a car from Fort Lauderdale Airport.

🕐 **Open** Hard Rock Cafe: 11am–midnight Sun–Thu & 11am–2am Fri–Sat

👫 **Age range** 5 plus

⏱ **Allow** 2–3 hours

🍽 **Eat and drink** SNACKS Constant Grind (*1 Seminole Way, 33314; 954 797 2328; www.seminole hardrockhollywood.com/ sweets-and-snacks.htm*) serves up sumptuous sandwiches, croissants and pastries. REAL MEAL Blue Plate (*1 Seminole Way, 33314; 954 327 7625; www. seminolehardrockhollywood. com*) serves casual food for breakfast as well as lunch, just across from the pool.

The tropical pool area in the Seminole Hard Rock Hotel and Casino

Picnic under $25; **Snacks** $25–50; **Real meal** $50–80; **Family treat** over $80 (based on a family of four)

Browsing through a variety of cowboy hats at Grif's Western, Davie

⑤ Davie

Cowboys, children's art and a trip to the stars

Lying 20 miles (32 km) inland, this Fort Lauderdale suburb is the unlikely venue for some intriguing family attractions. Davie is more like a cowboy outpost than a typical Florida town, a legacy of Florida's early cattle-ranching settlers. Kids will love watching the town rodeo, held intermittently between February and November. There is even a rodeo for kids in June. Fans of the Wild West should visit **Grif's Western**, the leading seller of cowboy boots, hats, and saddles in the state. Stop by the **Old Davie School Historical Museum**, a restored 1918 schoolhouse, with exhibits that bring Florida's pioneer history to life. Younger children will get more out of the **Young at Art Children's Museum**, which explores the history of art through five child-friendly themes. Finally, do not miss the **Buehler Planetarium & Observatory**, where planetarium shows are followed by star-gazing sessions. On a clear night, Jupiter, or even Saturn's rings, might be visible.

Letting off steam

Zip off to **Tree Tops Park** (*3900 SW 100th Ave, 33328; 954 357 5130; www.broward.org/Parks*), which has playgrounds, hiking trails, and guided horse-rides.

Prices given are for a family of four

The Lowdown

🌐 **Map reference** 10 H2
Address Grif's Western: 6211 Orange Dr, 33314; 954 587 9000; *grifswestern.com*. Old Davie School Historical Museum: 6650 Griffin Rd, 33314; 954 797 1044; *olddavieschool.org*. Young at Art Children's Museum: 751 SW 121 Ave, 33325; 954 424 0085; *www.youngatartmuseum.org*. Buehler Planetarium & Observatory: 3501 Davie Rd, Broward College campus, 33314; 954 201 6681; *www.broward.edu/studentlife/planetarium/Pages/default.aspx*

🚗 **Car** Rent a car from Fort Lauderdale Airport.

🕐 **Open** Grif's Western: 10am–8pm Mon–Sat & 11am–6pm Sun. Old Davie School Historical Museum: 10am–4pm Tue–Sat. Young at Art Children's Museum: 10am–5pm Mon–Thu (till 6pm Fri–Sat), 11am–6pm Sun. Buehler Planetarium: 8–10pm Wed (public viewings); check website for show timings.

💲 **Prices** Old Davie School Historical Museum: $24–34. Young at Art Children's Museum: $56, under 1s free. Buehler Planetarium: free on public viewing nights; shows $16–28

👫 **Age range** 5 plus

⏱ **Allow** A day

☕ **Eat and drink** SNACKS La Spada's Original Hoagies (*2645 S University Dr, 33328; 954 476 1099; www.laspadashoagies.com*) offers some of the best sandwiches in southern Florida. REAL MEAL Delvecchio's pizzeria (*2060 S University Dr, 33324; 954 476 9336; www.delvecchiospizza.com*) is a family-friendly pizza joint.

🎪 **Festival** Bergeron Rodeo Grounds (*4271 Davie Rd*) hosts 6 to 8 rodeos (*daviprorodeo.com*; Feb–Nov).

⑥ Flamingo Gardens

The home of pink flamingos

This botanical garden, smothered with subtropical plants and trees, is a serene preserve that attracts butterflies and hummingbirds in winter. The gardens are set up with families in mind – children are encouraged to touch and smell herbs and plants in the Children's Garden. But, inevitably, most kids will be asking, "where are the flamingos?" Fear not, the on-site Everglades Wildlife Sanctuary is home to 83 species of Florida's native birds and animals, including alligators, panthers, bobcats, otters, eagles, and pink flamingos. Around 250 birds, including plenty of noisy waders, are seen inside the huge Free-flight Aviary. Also visit the Wray Home Museum, restored to its appearance in the 1930s, when it was the home of Floyd and Jane Wray, the founders of the gardens.

Take cover

If it rains, head for the **Old Davie School Historical Museum**, located 6 miles (10 km) east of Flamingo Gardens. The museum houses artifacts and photographs that tell the story of the journey of the pioneers into the Everglades.

Visitors aboard a tram tour in Flamingo Gardens, Davie

The Lowdown

🌐 **Map reference** 10 G2
Address 3750 S Flamingo Rd, (between Griffin Rd and I-595), Davie, 33330; 954 473 2955; *www.flamingogardens.org*

🚗 **Car** Rent a car from Fort Lauderdale Airport.

🕐 **Open** 9:30am–5pm daily; Jun–Oct

💲 **Price** $53–66; under 2s free

🚩 **Guided tours** Guided tours of Wray Home Museum take place 10am–5pm daily. Narrated tram tours of the gardens depart on the hour and half-hour 11am–4pm daily.

👫 **Age range** 5 plus

🐾 **Activities** Live Wildlife Encounter Shows (weather permitting) at 11:30am, 1:30pm & 3:30pm daily

⏱ **Allow** 2–3 hours

☕ **Eat and drink** SNACKS Publix Countryside Shops (*5630 S Flamingo Rd, Cooper City, 33330; 954 434 2803; www.publix.com*) is the nearest major supermarket to Flamingo Gardens. REAL MEAL Marola's Trattoria (*5822 S Flamingo Rd, Cooper City, 33330; 954 434 3420; marolas.com*), a family-friendly Italian restaurant, serves salads, pasta, and pizza.

Walking across the Tinalandia Suspension Bridge in Butterfly World

⑦ Butterfly World
Birds, butterflies, and bugs

Few places are as enchanting as this nature park, located in Tradewinds Park, where hundreds of brilliantly colored butterflies flutter through tropical greenhouses, and exotic birds nestle in the palms. Inside the Tropical Rain Forest Aviary, bright blue, amber, and yellow butterflies land gently on children's hands and shoulders. Kids also love the Lorikeet Encounter, where multicolored parrots feed from cups of nectar right out of visitors' hands.

The Tinalandia Suspension Bridge, which sways as kids romp across it, is another favorite, while the main attractions inside the blossom-filled Jewels of the Sky Aviary are the fearless hummingbirds, which feed on nectar in the flowers. Do not miss the Bug Zoo, where giant water bugs, creepy spiders, and mean-looking wasps are sure to elicit gasps of horror/pleasure.

Letting off steam

Kids can run around in **Tradewinds Park** *(www.broward.org/Parks/Trade windsPark)*, an expanse of green that has playgrounds, picnic areas, and a fishing lake. Pony rides and trips in a model steam train are also available.

A butterfly on foliage in Butterfly World, Coconut Creek

The Lowdown

- 🌐 **Map reference** 10 H1
  Address Tradewinds Park, 3600 W Sample Rd, Coconut Creek, 33073; 954 977 4400; www.butterflyworld.com
- 🚗 **Car** Rent a car from Fort Lauderdale Airport.
- 🕐 **Open** 9am–5pm Mon–Sat & 11am–5pm Sun
- 💲 **Price** $82–104; under 2s free
- 🧍 **Age range** All ages
- 🧍 **Activities** The *Bring Back the Butterflies* guide tells you what

flowers and shrubs to plant in your garden at home in order to attract butterflies.

- ⏱ **Allow** 2 hours
- 🍽 **Eat and drink** SNACKS The Lakeside Café *(on site)* is the best place for sandwiches, salads, iced drinks, and coffee. REAL MEAL Pollo Tropical *(2320 N Federal Hwy, 33064; 954 946-9592; www.pollotropical. com)* a Caribbean-inspired chain restaurant a few miles away in Pompano Beach, serves up grilled meats, vegetables and sandwiches.

Elevated viewing platform in the Gumbo Limbo Nature Center, Boca Raton

⑧ Boca Raton

A Mediterranean fantasy

This lovely city started to develop during the Florida land boom of the 1920s, when famous architect Addison Mizner built the ultra chic pink building called the Boca Raton Resort & Club. Kids will probably spot this fortress from the car. Mizner inspired the Mediterranean Revival style of architecture that still dominates downtown and gives Boca Raton a Continental feel.

Younger kids will find the **Boca Raton Children's Museum** enticing. Set within a 1913 driftwood Cracker cottage – the simple abode of early Florida farmers – it has many hands-on exhibits that will keep children occupied for hours. The KidsCents Bank exhibit shows how a bank works, with teller windows and a working vault, while Pirate Island brings the seafaring world to life with interactive games, stories, and a treasure map. Nearer to the ocean, stroll around **Gumbo Limbo Nature Center**, where boardwalks wind through a tropical hardwood hammock and a mangrove forest. Spot ospreys, brown pelicans, and the occasional manatee lurking in the warm waters.

Letting off steam

There are plenty of public beaches in Boca Raton, but parking tends to be expensive. The **Red Reef Park**, next to the Gumbo Limbo Nature Center on Highway-A1A, is good for swimming, sunbathing, and snorkeling. The nearby **Delray Beach** is a cheaper alternative. **Boomers** (3100 Airport Rd, Boca Raton, 33431; 561 347 1888;

Prices given are for a family of four

www.boomersparks.com/site/dania) is an old-fashioned fun park, with high-speed go-karts, mini-golf, laser tag, and a huge video arcade.

The Lowdown

🌐 **Map reference** 10 H1

Address Boca Raton Children's Museum: 498 Crawford Blvd, 33432; 561 368 6878; www.cmboca.org. Gumbo Limbo Nature Center: 1801 N Ocean Blvd, 33432; 561 544 8605; www.gumbolimbo.org

🚗 **Car** Rent a car from Fort Lauderdale Airport.

ℹ️ **Visitor information** Boca Raton Chamber of Commerce, 1800 N Dixie Hwy, 33432; 561 395 4433; www.bocaratonchamber.com

🕐 **Open** Boca Raton Children's Museum: 10am–1pm Tue & Wed, 10am–5pm Thu–Sat. Gumbo Limbo Nature Center: 9am–4pm Mon–Sat, noon–4pm Sun

💲 **Prices** Boca Raton Children's Museum: $20–30; under 1s free. Gumbo Limbo Nature Center: free; $5 donation per person

🚩 **Guided tours** Gumbo Limbo Nature Center runs guided walks to observe sea turtles laying eggs (Jun–Jul) and eggs hatching (Jul–Aug).

🧑‍🤝‍🧑 **Age range** 5 plus

⏱️ **Allow** A day

🍴 **Eat and drink** PICNIC 4th Generation Organic Market (75 SE 3rd St, 33432; 561 338 9920; www.4thgenerationmarket.com) stocks salads, sandwiches, wraps, and desserts. Enjoy the picnic in the Red Reef Park. REAL MEAL Tom Sawyer Restaurant & Pastry Shop (1759 NW 2nd Ave, 33432; 561 368 4634; www.tomsawyer restaurant.com; 7am–2pm daily) is an old-fashioned diner with excellent breakfasts. It also serves soups, salads, and seafood.

⑨ Delray Beach

Fun with water and sand

Delray Beach is one of the most popular, family-friendly destinations in South Florida – this small and welcoming beach town has even received awards for being the "Most Fun Small Town in America." The 2-mile (3-km) beach, with good facilities, is ideal for fun activities, while the calm waters allow for numerous watersports, from paddleboarding to snorkeling. The nearby Atlantic Avenue has

plenty of fine restaurants and bars, upscale shops, and art galleries.

When kids tire of the beach, take a stroll along the three-quarter-mile (1-km) boardwalk that winds around the **Wakodahatchee Wetlands**. This swamp area has become home to a variety of wildlife, including alligators, turtles, frogs, and over 140 different species of birds. More water-related activities can be found at the **Sandoway Discovery Center**, which has reptiles, shark feedings, a shell collection, and an exhibit on the Delray Wreck, a steamship that sunk off the coast in 1903. The restored **Cason Cottage Museum**, run by the Delray Beach Historical Society, takes you back to Florida's pre-boom era, from 1915 to 1935, with a focus on local architecture and history.

The Lowdown

🌐 **Map reference** 10 H2

Address Wakodahatchee Wetlands: 13026 Jog Rd, 33446; www.pbcgov.com/waterutilities/wakodahatchee/. Sandoway Discovery Center: 142 S Ocean Blvd, 33483; 561 274 7263; www.sandoway.org. Cason Cottage Museum: 5 NE First St, 33444; 561 243 2577; www.delraybeachhistory.org/cason_cottage

🚗 **Car** Rent a car from West Palm Beach Airport.

ℹ️ **Visitor information** 140 NE 1st St, 33444; 561 279 1380; www.visitdelraybeach.org

🕐 **Open** Wakodahatchee Wetlands: 7am–sunset daily. Sandoway Discovery Center: 10am–4pm Tue–Sun. Cason Cottage Museum: Nov–Apr: 11am–3pm Thu–Sat

💲 **Prices** Wakodahatchee Wetlands: free. Sandoway Discovery Center: $20; under 3s free. Cason Cottage Museum: $10; under 16s free

🧑‍🤝‍🧑 **Age range** 5 plus

🧑‍🤝‍🧑 **Activities** Download a walking tour brochure and coloring book from the Delray Beach Historical Society website.

⏱️ **Allow** A day

🍴 **Eat and drink** SNACKS Sandwiches by the Sea (1214 E Atlantic Ave; 561 272 2212) serves good-value subs to go with the superb milkshakes and smoothies. REAL MEAL Caffe Luna Rosa (34 S Ocean Blvd; 561 274 9404; www.caffeluna rosa.com) offers top-quality seafood dishes, Italian specialties such as antipasti and homemade pasta, and desserts.

Stone sculptures and flower beds in the Japanese Gardens, Delray Beach

Letting off steam

The **Catherine Strong Splash Park** (1500 SW 6th Ave, 33444; 561 243 7194) is good for a cool-down, and there's a playground as well. For something calmer, opt for picking strawberries and explore the hydroponic garden at **The Girls Strawberry U-Pick** (14466 S Military Trail, 33484; www.thegirlsstrawberryupick.com).

⑩ Morikami Museum and Japanese Gardens

A day out in the Far East

Southern Florida is an unlikely place for an outpost of classical Japan, but this museum and its beautifully landscaped grounds give visitors an authentic taste of the Far East. See six beautiful Japanese gardens, a Shinto shrine, a teahouse, and a museum – the legacy of a Japanese agricultural colony established in Boca Raton in the early 20th century. The main section of the museum displays Japanese art, but kids might find this hard-going; aim instead for the Yamato-kan house, where the Japan through the Eyes of a Child exhibit offers a taste of modern Japanese life specially designed for younger kids. Explore a Japanese classroom, a shopping street, and a typical home complete with *tatami* mats (straw mats used to cover floors), a huge bathtub, and a high-tech toilet. The gardens, with zigzag bridges, hidden waterfalls, Zen-inspired rock gardens, and many bonsai trees, are ideal for strolling.

Letting off steam

The museum and gardens form part of the greater **Morikami Park**, a public space containing Lake Biwa and Saki Pavilion. Visitors can picnic here, and there is also a playground and a nature trail.

The Lowdown

🌐 **Map reference** 8 H6
Address 4000 Morikami Park Rd, Delray Beach, 33446; 561 495 0233; www.morikami.org

🚗 **Car** Rent a car from West Palm Beach Airport.

🕐 **Open** 10am–5pm Tue–Sun

💲 **Price** $39–48; under 6s free

👫 **Age range** All ages

⏱ **Allow** At least 2–3 hours

🍴 **Eat and drink** SNACKS Cornell Café (on site; 11am–3pm Tue–Sun) is an open-air place selling pan-Asian snacks, light meals, and desserts. REAL MEAL Henry's (16850 Jog Rd, 33446; 561 638 1949; henrysofbocaraton.com) offers contemporary American and Continental cuisine near the gardens.

🎌 **Festival** Hatsume Fair, spring festival (Mar)

Japanese-style schoolboy's bedroom at the Morikami Museum, Delray Beach

Picnic under $25; **Snacks** $25–50; **Real meal** $50–80; **Family treat** over $80 (based on a family of four)

⑪ Palm Beach
Hang out with America's mega-rich

One of the wealthiest places in the US, Palm Beach is peppered with grand mansions, pristine gardens, and upscale shopping streets. The town was founded in the 1890s, when Henry Flagler brought his railroad south and built two luxury hotels here. In the 1920s, Addison Mizner added Mediterranean-style homes and plazas, lending the town a refined European air. Ever since, it has attracted tycoons, sports stars, and even royalty.

Impressive facade of The Breakers

Key Sights

① **Lake Trail** Bike or walk along this tree-shaded 3-mile (5-km) path that borders the waters of Lake Worth to take in scenic lake views and admire Palm Beach mansions.

② **Green's Pharmacy** Open since 1937, this old-fashioned diner is known for its breakfasts, burgers, and ice cream sodas. Hit the pharmacy section for all sorts of beach gear, toys, and old-style sweets.

③ **The Breakers** Established by Henry Flagler in 1896, this hotel is a spellbinding place to visit for a guided tour. The present Italianate building dates from 1926.

④ **Episcopal Church of Bethesda-by-the-Sea** This Neo-Gothic church was built in 1926. Stroll in its lush Cluett Memorial Garden, amid the cloisters, with gazebos and a fountain pond filled with colorful koi.

⑤ **Society of the Four Arts** While art exhibitions are held inside this Italianate building, the beautifully landscaped grounds contain a series of lush botanical gardens, and a selection of elegant modern sculptures.

⑥ **Norton Museum of Art** This museum houses several masterpieces by great artists such as Picasso and Gauguin, as well as modern American art by Jackson Pollock, Georgia O'Keeffe, and glass artist Dale Chihuly.

Letting off steam

Spend time on the wide, clean **public beach** off Ocean Boulevard. Further afield, little ones will enjoy Playmobil toys at the **Playmobil FunPark** (*8031 N Military Trail, 33410; 561 691 9880; www.playmobilusa.com*).

Eat and drink

Picnic: under $25; Snacks: $25–50; Real meal: $50–80; Family treat: over $80 (based on a family of four)

PICNIC Publix on Palm Beach (*135 Bradley Pl, 33480; 561 655 4120; www.publix.com*) is a great

place to pick up delicious goodies for a picnic on the beach or in Cluett Memorial Garden.

Dining in the charming courtyard of Pizza Al Fresco

SNACKS Sprinkles Ice Cream & Sandwich (*279 Royal Poinciana Way, 33480; 561 659 1140; 9am–10pm Sun–Thu, 9am–11pm Fri–Sat*) offers luscious ice cream in several flavors.
REAL MEAL Pizza Al Fresco (*14 Via Mizner, 33480; 561 832 0032; pizzaalfresco.com*) has courtyard seating and serves fabulous brick-oven pizza and baked pasta.
FAMILY TREAT Charley's Crab (*456 S Ocean Blvd, 33480; 561 659 1500; www.muer.com*) offers fine seafood right on the beach. Try the Alaskan king crab or the filet mignon.

Prices given are for a family of four

Map labels
0 meters 600
0 yards 600
WELLS RD
Lake Trail ①
BRADLEY PLACE
N COUNTY RD
N OCEAN BLVD
② Green's Pharmacy
SUNRISE AVENUE
ROYAL POINCIANA WAY
Breakers Ocean Golf Course
N COUNTY RD
③ The Breakers
Lake Worth
Episcopal Church of Bethesda-by-the-Sea ④
BARTON AVE
Atlantic Ocean
COCOANUT
S COUNTY RD
⑤ Society of the Four Arts
ROYAL PALM WAY
⑥
Norton Museum of Art 1 mile (2 km)
ROW
SOUTH OCEAN BLVD
WORTH AVENUE

Shopping

Teenagers might like to window shop in **Worth Avenue** (www. worth-avenue.com) in downtown Palm Beach, which is packed with designer stores and art galleries. Try Palm Beach's high-class thrift stores, such as **Church Mouse** (378 S County Rd, 33480; 561 659 2154) for more affordable bargains.

Find out more

DIGITAL Check out www.pbpulse. com for information on events, dining, shopping, arts, and culture.

Next stop...

POLO AND SWIMMING The Palm Beach area is famous for polo. For fun tournaments held on weekends (Jan–Apr), visit the **International Polo Club of Palm Beach** (3667 120th Ave S, Wellington, 33414; 561 204 5687; www.international poloclub.com). **Peanut Island** (www.pbcgov.com/parks/peanut island), in the middle of Lake Worth, is a county park good for swimming and snorkeling. It is home to John F. Kennedy's Cold War bunker. The park also has a campground, and picnic areas with grills.

A polo match in progress at the International Polo Club of Palm Beach

The Lowdown

🌐 **Map reference** 8 H5
Address Green's Pharmacy: 151 North County Rd, 33480; 561 832 0304. The Breakers: 1 South County Rd, 33480; 888 273 2537; www.thebreakers.com. Episcopal Church of Bethesda-by-the-Sea: 141 South County Rd, 33480; 561 655 4554; www.bbts.org. Society of the Four Arts: 2 Four Arts Plaza, 33480; 561 655 7226; www.fourarts.org. Norton Museum of Art: 1451 S Olive Ave, West Palm Beach, 33401; 561 832 5196; www.norton.org

🚌 **Bus** Palm Tran bus 44 (www. pbcgov.com/palmtran) from airport to downtown West Palm Beach. Palm Tran bus 41 (Mon–Sat) from downtown Palm Beach to West Palm Beach Tri-Rail station (www.tri-rail.com).
Car Metered parking available on the Palm Beach seafront.

ℹ️ **Visitor information** 1555 Palm Beach Lakes Blvd, Suite 800, West Palm Beach, 33401; 800 544 7256; www.palmbeachfl.com

🕐 **Open** Green's Pharmacy: 7am–4pm Mon–Fri (till 3pm Sat & Sun). Episcopal Church of Bethesda-by-the-Sea: 8am–5pm daily. Society of the Four Arts: 10am–5pm daily. Norton Museum of Art: noon–5pm Fri–Wed, noon–9pm Thu

💲 **Prices** Episcopal Church of Bethesda-by-the-Sea, Society of the Four Arts, and Norton Museum of Art: free

🚩 **Guided tours** Norton Museum of Art runs tours Nov–Apr: 2pm Thu–Sun; check website. The Breakers offers a historical tour; call ahead for reservations.

🏃 **Activities** Rent bikes from Palm Beach Bicycle Trail Shop (www. palmbeachbicycle.com; $15 per hour, $29 half a day & $39 for 24 hours).

⏱️ **Allow** 1–2 days

Good family value?
Palm Beach is an expensive town, but it does not cost a cent to explore its pristine streets and shops, or enjoy its lovely beaches.

⑫ Flagler Museum
A palace fit for a merchant prince

While traveling along the east coast of Florida, it is impossible not to hear about Henry Flagler, the man who probably did more to develop the state than any other. Before Flagler's East Coast Railway reached Miami in 1896, most of Florida was a wilderness. By the time the trains made it to Key West in 1912, the region was firmly established as a winter getaway. Flagler's lavish Palm Beach home, Whitehall, is now the Flagler Museum, a fascinating monument to the man and his legacy.

Grand piano in the Drawing Room

Key Features

▌ **Illustrated area** Constructed in 1902.

▌ **Extension** Added in 1925.

▌ **Pavilion** Added in 2005.

Yellow Roses Room

Flagler-Kenan History Room Learn about Flagler's achievements as a founding partner in Standard Oil and as a developer of Florida's east coast here. An 18-carat gold replica of the telegram announcing the completion of his Key West Railway is also on display.

The Grand Hall Seven types of marble were used to create the largest and grandest room built in America's Gilded Age. It contains a bust of Caesar Augustus and a portrait of Henry Flagler himself.

Music Room Flagler employed his own organist to play a 1,249-pipe Odell organ in this room, a favorite with Mrs. Flagler for holding parties.

Entrance

Master Suite

Drawing Room

West Room Part of the 1925 hotel extension, this room originally served as the dining room. Look out for the medieval crests that circle the walls below the ceiling.

Vacationers at a public beach, Palm Beach

Letting off steam

The Flagler Museum lies on the route of the **Lake Trail** (see p88), while the beach is a short drive away on South Ocean Boulevard.

Prices given are for a family of four

Eat and drink

Picnic: under $25; Snacks: $25–50; Real meal: $50–80; Family treat: over $80 (based on a family of four)

PICNIC Amici Market (155 North County Rd, 33480; 561 832 0201; www.myamicimarket.com) is a gourmet market and deli just north of the museum. Picnic on the beach.

SNACKS Toojay's Original Gourmet Deli (313 Royal Poinciana Way, 33480; 561 659 7232; www.toojays. com) tempts with chicken noodle soup, overstuffed sandwiches, potato pancakes, and vegetable quesadillas. There is also a good kids' menu.

REAL MEAL Palm Beach Grill (340 Royal Poinciana Way, 33480; 561 835 1077; www.hillstone.com; dinner only), a short walk from the museum, serves excellent seafood. Do sample their Key lime pie.

FAMILY TREAT Buccan (350 South County Road, 33480; 561 833 3450; buccanpalmbeach.com) is the place for a real splurge. The tapas plates are perfect for sharing and there are plenty of creative pizzas on the menu, as well as more innovative dishes such as grilled quail with jalapeño biscuit. An extensive wine list is available too.

The Lowdown

🌐 **Map reference** 8 H5
Address 1 Whitehall Way, Palm Beach, 33480; 561 655 2833; *www.flaglermuseum.us*

🚗 **Bus** Palm Tran bus 41 connects downtown Palm Beach with West Palm Beach Tri-Rail station (Mon–Sat).

🕐 **Open** 10am–5pm Tue–Sat, noon–5pm Sun

💲 **Price** $42–56; under 6s free (kids 6–12: $3)

🔫 **Guided tours** Free guided tours run 11am–2pm Tue–Sat and at 12:30pm & 2:30 pm on Sun. Free audio guides are also available.

👫 **Age range** 7 plus

👪 **Activities** Pick up the free *Tour & Activity Guide for Kids* at the entrance, which is designed to engage and entertain children as they tour the museum. The guide features questions to be answered and items to be drawn; and includes

a pencil. At the Museum Store, kids receive a souvenir penny and two quarters for the Penny Stretching Machine.

⏱ **Allow** 2 hours

♿ **Wheelchair access** Yes

🍽 **Café** Café des Beaux-Arts (on site; Thanksgiving–Easter: 11:30am–2:30pm Tue–Sat & noon–3pm Sun) serves a set lunch, which is more like an elaborate afternoon tea with sandwiches and cakes.

🚻 **Restrooms** Outside the Café des Beaux-Arts and on the first floor next to the West Room

Good family value?

Though there are no family tickets, the entrance charge is relatively low. Kids are well-catered for with the great activity guide, friendly docents, and plenty of curious, rare objects to see.

Master Suite Henry Flagler and his wife shared this, the most lavish bedroom in the house. The furniture and gold color are in French Louis XIV style.

Drawing Room Flagler used delicate aluminum leaf, coated with shellac, to highlight the plaster ornaments in this gorgeous room.

Henry Flagler's private Railcar No. 91 The Flagler Kenan Pavilion has Flagler's very own "palace on wheels," with a bedroom, a bathroom, guest quarters, and a kitchen.

Lily pond in the gardens at the Society of the Four Arts, Palm Beach

Find out more

DIGITAL Read about the house and the life of Henry Flagler on *www.flaglermuseum.us*, the official website. Find more on Flagler at *www.keyshistory.org/flagler.html*.

Next stop...

GLIMPSES OF THE GILDED AGE Head up the road to the beautifully landscaped grounds of the **Society of the Four Arts** (see p88), or walk across the street to **The Breakers** (see p88), the extravagant hotel built by Henry Flagler in 1896.

KIDS' CORNER

Do you know...

Visit the Flagler-Kenan History Room and see if you can answer these questions:

1 When was Henry Flagler born?

2 Which company made the original gold telegram? (Hint: it's a girl's name.)

3 Which town in Florida did Flagler's railway reach in 1912?

Answers at the bottom of the page.

FLAGLER'S LONG-LOST RAIL CAR

Henry Flagler's private Railcar No. 91 wasn't always at the Flagler Museum. In 1935 it was sold to a railway in Georgia; 14 years later it was sold again. By the time it was rediscovered in 1959 it was being used as a dormitory for farm workers in Virginia! It took another nine years to restore it at the museum.

Color it pretty
Did you visit the Yellow Roses Room? Flowery wallpaper was popular in the early 1900s. Draw the most colorful wallpaper pattern you can think of – try to use at least three shapes and three colors.

Dream house

Flagler's mansion had 75 rooms, including 22 bathrooms. If you could design a mansion or a palace, how many rooms would you have? What kind of rooms would you include? Draw a floor plan of your dream house. Be sure to mark the front door on the plan.

Answers: 1 1830. **2** Tiffany **3** Key West.

A rare Florida panther in Palm Beach Zoo, West Palm Beach

⑬ Palm Beach Zoo

Pyramids, an interactive fountain, and wild things

This wildlife park has an intriguing array of themed areas and plenty of showstopping animal attractions, including eagles, panthers, black bears, otters, tigers, and alligators. Don't miss the stunning Harriet W. & George D. Cornell Tropics of the Americas exhibit – a re-creation of the Central and South American rain forest, where jaguars and giant anteaters pad around Mayan pyramids. The zoo, with its naturalistic environments and friendly, informative staff, is especially good for families. There are plenty of things to touch and climb onto, and opportunities to

The Lowdown

🌐 **Map reference** 8 H5
Address 1301 Summit Blvd, West Palm Beach, 33405; 561 547 9453; www.palmbeachzoo.org

🚌 **Bus** Palm Tran bus 45 connects West Palm Beach and the Tri-Rail station with the zoo (Mon–Sat only).

🕐 **Open** 9am–5pm daily

Ⓢ **Price** $69–80; under 3s free

👫 **Age range** All ages

👟 **Activities** Watch Wings over Water bird show 2:30pm daily, as well as Wild Things Show 1pm daily.

⏱ **Allow** At least 2–3 hours

🍴 **Eat and drink** SNACKS The zoo concession stand (on site; closes 4pm) offers cold drinks, ice cream, hot dogs, and other snacks. REAL MEAL Tropics Café, (on site; closes 3pm) serves salads, roast chicken, pasta, and healthy snacks for kids such as raisins, applesauce, and granola bars.

feed pelicans. The daily Wild Things Show features a rainbow boa, singing dogs, and a pygmy hedgehog named Xena. Be sure to bring the kids' bathing suits – they get to cool off in the water jets at the Interactive Play Fountain. Kids also love taking rides on the Wildlife Carousel and browsing the outdoor gift shop.

Take cover

If it rains, head to the **South Florida Science Center and Aquarium** (4801 Dreher Trail North, West Palm Beach, 33405; 561 832 1988; www.sfsciencecenter.org), next to the zoo. The museum features more than 50 hands-on exhibits, a planetarium, aquariums, and natural history displays.

A demonstration in progress at South Florida Science Museum, Palm Beach

⑭ Lion Country Safari

Journey to the African savanna

A wildlife preserve, Lion Country Safari does a fine job of re-creating the African plains, with elephants, giraffes, chimpanzees, zebras, ostriches, and lions roaming free. This is a drive-through safari park, with a 4-mile (6-km) road and 900

The Lowdown

🌐 **Map reference** 8 G5
Address 2003 Lion Country Safari Rd, Loxahatchee, 33470; 561 793 1084; www.lioncountrysafari.com

🚗 **Car** Rent a car from Palm Beach Airport.

🕐 **Open** 9:30am–5:30pm daily

Ⓢ **Price** $96–122; under 3s free. Parking $8 per vehicle

👫 **Cutting the line** Book online and get $2 discount on tickets and free parking.

🚩 **Guided tours** VIP private tours, insider tour, and photo-guided tour are available; check website for details.

👫 **Age range** 3 plus

👟 **Activities** Visit the Safari World theme park for rides and amusements. The preserve holds Flamingo talks 2pm daily and Alligator chit chat 3pm daily.

⏱ **Allow** Half a day to a full day

🍴 **Eat and drink** SNACKS Safari Snacks (on site) offers pizza, hot dogs, funnel cakes, and ice cream. REAL MEAL Los Agaves (1179 Royal Palm Beach Blvd, 33411; 561 798 1229; www.losagavesfl.com) serves great tacos, salads, and quesadillas.

wild animals, which means visitors are confined to their cars. In addition to the African areas, there are sections dedicated to the South American pampas and the Gir Forest in India.

The chimpanzees live on a five-island system: part of ChimpanZoo, an international research program to study chimps in captivity. Students, caretakers, and volunteers are trained by the Jane Goodall Institute to record and compare the behaviors of chimps in captivity to those in the wild.

Antelopes resting in shade at Lion Country Safari, Loxahatchee

Kayaking in John D. MacArthur Beach State Park, near Juno Beach

After the safari, families can stretch their legs at Safari World. This is a theme park with interactive fountains, a Ferris wheel, and a petting zoo, as well as camel rides and a giraffe-feeding exhibit.

Letting off steam

Bring bathing suits to cool off in **Safari Splash** inside the Lion Country Safari. Kids can play a round of mini-golf, or slide down the bouncy waterslide. Paddleboats are available by the lake in the park.

⑮ Juno Beach: Loggerhead Marinelife Center

Saving turtles and feeding fish

The sands of Juno Beach, 13 miles (21 km) north of West Palm Beach, make for a pleasant visit any time, but this small seaside town is enhanced by the family-friendly Loggerhead Marinelife Center. The focus here is the Sea Turtle Hospital, where sick and injured turtles are cared for. See feeding, medication being given, and even physical therapy sessions, depending on the time of day.

The center's exhibit hall chronicles turtle life cycles and Florida's coastal ecosystems. There are also five small aquariums with fish, corals, and anemones. Catch the 30-minute Dr. Logger show, which reveals the life of a sea turtle, highlighting not just its diet and habits, but the threats it faces in an interactive way that engages kids of all ages. At Hatchling Tales, younger kids are entertained with ocean-inspired stories and crafts, and there is also a weekly marine-related Kids' Story Time. In June and July, there are turtle walks

The Lowdown

🌐 **Map reference** 8 H5
Address 14200 US-1, Juno Beach, 33408; 561 627 8280; www.marinelife.org

🚗 **Car** Rent a car from Palm Beach Airport.

ℹ️ **Visitor information** Northern Palm Beach County Chamber of Commerce, 5520 PGA Blvd #200, Palm Beach Gardens, 33418; 561 746 7111; www.pbnchamber.com

🕐 **Open** 10am–5pm daily

💲 **Price** Free; turtle walks $18 per person

🚩 **Guided tours** The center runs a 1-hour guided tour at noon every Sunday.

👫 **Age range** All ages

🏃 **Activities** Visit the Junior Vet Learning Lab for kids (5 plus) Wed, Fri & Sat. There is fish feeding 3pm Tue, Thu & Sat, Hatchling Tales 10:30am Wed, and Dr. Logger 2pm Sun.

⏱️ **Allow** 1–2 hours; more time for activities

🥡 **Eat and drink** SNACKS Hurricane Café (14050 US-1, 33408; 561 630 2012; www.hurricanecafe. com) has outdoor seating and great selections for kids. REAL MEAL Captain Charlie's Reef Grill (12846 US 1, 33408; 561 624 9924) is justly famous for its seafood.

in the evening – expeditions to watch the turtles as they crawl ashore to lay eggs under cover of darkness. Reservations for this are essential, and accepted from May onward.

Letting off steam

Just south of Juno Beach, **John D. MacArthur Beach State Park** (10900 Jack Nicklaus Dr, North Palm Beach, 33408; 561 624 6952; www.macarthur beach.org) offers plenty of outdoor activities, with a nature walk, a pretty beach with dunes, and kayak rental.

⑯ Vero Beach
Let's hunt for treasure!

North of Palm Beach, the cities, resorts, and grand mansions give way to the less developed Treasure Coast, which boasts waters where manatees can be spotted, great sweeps of sandy beaches, and seaside towns such as Vero Beach. Much of the area's appeal lies in its state parks and sandy barrier islands, but there are plenty of museums and wildlife-related activities to keep families busy.

Trial Scene by Tom Otterness, Vero Beach Museum of Art

Key Sights

① **Sebastian Inlet State Park** The wild and enchanting beaches here lure plenty of surfers and swimmers, and the McLarty Treasure Museum provides a cultural diversion.

② **Mel Fisher's Treasures** Dedicated to Mel Fisher, a modern treasure hunter, this museum displays Spanish booty dredged up from the 1715 fleet wrecked just offshore.

③ **Environmental Learning Center** Learn about the mangroves and wetlands of the Indian River Lagoon here, with hands-on exhibits, boat tours, and touch tanks full of local sea life.

④ **Riverside Children's Theater** Watch plays and musicals performed by kids for kids here – from Roald Dahl's The Twits, to The Wiz, and a jazz version of The Nutcracker.

⑤ **Driftwood Resort** This bizarre-looking hotel – a giant beach shack right on the water – is worth a visit even for non-guests. The entire edifice was built in 1935 from ocean-washed timbers and planks.

⑥ **Vero Beach Museum of Art** See modern art in a variety of media, from the stunning glasswork of Dale Chihuly to the horse sculptures of Deborah Butterfield.

⑦ **Indian River Citrus Museum** Citrus farming has been an important part of life in Florida since the 1860s, and this museum chronicles the struggles and successes of the early pioneers.

⑧ **McKee Botanical Garden** This lush, blossom-smothered garden features an extensive subtropical jungle laced with streams, ponds, and trails dating back to the 1920s.

The Lowdown

Map reference 8 G2
Address Sebastian Inlet State Park: 9700 S State Rd A1A, Melbourne Beach, 32951; www.floridastateparks.org. Mel Fisher's Treasures: 1322 US-1, Sebastian, 32958; www.melfisher.com. Environmental Learning Center: 255 Live Oak Dr, 32963; www.discoverelc.org. Riverside Children's Theater: 3280 Riverside Park Dr, 32963; riversidetheatre.com. Driftwood Resort: 3150 Ocean Dr, 32963; www.thedriftwood.com. Vero Beach Museum of Art: 3001 Riverside Park Dr, 32963; www.verobeachmuseum.org. Indian River Citrus Museum: 2140 14th Ave, 32960; www.vero

heritage.org/CitrusMuseum.html. McKee Botanical Garden: 350 US-1, 32962; mckeegarden.org

🚆 **Train** Amtrak from West Palm Beach. **Car** Rent a car from Palm Beach Airport.

ℹ **Visitor information** Indian River County Chamber of Commerce, 1216 21st St, 32960; 772 567 3491; www.indianriverchamber.com; 9am–5pm Mon–Fri

🕙 **Open** Sebastian Inlet State Park: daily (McLarty Treasure Museum: 10am–4pm daily). Mel Fisher's Treasures: 10am–5pm Mon–Sat & noon–5pm Sun; closed Sep. Environmental Learning Center: 10am–4pm Tue–Fri, 9am–noon Sat

(till 4pm in winter) & 1–4pm Sun. Riverside Children's Theatre: check website for shows. Vero Beach Museum of Art: 10am–4:30pm Mon–Sat & 1–4:30pm Sun; closed Mon in summer. Indian River Citrus Museum: 10am–4pm Tue–Fri. McKee Botanical Garden: 10am–5pm Tue–Sat & noon–5pm Sun

💲 **Prices** Sebastian Inlet State Park: $8 per vehicle, $2 per pedestrian or cyclist (McLarty Treasure Museum: $2). Mel Fisher's Treasures: $17–20. Environmental Learning Center: $18–20; under 13s free. Riverside Children's Theatre: tickets $40–50. Vero Beach Museum of Art: $20;

The tranquil Treasure Shores Beach Park, Vero Beach

Playground for kids in Humiston Park, Vero Beach

Letting off steam

About 10 miles (16 km) north of Vero Beach lies **Treasure Shores Beach Park** (11300 Hwy-A1A, 32963) which also has a playground for little ones. **Humiston Park** (3000 Ocean Dr, 32963; 772 231 5790), closer to downtown, also has a playground, but the beach here is smaller and hemmed in by development. Lifeguards are on duty 9am–5pm in summer and 10am–3pm in winter.

Eat and drink

Picnic: under $25; Snacks: $25–50; Real meal: $50–80; Family treat: over $80 (based on a family of four)

PICNIC Publix at Vero Mall (1255 US-1, 32960; 772 778 1984; www.publix.com) offers a huge selection of fresh groceries, a deli, and an in-store bakery. The beach is a short drive away.
SNACKS The Barefoot Cafe (2036 14th Ave, 32960; 772 770 1733; www.thebarefootcafe.com) has seating, but mostly caters to a take-out crowd with a tasty menu of healthy wraps, soups, and salads.

under 17s free. Indian River Citrus Museum: free. McKee Botanical Garden: May–Oct: $30–40; Nov–Apr: $40–48; under 3s free

Guided tours The Environmental Learning Center runs daily Trek & Tracks nature walks in its grounds.

Age range All ages

Activities Download the McKee Botanical Garden's Children's Guide at www.mckeegarden.org.

Allow 2 days

Good family value?
Low entrance charges make this town suitable for all budgets. The beaches offer endless fun for kids.

REAL MEAL The Lemon Tree (3125 Ocean Dr, 32963; 772 231 0858; www.lemontreevero.com) overlooks the ocean and is an especially good place for a diner-style breakfast or lunch. It also offers a kids' menu.
FAMILY TREAT Ocean Grill (1050 Sexton Plaza, 32963; 772 231 5409; www.ocean-grill.com; closed Sun lunchtime) is a local legend situated right on the beach. It serves classic seafood and has a great kids' menu.

Island-style decor of the Barefoot Cafe, Vero Beach

Find out more

DIGITAL Visit www.kidsrecyclingzone.com and www.nps.gov/webrangers, fun sites with an environmental theme. Older kids might want to check out 1715treasurefleet.com for more on the Spanish treasure fleet.

Next stop...

FORT PIERCE Head 15 miles (24 km) south to Fort Pierce (see p96) for a day to learn about Florida's marine life at the Manatee Observation & Education Center and Harbor Branch Ocean Discovery Center.

KIDS' CORNER

Tables, trees, and Tikis
You might think that the McKee Botanical Garden is just full of plants and trees, but if you look hard enough you might find some special things:
1 Somewhere in the garden is a wooden table – not just any table, but the biggest mahogany table in the world!
2 A Tiki is a large Polynesian carving of a scary face usually made on Pacific islands. But there is one here guarding a secret seating area: can you find it?
3 There is a strange-looking tree called "the dragon tree." Can you see why it is called that?
4 The pineapples you can eat look green and yellow. You can see tiny pink pineapples in the gardens. Don't try to pick them!

TREASURE QUEST
Take a sketchbook and draw your own treasure island map. Add scary names such as Blood Valley, Skull Cave, and Terror River. Make sure you mark the treasure with a special symbol, and draw arrows to show how to find it.

What lies beneath
The Spanish treasure fleet of 1715, sailing from Cuba to Spain, was made up of 12 galleons loaded with silverware, and lots of gold. As the fleet sailed past Florida, it was hit by a fierce hurricane that wrecked 11 of the ships. Over 1,000 sailors were drowned, and many more died of starvation. Much of the treasure was never recovered – experts think that treasure worth $550 million remains hidden on the seabed.

⑰ Fort Pierce
On top of the lagoon, and deep beneath the sea

Much of Fort Pierce is industrial, but there are a few attractions on the outskirts. The **Manatee Observation & Education Center**, overlooking the Indian River Lagoon, is the favored grazing spot of the local manatee population. The best time to see them is from mid-November to early April. Dolphins and pelicans are also regular visitors. The center houses a butterfly garden and hands-on exhibits that provide information about manatees, butterflies, their habitats, and more.

Just 5 miles (8 km) north of Fort Pierce, the Harbor Branch Oceanographic Institute is a well-equipped deep-sea research center belonging to Florida Atlantic University. Visit the **Ocean Discovery Center** to learn about the incredible work done in the underwater labs – developing food aquaculture and deep-ocean exploration. The interactive exhibits are educational, but still fun for kids 7 plus. There is also a small aquarium for little ones.

Letting off steam
Head to **Fort Pierce Inlet State Park** *(905 Shorewinds Dr, 34949; 772 468 3985; www.floridastate parks.org)*, on the other side of the North Causeway (Hwy-A1A). It has a small unspoiled beach.

⑱ Hutchinson Island
Bathtubs on the beach

This island is a slim, 20-mile (32-km) stretch of mangroves, scrub, and idyllic sandy beaches. It has only one road, Highway-A1A, which runs from north to south. The best attractions lie at the southern end of the island, across from the town of Stuart. **Bathtub Reef Park** is a popular destination for families. At low tide, a series of exposed reefs just offshore create a protected, bathtub-like swimming area ideal for kids. A short drive north, the **Elliott Museum**, in eco-friendly premises, charts the history of the area with interactive exhibits and hands-on learning experiences. The museum also has a collection of over 50 vintage cars.

Fishing along the shore of Hutchinson Island

The Lowdown

🌐 **Map reference** 8 H3
Address Stuart 34996. Bathtub Reef Park: 1585 SE McArthur Blvd. Elliott Museum: 825 NE Ocean Blvd; 772 225 1961; *www.elliottmuseum.org*. Florida Oceanographic Coastal Center: 890 NE Ocean Blvd; 772 225 0505; *www.floridaocean.org*

🚗 **Car** Rent a car from Palm Beach Airport.

ℹ️ **Visitor information** Stuart/Martin County Chamber of Commerce, 1650 S Kanner Hwy, 34994; *www. stuartmartinchamber.org*

🕐 **Open** Elliott Museum: 10am–5pm daily. Florida Oceanographic Coastal Center: 10am–5pm Mon–Sat & noon–4pm Sun

💲 **Price** Elliott Museum: $34–40; under 6s free. Florida Oceanographic Coastal Center: $30–36; under 3s free

👫 **Age range** All ages

👫 **Activities** The Florida Oceanographic Coastal Center offers a children's activity pavilion and lagoon fish feeding program.

⏱️ **Allow** Half a day to a full day

☕ **Eat and drink** SNACKS The Chef Shack *(899 N E Ocean Blvd, 34996; 772 334 0820)* serves grouper sandwiches and burgers. REAL MEAL Shuckers Restaurant *(9800 S Ocean Dr, Jensen Beach, 34957; 772 229 1224; islandbeach resort.net)* has pasta and seafood.

Rocky shoreline of Fort Pierce Inlet State Park, Fort Pierce

The Lowdown

🌐 **Map reference** 8 G3
Address Manatee Observation & Education Center: 480 N Indian River Dr, 34950; 772 429 6266; *www.manateecenter.com*. Harbor Branch Ocean Discovery Center: 5600 US-1, 34946; 772 242 2293; *www.fau.edu/hboi/ community/odc.php*

🚌 **Bus** Greyhound from Miami, Orlando or Jacksonville. It's best to drive.

ℹ️ **Visitor information** St Lucie County Chamber of Commerce, 482 N Indian River Dr, 34950; 772 468 9152; *www.stluciechamber.org*

🕐 **Open** Manatee Observation & Education Center: 10am–5pm Tue-Sat, noon–4pm Sun. Ocean Discovery Center: 10am–5pm Tue–Sat

💲 **Prices** Manatee Observation & Education Center: $4; under 6s free. Ocean Discovery Center: free

🚩 **Guided tours** Indian River Lagoon Wildlife Boat Tours from Fort Pierce City Marina; call 772 464 4445.

👫 **Age range** All ages. Ocean Discovery Center: 7 plus

👫 **Activities** Manatee Observation & Education Center runs family-friendly kayak tours some Sat Jan–May.

⏱️ **Allow** Half a day to a full day

☕ **Eat and drink** SNACKS Uncle Carlo's Gelato *(141 Melody Lane, 34950; 772 672 4401)* has gelato, cookies and paninis. REAL MEAL 12A Buoy *(22 Fisherman's Wharf, 34950; 772 672 4524)* is a fish shack with an old Florida vibe and an outdoor deck.

The **Florida Oceanographic Coastal Center** across the street from the museum, takes a practical approach to learning about Florida's marine life, offering a stingray touch tank, a huge game-fish lagoon, and a looping nature trail to the Indian River Lagoon.

Letting off steam
Just across Ocean Boulevard from the Elliott Museum, **Stuart Beach** is a tranquil stretch of sand with lifeguards, boardwalk access points, parking, a snack bar, and restrooms.

⑲ Jupiter Island
Turtle walks and blowing rocks
A long, thin strip of pine, sand, and scrub, Jupiter Island is 17 miles (27 km) of affluent homes and wonderfully pristine beaches. The only north–south thoroughfare on the island is Beach Road, but with the sea blocked from view most of the way, it is not especially scenic, so plan to make several stops.

The northern end of the island is protected within **Hobe Sound National Wildlife Refuge**, a major nesting site for sea turtles and best experienced on an organized turtle walk. At other times, stroll up the 2-mile (4-km) beach trail to Peck Lake, looking out for scrub jays, gopher tortoises, and tiny snakes. The refuge's small nature center, on US-1, has a few exhibits, including tanks with baby alligators, and there is a short nature trail that leads down to the shores of the Indian River Lagoon.

Toward the southern end of the island, **Blowing Rocks Preserve** contains a rare limestone outcrop that covers much of the beach – it is fun to watch the waves driving under the rocks and spraying out at the top. The Hawley Education Center across the road has displays on Jupiter Island habitats and more trails into the thick mangroves on the lagoon.

Letting off steam
Visit **Jonathan Dickinson State Park** *(16450 SE Federal Hwy, Hobe Sound, 33455; 772 546 2771; www.florida stateparks.org)*, located south of Stuart. It has a swath of pine scrub, mangroves, and river swamps just across the water from Jupiter Island.

The Lowdown
🌐 **Map reference** 8 H4
Address Hobe Sound National Wildlife Refuge: 13640 SE Federal Hwy, Hobe Sound, 33475; 772 546 6141; www.fws.gov. Blowing Rocks Preserve: 574 South Beach Rd, Hobe Sound, 33455; 561 744 6668; www.nature.org

🚗 **Car** Rent a car from Palm Beach Airport.

ℹ **Visitor information** Northern Palm Beach County Chamber of Commerce, 5520 PGA Blvd #200, Palm Beach Gardens, 33418; 561 746 7111; npbchamber.com

🕐 **Open** Hobe Sound National Wildlife Refuge: sunrise–sunset daily. Blowing Rocks Preserve: 9am–4:30pm daily

💲 **Prices** Hobe Sound National Wildlife Refuge: $5 per car per day. Blowing Rocks Preserve: $4; under 13s free

👫 **Age range** All ages

👪 **Activities** Hobe Sound National Wildlife Refuge runs turtle hikes. Call 772 546 2067 for details.

⏱ **Allow** A day

🍴 **Eat and drink** SNACKS Harry & the Natives *(11910 SE Federal Hwy, 33455; 772 546 3061; harryandthe natives.com)* has fish sandwiches and gator burgers. REAL MEAL Flash Beach Grille *(9126 SE Bridge Rd, 33455; 772 545 3969; www. flashcatering.com)* serves mermaid pasta & popcorn shrimp.

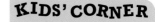
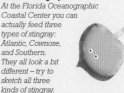

Visitors canoeing down the river in Jonathan Dickinson State Park

Picnic under $25; Snacks $25–50; Real meal $50–80; Family treat over $80 (based on a family of four)

Where to Stay on the Gold and Treasure Coasts

This region offers plenty of choice in family-friendly lodging, from budget motels to luxury resorts on the beach. Finding campgrounds close to the beach is tough, but state parks often have good camping options. There is a wide range of self-catering apartments and cottage rentals to choose from, too.

AGENCIES
Vacation Rentals
www.vacationrentals.com
This website lists over 13,000 properties across Florida, from vacation homes and beach houses to condos and apartments.

VRBO
www.vrbo.com
This agency offers a wide choice of lodging in southern Florida, including Boca Raton and Miami.

Boca Raton   Map 8 H6

RESORT
Boca Beach Club
900 S Ocean Blvd, 33432; 561 447 3000; www.bocabeachclub.com
This plush place sits right on the beach and offers lots of activities, as well as the dedicated Quest Club for kids. Rooms and suites are stylish, with plenty of amenities, but no kitchen. There is also a surf school, and tennis clinics for ages 3 to 18.
🌐 🍴 ⚡ 🔄 ⚪   **$$$**

HOTEL
Ocean Lodge
531 N Ocean Blvd, 33432; 561 395 7772; www.oceanlodgeflorida.com
Just off the beach, this hotel has spotless rooms, granite kitchenettes and dining areas, as well as flat-screen TVs, barbecue grills, and complimentary continental breakfast.
🌐 🔄 ⚪ 🍽️   **$$**

Fort Lauderdale Map 10 H1

RESORTS
Harbor Beach Marriott Resort & Spa
3030 Holiday Dr, 33316; 954 525 4000; www.marriottharborbeach.com
A luxurious beachfront property with large, comfy suites, this resort has a private beach and a complimentary Surf Club for kids with a Hawaiian

surf simulator and a clubhouse. Resort activities include beach sports and face-painting.
🌐 🍴 ⚡ 🔄 ⚪   **$$$**

Lago Mar Resort & Club
1700 S Ocean Lane, 33316; 954 678 3945; www.lagomar.com
This sprawling beachfront property has 164 suites with refrigerators and microwaves. Centrally located and with its own secure, private beach, it offers beach volleyball, shuffleboard, and a giant outdoor chessboard.
🌐 🍴 🔄 ⚪ 🏄   **$$$**

Palm-fringed pool at Birch Patio, Fort Lauderdale

HOTELS
Birch Patio
617 N Birch Rd, 33304; 954 563 9540; www.birchpatio.com
This retro-looking hotel is a 5-minute walk fr om the beach, with spacious efficiency apartments. Free parking, a coin-operated washer and dryer, and barbecue grills are available.
🌐 ⚡ 🔄 🍽️   **$**

Premiere Hotel
625 N Fort Lauderdale Beach Blvd, 33304; 954 566 7676; www.premierehotel.com
Located close to the beach, this hotel offers efficiency rooms with two beds and fully equipped kitchens, as well as suites. Although this is an older property, everything is spotless.
🌐 🔄 🍽️   **$**

Fort Pierce/ Port St. Lucie   Map 8 G3

RESORT
Club Med Sandpiper Bay
4500 SE Pine Valley St, Port St Lucie, 34952; 772 398 5100; www.clubmed.us
This all-inclusive resort is especially fun for families, with a Baby Welcome program, Baby Club Med, beautifully furnished family rooms and heaps of kids' programs.
🌐 🍴 ⚡ 🔄 ⚪   **$$$**

HOTEL
Holiday Inn Express
7151 Okeechobee Rd, Fort Pierce, 34945; 772 464 5000, www.hiexpress.com
Located close to the Florida Turnpike and I-95, and a 10–15-minute drive into downtown Fort Pierce, this hotel offers modern rooms with mini-fridges and microwaves.
🌐 🔄   **$**

CAMPING
Savannas Campground
1400 E Midway Rd, Fort Pierce, 34982; 772 464 7855; www.stlucieco.gov/parks/savannas.htm.
This county-run campsite is situated 7 miles (11 km) south of downtown Fort Pierce. It lies on reclaimed marshland beside the Indian River, and offers both primitive pitches and some with electricity and water.
🏕️ 🚿 🌐 🍴   **$**

Hutchinson Island   Map 8 H3

RESORT
Hutchinson Island Marriott Beach Resort & Marina
555 NE Ocean Blvd, Stuart, 34996; 772 225 3700; www.marriott.com
Just across the causeway from Stuart, this resort has rooms with pull-out sofa beds for kids, and

well-equipped kitchens. Family-friendly activities are planned each week.

📶 🍴 ⇆ ⊘ ◑   **$$**

Juno Beach   Map 8 H5

HOTEL
Hampton Inn Jupiter
13801 US-1, 33408; 561 626 9090; hamptoninn.hilton.com
This convenient, family-friendly hotel, near the Loggerhead Marinelife Center, offers two queen-deluxe rooms that accommodate up to five and are equipped with microwaves and mini-fridges. Breakfast is included. A coin-operated laundry is on site.

📶 🔋 ⇆ ⊘   **$$**

Palm Beach   Map 8 H5

RESORT
The Breakers
1 S County Rd, 33480; 888 273 2537; www.thebreakers.com
A fabulous option for families, this resort has a self-contained Family Entertainment Center, babysitting services, and kids' camps. All rooms are luxuriously furnished; standard rooms are big enough for most families with young children.

📶 🍴 ⇆ ⊘ ◑   **$$$**

HOTELS
Palm Beach Historic Inn
365 S County Rd, 33480; 561 832 4009; www.palmbeachhistoricinn.com
This charming old guesthouse offers clean rooms with two double beds, as well as four spacious suites with a king bed, trundle bed, VCR, and refrigerator. Breakfast is included.

📶 ⇆   **$$**

The Chesterfield
363 Cocoanut Row, 33480; 561 659 5800; www.chesterfieldpb.com
A historic hotel with bright and luxurious rooms that lodge two adults and two children. Kids aged 12 and under stay and eat free when sharing a room with parents.

📶 🍴 ⇆ ⊘   **$$$**

Vero Beach   Map 8 G2

RESORTS
Driftwood Resort
3150 Ocean Dr, 32963; 772 231 0550; www.thedriftwood.com
The most atmospheric place to stay on the Treasure Coast offers spacious rooms and villas. Families can go for a large two-room suite in the "Breakers" section. Kids will love the scavenger hunts and shuffleboard.

📶 ☕ ⇆ ⊘ ◑   **$**

Disney's Vero Beach Resort
9250 Island Grove Terrace, 32963; 772 234 2000; www.disneybeach resorts.com/vero-beach-resort
A plush resort set on the beach, this place has a variety of elegant accommodations, from studios to two-bedroom villas. There is a 163-ft (50-m) waterslide, treasure hunts, and sing-a-long campfires.

📶 🍴 ⇆ ⊘ ◑   **$$$**

Vero Beach Hotel & Spa
3500 Ocean Dr, 32963; 772 231 5666; www.verobeachhotelandspa.com
This family-friendly luxury resort has one-, two- and three-bedroom suites, all with kitchens. The "Kimpton Kids" program provides babysitting, cribs, and high chairs.

📶 🍴 ⇆ ⊘ ◑   **$$$**

MOTEL
Comfort Suites Vero Beach
9050 Americana Way, 32963; 772 257 3400; www.comfort suites.com
This excellent motel off I-95 is just 12 miles (19 km) from the beach. All rooms come with flat-screen TVs, microwaves, and refrigerators. There is a coin-operated laundry, and breakfast is included.

📶 ⊘   **$**

CAMPING
Sebastian Inlet State Park
9700 S State Rd A1A, Melbourne Beach, 32951; 321 984 4852; www.floridastateparks.org
The park's attractive tent and RV campground is just a short stroll from the beach. All 51 sites have water and electrical hook-ups.

📶   **$**

West Palm Beach   Map 8 H5

MOTEL
Best Western Palm Beach Lakes Inn
1800 Palm Beach Lakes Blvd, 33401; 561 683 8810; www.bestwestern westpalm.com
Across from the Palm Beach Mall, which is about 15 minutes from downtown, this motel has standard rooms arranged around a central pool area. All rooms have microwaves and refrigerators, and rollaway beds are available. Continental breakfast is included.

📶 ⊘   **$**

CAMPING
Lion Country Safari KOA Campground
2003 Lion Country Safari Rd, Loxahatchee, 33470; 561 793 9797; www.lioncountrysafari.com
This campground, adjacent to Lion Country Safari, has tent sites with water and electricity, a grill and picnic table, as well as cabins, which offer a bit more comfort. There is a general store, playground, and laundry, and plenty of sports are on offer.

📶 ⊘   **$**

A double room with a view of the ocean in The Breakers, Palm Beach

Price Guide
The following price ranges are based on one night's accommodation in high season for a family of four, inclusive of service charges and additional taxes.
$ Under $150 **$$** $150–300 **$$$** over $300

Key to symbols *see back cover flap*

Orlando
and the Parks

With a wide choice of theme parks, central Florida might seem like one big roller coaster, but there is also much natural and cultural beauty to explore. Orlando and its upscale neighbor, Winter Park, have museums, world-class restaurants, festivals, and sporting events that enhance the joy of the thrill rides, and add to the experience of visiting this colorful area.

Highlights

Walt Disney World® Resort
See Walt Disney's vision come alive in four famous theme parks (see pp106–17).

Universal Studios Florida® and Universal's Islands of Adventure®
Meet the Simpsons™ or visit Harry Potter's™ Hogwarts™ at these entertainment theme parks (see pp118–21).

SeaWorld®, Aquatica, and Discovery Cove®
Take a closer look at penguins and sea lions at SeaWorld®, watch dolphins at Discovery Cove®, and hop aboard thrilling water rides at Aquatica (see pp122–3).

The Orlando Eye
Soar high above to get a spectacular bird's-eye view of Central Florida from this observation wheel (see p124).

Orlando and Winter Park
Visit museums of art and science, watch championship basketball, and marvel at leaping alligators – a combination possible only in Orlando (see pp127–31).

LEGOLAND® Florida Resort
At this LEGO®-themed park, kids can learn how many LEGO® blocks it would take to build the Statue of Liberty, and how they could do it at home (see pp132–5).

Left The bustling main street at Disney's Magic Kingdom®
Above right Massive LEGO® giraffe at the entrance to the thrilling Imagination Zone, LEGOLAND® Florida Resort

The Best of
Orlando and the Parks

The fantasylands, wild animals, movie history, and world culture of the Walt Disney® theme parks have been drawing millions of visitors since 1971. Universal Studios Florida® adds to the adventure, celebrating movies and the world of Harry Potter™, along with the water wonderland of SeaWorld®. The city of Orlando, and its suburb Winter Park, have excellent historical museums, cultural sites, and entertainment options.

The wonderful world of Disney

Look up in **Magic Kingdom®** *(see pp108–9)* to see the soaring castle towers where Cinderella and Beauty's Beast live, or get an adrenaline rush on the Space Mountain®, Splash Mountain®, and Big Thunder Mountain® coasters. Ride with Ariel on Under the Sea: Journey of the Little Mermaid, and on a flying carpet in The Magic Carpets of Aladdin.

Soarin'™ lets visitors glide over the global landscape in **Epcot®** *(see pp110–11)*; Test Track allows them to design and test custom vehicles; and Mission: Space® goes beyond the atmosphere. World Showcase displays cultures of 11 countries in a 2-mile (3-km) circle with booming *taiko* drummers in the Japan Pavilion, and stunning acrobats at the Chinese Pavilion.

Visit living toys, Star Wars characters, and Indiana Jones™ in **Disney's Hollywood Studios®** *(see pp114–15)*. All Kermit fans will love Muppet*Vision 3D, and thrills await at the Rock 'n' Roller Coaster® Starring Aerosmith. At **Disney's Animal Kingdom®** *(see pp112–13)*, Pandora – The World of Avatar is an exciting ride. Take the Kilimanjaro Safaris® to see lions and wildebeests.

Right *Kids playing with LEGO® dinosaurs, LEGOLAND® Florida Resort*
Below *Riding the Kali River Rapids, Disney's Animal Kingdom®*

Above Crazy curves and weird shapes at High in the Sky Seuss Trolley Train Ride™, Universal Studios Florida®

Movie magic

Universal Orlando® Resort offers entertainment for the whole family, featuring the amazing **Universal Studios Florida®** *(see pp118–19)* and **Universal's Islands of Adventure®** *(see pp120–21)*. Men In Black™ and The Simpsons™ rides bring movies and TV to life at **Universal Studios Florida®**, while Harry Potter fans will enjoy visiting Gringotts Bank™ at Diagon Alley™. Over at **Universal's Islands of Adventure®** kids can cast a spell aboard Harry Potter and the Forbidden Journey™ or travel at 40 mph (64 km/h) on The Incredible Hulk Coaster®.

Culture vultures

International Drive *(see p126)*, Orlando's bustling strip of restaurants and hotels, features **ICON Orlando** *(see p124)*, **Wonderworks**, which includes a simulated earthquake and an upside-down building, and the fascinating **Ripley's Believe It or Not! Odditorium**. **Downtown Orlando's** big draw is the 20,000-seat **Amway Center** *(see p130)*, home of NBA basketball, arena football, concerts, and circuses. Check out the fine restaurants and music clubs nearby, as well as the charming Lake Eola Park, which has plenty of space to run around. While **Downtown Orlando** holds the **Orlando Museum of Art** and the **Orlando Science Center** *(see pp128–9)*, **Winter Park** *(see pp130–31)* is home to the world's best collection of Tiffany art at the **Morse Museum**, and a wonderfully casual main street filled with shops and restaurants called Park Avenue. The **Scenic Boat Tour** *(see p131)* winds through the picturesque lakes and canals of this historic area, with views of grand mansions and beautiful natural life.

The best of the rest

SeaWorld® *(see pp122–3)* boasts multiple thrilling water rides, while **Discovery Cove®** *(see pp122–3)* offers visitors a relaxed resort-like experience.

Kids can walk through the amazing LEGO® city replicas at Miniland USA in the **LEGOLAND® Florida Resort** *(see pp132–5)*, unearth Egyptian treasures in the Lost Kingdom Adventure, and have an exciting driving experience at the Ford Driving Schools.

ICON Orlando *(see p124)* offers stunning views of Orlando and its landmarks.

Left The dazzling Tiffany Chapel exhibit in the Morse Museum, Winter Park

Orlando and the Parks

Orlando is the undisputed theme park capital of the world, with Walt Disney World® Resort, Universal Orlando® Resort, LEGOLAND® Florida Resort, and the water parks making the city a family-oriented fantasyland. But it has a lot more to offer. International Drive is chock-full of kid-friendly attractions and good restaurants, and sports fans will delight in the spectacular basketball arena at the Amway Center. With so many sights spread out over the city, it is best to hire a car to get around.

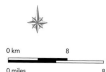

Scenic view of a lakefront mansion, Winter Park

Places of interest

◖ SIGHTS

1 Walt Disney World® Resort
2 Universal Studios Florida®
3 Universal's Islands of Adventure®
4 SeaWorld®, Aquatica, and Discovery Cove®
5 Icon Orlando
6 Crayola Experience
7 International Drive
8 Gatorland
9 Orlando Science Center
10 Loch Haven Park
11 Downtown Orlando
12 Winter Park
13 Winter Park Scenic Boat Tours
14 LEGOLAND® Florida Resort

Kids playing with an interactive exhibit at Orlando Science Center

The TriceraTop Spin in DinoLand U.S.A., Disney's Animal Kingdom®

Altamonte Springs
Casselberry
t Eatonville Maitland
Winter Park
For sights 9–13, see Orlando and Winter Park (p127)
Pine Hills
Orlando
Conway
ersal ios Florida®
Edgewood
International Drive
Sky Lake
Tangelo Park
Crayola Experience
Orlando International
N Orlando
World®, Aquatica, Discovery Cove®
ers eek
Gatorland
Meadow Woods
Kissimmee
Campbell
Lake Tohopekaliga
Poinciana

LEGO® pirates at the entrance to Pirates' Cove, LEGOLAND® Florida Resort

The Lowdown

Getting there and around
Air Fly to Orlando International Airport (*www.orlandoairports.net*) or Orlando Sanford International Airport (*www.orlandosanfordairport.com*). **Bus** Greyhound (*1 800 231 2222; www.greyhound.com*) has a station in Orlando. Red Coach (*1 877 733 0724; www.redcoachusa.com*) has terminals near Orlando International Airport and downtown. Megabus (*1 877 462 6342; us.megabus.com*) has a terminal 10 miles north of the airport. See Walt Disney World Resort® (*see pp106–17*) for transportation across parks. **Train** Amtrak (*1 800 872 7245; www.amtrak.com*) has stations in Orlando and Winter Park. SunRail (*www.sunrail.com*), the north-south commuter train has 12 stations. **Car** Rentals, such as Enterprise (*www.enterprise.com*) and Avis (*www.avis.com*) are located at the airport and across Orlando. Ride shares Lyft (*www.lyft.com*) and Uber (*www.uber.com*) are also available.

Visitor information Orlando Visitor Center, 8723 International Dr, Orlando, 32819; 407 363 5872; *www.visitorlando.com*

Supermarkets Publix (*www.publix.com*) is the premier supermarket with outlets throughout the region. The upscale organic food chain Whole Foods (*www.wholefoodsmarket.com*) also has branches in Orlando and Winter Park. **Markets** Downtown Orlando Farmers' Market, located near Lake Eola, offers seasonal produce, ethnic foods, and local crafts and artwork every Sun.

Festivals Walt Disney World® Marathon (Jan). Zora Neale Hurston Festival of the Arts; *www.zorafestival.com* (Jan). Universal Studios Florida® Mardi Gras (mid-Feb–Apr). Orlando International Fringe Theatre Festival; *www.orlandofringe.org* (May). Epcot® International Flower & Garden Festival (Feb–May). Seaworld® Viva La Musica; *www.tinyurl.com/SWViva* (Apr–May). Disney® Star Wars™ Weekends (May–Jun). Universal® Summer Nights (Jun–Aug). Mickey's Not-So-Scary Halloween Party (Sep–Oct). Universal® Halloween Spooktacular (Oct). Epcot® International Food & Wine Festival (Aug–Nov). LEGOLAND® Florida Resort Christmas Bricktacular (Dec). Universal® Grinchmas (Dec). For festivals across Walt Disney World®, visit *disneyworld.disney.go.com/special-events*. For Universal Studios® and Islands of Adventure® festivals, visit *www.universalorlando.com/Events/Year-Round-Events.aspx*.

Pharmacies Walgreens (*www.walgreens.com*) and CVS (*www.cvs.com*) are the two major pharmacies in the region; some of their branches in cities are open 24 hours.

Restrooms All major attractions, shopping malls, and gas stations have public restrooms.

① Walt Disney World® Resort
The house of The Mouse

Walt Disney changed Orlando from a sleepy cattle-rearing and orange-growing town into a family vacation hot spot. Spread over four exciting theme parks, the resort's attractions are based on cartoon animals invented 90 years ago, as well as characters out of 3-D movies. While Magic Kingdom® and Disney's Hollywood Studios® play with the imagination, Epcot® showcases world culture and Disney's Animal Kingdom® entertains with animal-themed rides.

DinoLand, U.S.A., Disney's Animal Kingdom®

Key Sights

① Magic Kingdom® Splash down a 52-ft (16-m) mountain, learn the ways of a pirate, or wander through Cinderella Castle at the best known of the Disney parks.

② Epcot® This park is divided into two sections: the modernistic Future World, with the iconic Spaceship Earth ride, and the World Showcase, which features the attractions, shops, and cuisines of 11 countries.

③ Disney's Animal Kingdom® Besides thrill rides, musical shows and parades, and animals from Africa and Asia in re-creations of their natural habitats, this unique zoo also has dizzying roller coasters zipping through mountains.

⑤ Water Parks Cool off aboard one of the world's tallest waterslides at Blizzard Beach, a snow-covered ski resort. The tropical Typhoon Lagoon has water-soaked attractions to suit all ages, including a surf pool with 6-ft (2-m) waves.

④ Disney's Hollywood Studios® High-speed rides, thrilling stunt and stage shows, and film extravaganzas – from The Muppets to Beauty and the Beast – lure visitors of all ages to this theme park.

Prices given are for a family of four

The Lowdown

Map reference 6 E6
Address 4600 N World Dr, Lake Buena Vista, 32830; 407 939 6244 or 407 939 7679 (for tickets); disneyworld.disney.go.com

Bus Lynx bus 50 & 56 from Orlando to Magic Kingdom® and the Ticket and Transportation Center (TTC). Many free buses and water crafts take guests to Disney Springs® as well as to other Disney parks. Free airport shuttle for resort guests. Free Disney buses connect every park. **Taxi** Water taxis from the TTC to Magic Kingdom®, Epcot®, Disney Springs®, and resorts. **Train** Monorails from the TTC to Magic Kingdom®, Epcot®, and resorts. **Car** From Orlando International Airport take South exit (FL 417S – toll) to Osceola Pkwy West (Exit 3) to Disney exits. Parking $20/day

Open Parks open from between 8am and 11am to between 5pm and 1am. Hours vary by park and season; check website for details. Every day, one theme park opens an hour early and closes 2 hours later for guests staying at the Walt Disney World® Resort hotels – Extra Magic Hours.

Prices $381–504 per day for Magic Kingdom; under 3s free. The Park-Hopper® Pass for multiple parks is an additional $55. Multiday tickets range from 3 days ($897–1,184; under 3s free) to 5, 7, 14 and 21 days. Check website for offers on park tickets and vacation plans at Disney hotels with discounted park prices.

Cutting the line Parks are busiest in mid-Feb, mid-Mar–late Apr,

⑥ Disney's Fort Wilderness Resort & Campground This resort has some of the best kid-centered dining options. Mickey's Backyard BBQ offers a chance to dance with Mickey Mouse.

⑦ Disney Springs® Live music at the House of Blues as well as interactive games and competitions at the NBA Experience are some of the highlights of this entertainment and shopping complex.

⑧ Winter Summerland Miniature Golf Course™ Play putt-putt in two Santa Claus-themed courses: the sunny Sand Course or the wintry Snow Course.

Colorful exterior of Pizzafari restaurant, in Disney's Animal Kingdom®

Eat and drink

Each park has a multitude of dining options, from fast-snack carts to full-service restaurants and themed dinner shows (see individual entries for details). Signature restaurants throughout the parks require a credit card for reservations; if the reservation is not canceled at least 24 hours ahead, there is a $10 charge per person. Restaurants that request full prepayment will not make a refund unless the reservation is canceled sufficiently in advance.

Shopping

Find everything from toys and kids' apparel to housewares, and jewelry in the park's shops. Kids will love the Captain Jack-themed gifts near the Pirates of the Caribbean® ride in Magic Kingdom®, and carved animal toys in Animal Kingdom®.

Find out more

DIGITAL Visit *www.wdwmagic.com/walt-disney-world-history.htm* to learn about the history of Walt Disney World® Resort. The website has a timeline that highlights events in the park's story. Younger kids will like *www.disney.co.uk/disney-junior*.

Memorial Day weekend (May), mid-Jun–Labor Day (Sep), Thanksgiving weekend (Nov) and Christmas week–New Year's Day. A high-tech system that allows guests to book time slots for Disney World's major attractions in advance is in place. Check the website for the latest information.

🔫 **Guided tours** The 7-hour Backstage Magic tour takes visitors behind the scenes at three Disney parks – Epcot®, Disney's Hollywood Studios®, and Magic Kingdom® – and shows how thrill rides, landscaping, and parades are put together; tickets include lunch at Wilderness Lodge.

👫 **Age range** The parks are most suitable for ages 7 and above.

Younger kids will enjoy Magic Kingdom® the most, as well as some parts of Disney's Animal Kingdom® and Disney's Hollywood Studios®. Age and height restrictions apply for most rides.

🧗 **Activities** Some Disney resorts run kids' programs that feature supervised activity centers. There are playgrounds, tennis courts, and a marina with watercraft rental.

⏱ **Allow** At least a day for each park

♿ **Wheelchair access** Yes

☕ **Cafés** Many across the park

👥 **Restrooms** Across the park

Good family value?

Although expensive, Disney is every child's dream come true and an unforgettable experience.

① **Walt Disney World® Resort continued ▶**

Magic Kingdom®
Let the enchantment begin!

A world full of the romance of princesses and magicians, and the frights of haunted houses – with a few nerve-testing roller coasters thrown in – Magic Kingdom® is the most popular Disney park. Divided into six areas, it is filled with rides and attractions that show off Walt Disney's best-loved characters, and a Disney-style cartoon version of the future.

Balloon vendor at Main Street, USA®

Key Features

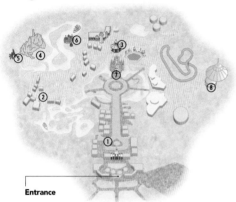

③ **Fantasyland®** Attractions in this delightful area include the Storybook Circus, with the Great Goofini Coaster.

④ **Frontierland®** Ride a runaway mining car through the Wild West, then board a wooden raft to look for hidden treasure on Tom Sawyer Island.

⑤ **Splash Mountain®** This log flume ride runs through swamps and caves before plummeting 52 ft (16 m) down into a pond.

⑥ **Liberty Square** Themed around the Colonial era, this area features the thrilling Haunted Mansion® and the educative Hall of Presidents.

① **Main Street, USA®** Shop, dine, and see dazzling parades on Main Street, USA®. Visitors can board a steam train or a horse-drawn trolley from here for a relaxing trip around the park.

② **Adventureland®** A mix of tropical jungles and Colonial buildings, this area features the ever popular Pirates of the Caribbean® and the Magic Carpets of Aladdin carousel.

⑦ **Cinderella Castle** This most-photographed Disney attraction houses glass murals depicting the fairy tale. At night, spectacular shows illuminate the stunning castle in a riot of colors.

⑧ **Tomorrowland®** From the sharp turns and steep drops of Space Mountain® to the humor of Monsters, Inc. Laugh Floor, this area is filled with attractions for all ages.

The Lowdown

🌐 **Map reference** 6 E5
Address 1180 Seven Seas Dr, Lake Buena Vista, 32830; 407 939 6244; *disneyworld.disney.go.com*

🚌 **Bus, water taxi, or monorail** from the TTC and resorts *(see p106)*

🕐 **Open** From between 8am and 9am to between 8pm and 1am. Check the park's "Calendar" page for seasonal variations and Extra Magic Hours.

💲 **Price** see p106

🚶 **Cutting the line** Avoid Mon and Thu, when the park is busiest.

🚩 **Guided tours** The 5-hour Keys to the Kingdom walking tour ($79 per person) highlights the behind-the-scenes workings of Magic Kingdom®, including a walk through the legendary underground tunnels. The tour is for ages 16 and above.

👫 **Age range** All ages

🎭 **Shows** Kids will love Mickey's PhilharMagic, a 12-min 3-D movie, and Country Bear Jamboree, a musical revue featuring singing bears. One-eyed monster Mike Wazowski will have kids laughing at the interactive Monsters, Inc. Laugh Floor comedy show; contact the Guest Relations office (407 939 6244) for times.

⏱ **Allow** Half a day to 2 days

♿ **Wheelchair access** Yes

🍴 **Eat and drink** SNACKS The Lunching Pad *(in Tomorrowland®)* serves hot dogs, chips, and beverages. FAMILY TREAT Cinderella's Royal Table *(inside Cinderella Castle)* offers the experience of dining with Disney princesses and family,

Top 10 Attractions

1. **BUZZ LIGHTYEAR'S SPACE RANGER SPIN®**
Shoot a laser cannon at aliens from a spinning XP-37 Space Cruiser on this ride in Tomorrowland®.

2. **SPLASH MOUNTAIN®**
A theme park in itself, this water-soaked ride in Frontierland® has a track running through swamps, caves, and bayous.

3. **PIRATES OF THE CARIBBEAN®**
Find Captain Jack Sparrow aboard a boat cruise in Adventureland®, meet pirates, and see blazing cannons before plunging down a 14-ft (4-m) waterfall.

4. **HAUNTED MANSION®**
Ride through dark and dusty rooms looking for – or trying to avoid – 999 ghosts, ghouls, and goblins in Liberty Square.

5. **STITCH'S GREAT ESCAPE!™**
This slightly scary audio and video extravaganza in Tomorrowland® recruits riders as Galactic Federation Security Agents to guard an alien called Stitch.

with a choice of breakfast, lunch, and dinner menus.

Shops Visit the shops at Main Street, USA® for Disney souvenirs.

Restrooms Many throughout the park – the least crowded ones are next to the Pirates of the Caribbean® gift shop, near the Town Hall on Main Street, USA®, and in Tomorrowland®.

Good family value?
Colorful parades, thrilling rides, and spectacular fireworks make this park a treat for all ages.

6. **TOMORROWLAND® SPEEDWAY**
Drive mini gas-powered sports cars around a 2,000-ft- (609-m-) long track on this exciting ride.

7. **ENCHANTED TIKI ROOM™**
Hundreds of singing Animatronic® birds – from crooning parrots to *Aladdin's* wisecracking Iago and *The Lion King's* Zazu – delight the audience at this musical show in Adventureland®.

8. **SPACE MOUNTAIN®**
Climb into a rocket ship to blast into outer space and spiral through a black hole on this intense ride in Tomorrowland®.

9. **BIG THUNDER MOUNTAIN RAILROAD®**
Zip through an abandoned Wild West-themed mine, with extreme twists and steep drops, on board this dizzying roller coaster in Frontierland®.

10. **MAGIC CARPETS OF ALADDIN**
Work the controls of a flying carpet to ride high or low around a giant genie bottle in Adventureland®. Watch out for the spitting camels!

Epcot®
Back to the future

The Experimental Prototype Community of Tomorrow (Epcot®) was Walt Disney's neighborhood of the future, designed to connect people with technology. Enjoy exploring the history of science and technology in this complex of two different, but connected, parks. Future World takes visitors from the bottom of the sea to the outer reaches of space, while World Showcase introduces the cultures of 11 countries through their food, architecture, and music.

Visitors enjoying the Test Track ride

Key Features

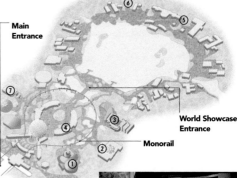
Main Entrance

World Showcase Entrance

Monorail

① **The Seas with Nemo & Friends** In this tribute to the world's oceans, the eponymous ride leads to the majestic Caribbean Coral Reef, a 5.7 million gallon (22 million liter) saltwater aquarium home to 6,000 underwater inhabitants.

② **The Land** Parasail above global landscapes in the Soarin'™ flying simulator, and take the Living with the Land boat tour through a simulated rainforest to experimental working greenhouses.

③ **Imagination!** Make a dragon sing just by moving, operate the world's largest digital camera, and watch Figment create mischief in Journey into Imagination.

④ **Innoventions** Learn how science affects daily life in this interactive museum of the technology of the past and future. Design a roller coaster and then "ride" it at The Sum of All Thrills™ in Innoventions East.

⑤ **World Showcase** These country-specific pavilions have architectural models and replicas from Mexico, Norway, China, Germany, Italy, the United States, Japan, Morocco, France, the United Kingdom, and Canada. They house a variety of ethnic restaurants and shops.

⑥ **Frozen Ever After** at the Norway Pavilion welcomes guests on a boat ride through the wintery world of Elsa, Anna, Olaf, Kristoff and friends. Meet Norsemen, enjoy Frozen-themed desserts and explore Elsa and Anna's summer cabin as part of this exciting adventure.

The Lowdown

🌐 **Map reference** 6 F6
Address 1510 North Ave of the Stars, Orlando, 32830; 407 824 4321; disneyworld. disney.go.com/parks/epcot

🚌 **Bus** From all Disney locations. **Monorail** From TTC to Future World. **Taxi** Water taxis from several resorts; check website. Epcot® has two entrances; park at a resort and take the water taxi to avoid the "front door" lines.

🕐 **Open** Future World: 9am–9pm; World Showcase: 11am–9pm. Check the park's "Calendar" page for seasonal variations and Extra Magic Hours.

💲 **Price** see p106

🚶 **Cutting the line** The park is most crowded on Tue and Fri;

⑦ **Mission: SPACE®** This motion-simulation thrill ride blasts off on a realistic training mission for space travel, which leads to the Advanced Training Lab for testing of skills in space-related games, and culminates in a landing on Mars.

Prices given are for a family of four

Top 10 Attractions

1. **SPACESHIP EARTH**
   This ride travels through the 40,000-year history of communications, from hieroglyphs to computers, while Project Tomorrow, an interactive play area, lets guests play virtual reality games.

2. **TEST TRACK**
   On this Future World ride, kids go through rigorous crash tests before riding a self-designed car along a three-story high track at 65 mph (105 km/h).

3. **MISSION: SPACE®**
   Dodge meteors, feel the force of twice the Earth's gravity, and train for a Mars landing on this motion simulation ride.

4. **SOARIN'™**
   Hang-glide around the world in this ultra-realistic simulator ride in the Land Pavilion, suspended in a giant panoramic movie theater filled with the sights, sounds, and feeling of flying.

5. **THE SEAS WITH NEMO & FRIENDS**
   Join Dory and Marlin in their search for Nemo on the sea floor aboard a "clamobile," among live fish and colorful coral reefs in this massive saltwater tank in the Seas Pavilion.

6. **FERRY ACROSS THE LAGOON**
   Four boats provide superb views of the whole World Showcase and a relaxing way to cool down and get from one country to another across the central lagoon.

7. **JOURNEY INTO IMAGINATION WITH FIGMENT**
   A flying dragon explores and plays with sight, smell, sound, touch, and taste in this whimsical tour of the senses, in the Imagination! Pavilion.

8. **FROZEN EVER AFTER**
   Climb onto the ancient Norwegian ship of Arendelle and sail through the sparkling, wintery land of *Frozen*.

9. **TURTLE TALK WITH CRUSH**
   Interact with Crush, Finding Nemo's surfing turtle, about the wonders of the ocean at this live 3-D show at the Seas Pavilion.

10. **ILLUMINATIONS: REFLECTIONS OF EARTH**
    This nightly sound and light show uses spectacular fireworks and lasers to tell the history of the world.

KIDS' CORNER

Find the chatterboxes!
There are three talking water fountains in Epcot®. See if you can find them.

Answer at the bottom of the page.

Thirsty?
Club Cool in Innoventions West is the coolest place in Epcot®, offering free samples of soda from all over the world. Try lemon soda from Israel and a Japanese bubbly vegetable drink.

PEEK-A-BOO!
A surprise treat awaits at the Germany Pavilion. Stand in the middle of the square to see hidden cuckoo clocks emerge from almost every building to strike the hour.

Go around the world
1 Be sure to get a World Showcase Passport, which you can have stamped at each "country" you visit.
2 Make your way through the hedge maze in the hidden park behind the United Kingdom Pavilion.
3 Don't miss the acrobat show in front of the China Pavilion, the juggling waiters of Serveur Amusant™ outside the France Pavilion, and the drummers of Japan.

---

it is busiest during the Flower & Garden Festival (early Mar–mid-May) and Food & Wine Festival (late Aug–mid-Nov).

Guided tours Behind the Seeds is a 1-hour walking tour of Living with the Land greenhouses. There are several tours inside the The Seas Pavilion. Check website for prices. Call 407 939 8687 for reservations.

Age range 3 plus

Shows Watch the World Showcase Players in the United Kingdom Pavilion, Circle of Life in the Land Pavilion, and Phineas & Ferb: Agent P's World Showcase Adventure.

Allow At least 6 hours

Wheelchair access Yes

Eat and drink SNACKS Electric Umbrella Restaurant (in Future World) has meatball subs and cheeseburgers. FAMILY TREAT Coral Reef Restaurant (in Living Sea) offers fresh seafood with views of a live coral reef.

Shops Regional choices in World Showcase, notably Der Teddybar in the Germany Pavilion, and kimonos, chopsticks, and candy in the Japan Pavilion.

Restrooms At every pavilion and restaurant. Baby care center between the Mexico Pavilion and Test Track.

Good family value?
Though pricey, the variety of rides and informative tours will engage kids of all ages, and grown-ups.

Answer: Outside the Mouse Gear shop, behind Innoventions West, and in the area between Future World and World Showcase, alongside the kiddie fountain.

① Walt Disney World® Resort continued ▶

Disney's Animal Kingdom®

Explore the world's jungles

Disney invented the term "notazoo" to describe Animal Kingdom®, and it is certainly different from a traditional zoo. Families can see Asian tigers padding through ruins, daintily swimming hippos, and majestic mountain gorillas, all of whom live here happily. In addition, there are thrilling rides and even an area that takes you to an alien world.

Pandora – The World of Avatar

Key Features

1. **Pandora – The World of AVATAR** Experience the world of Pandora, with its floating mountains and glowing plants, as you ride down the mystical Na'vi River.

2. **Discovery Island®** Wooden bridges and cave-like tunnels lead to giant tortoises, lemurs, kangaroos, and other exotic creatures. There is also a glass-paneled viewing area where playful otters can be seen.

3. **The Tree of Life** This 145-ft- (44-m-) tall structure is decorated with around 325 super realistic animal carvings. It also houses the It's Tough to be a Bug® show.

4. **Disney's Animal Kingdom Lodge** This majestic lodge, located close to the park, has a six-story lobby with a view of the surrounding savannas, and some of the best African cuisine around.

5. **Rafiki's Planet Watch** Pet the goats, sheep, and llamas in the Affection Section, then head to Habitat Habit! to meet frisky South American cotton-top tamarins.

6. **Asia** The Asia section of the park thrills with the Expedition Everest® roller coaster, and is the setting for tigers, Komodo dragons, and a bird show.

2 miles (3 km)

Entrance

7. **DinoLand, U.S.A.** Travel under the sea with Finding Nemo – The Musical, and into the prehistoric past on the TriceraTop Spin carousel and Primeval Whirl® – two facing coasters with spinning cars.

8. **Africa** Explore the African savanna in the Kilimanjaro Safaris® Expedition, walk along the Pangani Forest Exploration Trail® to the gorilla habitat, and then take the steam-powered Wildlife Express Train.

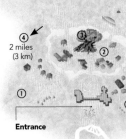

Top 10 Attractions

1. **FESTIVAL OF THE LION KING**
   This elaborate 30-minute musical show in the Harambe Theatre, in the Africa zone, features puppets, dance, and music, and occasionally invites children from the audience to dance along.

2. **PANGANI FOREST EXPLORATION TRAIL®**
   Walk this self-guided trail in Africa to see massive silverback gorillas, exotic birds, meerkats, and hippos.

3. **KALI RIVER RAPIDS®**
   Enter a lush rain forest, in a ride that leads through steaming

geysers and misty waterfalls, on the churning Chakranadi River in the Asia section, before dropping down a 30-ft (9-m) waterfall for a soaking good time *(left)*.

4. **THE AFFECTION SECTION**
   This petting zoo is the only place in Animal Kingdom® where kids can touch and feed a variety of friendly, domesticated animals, such as goats, chickens, and sheep.

5. **FINDING NEMO – THE MUSICAL**
   Performers dressed as colorful fish bring the much-loved animation to life with music, puppets, and Elton John tunes, in this live 30-minute show at DinoLand, U.S.A.

Prices given are for a family of four

The Lowdown

🌐 **Map reference** 6 E6
Address 1375 E Buena Vista Dr, Lake Buena Vista, 32830; 407 824 4321; www.disney world.disney.go.com/parks/animal-kingdom

🚌 **Bus** Lynx 301 from downtown Orlando. Disney buses connect from TTC and resort hotels.

🕐 **Open** From between 8 and 9am to between 5 and 8pm. Check the park's "Calendar" page for seasonal variations and Extra Magic Hours.

💲 **Price** see p106

🏃 **Cutting the line** Avoid Mon–Wed, when park is busiest.

🚩 **Guided tours** Backstage Tales ($360), a 3-hour inside look at the care and feeding of the animal inhabitants, ages 16 and above. Wild Africa Trek ($876–996), small group excursions into Pangani Forest for close encounters with animals. Call 407 939 8687 to reserve.

👫 **Age range** All ages

⏱ **Allow** 6 hours–2 days

♿ **Wheelchair access** Yes

🍽 **Eat and drink** REAL MEAL Tusker House Restaurant *(in Africa)* has an extensive buffet of modernized African cuisine. FAMILY TREAT Sanaa *(in Disney's Animal Kingdom Lodge)* offers an extraordinary blend of African and Indian food. Dine while enjoying the view of the animals in their habitats.

🛍 **Shops** Zawadi Marketplace gift shop *(in Disney's Animal Kingdom Lodge)* has African clothing, masks, and toys. Mombasa Marketplace *(in Africa)* sells African art, wines, jewelry, and musical instruments.

🚻 **Restrooms** Throughout the park. Baby Care Center near Discovery Island

Good family value?
With several outdoor adventures alongside shows for the young ones, there's something for everyone at Animal Kingdom®.

6. **IT'S TOUGH TO BE A BUG!®**
Inside The Tree of Life, see what it means to be a bug, as *A Bug's Life* characters turn this 3-D movie into a creepy, crawly experience.

7. **KILIMANJARO SAFARIS®**
Hop aboard a jungle taxi to ride across a dry savanna in Africa, within feet of live zebras, giraffes, rhinos, and elephants.

8. **PRIMEVAL WHIRL®**
Spin on two dipping, twisting coasters that go back to the age of the dinosaurs, in DinoLand, U.S.A.

9. **EXPEDITION EVEREST®**
A leaping Abominable Snowman interrupts this hair-raising coaster as it goes up a treacherous

mountain in Asia, at which point the car slams into reverse, to travel downhill at 50 mph (80 km/h).

10. **THE TREE OF LIFE**
Spot elephants, iguanas, lemurs, sea horses, and serpents among the 325 animals carved into this exquisite man-made tree in Discovery Island® *(below)*.

Disney's Hollywood Studios®

Hollywood magic meets the wizardry of Disney

From adventuring treasure hunters and swashbuckling spacemen to living toys and friendly monsters, the attractions at Hollywood Studios® immerse visitors in the history of Hollywood, Disney-style. Opened in 1989 as a working film- and TV- production facility, today it has shows and rides based on films and TV. While Toy Story Land opened in 2018, the long-anticipated Star Wars: Galaxy's Edge is slated to open in 2019.

Arched entrance leading to the park

Key Features

⑤ Sunset Boulevard Ride a runaway elevator on The Twilight Zone Tower of Terror™ or zoom away on the Rock 'n' Roller Coaster® Starring Aerosmith, before ending your day at an awesome fireworks show.

⑥ Animation Courtyard Meet Disney and Pixar characters before the Magic of Disney Animation show. Puppets take the stage during the Voyage of the Little Mermaid live show.

Entrance

① Hollywood Boulevard The whole family will love the Citizens of Hollywood improv acting troupe, which calls the audience into play while bringing the silver screen to life.

② Star Tours® – The Adventures Continue The most popular attraction in this park, "Star Tours®" uses characters and scenes from the Star Wars™ films and leads guests on a multiple-storyline intergalactic adventure in the Backlot.

③ Echo Lake The Indiana Jones™ Epic Stunt Spectacular! offers pyrotechnics of another sort. The Force grows stronger as 2019 and the opening of the new Star Wars: Galaxy's Edge land approaches

⑦ Toy Story Land Board a spinning car in Toy Story Mania!® to practice pie-throwing and play ring toss with Toy Story characters and giant green Army men.

④ Muppet Courtyard Enter the madcap world of the Muppets, where the Muppet*Vision 3D film, with its hilarious pre-show and 4D special effects, entertains young and old alike.

The Lowdown

🌐 **Map reference** 6 F6
Address 351 South Studio Dr, Lake Buena Vista, 32830; 407 824 4321; disneyworld.disney.go.com/parks/hollywood-studios

🚌 **Bus** Lynx bus 303 from downtown Orlando to Disney's Hollywood Studios®. Disney buses run from the TTC. **Taxi** Water taxis from BoardWalk and Yacht Club Resorts, as well as Swan and Dolphin resorts.

🕐 **Open** 9am–10pm daily. Check the park's "Calendar" page for seasonal variations and Extra Magic Hours.

💲 **Price** see p106

👫 **Cutting the line** Busiest days are Sun and Wed. Star Wars™ Weekends (May–Jun) and Christmas are the busiest periods.

👫 **Age range** 4 plus

🌐 **Shows** Beauty and the Beast, at the Theater of the Stars, tells of

the beast who was saved by love. Fantasmic! combines lasers, water, and fireworks with dozens of Disney characters. Both shows take place in Sunset Boulevard.

⏱ **Allow** 3–8 hours

♿ **Wheelchair access** Yes

☕ **Eat and drink** SNACKS Fairfax Fare (in Sunset Boulevard) has salads and specialty hot dogs. REAL MEAL Sci-Fi Dine-In (in Backlot) has sci-fi movies playing while families sit at

Top 10 Attractions

1. STAR TOURS® – THE ADVENTURES CONTINUE
Board a Starspeeder 1000 and ride along with C-3PO and R2-D2 from *Star Wars*™ through a 3-D universe.

2. INDIANA JONES™ EPIC STUNT SPECTACULAR!
Amid explosions and fire, daredevil stunt artists re-enact scenes from *Raiders of the Lost Ark* in this 30-minute show in the Backlot.

3. BEAUTY AND THE BEAST LIVE ON STAGE
The magic and romance of the film are re-created in this kid-friendly live show in Sunset Boulevard, featuring dancing, music, brilliant colors, and hilarious characters.

4. VOYAGE OF THE LITTLE MERMAID
Experience the land of Ariel and friends in this 15-minute live show in Animation Courtyard, in which water, lasers, music, and glow-in-the-dark puppets re-create scenes from the movie.

5. TOY STORY MANIA!®
Located in Toy Story Land, this carnival-themed ride is straight out of the beloved *Toy Story* movies. Kids can shoot virtual darts and eggs at 3-D targets, as Woody, Buzz, and Jessie offer helpful hints and cheer them on.

6. FOR THE FIRST TIME IN FOREVER: A FROZEN SING-ALONG CELEBRATION
This 30-minute live show is a crowd favorite, with live actors and a movie screen bringing to life the *Frozen* saga and inviting the audience to sing along to some of the movie's popular songs.

7. MUPPET*VISION 3D
Join Jim Henson's creations on a 17-minute, multiscreen kids' delight while Kermit, Miss Piggy, and Fozzie sing, dance, and play along inside the theater, in Muppet Courtyard.

8. THE TWILIGHT ZONE TOWER OF TERROR™
Take a ride on an out-of-control elevator in the Hollywood Tower Hotel, where guests are taken to a height of 170 ft (52 m) in a dizzying combination of lifts and faster than gravity drops.

9. MAGIC OF DISNEY ANIMATION
Go behind the scenes with real Disney animators and discover the tricks of making cartoons like *Mulan*, *Aladdin* and *The Lion King*, in Animation Courtyard.

10. ROCK 'N' ROLLER COASTER® STARRING AEROSMITH
Rock out on this very fast, very loud roller coaster in Sunset Boulevard, where guests sit in souped-up limousines and are launched from a full stop to 60 mph (96 km/h) in 2.8 seconds, upside down, in the dark.

car-shaped tables and eat burgers, pasta, and steaks.

Shops Each attraction has its own gift shop. Tatooine Traders, the *Star Wars*™ store, is one of the most popular.

Restrooms Throughout the park

Good family value?
It's a little expensive, like all Disney parks, but with rides and shows geared to kids of all ages, this is an excellent place to spend a day.

Blizzard Beach
A water park – with snow

Walt Disney World® Resort's creatively designed winter ski resort-turned adventure park looks like a snowy wonderland, and has plenty of thrilling rides. The waterslides of Summit Plummet shoot straight down 120 ft (37 m) at 60 mph (97 km/h) and the twisty-turny double slides of Downhill Double Dipper are 50 ft (15 m) high and 200 ft (61 m) long. Try the family white-water raft ride Teamboat Springs, which drops down 1,200 ft (366 m) of waterfalls, or take a water-slicked bobsled ride down Mt. Gushmore on the eight-lane Toboggan Racers. The **Winter Summerland** mini-golf course is right at the entrance.

Take cover

If inclement weather threatens, head to the **Coronado Springs Resort** (disneyworld.disney.go.com/resorts/coronado-springs-resort). It has many dining options, including Pepper Market, which offers buffet-style breakfast and lunch, and the quick-service

The thrilling 90-ft- (27-m-) high Slush Gusher ride, Blizzard Beach

restaurant Café Rix, which serves delicious salads, paninis, and freshly baked goods.

Typhoon Lagoon
Ten ways to get really soaked

This Disney water park has everything from gentle raft rides for the whole family to daredevil waterslides for the fearless. The tropical island theme is reflected in the park's lush palm trees and the white-sand beach. The incredible Surf Pool with its 6-ft (2-m) waves tempts experienced board riders. The roller-coaster-like slides of Crush 'n' Gator let three people take the plunge, and the slides of Gang Plank Falls can take four people for a wet ride. Go over the edge at the three raft rides of Mayday Falls, the winding waterways of Storm Slides, or the five-story high-speed drop of Humunga Kowabunga.

Take cover

While getting wet is the whole point of a water park experience, an escape can be found at **Disney**

The Lowdown

- 🌐 **Map reference** 6 E6
- 📍 **Address** 1524 W Buena Vista Dr, Lake Buena Vista, 32830; 407 824 4321; disneyworld.disney.go.com/parks/blizzard-beach
- 🚌 **Bus** Disney bus from the TTC and resort hotels
- 🕐 **Open** Hours vary by season; check website for details.
- 💲 **Price** $195–260; under 3s free. Winter Summerland: $40–52; under 3s free
- 👫 **Cutting the line** The park is least crowded from mid-Feb to mid-Mar, and mid-Sep to early Nov.
- 👫 **Age range** 2 plus. Swim diapers required for toddlers.
- ⏱ **Allow** 2–6 hours
- ♿ **Wheelchair access** Yes
- 🍴 **Eat and drink** SNACKS Cooling Hut (near the entrance) offers pretzels, nachos, muffins, tuna sandwiches, and popcorn. REAL MEAL Lottawatta Lodge (straight ahead from the entrance) serves chili dogs, chicken wraps, french fries, salads, and burgers.
- 👫 **Restrooms** Throughout the park

The Lowdown

- 🌐 **Map reference** 6 F6
- 📍 **Address** 1195 E Buena Vista Dr, Lake Buena Vista, 32830; 407 824 4321; disneyworld.disney.go.com/parks/typhoon-lagoon
- 🚌 **Bus** Disney bus from the TTC and resort hotels
- 🕐 **Open** Hours vary by season; check website for details
- 💲 **Price** $195–260; under 3s free
- 👫 **Cutting the line** The park is least crowded from mid-Feb to mid-Mar, and mid-Sep to early Nov.
- 👫 **Age range** 2 plus. Swim diapers required for toddlers.
- ⏱ **Allow** 2–6 hours
- ♿ **Wheelchair access** Yes
- 🍴 **Eat and drink** SNACKS Happy Landings Ice Cream (near the shallow end of Surf Pool) serves ice cream sundaes and sodas. REAL MEAL Typhoon Tilly's (between Hidaway Bay and Castaway Creek) offers shrimp, fish, and salads.
- 👫 **Restrooms** Throughout the park

Springs® (see p117). It has a variety of shops and restaurants, an extensive LEGO® Imagination Center, as well as a massive movie theater.

Disney's Fort Wilderness Resort & Campground
Hoop-Dee-Doo!

More than just a themed camping resort, the Disney's Fort Wilderness Resort & Campground (see p137) offers visitors the opportunity to hike, ski, and take horse-drawn carriage rides, or sit by the campfire and sing along with Chip and Dale

A water ride at the Typhoon Lagoon

Prices given are for a family of four

behind the Meadow Trading Post. Families come year after year, and during the holiday season, the campground is ablaze with lights. Kids will enjoy the dinner show Hoop-Dee-Doo Musical Revue.

Letting off steam

Kids will have fun climbing and sliding at **Creekside Meadow** and at the **Bay Lake** in the beach area.

The Lowdown

- 🌐 **Map reference** 6 F6
  Address 901 Timberline Dr, Lake Buena Vista, 32830; 407 824 3200; disneyworld.disney. go.com/resorts/wilderness-lodge-resort
- 🚌 **Bus** Disney bus from the TTC and resort hotels
- 💲 **Price** Hoop-Dee-Doo Musical Revue: $180–240
- 🔫 **Guided tours** A 45-min guided trail rides around Fort Wilderness ($46 horseback; $45 carriage ride). Wilderness Back Trail Adventure is a 2-hour Segway tour of the grounds ($96 per person; must be 16 or above).
- 👫 **Age range** 3 plus
- 🏃 **Activities** Rent a bike or pontoon boat or take a pony ride at the Tri-Circle-D Ranch.
- ⏱ **Allow** 1–3 hours
- ♿ **Wheelchair access** Yes
- 🍽 **Eat and drink** SNACKS The Roaring Fork (in Disney's Wilderness Lodge) has sandwiches, burgers, and omelets. FAMILY TREAT Artist Point (in Disney's Wilderness Lodge) serves specialties from the Pacific Northwest, including seafood, sirloin, and game.
- 🚻 **Restrooms** In all comfort stations

Disney Springs®
Everything at this attraction is really big

Disney Springs® has no shortage of options to occupy the whole family's time. In addition to some superb dining venues, West Side is home to Cirque du Soleil® and to the 24-screen AMC. Marketplace has the world's largest Disney merchandise outlet, a Harley-Davidson store, a gigantic LEGO® Imagination Center, and even a three-story Planet Hollywood®. To sample world cuisine, head to Morimoto Asia, Raglan Road Irish Pub, and Paradiso 37.

Letting off steam

Take a quick trip on the Disney bus system to the **Typhoon Lagoon** (see p116).

A variety of plush toys in the World of Disney® store, Disney Springs®

The Lowdown

- 🌐 **Map reference** 6 F6
  Address 1590 E Buena Vista Dr, Lake Buena Vista, 32830; 407 828 3800; www.disneysprings.com
- 🚌 **Bus** Disney bus from the TTC and resort hotels
- 🕐 **Open** Hours vary; check website
- 💲 **Price** Cirque du Soleil®-La Nouba™: $228–540; under 3s free. DisneyQuest®: $170–200; under 3s free
- 🏃 **Activities** Play interactive virtual reality games such as virtual jungle cruise, Buzz Lightyear's Astroblasters, and design-your-own roller coaster at DisneyQuest®. Splitsville (in West Side) combines family bowling and billiards with dining. The Characters

in Flight ($80–100; under 3s free), a hot-air balloon ride, takes 29 guests a breathtaking 400 ft (122 m) above Disney Springs®.
- ♿ **Wheelchair access** Yes
- 🍽 **Eat and drink** SNACKS Earl of Sandwich (1750 E Buena Vista Dr, 32830; 407 938 1762; www.earlof sandwichusa.com) offers soups, salads, and sandwiches. FAMILY TREAT Fultons Crab House (1670 Buena Vista Dr, 32830; 407 934 2628; www.fultonscrabhouse.com) serves some of the freshest fish in town.
- 🚻 **Restrooms** At all restaurants, some shops, and Cirque du Soleil®

---

② Universal Studios Florida®
Rock 'n' roll and lots of aliens

This Universal Orlando® Resort theme park takes movies and television very seriously, but in a fun way. See Hollywood's history come alive through classic horror films, characters from famous movies, and vintage cartoon creatures that younger guests may not know. The thrilling rides, based on Harry Potter's adventures, mummies, aliens, and animated ogres, incorporate state-of-the-art technology in themed zones.

Universal Globe at the entrance to Universal Studios Florida®

Key Features

Hollywood Hang out with Hello Kitty and her friends at the Hello Kitty Shop, and meet a cyborg time traveler at Terminator 2®: 3-D Battle Across Time.

Woody Woodpecker's KidZone®
Everything young kids could hope for is here, from Woody Woodpecker's Nuthouse Coaster® and the E.T. Adventure®, to the Curious George Goes to Town™ playground, with its cartoonish buildings and plenty of activities for toddlers.

Production Central Shrek 4D lets guests ride a dragon, while Despicable Me Minion Mayhem hosts a dance party. But the highlight is the thrilling 17-story-high Hollywood Rip Ride Rockit® coaster.

London The Wizarding World of Harry Potter™: Diagon Alley™ is a hair-raising ride from Gringotts Bank™, through Platform 9¾™, and onto the Hogwarts™ Express, heading to Hogsmeade™.

Lagoon front Embark on a thrilling adventure in the heart-stopping world of Fast & Furious: Supercharged. Guests can enjoy high-octane underground racing on this Hollywood action series ride, or alternatively, face realistic fears in the interactive Fear Factor Live show.

World Expo Wily aliens await in the streets of New York in MEN IN BLACK™: Alien Attack™, and Bart and the gang hang out at Krustyland at the simulated The Simpsons Ride™.

The Lowdown

Map reference 6 F5
Address 6000 Universal Blvd, Orlando, 32819; 407 363 8000, or 407 224 7840 (for tickets); *www.universalorlando.com*

Bus Lynx bus 40 ($2 one way) from downtown Orlando.
Car From Orlando International Airport to Interstate 4 East. Parking $15 per day. Park at Loews Royal Pacific Resort to take the free water taxi to CityWalk®.

Open Park usually open 9am–7pm; closing times vary; check website for seasonal hours. Universal CityWalk®: 11am–2am

Price $352–460. $510–680 park-to-park pass for both parks. Multiday packages available; check website for details.

Cutting the line The park is busiest Tue–Fri. Avoid visiting in the months of Mar–Aug, Oct, and late Nov–Dec. Most hotel guests get a free Express Pass ($99 for non-hotel guests) that helps in avoiding queues.

Guided tours VIP guided walking tours with Express Pass to rides: $600 one park; $740 both parks.

Shows Little ones adore the big purple dinosaur at A Day in the Park with Barney™. Families love Universal's Horror Make-Up Show, and older kids will get a kick out of Fear Factor Live.

Age range 3 plus. Age and height restrictions apply for most rides.

Allow 1–2 days

Wheelchair access Yes

Restrooms Throughout the park

Good family value?
Every moviegoer's dream, this park brings blockbuster movies to life and offers a variety of rides and attractions for both kids and adults.

Prices given are for a family of four

Letting off steam

Enjoy a round of sci-fi and horror film-themed golf at CityWalk's® Hollywood Drive-in Golf™ course.

Eat and drink

Picnic: under $25; Snacks: $25–50; Real meal: $50–80; Family treat: over $80 (based on a family of four)

PICNIC Richter's Burger Co. *(near the Lagoon)* has cheeseburgers, salads, and sandwiches to take away.
SNACK Kid Zone Pizza Company *(in Woody Woodpecker's KidZone®)* has pizza, chicken, and salads.
REAL MEAL Classic Monsters Cafe *(at Production Central)* offers a kid-friendly menu in themed environs.
FAMILY TREAT The Kitchen *(at Hard Rock Hotel)* has fine dining with a rock 'n' roll attitude.

Children explore a themed golf course at Hollywood Drive-in Golf™

Shopping

Everything movie- and cartoon-related can be found at **Woody Woodpecker's KidZone®**, in stores such as **The Barney® Store**, **E.T.'s Toy Closet & Photo Spot®**, and **Universal's Cartoon Store**, while stores such as the Simpsons'™ **Kwik-E-Mart** have customized goodies. There are also acres of shopping in **CityWalk®**.

Top 10 Attractions

1. **THE WIZARDING WORLD OF HARRY POTTER™: DIAGON ALLEY™**
   Ride the rails at Escape from Gringotts™, shop for quills, robes, Quidditch™ brooms, and wands, then hop on the Hogwarts™ Express and head for Hogsmeade™.

2. **THE SIMPSONS RIDE™**
   There are many surprises and twists on this flying, crashing visit to the Krustyland carnival with the Simpson family, in World Expo.

3. **MEN IN BLACK™: ALIEN ATTACK™**
   Join the famous alien hunters in their underground headquarters, and then ride through the streets of New York blasting escaped aliens – who may shoot back.

4. **TERMINATOR 2®: 3-D BATTLE ACROSS TIME**
   Join forces with Terminator robots in this live show that pits humans against futuristic cyborgs in Hollywood.

5. **REVENGE OF THE MUMMY®**
   The mummy awakes, along with fiery fireballs, and attacks in total darkness during the coaster's twists and turns on this New York ride.

6. **SHREK 4-D**
   Ride on a fire-breathing dragon, plunge over a churning waterfall with Shrek, Fiona, and Donkey, and gallop through a haunted forest in Production Central's hilarious motion simulation movie adventure.

7. **DESPICABLE ME MINION MAYHEM**
   The mischievous minions, as well as other characters from the hit film, join guests on a tour of Gru's house in this Production Central ride that ends in a wild dance party.

8. **WOODY WOODPECKER'S NUTHOUSE COASTER®**
   Visit the woodpecker's Nut Factory for a wacky kid-friendly ride full of small thrills, silly jokes, and gentle ups and downs.

9. **HOLLYWOOD RIP RIDE ROCKIT®**
   Pick your music and then strap in to a high-tech car on Orlando's highest coaster, which climbs 17 stories above the park before plummeting at 65 mph (104 km/h).

10. **E.T. ADVENTURE®**
    Bring E.T. back to his home on this part-movie, part-virtual flying bike ride that ends with a personalized farewell from E.T. himself.

③ Universal's Islands of Adventure®

Where superheroes hang out

When the snow-covered Wizarding World of Harry Potter™ opened here in 2010, Potter fanatics snatched up a year's worth of Butterbeer™ and Ollivanders™ wands in its opening weeks, and it continues to be a popular draw. But there's a lot more at this Universal Orlando® Resort theme park, including stunning pyrotechnics, thrilling roller coasters, and rides for younger kids, inspired by everyone's favorite movies.

The Pharos Lighthouse at the entrance

Key Features

Jurassic Park® Dinosaur-fueled excitement awaits, from the 85-ft (26-m) drop inside the Jurassic Park River Adventure® to the fun of the sky-high Pteranodon Flyers®.

Toon Lagoon® Children love the crashing log-ride adventure of Dudley Do-Right's Ripsaw Falls® and the water-based action of Popeye and Bluto's Bilge-Rat Barges® and Me Ship, The Olive.

Wizarding World of Harry Potter™ Explore Hogwarts™ Castle, ride the fun Hippogriff™, enjoy a thrilling Quidditch™ match, or shop for Bertie Bott's Every Flavor beans in Hogsmeade™ Village.

Lost Continent® Witness legends, myths, and heroes at the Eighth Voyage of Sindbad® Stunt Show, or talk to the Mystic Fountain, which squirts water in reply.

Marvel Super Hero Island® Meet your favorite superheroes and villains on the Amazing Adventures of Spider-Man® 3-D ride, the Incredible Hulk Coaster, and Doctor Doom's Fearfall®.

Seuss Landing™ From the house of The Cat In The Hat™ to the spinning fun of the Caro-Seuss-el™ and One Fish Two Fish Red Fish Blue Fish™ rides, this is the place for Dr. Seuss fans. Don't miss the High in the Sky Seuss Trolley Train Ride!™.

Take cover

Blue Man Group, the colorful show at **Universal CityWalk®**, offers guests a remarkable evening of outrageous humor, dance, and theater.

Eat and drink

Picnic: under $25; Snacks: $25–50; Real meal: $50–80; Family treat: over $80 (based on a family of four)

PICNIC Blondie's (in Toon Lagoon®) has towering made-to-order sandwiches for the family, with fresh meat, vegetables, and a variety of cheeses and dressings.
SNACKS The Watering Hole (in Jurassic Park®) has hot dogs, nachos, and chicken wings, as well as soft drinks.

Prices given are for a family of four

REAL MEAL Three Broomsticks™ (in Wizarding World of Harry Potter™) offers authentic British food such as fish and chips, Cornish pasties, and shepherd's pie.
FAMILY TREAT Mythos Restaurant® (in Lost Continent®), built inside a rocky cliff, is one of the best

The award-winning Mythos Restaurant® in Lost Continent®

restaurants in Orlando. It serves great soups and appetizers, excellent seafood, and fabulous desserts.

Shopping

The Wizarding World of Harry Potter™ has fun stuff, from Chocolate Frogs™ at Honeydukes™ to screaming yo-yos at Zonko's™ Joke Shop. Kids will also enjoy the shops at Toon Lagoon®, Marvel Super Hero Island®, Seuss Landing™, and Jurassic Park®.

Find out more

DIGITAL Visit www.mugglenet.com and www.universalorlando.com/harrypotter for insider information.

Top 10 Rides

1. **INCREDIBLE HULK COASTER**
Dive underwater and rocket upside down on this thrilling coaster on Marvel Super Hero Island®.

2. **HARRY POTTER AND THE FORBIDDEN JOURNEY™**
Fly a broomstick with the Hogwarts™ gang in the Wizarding World of Harry Potter™, an amazing 3-D experience that is one of the most popular attractions here.

3. **HARRY POTTER COASTER**
A new Harry Potter-themed coaster, scheduled to open in 2019, will take visitors on a thrilling ride deeper into the Wizarding World of Harry Potter™.

4. **SKULL ISLAND: REIGN OF KONG**
Enter the wild terrain of King Kong, and voyage through an ancient temple and a series of caves, to eventually meet the legendary ape.

5. **AMAZING ADVENTURES OF SPIDER-MAN®**
Spidey and his friends swing off the page in this 3-D living comic book on Marvel Super Hero Island®.

6. **POPEYE AND BLUTO'S BILGE-RAT BARGES®**
Head to Toon Lagoon® for a ride along rapids on giant rafts, as onlookers shoot water cannons.

7. **JURASSIC PARK RIVER ADVENTURE®**
Journey on a river, past quiet lagoons, before the raptors attack and the only escape from a giant T-Rex is an 85-ft (26-m) dark plunge.

8. **THE HIGH IN THE SKY SEUSS TROLLEY TRAIN RIDE!™**
The storytelling trolley in Seuss Landing™ roams over carousels and roller coasters, and even through the Circus McGurkus Café.

9. **THE CAT IN THE HAT™**
Join Things One and Two on this wacky tour of The Cat's home in Seuss Landing™.

10. **PTERANODON FLYERS®**
Fly under the outstretched wings of a pteranodon as it glides over the playground in Jurassic Park®.

The Lowdown

🌐 **Map reference** 6 F5
Address 6000 Universal Blvd, Orlando, 32819; 407 224 4233 or 407 224 7840 (for tickets); www.universalorlando.com

🚌 **Bus** Lynx bus 40 ($2 one way) from downtown Orlando to Universal Studios® parking garage. Park at Loews Royal Pacific Resort and take the free water taxi to Universal CityWalk®. **Car** Rent a car from Orlando.

🕐 **Open** 9am–6pm daily; check website for variations. Universal CityWalk®: 11am–2am daily

💲 **Price** $350–500; call for current prices. Multiday packages are available; check website for details and discounts.

🚻 **Cutting the line** The least crowded months are mid-Jan–Feb, Sep & early Nov. The busiest days are Mon–Fri. A Universal Express℠ pass to skip lines for rides is available; check website for details and discounts. An Unlimited Express℠ Ticket allows unlimited skipping of lines; check website for details.

👫 **Age range** 7 plus

⏱ **Allow** 1–2 days

🚻 **Restrooms** Throughout the park

Good family value?
Although expensive, the park has something to offer everyone, and Harry Potter™ fans will be thrilled to see the books brought to life.

④ SeaWorld®, Aquatica, and Discovery Cove®

A splashing good time

SeaWorld®, and its sister parks Aquatica and Discovery Cove®, are located close to each other, and provide opportunities for families to learn about marine life while having fun. Kids will enjoy the entertaining seals, sea lions, and penguins, and the thrilling rides at SeaWorld® and Aquatica, while Discovery Cove®, a resort-like park, features rivers and white sandy beaches.

Logo of SeaWorld® Orlando

Key Features

Thrill Rides SeaWorld® offers some of the fastest, wettest rides in town, such as the high-flying Manta®, the upside-down Kraken®, and Journey to Atlantis®, a flume-ride and roller-coaster hybrid – filling the air with screams of delight.

Antarctica: Empire of the Penguin® follows the fictional adventures of a penguin named Puck, before exploring the icy world of a penguins' colony.

The Animals Feed bottlenose friends at Dolphin Cove®, pet velvety rays in the Stingray Lagoon, and play with sea lions at Pacific Point Preserve®, in SeaWorld®.

Undersea Life SeaWorld®'s Manta® Aquarium holds 3,000 animals, from sea horses to octopuses. In Shark Encounter®, see thousands of sharks through glass.

Aquatica This water park features giant surfing pools, zooming underwater mazes, and racing rapids, as well as Loggerhead Lane, the laziest river in town.

Prices given are for a family of four

Clyde & Seamore's Sea Lion High® is a fun-filled show that follows the comic adventures of sea lions, walruses, and otters in an aquatic-themed high school.

Discovery Cove® Experience marine life: take an underwater stroll in a diving helmet, or meet otters and marmosets.

The Lowdown

🌐 **Map reference** 6 F6
Address SeaWorld®: 7007 SeaWorld Dr, Orlando, 32821; 407 351 3600; www.seaworld orlando.com. Aquatica: 5800 Water Play Way, Orlando, 32821; 1 888 800 5447; www.aquatica byseaworld.com. Discovery Cove®: 6000 Discovery Cove Way, Orlando, 32821; 1 877 557 7404; www.discoverycove.com

🚗 **Car** Rent a car from Orlando International Airport. Parking: SeaWorld® $14; Aquatica $12; Discovery Cove® free

🕐 **Open** SeaWorld®: 9am to between 6 and 10pm. Aquatica: 9am–6pm. Discovery Cove®: 9am–5:30pm. Check websites.

💲 **Prices** SeaWorld®: $316; under 3s free. Aquatica: $196. Discovery Cove®: $510–690 (inclusive of meals; cheapest in Sep). SeaWorld®/Aquatica 14-day unlimited entry: $556. Add $100 to Discovery Cove® for unlimited 14-day access to SeaWorld® and Aquatica.

SeaWorld® All Day Dining Deal: $110–40.

👥 **Cutting the line** The Quick Queue pass gives front-of-the-line access to Manta®, Kraken®, Journey To Atlantis®, and Wild Arctic® ($60–100). The parks are busiest late May–Sep and Nov. Thu–Sun are crowded.

👉 **Guided tours** There is a 90-minute SeaWorld® Behind the Scenes tour and a Wild Arctic® Up-Close Tour.

👫 **Age range** 2 plus. Age and height restrictions apply for most rides.

🕐 **Allow** 1–3 days

♿ **Wheelchair access** Yes

🚻 **Restrooms** Across the parks. Diaper-changing tables in restrooms near SeaWorld®'s front entrance.

Good family value?
Though pricey, the three parks have many entry options that ensure a great family experience.

Letting off steam

Shamu's Happy Harbor® is a great place for kids to burn off energy, with plenty of shady spots for parents.

Eat and drink

Picnic: under $25; Snacks: $25–50; Real meal: $50–80; Family treat: over $80 (based on a family of four)

PICNIC Mango Joe's *(near Wild Arctic®, SeaWorld®)* has delicious fajita sandwiches, wraps, and salads for a quick picnic in the park. **SNACKS Captain Pete's Island Hot Dogs** *(in Dolphin Cove®, SeaWorld®)* serves funnel cakes and hot dogs in an island atmosphere. **REAL MEAL Seafire Inn** *(in Waterfront, SeaWorld®)* has stir-fry and pasta, as well as fish and chips. **FAMILY TREAT Sharks Underwater Grill** *(in Shark Encounter®, SeaWorld®)* serves exceptional seafood with a view of a massive glass-walled shark tank.

Shopping

Across the parks, visit **Emporium** for hats, **Coconut Bay Traders** for souvenirs, and **Fins** for plush toys.

Find out more

DIGITAL Watch Shamu and the SeaWorld® penguins on webcams at *www.tinyurl.com/7t2umlf.*

Guests enjoying a seafood meal at Sharks Underwater Grill, SeaWorld®

Top 10 Attractions

1. **CLYDE & SEAMORE'S SEA LION HIGH®**
   Enjoy the fun adventures of these amazing animals in their wacky quest of high-school diplomas.

2. **MANTA®**
   Ride this manta ray-shaped suspended coaster in SeaWorld® that includes an up-close encounter with manta rays and other sea life.

3. **JOURNEY TO ATLANTIS®**
   Travel through the ruins of a sunken city on this part-boat, part-roller coaster in SeaWorld®, and explore dark passageways before being plunged into the waters below.

4. **KRAKEN®**
   This spiraling, upside-down, high-speed monster of a thrill ride suspends riders high above the Serpent's Lagoon in SeaWorld®.

5. **ANTARCTICA: EMPIRE OF THE PENGUIN®**
   Get up close with penguins and see what it's like to live on ice on this magical SeaWorld® ride, where the adventure is different every time.

6. **DOLPHIN COVE®**
   Observe bottlenose dolphins during feeding time in this massive but peaceful lagoon in SeaWorld®.

7. **SHAMU'S HAPPY HARBOR®**
   Younger kids will love this SeaWorld® mini-park that has boat rides, teacup spinners, an octopus carousel, and the Shamu Express teeny coaster.

8. **DOLPHIN PLUNGE®**
   This thrilling Aquatica ride has side-by-side enclosed tubes that slide through the underwater home of black-and-white dolphins.

9. **TURTLE TREK®**
   Witness the journey of a sea turtle in the world's first 3-D, 360-degree domed theater, surrounded by giant aquariums and thousands of fish, in SeaWorld®.

10. **WALHALLA WAVE® & HOOROO RUN®**
    In these two connected Aquatica waterslides, guests can ride through a six-story tunnel maze, which then takes them over the edge and racing to the bottom.

KIDS' CORNER

See more at SeaWorld®

1 Stop by the SeaWorld® Information Center (right of entrance turnstiles) to find out when you can see or even help feed the mammals.

2 Head to the Lakeside Patio to dance with Shamu at the all-day Shamu's Party Zone.

3 Climb the 400-ft (122-m) rotating Sky Tower for a bird's-eye view of Orlando, Walt Disney World® Resort, and Universal Orlando®.

"Secret" events

Shamu & Crew sign autographs at the SeaWorld® front gate from 9am to noon, and there is a special pre-show, held just before Clyde & Seamore's Sea Lion High®..

TRICK A GROWN-UP!

Tell your parents to sit in the front row on the Journey to Atlantis® coaster, but don't tell them how wet they'll get!

Whirlwind spin

Aquatica's quiet Loggerhead Lane lazy river has a thrilling secret: from the island in the middle, climb the tower and dive into Tassie's Twisters – a series of lightning-fast tubes that spin into a giant bowl – for a dizzying ride back into the river.

⑤ ICON Orlando

For a view from the top

ICON Orlando, offering visitors a grand view of the city

This stunning observation wheel is a fairly recent addition to the spectrum of Orlando's attractions. Similar to the installation in London, ICON Orlando takes visitors on a 20-minute ride in an air-conditioned capsule, traveling to a height of 400 ft (122 m). The ride offers spectacular views of the Orlando skyline and the lights of International Drive. The theme parks and lakes are all within sight, and on really clear days, visitors can catch sight of the Vertical Assembly Building at Cape Canaveral, nearly 60 miles (97 km) away. At night, the the wheel is set ablaze with 64,000 lights, and is an incredible spectacle visible for miles.

The ICON Orlando wheel is part of the ICON Orlando 360 complex, which includes Madame Tussauds (*see p126*), with its many waxworks of celebrities from the worlds of music, movies, television, science, art, history, sports, and popular culture, as well as Skeletons: Museum of Osteology, and the Orlando Starflyer – the world's tallest swing ride at 450 ft (137 m).

Located close by, **SEA LIFE Aquarium Orlando** offers visitors a glimpse into the underwater lives of more than 5,000 sea animals, scattered over 32 displays. These are arranged in tanks reflecting the different oceans of the world, such

as the Atlantic Ocean, Indian Ocean, and Pacific Ocean. There are varieties of sea creatures – from beautiful, dangerous jellyfish, green sea turtles, and eels, to playful octopi, such as the Giant Pacific Octopus, that wanders and drifts through a shipwreck. Sharks and manta rays swim above and below visitors walking through a 360-degree ocean tunnel, making it an arresting and intensely visual experience. In one room, sardines swim in a silvery vortex above visitors' heads; another area offers starfish and other rock-pool inhabitants.

Staff members are at hand to offer visitors information on rescuing, protecting, and breeding the animals. The aquarium has also set up six sea animal sanctuaries that are currently situated around the world. As many as 150 seals and turtles have had their injuries treated, in order to be released back into the wild.

Letting off steam

For rides that defy gravity, Starflyer mega-swings, and go-karts, visit **Magical Midway** (*7001 International Dr, 32819; 407 370 5353, www.magicalmidway.com*), located less than two miles (3 km) from ICON Orlando. There are arcade games and low-key rides as well, such as merry-go-rounds and bumper boats, which the kids will love.

An I-Ride Trolley that helps visitors get around in the International Drive area

Prices given are for a family of four

The Lowdown

🌐 **Map reference** 10 H2
Address ICON Orlando 360: 8401 International Dr, 32819; 866 228 6438; www.iconorlando.com. SEA LIFE Aquarium Orlando: 8449 International Dr, 32819; 866 602 0607; www.visitsealife.com/

🚗 **Bus** Lynx bus 8, 38, 42, 50, 58 & 111 to International Dr. I-Ride Trolley (*407 354 5656; 8am–10:30pm daily*) on the Green Line to south-bound stop G9, and on the Red Line to north-bound stop 17. **Car** Rent a car from Orlando. Take exit 74A onto Sand Lake Rd off I-4 to International Dr.

🕐 **Opening times** ICON Orlando: 10am–10pm Sun–Thu, 10am–midnight Fri & Sat. SEA LIFE Aquarium Orlando: 10am–9pm daily

💲 **Price** ICON Orlando: $78–104; under 3s free. Combination tickets for SEA LIFE Aquarium, Madame Tussauds, or Skeletons: Museum of Osteology: $120–$160. Book online to get discounts.

🔫 **Guided tours** ICON Orlando offers private rides ($375 per capsule; book ahead).

👫 **Age range** 5 plus

🕐 **Allow** 1–3 hours

♿ **Wheelchair access** Yes

🍴 **Eat and drink** SNACKS Friendly's (*8418 International Dr, 32819; 407 345 1655*) offers good diner fare and delicious ice-cream. REAL MEAL Brick House Tavern and Tap (*8440 International Dr, 32819; 407 355 0321; www.brickhousetavernandtap.com*) serves pizzas and burgers, and fun starters for kids, such as pork meatballs and pretzels.

👫 **Restrooms** At all venues

⑥ Crayola Experience

Sculpt, create, and play

Founded in 2015, Crayola Experience offers over two dozen distinct attractions for children to be creative, and to play with colors. Digital versions of art, projected onto the walls, can be created at Art Alive!, while charming spin-board art can be fashioned from wax at the Drip Art station. At Melt & Mold, kids can create cars, seahorses, rings, and much more, with the help of crayon wax and a machine. Imaginative shapes can be sculpted out of tinted clay at Modeling Madness. Visitors should begin at the Crayola Factory, where Scarlet and Turk (short for turquoise) guide you through the Crayola manufacturing process, while the resident 'Crayonologist' answers questions about Crayola's products.

Over the years, the company has expanded phenomenally and its products are innumerable, from markers and colored pencils to pigments and fine art supplies. Stop by at the Crayola Store for a taste of this – and catch eccentric crayon names like Macaroni & Cheese, Robin's Egg Blue, and Inchworm.

Letting off steam

There are two children's play areas in the **Florida Mall** – one near Macy's, and the other next to American Girl. You can also find several stores that sell children's games and toys, such as Build-A-Bear Workshop *(407 438 8882; www.buildabear.com)*.

Entrance to the Florida Mall, where the Crayola Experience is located

The Lowdown

🌐 **Map reference** 10 H2
Address 8001 S Orange Blossom Trail, Florida Mall, 32809; 407 757 1700; www.crayolaexperience.com/orlando

🚗 **Car** Rent a car from Orlando. Take the Sand Lake Rd exit off I-4, or Exit 8 from eastbound, or Exit 4 from westbound

🕐 **Opening times** 10am–8pm daily

💲 **Price** $96; under 2s free

🕑 **Cutting the line** The best time to visit is before noon.

👫 **Age range** 2 plus

⏱ **Allow** 3–4 hours

♿ **Wheelchair access** Yes

🛍 **Shop** The Crayola Store *(on site)* sells Crayola products, plush toys, and customized apparel.

🍴 **Eat and drink** SNACKS Café Crayola *(on site)* has a choice of sandwiches, pizzas, and gluten-free items. REAL MEAL Spoleto Italian Kitchen *(8001 S Orange Blossom Trail, Florida Mall, 32809; 561 274 9404; www.spoletoitalian.com)* offers customized dishes with over 30 sauces and toppings options.

KIDS' CORNER

Colorful beginnings

While Crayola had a humble start in the mid-1800s, today it produces over 1,500 different items.
1 Do you know what Crayola first produced?
2 In 1903, Crayola released a box of wax coloring sticks. How many colors did the box contain?
3 What were the original colors in the pack?
4 There are several popular phrases used today, that involve color. Can you guess what "I'm feeling blue" means?

COLOR BLIND?

Being color blind doesn't mean you can't see colors – it just means your perception of specific colors is inaccurate. You simply may not be able to see a green leaf or a red fire engine the same way others do.

The Highest Eye

ICON Orlando offers a panoramic view from the sky, but it is still not the highest!. There are four Ferris wheels in the world that are taller than ICON Orlando – in London, China, Singapore, and Las Vegas – the last of which is the tallest, at a whopping 550 ft (168 m).

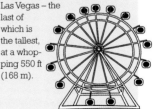

Answers: 1 Industrial pigments. **2** Eight colors. **3** Green, yellow, orange, red, violet, blue, brown, and black. **4** It means "I'm feeling sad".

The colorful entry welcoming young children at the Crayola Experience

⑦ International Drive

Watch out for falling buildings

With Universal Studios Florida® at one end and SeaWorld® at the other, I-Drive features more great attractions for kids. It is hard to miss the upside-down building of **Wonderworks** and its science-oriented exhibits, or the giant wheel of ICON Orlando towering over the whole area. **Monkey Joe's** has wall-to-wall bouncing fun for ages 4 to 12, and an adult lounge for parents. The dramatically tilted building of **Ripley's Believe It or Not! Odditorium** contains the world's largest collection of weird stuff, and **Madame Tussauds** keeps its life-like wax statues in air-conditioned surroundings.

Letting off steam

Head to **Fun Spot Action Park** (5700 Fun Spot Way, 32819; 407 363 3867; www.funspot.tuten graphics.com) for go-karts, bumper

Bizarre-looking building housing Wonderworks, International Drive

cars, Ferris wheels, and tilt-a-whirls. Or try the 14-slide water park at the **Coco Key Resort** (7400 International Dr, 32819; 407 351 2626; www.cocokeyorlando.com).

⑧ Marsh Landing Adventures

Gators and wildlife galore

Head out onto the water at Lake Tohopekaliga (Lake Toho to locals), one of Florida's largest lakes. To take in the natural beauty and get a taste of Florida's wild side, climb aboard one of Marsh Landing's five airboats. Tours range from a one-hour overview of the lake and its environs, to a four-hour adventure that includes a picnic stop on a remote island. Coast Guard trained captains stop by often to share knowledge, as the boats pass moss-laden cypress trees and grassy swamp lands. Wildlife includes herons, egrets, pelicans, and bald eagles, along with alligators, deer, and wild pigs.

Letting off steam

After zipping across the water, visit the **Partin Triangle Neighborhood Park** (on site) that offers a shaded playground with swings as well as tennis and racquetball courts. Pavilions offer shade, and the picnic area has grills, the perfect place for an after-boating meal.

A Marsh Landing Adventures' airboat zipping through the water

Orlando, Winter Park, and around

Entertainment, gardens, and the promise of warm winters have been luring visitors to Orlando since the 1880s. About an hour's drive from both east and west coasts, it usually escapes the worst of the hurricane season while benefitting from pleasant temperatures in winter. Bordering greater Orlando, Winter Park's appeal lies in its great museums, cafés, and scenic waterways.

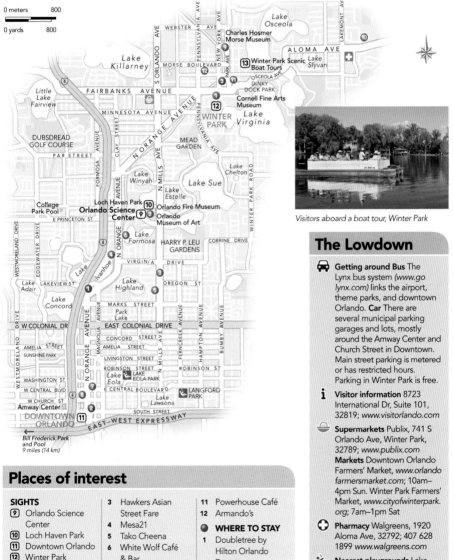

Visitors aboard a boat tour, Winter Park

The Lowdown

Getting around Bus The Lynx bus system (www.go lynx.com) links the airport, theme parks, and downtown Orlando. **Car** There are several municipal parking garages and lots, mostly around the Amway Center and Church Street in Downtown. Main street parking is metered or has restricted hours. Parking in Winter Park is free.

Visitor information 8723 International Dr, Suite 101, 32819; www.visitorlando.com

Supermarkets Publix, 741 S Orlando Ave, Winter Park, 32789; www.publix.com
Markets Downtown Orlando Farmers' Market, www.orlando farmersmarket.com; 10am–4pm Sun. Winter Park Farmers' Market, www.cityofwinterpark. org; 7am–1pm Sat

Pharmacy Walgreens, 1920 Aloma Ave, 32792; 407 628 1899 www.walgreens.com

Nearest playgrounds Lake Eola Park, 712 E Washington St, 32801, 7am–midnight daily. Langford Park, 1808 E Central Blvd, 32803; 5am–sunset daily

Places of interest

SIGHTS
9 Orlando Science Center
10 Loch Haven Park
11 Downtown Orlando
12 Winter Park
13 Winter Park Scenic Boat Tours

● **EAT AND DRINK**
1 Ethos Vegan Kitchen
2 SUBWAY
3 Hawkers Asian Street Fare
4 Mesa21
5 Tako Cheena
6 White Wolf Café & Bar
7 Beth's Burger Bar
8 The Rusty Spoon
9 Panera Bread
10 Tibby's New Orleans Kitchen
11 Powerhouse Café
12 Armando's

● **WHERE TO STAY**
1 Doubletree by Hilton Orlando Downtown
2 Grand Bohemian Hotel
3 Park Plaza Hotel

⑨ Orlando Science Center
Explore the past and the future

Walking across the glass bridge from the parking garage into the Science Center's spaceship-like rotunda is like stepping into another world. Science-hungry kids and curious adults alike will enjoy the interactive exhibits, live programs, and films on giant screens. Hands-on learning and tricks teach kids about the small wonders of science, while astronomy exhibits and an observatory let them consider the enormity of the universe.

Exterior of Orlando Science Center

Key Features

Level 4 DinoDigs, Our Planet, Science Stations

Level 3 Engineer It!, Fusion: A STEAM Gallery

Level 2 New KidsTown, Kinetic Zone, Digital Adventure Theater: A National Geographic Experience, The Science Store

Level 1 NatureWorks, KidsTown, Dr. Phillips CineDome

① **NatureWorks** Exhibits of animal habitats and diverse ecosystems start with an exhibit on Florida's natural fish and alligator habitats.

② **DinoDigs** Find fossils buried in the Dig Pit, look into a triceratop's eye, and see life-size replicas of a T-Rex and a 40-ft- (12-m-) long plesiosaur skeleton.

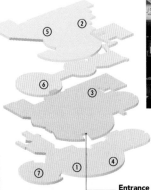

③ **Kinetic Zone** Kids can learn about gravity and electricity, and build their own creations, such as rockets and air cars.

④ **KidsTown** Young visitors float boats on a multilevel waterfall, work in an orange grove, and interact with creative exhibits that accelerate cognitive development.

⑤ **Our Planet** Explore the stars, and learn how planets were formed, what happens when galaxies collide, and why the sky is blue.

⑥ **Engineer It!** Create prototypes of anything imagined, from bridges and LEGO® boats to much more, and develop the model, so that you can test it here.

⑦ **Dr. Phillips CineDome** Watch films about the bottom of the sea and the Grand Canyon on this spectacularly huge screen.

Entrance

Swans on the grassy banks in Lake Eola Park, south of the Orlando Science Center

Letting off steam

Kids can tire themselves out harvesting plastic oranges and loading crates by hand in the juice factory in KidsTown. **Lake Eola Park**, 3 miles (5 km) south, offers lots of running space, a jogging lane around the lake, and boating.

Eat and drink

Picnic: under $25; Snacks: $25–50; Real meal: $50–80; Family treat: over $80 (based on a family of four)

PICNIC Ethos Vegan Kitchen *(601-B S New York Ave, 32804; 407 228 3898; www.ethosvegankitchen. com)* has meat-free sandwiches and salads to take away for a picnic at **Loch Haven Park** *(see p130).*

SNACKS SUBWAY *(Level 1)* is a sandwich shop that also has fresh salads and kids' meals.

REAL MEAL Hawkers Asian Street Fare *(1103 Mills Ave, 32803; 407 237 0606; www.eathawkers.com)* presents a menu of street food delights from China, Vietnam, Malaysia, and Singapore in small sharing plates.

Prices given are for a family of four

The Lowdown

🌐 **Map reference** 6 F5
Address 777 E Princeton St, Orlando, 32803; 407 514 2000; www.osc.org

🚗 **Bus** Lynx bus 125 from downtown Orlando or SunRail commuter train to SunRail Florida Hospital Health station.
Car Rent a car from Downtown Orlando and head onto Interstate 4, exit 85. Parking $5

🕐 **Open** 10am–5pm Mon–Sun. Hours vary; check website. Crosby Observatory: Sat and some Fri

💲 **Price** $57–72. $165 for an annual family membership

👪 **Cutting the line** Visit during extended hours to avoid crowds. Members have the benefit of the members-only line.

👫 **Age range** All ages

🧑‍🔬 **Activities** Live Science! Programming brings science to life with demos for visitors around the building.

⏱ **Allow** 3–6 hours

☕ **Café** SUBWAY (see p128)

🛍 **Shop** The Science Store (Level 2) sells puzzles, interactive science kits, and toys.

🚻 **Restrooms** On each level near the elevator

Good family value?
From dinosaurs to space exploration, this museum has a great variety of exhibits and activities for the whole family.

The Crosby Observatory This silver dome on top of the Orlando Science Center hides a custom telescope powerful enough to see Saturn's rings, Jupiter's moons, and distant stars.

Science Live! Mad scientists in training will enjoy conducting experiments at Dr. Dare's Lab, and observing images of Earth, the Moon, and Mars projected on the hovering Science on a Sphere globe that hangs high above the audience.

FAMILY TREAT Mesa21 (1414 N Orange Ave, Orlando, 32804; 407 930 8000; www.mesa21.com) is a popular place for authentic Mexican food. Located in a beautiful park, it overlooks the picturesque Lake Ivanhoe, and also has a play-ground for kids.

Next stop...
Head to the **Orlando Museum of Art** (see p130) located in the Loch Haven Park, close to the Orlando Science Center. Here, you can see ancient Aztec pottery share space with contemporary American art, along with African handicrafts and many incredibly fascinating touring exhibitions.

SUBWAY on Level 1 of the Orlando Science Center

⑩ Loch Haven Park

Art in the green

This extensive park is a cultural mecca, home to the Orlando Science Center (see pp128–9), and several theaters and museums. The **Orlando Shakespeare Theater** performs plays by the Bard and modern playwrights, as well as children's theater and productions from the Orlando International Fringe Theatre Festival. Across the parking lot, the multiple galleries of the **Orlando Museum of Art** hold American contemporary art, glass works by Dale Chihuly, and large collections of African handicrafts. Behind the Shakespeare Theater is the small **Orlando Fire Museum**, with rebuilt engines, and pumpers dating from 1911.

Letting off steam

Cool off at the **College Park Pool** (*2411 Elizabeth Ave, 32804; 407 246 2764*), located just a few minutes away from Loch Haven Park.

The Lowdown

- 🌐 **Map reference** 6 F5
  Address Orlando Shakespeare Theater: 812 E Rollins St, 32803; *orlandoshakes.org*. Orlando Museum of Art: 2416 North Mills Ave, 32803; *www.omart.org*. Orlando Fire Museum: 814 E Rollins Rd, 32803; *407 246 2033*

- 🚌 **Bus** Lynx bus 102 from Winter Park
  Car Rent a car from the airport.

- 🕐 **Open** Orlando Shakespeare Theater: check website. Orlando Museum of Art: 10am–4pm Tue–Fri, noon–4pm Sat & Sun. Orlando Fire Museum: 9am–3pm Fri–Sat

- 💲 **Price** Orlando Shakespeare Theater: prices vary with events; check website. Orlando Museum of Art: $35–40; under 4s free

- 🚶 **Cutting the line** Busiest during the Orlando International Fringe Theatre Festival in May.

- 👉 **Guided tours** Free docent-led tours of Orlando Museum of Art at 1:30pm Thu

- 🚶 **Age range** 4 plus

- ⏱ **Allow** 2–8 hours

- 🍴 **Eat and drink** SNACKS Tako Cheena (*932 N Mills Ave, 32803; 321 236 7457*) has tacos stuffed with exotic fillings. REAL MEAL White Wolf Café (*1829 N Orange Ave, 32804; 407 895 9911; whitewolfcafe.com*) serves pasta dishes, steaks, and seafood.

- 🚻 **Restrooms** In all attractions

Strolling along a lush lawn in Harry P. Leu Gardens, Downtown Orlando

⑪ Downtown Orlando

Basketball, great food, concerts, and pretty gardens

The heart of Orlando is the corner of Church Street and Orange Avenue – with nightclubs, restaurants, and bars. Visit the **Amway Center** for concerts, circuses, and to watch the NBA team Orlando Magic. The **Dr. Phillips Center for the Performing Arts** often has children's theater and shows. Church Street's restaurants serve some great food, and Lake Eola has an iconic fountain and an easy, mile-long walking path. The **Orange County Regional History Center** houses exhibits representing Orlando's past, present, and future. Nearby are the vast **Harry P. Leu Gardens**, with roses, azaleas, a giant bamboo collection, and more.

Letting off steam

Dubsdread (*www.historical dubsdread.com*) welcomes kids aged 17 and under to play golf.

The Lowdown

- 🌐 **Map reference** 6 F5
  Address Amway Center: 400 W Church St, 32801; 407 440 7000; *www.amwaycenter.com*. Orange County Regional History Center: 65 E Central Blvd, 32801; 407 836 8500; *thehistorycenter.org*. Harry P. Leu Gardens: 1920 N Forest Ave, 32803; 407 246 2620; *www. leugardens.org*. Dr. Phillips Center, 445 S. Magnolia Ave, 32801; 844 513 2014; *www.drphillipscenter.org*

- 🚌 **Bus** Lynx bus 102 from Winter Park

- 🕐 **Open** Amway Center and Dr. Phillips Center: check website Orange County Regional History Center & Harry P. Leu Gardens: daily

⑫ Winter Park

Art and culture in the suburbs

Suburban Winter Park became a warm-weather escape for wealthy Northerners in the early 1900s, and today its museums, high-end stores, and great restaurants retain an air of sophistication.

At the north end of the beautiful one-mile stretch of green called Park Avenue stands the **Charles Hosmer Morse Museum of American Art**, which holds the world's largest collection of art, stained glass, jewelry, and furnishings made by

Elegant Tiffany lamps in the Morse Museum, Winter Park

- 💲 **Prices** Amway Center and Dr. Phillips Center: check website. Orange County Regional History Center: $22–28; under 5s free. Harry P. Leu Gardens: $25–30; under 5s free

- 🚶 **Age range** 2 plus

- ⏱ **Allow** A day

- 🍴 **Eat and drink** SNACKS Beth's Burger Bar (*24 E Washington St, 32801; 407 650 4950; www.bethsburger-bar.com*) serves burgers with inventive toppings. REAL MEAL The Rusty Spoon (*55 W Church St, 32801; 407 401 8811; www.the rustyspoon.com*) uses organic produce from local farmers, served in a casual, upscale setting.

Louis Comfort Tiffany (1848–1933). At the south end of Park Avenue is Rollins College, the oldest university in the southeast, which is home to the **Cornell Fine Arts Museum**. The museum has a stellar collection of American and European art.

Letting off steam

Next to Rollins College is **Dinky Dock**, a public park with grills and tables for picnicking, and a sand beach with opportunities to swim.

The Lowdown

- **Map reference** 6 F5
  Address Morse Museum: 445 N Park Ave, 32789; 407 645 5311; www.morsemuseum.org. Cornell Fine Arts Museum: 1000 Holt Ave, 32789; 407 646 2526; www.rollins.edu/cfam

- **Train** Amtrak or SunRail train from downtown Orlando. **Bus** Lynx bus 102 from Downtown Orlando

- **Visitor information** Winter Park Welcome Center & Chamber of Commerce, 151 West Lyman Ave, 32789; 407 644 8281

- **Open** Morse Museum: 9:30am–4pm Tue–Sat, 1–4pm Sun. Cornell Fine Arts Museum: 10am–4pm Tue–Fri, noon–5pm Sat & Sun

- **Price** Morse Museum: $12–14; under 12s free. Cornell Fine Arts Museum: free

- **Cutting the line** Busiest during the two annual arts festivals in March and October.

- **Guided tours** Morse Museum has docent-led tours during public hours.

- **Age range** 5 plus

- **Allow** 3–8 hours

- **Eat and drink** SNACKS Panera Bread (329 N Park Ave, 32789; www.panerabread.com) offers bagels, sandwiches, and a kids' menu. REAL MEAL Tibby's New Orleans Kitchen (2203 Aloma Ave, 32792; www.tibbys.com) has authentic New Orleans gumbo, and po-boy sandwiches.

⑬ Winter Park Scenic Boat Tours

Behind the scenes and houses of Winter Park

The Scenic Boat Tour glides along a chain of magnificent lakes, past some of the finest homes in Florida. The lush canals that connect Lake Osceola, Lake Virginia, and Lake Maitland were renovated in the 1930s especially for tourism, and

Boat cruising along a picturesque canal in Winter Park

the flat-bottom pontoon boats have been plying them ever since. Mansions built by Goodyear and Walgreen, the Rollins College campus, and the home of noted American architect James Gamble Rogers II can be seen on the tour. Decades-old palm trees, bamboo, papyrus, and flowering vines overhang the canals, providing a cool break from the bright sun, but be sure to carry sunscreen and hats. Kids can spot gray herons, sunning anhingas, turtles, and even the rare alligator on the cruise.

Letting off steam

Go 11 miles (18 km) southwest to **Bill Frederick Park and Pool** (3401 S Hiawassee Rd, 32835; 407 246 4486), at Turkey Lake, for boat rentals, largemouth bass fishing, and a wooden playground with a maze of tunnels and swings.

The Lowdown

- **Map reference** 6 F5
  Address 312 E Morse Blvd, 32789; 407 644 4056; scenicboat tours.com

- **Car** Rent a car from the airport.

- **Open** 10am–4pm daily. Tours depart on the hour.

- **Price** $35–42; under 2s free

- **Cutting the line** Tour early or pick late tours (no reservations), when the sun isn't directly overhead.

- **Age range** 2 plus

- **Allow** 1 hour

- **Eat and drink** SNACKS Powerhouse Café (111 E Lyman Ave, 32789; 321 441 4888; www.powerhouse cafe.com) serves healthy juices, smoothies, and Middle Eastern snacks. FAMILY TREAT Armando's (463 W New England Ave, 32789; 407 951 8930) serves classic Neapolitan food.

- **Restrooms** At the boathouse

⑭ LEGOLAND® Florida Resort
Not just another brick in the wall

Built on part of the former site of Cypress Gardens, Florida's oldest theme park, this LEGOLAND® has captured everyone's imagination. With 50 acres (20 ha) of attractions, including a section of the original Cypress Gardens park, LEGOLAND® Florida Resort is the biggest of the seven parks of its kind across the world. A tribute to the popular little Danish building blocks, this spectacular park is full of roller coasters, rides, and shows that challenge as well as entertain. The inventive and often humor-filled constructions make adults giggle, while children gaze in awe as they discover an entire city made of LEGO® bricks.

LEGO® model of Windra, one of the characters found in the World of Chima™

Key Features

① **The Beginning** This colorful area right at the entrance features the Island in the Sky, a 150-ft (46-m) rotating platform that offers a panoramic view of the park.

② **Fun Town** Stroll past the Island in the Sky to enter this area, which is home to the 700-seat Wells Fargo Fun Town Theater. See how LEGO® bricks are transformed from raw plastic into building blocks in the Factory Tour. Younger kids will enjoy riding the two-tier Grand Carousel.

③ **DUPLO® Valley** Playgrounds, planes, and trucks designed for little kids with big imaginations can be found in this play area. Don't miss the DUPLO® Farm, full of plastic animals, fire engines, and drivable cars.

④ **LEGO® Kingdoms** Little princesses and knights joust and battle wizards in this medieval castle. Climb aboard the Dragon coaster for a ride through the LEGOLAND® castle, before heading to Royal Joust for a quiet time on the cantering LEGO® horses.

⑤ **Heartlake City** The LEGO® Friends line of toys comes to life with a live stage show, an interactive musical fountain, and the Mia's Riding Adventure disc coaster ride.

Entrance

⑥ **Land of Adventure** Steer around brick jungle beasts on the Safari Trek, or brave the rollicking wooden tracks of Coastersaurus that rumble past giant LEGO® dinosaurs. Shoot back at glowing skeletons and spiders to score points in the Lost Kingdom Adventure.

⑦ **Miniland USA** Marvel at miniature LEGO® replicas of American cities spread over seven themed areas. Look for movie stars in Los Angeles in California and street musicians in Times Square in New York, and see the space shuttle smoke and rumble at the Kennedy Space Center. Then check out the battle of miniature galleons at Pirate's Shores.

Prices given are for a family of four

⑧ LEGO® City
Children can learn to drive at one of the two Ford Driving Schools, steer a boat in hopefully the right direction at the Boating School, and soar in the air on Flying School, a thrilling roller coaster. Rescue Academy gets the whole family to pump, drive, and fight fire in a muscle-powered fire engine.

⑨ LEGO® TECHNIC™ Filled with hair-raising rides on the ground, in the water, and in the air, this area is the most extreme of all the zones in the park. Hop onto the wind-powered speedsters at AQUAZONE Wave Racers to dodge water blasters or cycle the way into the sky on Technicycle.

⑩ Imagination Zone Budding engineers can build and program real MINDSTORM™ robots in LEGO® MINDSTORMS® or build and race brick cars in Wheels Zone. There are other areas as well, for kids to design, build, and test their LEGO® creations.

⑪ World of Chima™ Get soaking wet on a fun interactive boat ride in The Quest for CHI™, battling with water cannons to help Laval the Lion Prince defeat Cragger the Crocodile King. Meet characters from the LEGO® Legends of Chima in a 4D movie experience. Little ones will enjoy playing with water in the Cragger's Swamp splash area.

⑫ LEGOLAND® Water Park Toddlers will love the DUPLO® Splash Safari with short slides and interactive DUPLO® creatures. Older kids can choose between racing their own boats at Build-A-Boat, the 375-ft (114-m) waterslides at Twin Chasers, or the playground with a 300-gallon (1,135-liter) bucket drop in Joker Soaker.

KIDS' CORNER

Sharp spotting

It could take hours to find everything tucked in Miniland USA, but here are a few fun things to keep an eye out for:

1 Cats. Find the cats jumping through flaming hoops in Key West, and a lady with kittens on the roof in California.

2 Pirates. Not only is there a big sea battle at Pirate's Shores, but there's also a Las Vegas version at the Treasure Island Hotel.

3 A giant chicken, and men lifting weights in Miami Beach.

4 People turning into babies at the Fountain of Youth in St. Augustine.

5 Penguins and parrots in Central Park in New York.

Brownie points
Take aim at the cobra in the Lost Kingdom ride in Land of Adventure, and keep shooting to rack up tons of extra points!

OLD, OLD TREE

Unsuspecting visitors will be astonished by a massive banyan tree – the giant trunk and roots having grown in this spot since 1939. Look out for the tree's "knobbly knees" for a giggle.

LEGO® mania

1 Kids around the world spend 5 billion hours a year playing with LEGO® bricks.

2 More than 400 billion LEGO® bricks have been produced since 1949. Stacked on top of each other, this is enough to connect the Earth and the Moon ten times over!

3 All the LEGO® bricks sold in one year would circle the world five times.

⑬ LEGOLAND® Florida Resort continued ▶

LEGOLAND® Florida Resort, continued

The colorful entrance to the attractive LEGOLAND Hotel

Canal Deck. The upscale menu concentrates on seafood such as oysters and shellfish, to go with meaty steaks, ribs, and some lighter dishes. A selection of wines and cocktails is also available.

Shopping

Find everything from LEGO® toy sets and LEGO® exclusives to T-shirts and souvenirs in the **LEGO® Studio Store** *(in Fun Town)*. Pick up *Star Wars™*, *The LEGO Movie™*, NEXO

Star Wars™ LEGO® sets lining the shelves of LEGO® Studio Store, Fun Town

Letting off steam

Run around in LEGOLAND® Florida Resort, or go to **Rotary Park** *(300–398 6th St NE, Winter Haven, 33881)* to burn off excess energy. The park offers a skate park, a sand volleyball court, and walking paths.

Eat and drink

Picnic: under $25; Snacks: $25–50; Real meal: $50–80; Family treat: over $80 (based on a family of four)

PICNIC Castle Burger *(in LEGO® Kingdoms)* serves grilled chicken salads, burgers and fries. Picnic in the shaded area in the Land of Adventure by the Safari Trek.

Logo of Granny's Apple Fries Stand, Fun Town

SNACKS Granny's Apple Fries Stand *(in Fun Town)* is the place for a tasty fried snack of warm apple sticks coated in cinnamon and sugar served with a vanilla cream dip. **Adventure Snacks** *(in Land of Adventure, next to Dino Ice Cream)* dishes out hot dogs, nachos and cheese, and chips.

Prices given are for a family of four

REAL MEAL The Market Restaurant *(in The Beginning)* serves coffee and pastries in the morning, and rotisserie chicken and Asian fusion dishes later in the day. **FAMILY TREAT Harborside** *(2435 7th St SW, Winter Haven, 33880; 863 293 7070; www.harborsidefl. com)* offers a superb view of Lake Shipp, especially from the

The Lowdown

🌐 **Map reference** 7 D1
Address One LEGOLAND Way, Winter Haven, 33884; 877 350 5346; www.legoland.com/florida

🚗 **Bus** Daily shuttle bus (8401 International Dr, 32819; www. legoland.com/florida/planning-your-visit/getting-here; $5 per person) leaves from I-Drive 360 (outside the parking deck near the ICON Orlando back entrance) at 9am and returns at park closing. Reserve online 24 hours in advance. **Car** Hire a car from Orlando Airport. Parking $12; preferred parking $20

🕙 **Open** Parks usually open from 10am to between 7pm and 8pm. Closed Tue–Wed year-round except Jun–Aug. Check www.legoland.com/florida/planning-your-visit/park-hours for details.

💲 **Price** $277–366; under 3s free. Additional fee of $20 for the Water Park. Second day add-on available at the park for $15. Discount coupons are sometimes available at fast food outlets, on LEGO® kit boxes,

and for AAA (Automobile Association of America) members. Lockers are available for rent in The Beginning and inside LEGOLAND® Water Park.

🧑 **Age range** 2 plus

🎭 **Show** Rescue Academy (in LEGO® City) features the City Volunteer Fire Department in a superb interactive show full of music and dance. Shows at 11am, 12:45pm, 2:15pm, & 4pm

⏱ **Allow** 1–2 days

♿ **Wheelchair access** Yes

☕ **Cafés** Many across the park

🛍 **Shops** Many across the park

🚻 **Restrooms** Plenty throughout the park. The Baby Care Center in DUPLO® Valley has baby-changing facilities, high chairs, and bottle warmers.

Good family value?

A mix of educative and entertaining attractions, as well as beautiful gardens, makes LEGOLAND® Florida Resort superb as a family destination.

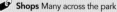

KNIGHTS™, NINJAGO™, and other such toys. There are also bins of individual parts for imaginative builders at **Pick-A-Brick** *(in Fun Town)*.

Find out more
DIGITAL LEGO® Club offers "Master builder" videos, how-to instructions, comic books, and a free magazine with discount coupons for toys and park admission. Check out *www.lego.com/en-us/club/member* for more information.

Take cover
If rough weather threatens, head for the **LEGOLAND Hotel** *(877 350 5346; www.legoland.com/florida/legoland-hotel/overview)* at the entrance of LEGOLAND® Florida Resort. A paradise for LEGO® lovers, the hotel has 152 themed rooms in LEGO® decor, interactive play areas, a pool, and a restaurant *(see p136)*.

Next stop...
FROM PRETTY GARDENS TO A RANCH Head 8 miles (13 km) southeast of LEGOLAND® Florida Resort to the **Bok Tower Gardens** *(1151 Tower Blvd, Lake Wales, 33853;*

The striking Neo-Gothic and Art Deco Singing Tower, Bok Tower Gardens

863 676 1408; boktowergardens.org), a huge botanical garden and bird sanctuary. Named for Edward W. Bok, an influential publisher, the gardens boast the Singing Tower, which is known for its 45-minute live carillon concert at 1pm and 3pm daily. Dotted with camellias, magnolias, and azaleas, these woodland gardens have plenty for families – picnic areas with sandboxes and toys, reading benches, a vine-covered arbor tunnel, and even secret garden areas.

Alternatively, the **Westgate River Ranch** *(3200 River Ranch Blvd, Frostproof, 33867; 863 692 1321; wgriverranch.com)*, 33 miles (53 km) southeast of LEGOLAND® Florida Resort near Lake Wales, holds a live rodeo every Saturday night, with bucking broncos, bull riding, rodeo clowns, and genuine cowboys. Kids will love petting and feeding barn animals such as lambs, calves, and baby goats in the petting farm. There are also pony rides on offer.

Top 10 Rides

1. **LOST KINGDOM ADVENTURE**
   Pick up a laser pistol and get points for firing at ancient Egyptian targets in this dark and slightly scary ride in the Land of Adventure.

2. **COASTERSAURUS**
   Ride this old-fashioned and noisy wooden roller coaster, in the Land of Adventure, as it zooms through a land filled with brick dinosaurs.

3. **BATTLE FOR BRICKBEARD'S BOUNTY**
   Watch this exciting live-action water battle featuring water-skiing pirates on Lake Eloise in Pirates' Cove. Those wanting to get soaked can sit in one of the first five rows.

4. **AQUAZONE WAVE RACERS**
   Daring riders get to control the speed of their jet skis by starting out slowly and then spinning out to dizzying and soaking heights in this LEGO® TECHNIC™ ride.

5. **MERLIN'S CHALLENGE**
   Battle a LEGO® Merlin as the wooden train spins around a roller coaster track in wild and possibly magical circles in LEGO® Kingdoms.

6. **SPLASH OUT**
   Climb to the highest point in the park, then plummet down one of the three 60-ft (18-m) slides to drop into the pool below in LEGOLAND® Water Park.

7. **FLYING SCHOOL**
   Board a suspended coaster and zoom above LEGO® City on this winding, twisting, and diving ride.

8. **BUILD-A-RAFT RIVER**
   Design and build a one-of-a-kind boat and launch it on a 1,000-ft- (305-m-) long lazy river in LEGOLAND® Water Park.

9. **WELLS FARGO FUN TOWN THEATER**
   Immerse yourself in the 4D movie experience with *The LEGO® Movie™ 4D: A New Adventure* and *LEGO® NEXO KNIGHTS™: The Book of Creativity*.

10. **PROJECT X**
    Race a full-size TECHNIC™ car along a twisting roller coaster track full of sharp twists and turns on this ride in LEGO® TECHNIC™.

Where to Stay in Orlando and the Parks

Orlando and the theme parks have lodgings to suit all tastes. Whether a night under the stars in a tent, or the luxury of a family suite in a tower appeals, there's no lack of choice, and most places offer pools, in-room entertainment, and more. Rooms range from standard to suites with kid-friendly themes.

AGENCY
HomeAway
www.homeaway.com
This website connects visitors with the private owners of a variety of accommodations ranging from a luxury pool home to a room in a condo.

Downtown Orlando and Winter Park Map 6 F5

HOTELS
Doubletree by Hilton Orlando Downtown
60 S Ivanhoe Blvd, 32804; 407 425 4455; doubletree1.hilton.com
Overlooking beautiful Lake Ivanhoe, just north of downtown Orlando, this Hilton hotel offers a heated rooftop pool with whirlpool for adults, children's activities, and a kids' menu at the restaurant. Free shuttle service to downtown restaurants.
📶 🍽 🚼 ✪ $

Grand Bohemian
325 S Orange Ave, 32801; 407 313 9000; www.grandbohemianhotel.com
The only AAA Four-Diamond hotel in downtown, this splendid building houses a great collection of art. Centrally located, it has a spa, a fitness center, and a heated outdoor pool overlooking the city.
💆 📶 🍽 🚼 ✪ $$

Park Plaza Hotel
307 S Park Ave, Winter Park, 32789; 407 647 1072; parkplazahotel.com
Overlooking the green space of Central Park, this charming hotel has cast-iron railings on flower-bedecked balconies. Complimentary valet parking available, or simply check out the shops along Park Avenue or walk to the nearby museums. Children under three are not allowed.
📶 🍽 🚼 $$$

LEGOLAND® Florida Resort Map 7 D1

HOTELS
Lake Roy Beach Inn
1823 Cypress Gardens Blvd, Winter Haven 32884; 863 324 6320; www.lakeroybeachinn.com
Located on an interconnected chain of 14 lakes and canals, this inn offers rooms and suites with kitchenettes, and three-bedroom townhouse suites, which can sleep up to eight people, with screened-in porches and balconies overlooking Lake Roy.
📶 🚼 ✪ 🍽 📺 $–$$

LEGOLAND Hotel
1 Legoland Way, 33884; 1 877 350 5346; www.legoland.com/florida/legoland-hotel/overview
One of two lodging options in the park, this inventive hotel offers its

guests themed rooms, and has 2,000 LEGO models across the hotel. There are plenty of activities and amenities for children, and a complimentary breakfast buffet as well.
📶 🍽 ✪ 🛎 $$

SeaWorld® Map 6 F5

RESORT
Floridays Resort Orlando
12562 International Dr, 32821; 407 238 7700; www.floridaysresort orlando.com
Just 6 miles (10 km) from SeaWorld®, this bright, Mediterranean-themed resort offers suites with separate living and dining rooms, full kitchens, and in-suite grocery delivery. There is a kids' pool area with fountains and dedicated special activities.
📶 🍽 ☕ ✪ 🍴 $$

HOTELS
Fairfield Inn & Suites Orlando at SeaWorld®
10815 International Dr, 32821; 407 354 1139; www.marriott.com
Within walking distance of Aquatica, this 200-room hotel has a game room, a fitness center, shuttles to SeaWorld® and Universal Studios Florida®, and views of the nightly fireworks. Free Quick Queue bracelets for SeaWorld® are available at the front desk, and guest have access to early park openings on some days.
💆 📶 🍽 ✪ $$

Marriott Harbour Lake
7102 Grand Horizons Blvd, 32821; 407 465 6100; www.marriott.com
Minutes away from SeaWorld®, this hotel offers rooms equipped with DVD players and laundry facilities, as well as suites with full kitchens. There is miniature golf, slide pools, water playground, a pirate ship in the pool, and a pirate-themed kids' camp.
📶 🍽 🚼 🐾 ✪ $$

A fully furnished family suite in Floridays Resort Orlando

Universal Orlando® & The Orlando Eye Map 6 F5

RESORT
Loews Royal Pacific Resort
6300 Hollywood Way, 32819; 888 464 3617; www.loewshotels.com/royal-pacific-resort
With its tropical ambience, this 1,000-room resort has a lagoon pool. It provides free Universal Express℠ passes, and early admission to the Wizarding World of Harry Potter™.
🌐 🍽 🚻 ♿   **$$**

HOTELS
The Enclave Suites
6165 Carrier Dr, 32819; 407 351 1155; www.enclavesuites.com
Directly across from Universal Studios Florida®, this hotel has suites with separate Scooby Doo-themed rooms, with bunk beds. Watch the Universal fireworks from the balcony.
🍽 🚻 ♿ 🚲   **$**

Wyndham Orlando Resort International Drive
8001 International Dr, 32819; 407 351 2420
Located next door to ICON Orlando 360 and its varied attractions, this hotel offers a pool, restaurant, and modern rooms, some with bunk beds.
🌐 ☕ 🚻 ♿ 🛏 🚌   **$$**

Hard Rock Hotel
5800 Universal Blvd, 32819; 407 490 1272; www.hardrockhotelorlando.com
Right on Universal property, this hotel features a pool with an underwater sound system, and supervised kids' activities at Camp Lil' Rock. Some suites have attached themed kids' rooms. Complimentary water taxi and shuttle buses to the parks.
🌐 🍽 🚻 ♿   **$$$**

Walt Disney World® Resort

RESORTS
Hilton Orlando Buena Vista Palace Disney Springs™ Area Map 6 F5
1900 E Buena Vista Dr, 32830; 407 827 2727; www.hilton.com
This huge resort has lovely rooms, activities for kids, and a float lagoon pool. Kids will love the Disney character breakfast on Sundays. Free shuttles to Disney parks.
🌐 🍽 ♿   **$**

The Hard Rock Hotel Orlando, with a view of the pool

Hyatt Regency Grand Cypress Map 6 F5
1 Grand Cypress Blvd, 32836; 407 239 1234; grandcypress.hyatt.com
This resort offers everything from standard guestrooms to massive VIP suites. There's a golf course, a huge lake with watersports, and a vast lagoon pool with slides and waterfalls. Kids' programs are available too.
🚲 🌐 🍽 ♿   **$$**

Disney's Art of Animation Resort Map 6 E6
1850 Century Dr, Lake Buena Vista, 32830; 407 938 7000; disney.go.com
Choose from *Nemo*-, *Cars*-, and *Lion King*-themed family suites that can sleep up to six people. Playgrounds, a jogging trail, in-room pizza delivery, and free Disney movies are some of the further lures at this Disney resort.
🚲 🌐 🍽 🚻 ♿ 🚌   **$$–$$$**

Marriott Orlando World Center Resort Map 6 F5
8701 World Center Dr, 32821; 407 239 4200; www.marriott.com
The world's largest Marriott, just outside Walt Disney World® Resort, has 2,000 rooms and suites, six pools, waterslides, a video arcade, and a golf course. There are organized arts and crafts programs, and scavenger hunts for kids.
🌐 🍽 🚻   **$$–$$$**

Swan and Dolphin Resort Map 6 E6
1500 Epcot Resorts Blvd, Lake Buena Vista, 32830; 407 934 3000 (Swan) & 407 934 4000 (Dolphin); www.swandolphin.com
Located in Walt Disney World® Resort, these adjoining hotels offer a massive pool grotto, complete

with a white-sand beach and waterfalls. The Camp Dolphin club offers programs for kids aged 4 to 12.
🌐 🍽 🚻 ♿ 🚲   **$$–$$$**

Disney's Animal Kingdom Lodge Map 6 E6
2901 Osceola Pkwy, Lake Buena Vista, 32830; 407 938 3000; disney.go.com
This beautifully designed Disney resort offers views of wild animals grazing on an extensive savanna. Free Continental breakfast, midday snacks, and evening wine and cheese.
🌐 🍽 🚻 ♿   **$$$**

Wyndham Bonnet Creek Resort Map 6 F6
9560 Via Encinas, Lake Buena Vista, 32830; 800 610 9558; www.wyndhambonnetcreek.com
This all-suite resort has great lodgings, with kitchens and private balconies. Children can enjoy the Play Days activities program.
🌐 🍽 🚻 ♿ 🚲 🛏 🚌   **$$$**

HOTEL
Best Western Lake Buena Vista Map 6 F5
2000 Hotel Plaza Blvd, Lake Buena Vista, 32830; 407 828 2424; www.lakebuenavistaresorthotel.com
This hotel is within walking distance of Disney Springs® restaurants and shops, as well as the Disney transportation system. Rooms above the sixth floor offer splendid views of the Epcot® fireworks. There is a children's pool and a video game parlor for kids.
🚲 🌐 🍽 P ♿   **$$**

CAMPING
Disney's Fort Wilderness Resort & Campground Map 6 F6
4510 N Fort Wilderness Trail, Lake Buena Vista, 32830; 407 939 7429; disneyworld.disney.go.com
Bring a tent, drive in with an RV, or rent a rustic but comfortable cabin for a stay in these woods, minutes away from the Disney parks. Attractions include horseback-riding, and nightly marshmallow roasts.
🚲 🌐 🍽 ♿ 🚲   **$–$$$**

Price Guide
The following price ranges are based on one night's accommodation in high season for a family of four, inclusive of service charges and additional taxes.
$ Under $150 **$$** $150–300 **$$$** over $300

The Space Coast

Ancient home to Native Americans, this part of Florida is where Spanish explorers first landed on American soil – and from where man's first voyage to the Moon took off. Today, the area's highlight is the cutting-edge Kennedy Space Center, from where NASA has launched all its space programs since 1968. Here, visitors get a chance to see the shuttles that orbited in space, and meet the astronauts who manned them.

The Space Coast

Highlights

Kennedy Space Center
Become a virtual astronaut and experience what a journey into outer space feels like at this stellar space center, the only one of its kind (see pp144–7).

Merritt Island National Wildlife Refuge
Step back in time to the area where Florida's early inhabitants lived, and where native wildlife thrives today (see pp148–9).

Canaveral National Seashore
Bask in the sun on beautiful, soft white sands that are frequented by migrating sea turtles (see p148).

Brevard Zoo
See animals native to Florida, as well as from lands as far away as Africa and Australia, in this 73-acre (30-ha) zoological park (see p151).

Cocoa Beach and Pier
Take a break at this famous resort, with a white-sand beach, and a pier with restaurants and souvenir shops (see p150).

Brevard Museum of History and Natural Science
Explore this little gem of a museum with exhibits on everything from 7,000-year-old Native American culture to astronauts (see p151).

Left The spectacular Saturn V shuttle displayed at the Apollo/Saturn V Center, Kennedy Space Center
Above right Fishing at Playalinda Beach, Merritt Island National Wildlife Refuge

The Best of
The Space Coast

With beaches located very close to Orlando's major theme parks, the Space Coast is a great destination for families looking for some sand and sun; lively Cocoa Beach is perfect for surfing and swimming. A visit to the Kennedy Space Center offers the thrill of seeing the shuttles that once journeyed into space and learning about astro-history. For a change of pace, visit the region's tranquil wildlife preserves, rich with flora and fauna.

Up in the air and higher

The biggest attraction for sky-gazing visitors is the **Kennedy Space Center** (see pp144–7). From its beginnings in 1969, the center has been the heart of America's space program. NASA's Orion program has picked up after a post-shuttle lull in launches, and commercial companies, such as SpaceX, Blue Origin, and United Launch Alliance, have lit up the Space Coast with rocket launches. The interactive exhibits and motion-simulation rides at the Shuttle Launch Experience, the Apollo/Saturn V Center, and the United States Astronaut Hall of Fame® provide comprehensive space information for budding astronauts. See rare items from the Moon

Right Splashing in the waters near the Pier, Cocoa Beach
Below A simulated pre-show briefing for visitors at the Shuttle Launch Experience, Kennedy Space Center

Above Kayaking past giraffes in a re-creation of their natural habitat in Brevard Zoo, Melbourne **Right** Roseate spoonbills in Merritt Island National Wildlife Refuge

missions, including the space suit that Apollo 14 Commander Alan Shepard wore on the Moon, in the Apollo Treasures Gallery in the Apollo/Saturn V Center. Admirers of all things aeronautic may also want to catch the Tico Air Show at the **Valiant Air Command Warbird Museum** *(see p147)* in Titusville in March, where vintage jets and old biplanes fly overhead.

Fun in the sun

The beaches around Cocoa, Titusville, and Melbourne are a natural draw for families. Some, such as **Cocoa Beach** *(see p150)*, are lined with resort hotels, restaurants and bars, and are popular with sun-lovers and surfing fanatics. By contrast, **Playalinda Beach** *(see p148)*, on the **Canaveral National Seashore** *(see p148)*, is protected by the Parks Department from development. Visitors here can enjoy pristine nature not far from high-tech rockets pointed at the stars.

Florida's wild side

Between the **Canaveral National Seashore** and **Merritt Island National Wildlife Refuge** *(see pp148–9)*, there is a large expanse of wild, untamed Florida. Saltwater marshes, pine flatwoods, hardwood hammocks, and wetlands are all found here, and are home to a host of plants and animals, including turtles, manatees, and alligators. Combine all this with the Wild Florida habitat at **Brevard Zoo** *(see p151)*, and families can see hundreds of native animals without having to look far.

In a week

Start with the **Kennedy Space Center**. Check out the Shuttle Launch Experience first, and then take a guided tour before catching an IMAX® movie. Visit Heroes and Legends *(see p144)* to virtually experience the dangers of early space flight. The next day, take bathing suits to **Playalinda Beach** for an undisturbed afternoon in the sun. On the third day, follow the **Black Point Wildlife Drive** *(see p148)* at the **Merritt Island National Wildlife Refuge**, enjoy a picnic lunch under the cypress trees, then take a free walking tour of the lagoon with a guide from the Visitor Center. Next, head to **Brevard Zoo** to let the kids feed giraffes in the Expedition Africa habitat. An early dinner on the Pier at **Cocoa Beach** is a good way to wrap up the day. The next day, watch the sunrise over the 24 miles (38 km) of **Canaveral National Seashore** beach. Stop at the **Brevard Museum of History and Natural Science** *(see p151)* for a look at prehistoric Florida's inhabitants and a run around the **Imagination Center** *(see p151)*.

The Space Coast

With swamps, flatlands, and beaches, and a temperate to subtropical climate, the Space Coast has more native wildlife than practically anywhere in the US. Due to the high influx of tourists, the major roadways are well kept; however, its location surrounding the Kennedy Space Center and preserves means development is limited. While there is a fairly usable public transportation system, especially along the trolley routes around Cocoa Beach, a car is mandatory for any excursions farther afield, and to get here from Orlando. Interstate 95 is the main highway for north–south travel, with US Route 1 the principal road through coastal tourist areas.

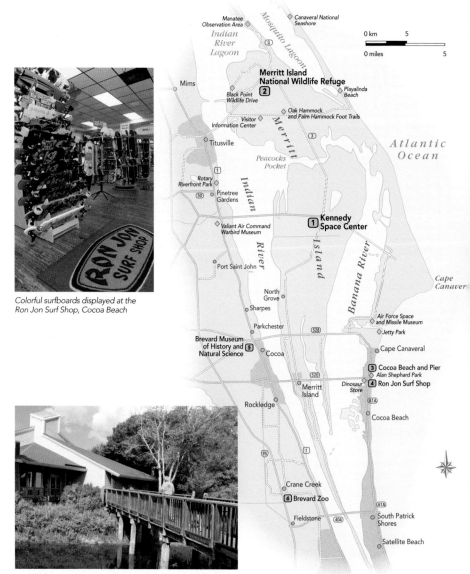

Colorful surfboards displayed at the
Ron Jon Surf Shop, Cocoa Beach

Visitor Information Center in Merritt Island National Wildlife Refuge

White rhinos in the Expedition Africa exhibit in Brevard Zoo, Melbourne

The Lowdown

🚗 **Getting there and around**
Air Fly into Orlando International Airport *(1 Jeff Fuqua, Orlando, 32827; 407 825 2001; www. orlandoairports.net)*, Daytona Beach International Airport *(700 Catalina Drive, Daytona Beach, 32114; 386 248 8069; www.flydaytonafirst.com)* or Melbourne International Airport *(1, Air Terminal Parkway, Melbourne, 32901; 321 723 6227; www.mlbair.com)*. **Bus** Greyhound *(1 800 231 2222; www.greyhound. com)* is ideal for interstate travel, with stations in Daytona Beach, Titusville and Melbourne. The Space Coast Area Transit or SCAT *(401 S Varr Ave, Cocoa, 32922; 321 633 1878; www.ridescat.com)* local bus service includes a trolley serving Cocoa Beach. **Car** Avis *(www.avis.com)* and Hertz *(www. hertz.com)* have offices at airports. Melbourne Airport Express *(321 724 1600; www.melbourneairport express.com)* offers services between Orlando International Airport and the cruise port.

ℹ️ **Visitor Information** Visit the Space Coast tourist center at 430 Brevard Ave, Cocoa Village, 32922; 877 572 3224; *www.visitspacecoast.com*

🛒 **Supermarkets** Publix *(www. publix.com)* and Winn-Dixie *(www.winndixie.com)* are the premier supermarket chains, with outlets throughout this region.

🎉 **Festivals** Beach 'N Boards Fest (early Mar). Ron Jon Easter Surfing Festival, Cocoa Beach; *www.eastersurffest.com* (mid-Mar). Thunder on the Beach: Space Coast Super Boat Grand Prix; powerboat races; *www.thunderoncocoa beach.com* (mid-May). NKF Pro-Am Surf Festival; surfing competition benefitting the National Kidney Foundation; *www.nkfsurf.com* (Labor Day, Sep); Brevard Caribbean Festival; live music, good food and family activities; *www.brevardcaribbeanfest.com* (Labor Day, Sep); Space Coast Art Festival; art competition and exhibition, with kids activities; *www.spacecoastart festival.com* (Thanksgiving weekend, Nov)

➕ **Pharmacies** Publix, CVS *(www.cvs.com/pharmacy)* and Walgreens *(www.walgreens. com/pharmacy)* are the main pharmacies in the region, with some outlets open 24 hours.

🚻 **Restrooms** Almost all major attractions, restaurants, parks, malls, and most gas stations have public restrooms.

Building sand castles at Playalinda Beach, Canaveral National Seashore

Places of interest

🔲 **SIGHTS**
1 Kennedy Space Center
2 Merritt Island National Wildlife Refuge
3 Cocoa Beach and Pier
4 Ron Jon Surf Shop, Cocoa Beach
5 Brevard Museum of History and Natural Science
6 Brevard Zoo

Spectacular view of the ocean from Turtle Mound, Canaveral National Seashore

① Kennedy Space Center
3-2-1 Blast off!

Every young space cadet dreams of being an astronaut, and this is the place where the dream comes true. Since its opening in 1963, the home of the National Aeronautics and Space Administration (NASA) has launched 135 shuttle missions, 26 manned space flights, and countless rockets from the Cape Canaveral base. The highlight of the Visitor Complex is the permanent display of Atlantis, which ended the shuttle orbiter program in 2011.

A command module on display in the Visitor Complex

Key Features

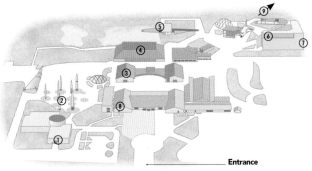

① **Heroes and Legends** America's space pioneers are honored at this exhibit, where superb interactive technology re-creates the dangers of early missions. The US Astronaut Hall of Fame® is housed here as well.

② **Rocket Garden** Eight vintage rockets from every stage of the US Space Program reach for the stars in this display area, beautifully lit at night. Walk among the real rockets and replicas of space capsules illustrating the Center's history of flight.

③ **Journey to Mars: Explorers Wanted** This 10,000-sq ft- (3,048-sq m-) exhibit features a live theater, interactive experiences, and large-scale multimedia presentations to help kids and adults learn about the future of space exploration. The model of Orion, NASA's next-generation spacecraft, takes visitors through the technology that helps astronauts explore deep space. The Explorers Wanted show runs live, twice an hour.

④ **IMAX® Theater** Two massive 50-ft (15-m) movie screens show films featuring footage shot by astronauts during actual missions in space, with sound and 3-D effects so realistic that viewers feel they are in space themselves. Films include *Hubble 3D*, where viewers can "float" alongside astronauts as they build the Hubble Space Telescope, and *Journey to Space*, narrated by Sir Patrick Stewart, where viewers can learn about NASA's plans for deep space exploration.

⑤ **Astronaut Memorial** This granite memorial, which stands outside the Atlantis exhibit, is inscribed with the names of those who have died in various space programs. Nearly 2,000 sq ft (186 sq m) of the Atlantis exhibit is dedicated to Forever Remembered, which contains a display of items that belonged to the crew of two shuttles – Challenger and Columbia.

⑥ **Space Shuttle Atlantis**ˢᴹ
This $100-million exhibit features the space shuttle Atlantis – an Earth orbiter that went into space more than 30 times between 1985 and 2011. This exhibit is one of only three shuttles on display in the world. Its cargo bay door is open and its robotic arm extended.

⑦ **Shuttle Launch Experience®**
Visitors can ride a thrilling space flight simulator to sample G-forces and zero gravity. After a pre-launch briefing held in a replica launch gantry, strap on as the countdown begins, and the sounds, lights, and sensation of being launched into space propel the imagination into orbit.

⑧ **Astronaut Encounter** In this 30-minute show, visitors meet the members of NASA's astronaut teams, who tell stories of their experiences and answer questions. The 3-D film *Eyes on the Universe: NASA's Space Telescopes* employs footage from the Hubble Telescope, allowing visitors to view the farthest reaches of the universe.

⑨ **Apollo/Saturn V Center** Explore a reproduction of the Apollo mission control room, marvel at a 370-ft- (112-m-) tall Saturn V rocket, and see space suits that Apollo 14 astronauts wore in outer space in this tribute to the Apollo Space Program.

KIDS' CORNER

Spacecraft have names too!

Walk around the Apollo/Saturn V Center and find the numbers on these Apollo capsules with sometimes funny names:

1 Gumdrop
2 Charlie Brown
3 Columbia
4 Kitty Hawk
5 Casper

Answers at the bottom of the page.

LEFT BEHIND

The US Space Program has left six landing modules, three lunar rovers, six flags, two pairs of boots, a hammer, and three golf balls on the Moon.

First and last words

Neil Armstrong was the first man to walk on the Moon, on July 21, 1969. He famously uttered the first words on the Moon, too: "That's one small step for man, one giant leap for mankind." Do you know what the last words on the Moon were? Eugene Cernan, the last man on the Moon aboard Apollo 17 in December 1971, said: "We leave now as we once came, with peace and with hope for all mankind."

Answers: 1 Apollo 9. **2** Apollo 10. **3** Apollo 11. **4** Apollo 14. **5** Apollo 16.

① Kennedy Space Center continued ▶

Kennedy Space Center, continued

Letting off steam

Kids can crawl and climb through tunnels, scamper over a rock wall, and command a mini-shuttle in the **Children's Play Dome** (on site), a play area with an outer space theme. If commanding rockets does not use up enough energy, head 8 miles (13 km) south to the **Rotary Riverfront Park** (4141 S Washington Ave, Titusville, 32780), which has a playground and a fishing pier along the Indian River.

Eat and drink

Picnic: under $25; Snacks: $25–50; Real meal: $50–80; Family treat: over $80 (based on a family of four)

PICNIC Publix Supermarket (2000 Cheney Hwy, Titusville, 32780; 321 267 9606 has sandwiches and salads made fresh daily in the deli.
SNACKS G-Force Grill (in Astronaut Encounter) serves tacos, sandwiches, and fish and chips.
REAL MEAL The Orbit Café (next to the IMAX® Theater), the largest eatery in the Kennedy Space

Kids exploring the play area in the Children's Play Dome

Center, has pizza, barbecue, and sandwiches. Buy a Souvenir Sipper Cup and get free soda refills all day.
FAMILY TREAT Lunch With an Astronaut (in Astronaut Encounter) gives visitors a rare chance to converse and eat with an actual spaceman. Call 866 737 5235 to make a reservation.

Meeting veteran space explorers at Lunch with an Astronaut

Shopping

More than 3,000 space-themed items are available at **The Space Shop** (NASA Central; www.kennedyspace center.com/shopping; 9am–3pm) which covers an area of 15,372 sq ft (1,428 sq m). It is said to be the largest store in the world dedicated to space memorabilia and NASA gear, including T-shirts, commemorative medals, space-themed LEGO®, and even full replica flight suits. Gear and souvenirs can be personalized at the Customization Station.

Find out more

DIGITAL Visit NASA Kids' Club at www.nasa.gov/audience/forkids/ kidsclub/flash for contests and space-themed games featuring Buzz Lightyear for younger kids, and news and pictures taken from space by astronauts for older kids. National Geographic offers an interactive guide to the solar system at science.nationalgeographic.com/ science/space/solar-system.

Next stop...

NEARBY SPACE HISTORY To discover more about space history, head 13 miles (21 km) west to the **US Space Walk of Fame Museum** (4 Main St, Titusville, 32796; 321 264 0434), with displays on Mercury, Gemini, Apollo, and other shuttles. Or head 12 miles (19 km) east to the **Air Force Space and Missile Museum** (191 Museum

Timeline

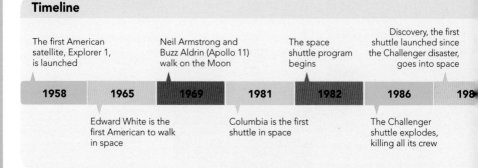

1958	1965	1969	1981	1982	1986	198

The first American satellite, Explorer 1, is launched — 1958

Neil Armstrong and Buzz Aldrin (Apollo 11) walk on the Moon — 1969

The space shuttle program begins — 1981

Discovery, the first shuttle launched since the Challenger disaster, goes into space — 1986

Edward White is the first American to walk in space — 1965

Columbia is the first shuttle in space — 1982

The Challenger shuttle explodes, killing all its crew — 1986

Circle, Patrick Air Force Base, 32925; 321 853 9171) to see restored items from the US Air Force's space launch activities. The **Valiant Air Command Warbird Museum** (6600 Tico Rd, Titusville, 32780; 321 268 1941; www.valiantair command.com), 8 miles (13 km) west of the Kennedy Space Center, is for those interested in terrestrial flight. The museum displays, repairs, and flies vintage airplanes.

Space shuttle model in the US Space Walk of Fame

The Lowdown

🌐 **Map reference** 6 H5
Address State Rd 405, Kennedy Space Center, 32899; 1 866 737 5235; www.kennedyspace center.com

🚗 **Car** Rent a car from Orlando.

🕑 **Open** 9am–6pm daily, closed Dec 25 and certain launch days

💲 **Prices** $140–180; under 3s free. Unlimited admission annual pass: $210–70; under 3s free

👥 **Cutting the line** Book tickets online and avoid visiting during holidays, the spring break in Mar, and late fall. Head for the Shuttle Launch Experience in the morning, as the lines get long later in the day.

🔫 **Guided tours** The KSC Bus Tour (included with admission) takes visitors to launch pads, the Vehicle Assembly Building (VAB), and the Apollo/Saturn V Center. For a comprehensive tour of the Center, visitors can try the KSC Explore Tour ($70–90 add-on to basic entry tickets; under 3s free), which is guided by an expert. Visitors can learn about sights such as the 525-ft

(160-m) tall VAB, where rockets are prepared for launch. Another tour, the Early Space Tour, takes visitors past historic launch sites at Cape Canaveral Air Force Station, and stops at the Air Force Space & Missile Museum. ($70–90; under 3s free). The free Rocket Garden tour (10:30am and 4pm daily) shows guests the rockets that helped power American astronauts into space.

👫 **Age range** 6 plus

👨‍👧 **Activities** Kids can ride in a Mars Rover simulator as well as a slowed-down G-force trainer in the Heroes and Legends exhibition.

⏱ **Allow** 4–8 hours

♿ **Wheelchair access** Yes

🚻 **Restrooms** At the Visitor Complex, IMAX® Theater, and all restaurants

Good family value?
Kids, and most adults, are fascinated by the space program, and the all-inclusive price is a bargain for an all-day experience.

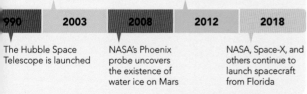

Space shuttle Columbia explodes on re-entry, killing all its crew

NASA's Curiosity Rover lands on Mars

| 990 | 2003 | 2008 | 2012 | 2018 |

The Hubble Space Telescope is launched

NASA's Phoenix probe uncovers the existence of water ice on Mars

NASA, Space-X, and others continue to launch spacecraft from Florida

② Merritt Island National Wildlife Refuge
The wildest place in Florida

With its dry coastal dunes and boggy marshes, the Merritt Island area is like a theme park built by nature. Established in 1963, the refuge covers an area twice the size of Orlando. More than 1,500 species of plants, mammals, and reptiles are found here, including endangered animals that live nowhere else. Many migratory birds visit between October and April, and many large birds, such as egrets and pelicans, live here year-round.

Manatees in the Observation Area

Key Sights

④ **Black Point Wildlife Drive** Follow the 7-mile (4-km) trail by car or set out on one of the hiking trails and look out for more than 50 species of birds. The connecting 5-mile (8-km) Cruickshank Trail loops through the marsh and back to the drive.

⑤ **Indian River Lagoon** The banks of these waterways, home to Native American tribes for thousands of years, offer the best spots to watch for wintering manatees and bottlenose dolphins.

⑥ **Manatee Observation Area** This deck on the northeast side of Haulover Canal offers close views of these endangered animals. In winter, when the sea temperature falls, several hundred can be seen.

⑦ **Canaveral National Seashore** White-sand beaches, tropical forest, lagoons, and cypress hammock make up this unspoiled 24-mile (39-km) stretch of coastline.

① **Playalinda Beach** This protected beach with pure, soft white sands and undisturbed vistas is one of the few beaches in Florida untouched by big hotels.

② **Visitor Information Center** Exhibits and hands-on presentations on the refuge's wildlife are regularly shown here. Climb the observation tower for fine views.

③ **Oak Hammock and Palm Hammock Foot Trails** The short Oak Hammock Trail is posted with educational signs explaining the area's ecology. The Palm Hammock Trail is a 2-mile (4-km) loop through hardwood forest with areas perfect for spotting songbirds.

The Lowdown

🌐 **Map reference** 6 H5
Address SR-402, Titusville, 32782; 321 861 0667; www.fws.gov/merrittisland

🚗 **Car** Rent a car from New Smyrna Beach or Orlando. The refuge begins at the east side of the Max Brewer Causeway.

🕐 **Open** Refuge: sunrise–sunset daily. Visitor Information Center: usually 10am–4pm. Hours vary by season; check website. Playalinda Beach: 6am–6pm daily (life guards are on duty May 30– Sept 1: 10am–5pm). Roads, trails, and boat ramps open daily from sunrise to sunset.

💲 **Price** Entry to the park is free, as are fishing permits. Black Point Wildlife Drive and boat docking: $5

🔫 **Guided tours** Driving tours of bird habitats (321 861 5601). Free guided hikes leave from the Visitor Information Center.

👫 **Age range** 9 plus (for walking trails); driving tours for younger children. Head for the southern end of Playalinda Beach, as the northern end is an unofficial clothing-free area.

👫 **Activities** The Visitor Center holds crafts workshops for kids.

⏱ **Allow** 1–8 hours

☕ **Café** No

🚻 **Restrooms** At the Visitor Center, Cruickshank Trail stop, and the parking areas at Playalinda Beach.

Good family value?
With free access to one of North America's last unspoiled wild areas, Merritt Island is great for outdoorsy families.

Prices given are for a family of four

View from the top of Turtle Mound, Canaveral National Seashore

Letting off steam

Merritt Island is a wilderness area, and disturbing the animals here by running and making a noise is frowned upon. Head for **Jetty Park Fishing Pier** in Cape Canaveral to catch and release fish in some of the best waters in the state, or check out **Seminole Rest** and **Turtle Mound** in the middle of the Canaveral National Seashore. These archaeological sites prove the presence of Native Americans here 4,000 years ago.

Eat and drink

Picnic: under $25; Snacks: $25–50; Real meal: $50–80; Family treat: over $80 (based on a family of four)

PICNIC Publix (*125 E Merritt Island Causeway, 32952; 321 452 0288*) stocks picnic supplies. Take your lunch to the Sendler Education Outpost Pavilion, near the Indian River Lagoon. It has picnic tables, running water, and restrooms.

SNACKS Taco City (*2955 S Atlantic Ave, Cocoa Beach, 32931; 321 784 1475; www.tacocity.net*) has a casual atmosphere and lots of easily-held-by-little-hands Tex-Mex items.

REAL MEAL Grills Seafood Deck & Tiki Bar (*505 Glen Cheek Dr, Cape Canaveral, 32920; 321 868 2226; www.grillsseafood.com*) offers locally caught seafood and outdoor seating by the water. Visitors can watch cruise ships and fishing boats sail by.

FAMILY TREAT The Fat Snook (*2464 S Atlantic Ave, Cocoa Beach, 32169; 321 784 1190; www.thefat snook.com*) is a modern Caribbean restaurant that serves interesting dishes such as coffee-rubbed steak and scallops with banana polenta. Call ahead to make a reservation.

Shopping

Choose from a variety of hats, caps, T-shirts, totes, badges, pins, and books at the gift shop in the **Visitor Center**.

Find out more

DIGITAL Go to *www.floridabirding trail.com* for a list of 500 sites across Florida ideal for bird-watching.
FILM *The Big Year* (2011), about watching rare birds, and starring Jack Black and Steve Martin, was partly filmed at Merritt Island.

Kids playing in the water near the Pier, Cocoa Beach

Take cover

If rain threatens, head 20 miles (32 km) south to the town of **Cocoa Beach** (*see p150*), which has ample restaurants and shops.

Next stop...

THE BOTANICAL GARDEN
Zip 40 miles (64 km) south to the Botanical Garden at the Florida Institute of Technology (*facilities.fit. edu/botanical_gardens.php*). This unique 15-acre (6-ha) garden is dotted with more than 300 species of ferns, palms, and tropical plants.

KIDS' CORNER

You're watching them...

It is easy to spot wild birds if you know what to look and listen for:
1 Bright colors. The blue wings of a scrub jay in the green trees, and a bright pink spoonbill in the dark water.
2 Songs. The high-pitched whistle of an osprey, or the "kuk-kuk-kuk" laugh of a pileated woodpecker.
3 Shadows. Eagles and hawks are usually silent, but they are very large and cast big shadows on the ground.
4 Movement. Wading birds like the gray Louisiana heron and the snow-white ibis stand still for a very long time to catch fish. See if you can spot them moving.

TREASURE HUNT

Borrow a GeoHunt kit and GPS device from the Visitor Center, and begin the hunt by car and on foot for the treasures of Merritt Island. Along the way, you'll be asked to find historical sites, spot birds of all kinds, and write down how long each trail is.

Not made of turtles
Turtle Mound, on Canaveral National Seashore, is called a midden – a big hill made from the shells of oysters eaten by early Native American settlers. It is more than 50 ft (15 m) high and can be seen 7 miles (11 km) out at sea.

...they're watching you

The freshwater ponds behind the Visitor Center have not-so-secret guests: live alligators who rest on the muddy banks and warm themselves in the sun. Look for the light reflected in their eyes, and if you're lucky, you'll hear the low, booming cough of a gator call.

Vacationers at the famous white-sand Cocoa Beach

③ Cocoa Beach and Pier

Eating, shopping, and fishing above; sunbathing below

The city of Cocoa Beach became famous because of its proximity to the Kennedy Space Center (see pp144–7), but it was popular long before rockets were launched from here. It nestles on a small barrier island bordered by a fertile lagoon and the warm waters of the Atlantic Ocean. Remains of ancient Native American villages prove that Cocoa was home to native Floridians for thousands of years, and shops, restaurants, and museums keep it lively today. The beach, with its soft white sand, stretches into relatively calm waters and has long been a major draw for visitors. There is always plenty of activity, from families building sand castles to surfers, and treasure-hunters with metal detectors. A landmark since 1962, the wooden **Pier** has bars, restaurants, and stores selling handcrafted gifts. Live concerts and festivals are also held right on the beach.

Take cover
Head for the **Dinosaur Store** (250 W Cocoa Beach Causeway, 32931; 321 783 7300; www.dinosaurstore.com), which has a vast selection of dinosaur teeth and replicas, meteorites, and toys. Kids will like the fake shrunken heads and arcade games.

④ Ron Jon Surf Shop, Cocoa Beach

Always open, always fun

Opened in 1964, this iconic shop has been here so long it has become a tourist destination in its own right. It has loads lined up for families: shop for swimsuits, board shorts, towels, or flip flops in the fun-looking two-story building

The Lowdown

🌐 **Map reference** 6 H6
Address 4151 North Atlantic Ave, Cocoa Beach, 32931; 321 799 8888; www.ronjons.com

🚗 **Car** Rent a car from Orlando International Airport.

🕐 **Open** 24 hours daily. Florida Surf Museum: 8am–8pm daily

👫 **Age range** 6 plus

⏱ **Allow** 30 mins–2 hours

♿ **Wheelchair access** Yes

🍴 **Eat and drink** SNACKS Simply Delicious Café & Bakery (125 N Orlando Ave, 32931; 321 783 2012) serves breakfast, sandwiches, and baked goods. REAL MEAL The Shark Pit (4001 N Atlantic Ave, 32931; www.cocoa beachsurf.com/SharkPit) has fish tacos, pizza, and a kids' menu.

👫 **Restrooms** On both floors

Wide variety of fascinating merchandise in the Ron Jon Surf Shop, Cocoa Beach

fronted by Hawaiian statues. The shop also has a huge selection of kitsch souvenirs, including Ron Jon stickers, tiki statues, keychains, and basically everything imaginable with the word "Florida" written on it. Serious surfers, too, shop here, and the assortment of boards and supplies is first-rate. Look out for discount coupons in hotel lobbies before visiting.

Visit the **Florida Surf Museum** (www.floridasurfmuseum.org), situated just north of the main store building. It screens movies and features exhibits on the history and heroes of surfing.

Letting off steam
Alan Shephard Park (299 E Cocoa Beach Causeway, 32931; 321 868 3258), two blocks away, offers ample opportunities to run around. There is also access to a white-sand beach, and restrooms.

The Lowdown

🌐 **Map reference** 6 H6
Address Pier: 401 Meade Ave, Cocoa Beach, 32931; 321 783 7549; cocoabeachpier.com/cbp

🚗 **Car** Rent a car from Orlando International Airport.

💲 **Price** Pier: $15 parking fee; check website for details.

👫 **Cutting the line** Avoid spring break in Mar, and surfing festivals in Apr and Sep, which draw massive crowds. On July 4, the firework display is spectacular.

🚶 **Guided tours** Wildside Tours (www.wildsidetours.com) runs a boat excursion from Cocoa Beach to the Banana River Lagoon to spot manatees and birds. A Day Away

Outfitters (www.adayawaykayak-tours.com) offers a nighttime kayak adventure on the Indian River Lagoon to observe bio-luminescence.

👫 **Age range** All ages

⏱ **Allow** 2 days

🍴 **Eat and drink** PICNIC Cocoa Beach Sunday Farmers' Market (City Hall, 2 S Orlando Ave, 32931; 321 917 0721; www.brevardfarmersmarkets.com) offers local produce and hand-made baked goods that can be enjoyed on the beach. REAL MEAL Pelican's Bar & Grill (on the Pier; 321 783 7549) offers freshly caught fish and a spectacular view from high above the Atlantic Ocean.

⑤ Brevard Museum of History and Natural Science

From mastodons to missiles

This charming museum offers a glimpse into the distant past and the technological present of central Florida – from prehistoric fossils to rocket ships. See re-creations of the archaeological dig of the area's oldest site and of ancient Native American villages to get an insight into Cocoa's origins. There are also exhibits on the space program and Brevard County's still-vibrant cattle-ranching. Items from the museum's own holdings about life in Florida are displayed alongside traveling collections.

Letting off steam

The ramped treehouse in the **Imagination Center** *(on site)* is a high-energy climb and run. The museum's park has nature trails that offer tree-shaded places to cool off.

The Lowdown

🌐 **Map reference** 6 H6
Address 2201 Michigan Ave, Cocoa, 32926; 321 632 1830; *www.brevardmuseum.org*

🚗 **Car** Rent a car from Orlando International Airport.

🕐 **Open** 10am–4pm Thu–Sat

💲 **Price** $21–31; under 4s free

🧍 **Cutting the line** Afternoon is the quietest time to visit.

🔫 **Guided tours** The museum runs a pre-arranged guided tour of the nature trails and exhibits for groups of 15 plus.

👫 **Age range** 6 plus

🖐 **Activities** There are hands-on activities in the Imagination Center.

⏱ **Allow** 1–3 hours

♿ **Wheelchair access** Yes

🍴 **Eat and drink** REAL MEAL Jabbers *(4365 Grissom Parkway, Cocoa, 32926; 321 638 4130)* offers hearty Southern food. FAMILY TREAT Heidelberg Restaurant *(7 N Orlando Ave, 32931; 321 783 4559)* serves German specialties and great home-made desserts.

👫 **Restrooms** In the lobby

Braving it on a zip line in Brevard Zoo, Melbourne

⑥ Brevard Zoo

Get up close to bobcats, whistling ducks, and giraffes

As if Florida were not wild enough, this modern, spacious zoo presents even more wild animals and habitats. In the Wild Florida area, see animals native to Florida such as alligators, bobcats, foxes, whistling ducks, and hawks. The also zoo has re-created African, Australian, and South American jungle habitats populated by exotic wildlife. Climb the 16-ft- (5-m-) high platform in the Expedition Africa zone to look into a giraffe's eye.

Letting off steam

The **Treetop Trek Chutes & Ladders** *(on site; www.treetoptrek.com)* activity course runs on rope bridges, tight-ropes, and zip lines through, around, and 20 ft (6 m) above the zoo.

The Lowdown

🌐 **Map reference** 6 H6
Address 8225 N Wickham Rd, Melbourne, 32940; 321 254 9453; *www.brevardzoo.org*

🚗 **Car** Rent a car from Orlando International Airport.

🕐 **Open** 9:30am–5pm daily (last admission 4:15pm)

💲 **Price** $60–70; under 2s free

🔫 **Guided tours** A host of tours are offered inside the zoo and in the connecting wetlands. A behind-the-scenes Wild Encounter tour is also available.

👫 **Age range** 2 plus

🖐 **Activities** Petting zoo, water park & Cape to Cairo Express train ride

⏱ **Allow** 1–3 hours

♿ **Wheelchair access** Yes

🍴 **Eat and drink** PICNIC Flamingo Café *(on site)* offers snacks and refreshments that can be eaten at the picnic tables outside the zoo. SNACKS Paws On Pizzeria *(on site)* serves sandwiches, pizza, and chicken.

Picnic under $25; **Snacks** $25–50; **Real meal** $50–80; **Family treat** over $80 (based on a family of four)

Where to Stay on the Space Coast

With more than 2,500 hotels and motels, prices and lodgings in this area range from low and basic to outrageous and ultra-luxurious. While most accommodations trumpet their proximity to the beaches, there are a few hidden gems that offer a unique experience in outdoor living.

AGENCY
Cocoa Beach Best
www.cocoabeachbest.com
Located in the heart of the Space Coast, this agency offers self-catering condominium rentals – from one-bedroom efficiency apartments and tower suites to five-bedroom pool homes – with nightly and weekly rates.

Cape Canaveral   Map 6 H6

RESORTS
Radisson Resort at the Port
8701 Astronaut Blvd, 32920; 321 784 0000; www.radisson.com
The closest resort to Port Canaveral allows views of incoming cruise ships from certain balconies. The outdoor recreation area features waterfalls and a hot tub. A microwave and refrigerator are available in each room, and breakfast is free. The Kennedy Space Center is a 30-minute drive away.
🜚 ⊙ $$

Royal Mansions Resort
8600 Ridgewood Ave, 32920, 321 784 8484; www.royalmansions.com
This resort offers oceanfront condo rentals on a private beach. Each apartment has a full kitchen, and outside there is a clubhouse with BBQ grills, hot tubs, and bike rentals, as well as a private walkway to the beach. Breakfast is included. A two-night minimum stay is required.
🜚 ⇴ P ⊙ ⊟ $$

Holiday Inn Club Vacations Cape Canaveral Beach Resort
1000 Shorewood Dr, 32920; 321 799 4900; www.ihg.com/ holidayinnclubvacations
Right on the white sand beach, this resort has a wild water park, a lazy river, and a large pool. Gaming facilities include those for mini-golf, tennis, and shuffleboard. Water sport rentals are available on the beach.
🜚 ⊙⃝ ⇴ ⊟ ⊙ ⊘ $$–$$$

Pirate-themed water park for kids at International Palms Resort, Cocoa Beach

HOTEL
Residence Inn Cape Canaveral Cocoa Beach
8959 Astronaut Blvd, 32920; 321 323 1100; www.marriott.com
Set amid lovely landscaped gardens and scenic beachside surroundings, these Key-West-style suites come with free breakfast and an evening social on Mondays through Wednesdays.
🜚 ⇴ ⊟ P ⊙ $$

CAMPING
Jetty Park Campground
400 Jetty Rd, 32920; 321 783 7111; www.jettyparkbeachand campground.com
A state-owned site offering over 150 pitches, from "rustic" – a tent beneath the trees – to "improved," with electricity and running water. There is fishing from the pier or beach, and facilities include a bait and tackle shop, laundry, and showers.
⊘ ⚲ $

Cocoa Beach   Map 6 H6

RESORTS
Beach Island Resort
1125 S Atlantic Ave, Cocoa Beach, 32931; 321 784 5720; www.beach islandresort.com
This family-friendly resort has one- and two-bedroom accommodations, with fully equipped kitchens and dining rooms. The white-sand beach is a short walk away, and

there is a heated pool and hot tub on the resort premises.
🜚 🜚 ⇴ ⊟ ⊙ $–$$

International Palms Resort
1300 N Atlantic Ave, 32931; 321 783 2271; www.internationalpalms cocoabeach.com
An extensive beachside resort, the Palms offers suites and bunked-equipped "family fun rooms." Youngsters will love the game room and pirate-themed water park. Adults can use the gym and fitness center, and tennis and shuffleboard courts. Surfboard rental is available.
🜚 ⊙⃝ ⇴ ⊙ ⊘ $–$$

Discovery Beach Resort
300 Barlow Ave, 32931; 321 868 7777; www.discoverybeachresort.com
This condo rental of one-, two-, and three-bedroom suites has views of the beach, perfect for watching giant cruise ships sail by on their way to Port Canaveral. Full kitchens, hot tubs and sauna, tennis and basketball courts, as well as an arcade room, keep everyone busy.
⊙⃝ ⇴ ⊟ ⊙ ⊘ $$

The Resort on Cocoa Beach
1600 N Atlantic Ave, 32931; 321 783 4000; www.theresorton cocoabeach.com
A few minutes from the Kennedy Space Center, this condo rental resort has two-bedroom suites with balconies and ocean views. Along with a fitness center, there are shuffleboard and beach volleyball courts, and screenings of family-friendly movies. Kids can play on the private beach or in the game room.
🜚 ⊙⃝ ⇴ ⊙ ⊘ $$

HOTELS
Four Points Cocoa Beach
4001 N Atlantic Ave, 32931; 321 783 8717; www.fourpointscocoabeach.com
Housed within the "World's Largest Surf Complex," this hotel has a bright, surfer-style decor that

makes it look like something from *SpongeBob SquarePants*. Some rooms come with views into the shopping and entertainment area, which offers a huge shark and exotic fish aquarium as well as shops and beach rentals.

🔊 |◎| P ⊗　　　　$$

The Inn at Cocoa Beach
4300 Ocean Beach Blvd, 32931; 321 799 3460; www.theinnatcocoa beach.com
Many of the 50 rooms in this French-country-style inn offer both pool and ocean views, while others have Jacuzzi tubs and private balconies with sea views. There are exercise and massage rooms, and a steam bath. Breakfast is free and there is an afternoon wine and cheese bar for adults.

🔊 ⊗ ◐　　　　$$$

MOTELS
LaQuinta Inn Cocoa Beach
1275 N. Atlantic Ave, 32931; www.lq.com
This property was once owned by the original astronauts, and is located just a two-minute walk from the beach and pier. Breakfast and Wi-Fi are free.

🔊 🗗 P ⊗　　　　$

Anthony's on the Beach
3499 S Atlantic Ave, 32931; 321 784 8829; www.anthonysonthebeach.com
Built in 1958, Anthony's is a slice of old Florida beach life. The 19 efficiency rentals have full kitchens and dining areas. The motel is off the main road and affords a bit of quiet in an otherwise traffic-heavy area. The beach is right outside the door.

🔊 ⇆ ⊡ ⊗　　　　$$

SELF-CATERING
Wakulla Suites
3550 N Atlantic Ave, 32931; 321 783 2230; wakullasuites.com
Family-owned since 1972, this property of two-bedroom suites offers a tropical courtyard setting and a backyard beach with volleyball nets. There is an arcade game room and a lobby snack bar. Beach chair and kayak rentals are available.

🔊 ⇆ ⊡ P ⊗　　　　$

Beach Place Guesthouses
1445 S Atlantic Ave, 32931; 321 783 4045; beachplaceguesthouses.com
This complex of 16 guesthouses, is located in a quiet residential neighborhood and is just steps from the beach. The property has three decks with ocean views, hammocks, oversize lounges, and a garden for relaxing.

🔊 ⇆ ⊗ ◐　　　　$$$

Melbourne Beach
RESORT　　　　Map 8 G1
Seashell Suites Resort
8795 S Hwy A1A, 32951; 321 409 0500; www.seashellsuites.com
An interesting combination of luxury resort and eco-friendly environment, this place was built with non-toxic, nature-friendly materials. A secluded getaway, it offers eight two-bedroom suites, a brick sundeck, and a private beach.

🔊 ⇆ ⊗　　　　$$

BED & BREAKFAST
Port d'Hiver Bed and Breakfast
201 Ocean Ave, 32951; 321 722 2727; www.portdhiver.com
This B&B has the air of a boutique hotel. Each of the 11 rooms and suites are individually styled. Room service is available at breakfast. Light hors d'oeuvres are served in the early evening.

🔊 ⇆ P ⊗　　　　$$–$$$

Titusville　　　　Map 6 G5
HOTELS
Days Inn Kennedy Space Center
3755 Cheney Hwy, 32780; 321 269 4480; www.wyndhamhotels.com
Located closer to Brevard Zoo than the Kennedy Space Center, this pet-friendly hotel offers laundry facilities and a 24-hour front desk service.

🔊 |◎| ⇆ ⊗　　　　$

Holiday Inn Titusville-Kennedy Space Center
4715 Helen Hauser Blvd, 32780; 321 383 0200; www.ihg.com
Up to four children aged 12 and under eat free at the on-site Bapa's Bistro restaurant with the Kids Eat Free program. In addition, every room comes with a mini-refrigerator and microwave. There is also a fitness center, and cribs are available.

🔊 |◎| 🗗 ⊗　　　　$

CAMPING
Manatee Hammock Camp Grounds
7275 South US Hwy 1, 32780; 321 264 5083; www.brevardcounty.us/parks recreation/north/ManateeHammock
Great wildlife-viewing opportunities await in the extensive grounds around these 35 campsites, which offer water and electricity, hot showers, and laundry facilities. A two-night minimum stay is required.

🔊 ⊗　　　　$

Spacious and elegantly styled suite in Port d'Hiver Bed and Breakfast, Melbourne Beach

Price Guide
The following price ranges are based on one night's accommodation in high season for a family of four, inclusive of service charges and additional taxes.
$ Under $150 **$$** $150–300 **$$$** over $300

The Northeast

The First Coast has been attracting visitors for centuries – the first European to set foot here was Spanish explorer Juan Ponce de León, in 1513. By 1562, Pedro Menendez had established a Spanish colony at St. Augustine. Long before the 1920s tourist boom in Miami, the Northeast's great weather and superb beaches meant it was a mecca for visitors; today's vacationers can add to these a host of newer family attractions.

Highlights

Fernandina Beach
From the shrimp fleet's docks to the Victorian-era homes, historic Fernandina Beach is a great place to stroll, shop, and restaurant-hop (see p166).

Timucuan Ecological and Historic Preserve
Hike through a maritime forest to the beach, investigate the past at a historic plantation, and learn to canoe, at the Talbot Islands park system (see pp164–5).

Jacksonville Zoo and Gardens
Pet the stingrays, feed the giraffes, roar with the jaguars, ride a tiger on the wildlife carousel, and see animals in their natural habitats in this award-winning zoo with more than 1,500 inhabitants (see pp162–3).

St. Augustine
Walk through this fascinating "Ancient City," founded in 1565, with its historic district allowing a look back into the past (see pp168–9).

Museum of Arts and Sciences (MOAS)
With its planetarium, Ice Age fossils, historic teddy bears, and an interactive children's center, this Daytona Beach museum is always a hit with families (see pp176–7).

Left A canopied street in the historic city of St. Augustine
Above right Row of Spanish cannons at the sprawling 17th-century Castillo de San Marcos, St. Augustine

The Best of
The Northeast

While central Florida has famous theme parks and southern Florida plenty of glamour, the Northeast showcases the state in all its natural beauty. The region not only has many miles of soft-sand beaches, but also remarkably diverse parks where families can swim, shell, hike, fish, and kayak. In addition, numerous attractions, historic sites, and kid-friendly museums keep every member of the family entertained.

Park it here

Northeastern Florida boasts a number of unusual sights – there are no cookie-cutter parks here. Begin the tour at **Big Talbot Island State Park's** *(see p164)* Boneyard Beach – its huge windswept skeletons of oaks and cedars create a landscape unlike any other. Head farther south to see herds of plains bison and Florida Cracker cows in **Paynes Prairie Preserve State Park** *(see p180)* near Ocala. Cool off at **Blue Spring State Park** *(see p178)*, close to Orange City, where manatees like to spend the winter. Round it off by going down all 236 steps into the miniature rain forest at the bottom of the sinkhole known as the **Devil's Millhopper Geological State Park** *(see p181)*, near Gainesville.

Historic encounters

Watch skilled re-enactors bring Florida's history to life at historic sites across the region. At **Fort Clinch State Park** *(see p166)* in **Fernandina**

Left Snorkelers in the clear waters of Blue Spring State Park, located a few miles southwest of Daytona Below Families go-karting at Adventure Landing, Jacksonville Beach

Above *Massive fossilized sharks' jaws at the Florida Museum of Natural History, University of Florda, Gainesville*
Right *A lioness basking in the sun in the Africa Loop section, Jacksonville Zoo and Gardens, Jacksonville*

Beach *(see p166)*, soldiers re-create life at the fort during the Civil War. But **St. Augustine** *(see pp168–9)* offers the best opportunity to see life as it was lived in the 1740s. There are several places in the Old Town area that feature costumed actors on a daily basis, and the city also hosts large-scale events regularly. Two of the most popular annual events are the **Sack of St. Augustine** *(see p14)* – with more than 60 buccaneers, Spanish soldiers, and townspeople – and the British Night Watch, when families can join the parade of British guards who march by the light of candles and lanterns to secure the city.

Scientifically speaking

Children who have an inclination for science will love the Northeast's great museums and research centers. Start a science trek in the **Museum of Science & History** *(see p160)* at **Jacksonville** *(see pp160–61)*, then spend some time at the **Environmental Education Center** *(see p171)* at Ponte Vedra beach. They offer great summer programmes, eco-educational activities as well as interpretive exhibits that are both, informative and enjoyable. Space buffs will not want to miss the planetarium in the **Museum of Arts and Sciences** *(see pp176–7)* in Daytona Beach *(see pp174–5)*. End the final leg of the trip at the **Florida Museum of Natural History** *(see p180)* in Gainesville – one of the top five natural history museums in the US and the largest "Smithsonian of the south."

The big three

Hit northern Florida's high spots with a trip to its three urban hubs. Begin at **Jacksonville**, which offers the lure of the local NFL team – the Jacksonville Jaguars – as well as real jaguars in its award-winning **Jacksonville Zoo and Gardens** *(see pp162–3)*. Kids will also like the fun games and water rides at **Adventure Landing** *(see p160)*. A half-hour drive south is **St. Augustine** and its myriad historic sites and outstanding restaurants. Cannon firings at **Castillo de San Marcos** *(see p170)*, and the ghost tour at **St. Augustine Lighthouse** *(see p172)* are true kid-pleasers. After a tour of **St. Augustine**, cruise down A1A to **Daytona Beach**, with a stopover at **Washington Oaks Gardens State Park** *(see p173)* for a picnic before heading for the city's famous **Public beaches** *(see p174)* and the **Boardwalk** *(see p174)*. Don't miss the **Museum of Arts and Sciences**, a hidden gem with an outstanding interactive children's section.

The Northeast

Some of the most intriguing views of Northeast Florida can be found along SR A1A as it winds through a string of quirky beach towns. Although it is hard to compete with 120 miles (193 km) of white-sand beaches, this region has many other sights worth visiting. Jacksonville and Daytona Beach offer the big-city experience; Fernandina Beach is a quaint town with superb state parks nearby; and St. Augustine boasts a venerable Spanish heritage. Jacksonville is the main transportation hub for the region. Several east–west routes link the coast and I-75, inland.

Splashing in the fountains near the Daytona Beach Boardwalk

The Lowdown

🚗 **Getting there and around**
Air Jacksonville (*www.flyjackson ville.com*) and Daytona Beach (*www.flydaytonafirst.com*) have international airports. **Train** Amtrak (*www.amtrak.com*) trains stop at Jacksonville, with two routes south – one inland through Gainesville and Ocala, and another route with stops in Palatka, Deland, and Sanford, which is the terminus of the Auto Train Amtrak. **Car** Avis (*www.avis.com*) and Hertz (*www.hertz.com*) have offices at airports.

ℹ️ **Visitor information** Visit the tourist information center at Jacksonville International Airport, which is located near the baggage carousel (*904 741 3044*), for information on Jacksonville, Amelia Island/ Fernandina Beach, and St. Augustine.

🛒 **Supermarkets** Publix (*www.publix.com*) and Winn-Dixie (*www.winndixie.com*) have outlets throughout this region. **Markets** The Jacksonville Farmers' Market (*www.jax farmersmarket.com*) sells fresh produce from more

than 200 farmers from dawn to dusk daily.

🎌 **Festivals** Daytona 500, Daytona Beach; *www.daytona internationalspeedway.com* (Feb). Hoggetowne Medieval Faire, Gainesville; *www.hogge townefaire.com* (Jan). Springing the Blues, Jacksonville Beach; *www.springingtheblues.com* (Apr). Jacksonville Jazz Festival; *www.jacksonvillejazzfest.com* (May)

🕐 **Opening hours** Business hours are usually 9am–5pm. Shops open at 10am. Smaller shops may close at 5 or 7pm, but larger stores are often open until 9pm, except Sundays, when stores generally open 11am or noon and close 6 or 7pm. Banks are usually open 8am–3pm Mon–Fri, although many stay open later.

➕ **Pharmacies** Check Publix, Walgreens (*www.walgreens.com/ pharmacy*) or CVS (*www.cvs.com/ pharmacy*) for 24-hour pharmacy locations throughout the region.

🚻 **Restrooms** Almost all major attractions, restaurants, and malls, and most gas stations, have public restrooms.

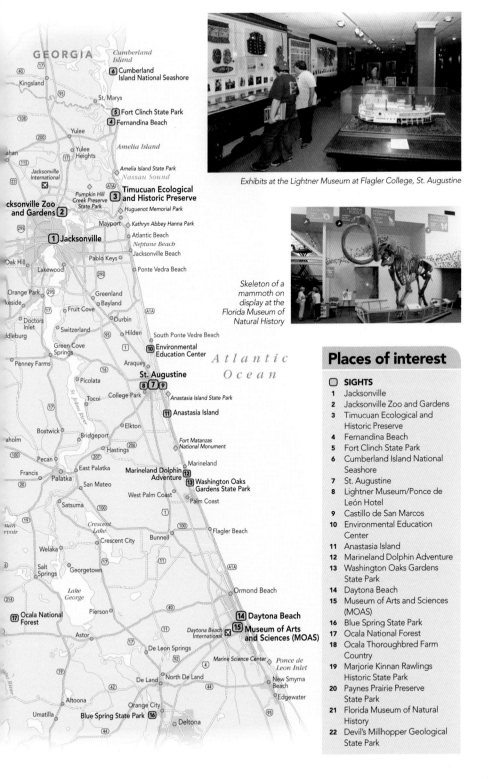

Exhibits at the Lightner Museum at Flagler College, St. Augustine

Skeleton of a mammoth on display at the Florida Museum of Natural History

Places of interest

☐ **SIGHTS**

1 Jacksonville
2 Jacksonville Zoo and Gardens
3 Timucuan Ecological and Historic Preserve
4 Fernandina Beach
5 Fort Clinch State Park
6 Cumberland Island National Seashore
7 St. Augustine
8 Lightner Museum/Ponce de León Hotel
9 Castillo de San Marcos
10 Environmental Education Center
11 Anastasia Island
12 Marineland Dolphin Adventure
13 Washington Oaks Gardens State Park
14 Daytona Beach
15 Museum of Arts and Sciences (MOAS)
16 Blue Spring State Park
17 Ocala National Forest
18 Ocala Thoroughbred Farm Country
19 Marjorie Kinnan Rawlings Historic State Park
20 Paynes Prairie Preserve State Park
21 Florida Museum of Natural History
22 Devil's Millhopper Geological State Park

① Jacksonville
A city for all seasons

Founded in 1822, Jacksonville flourished as a port and railroad hub in the late 19th century. The largest city in Florida, it has the lion's share of the Northeast's major cultural attractions – museums with outstanding kids' programs, large concert venues, and an award-winning zoo. With great weather almost year-round, the city and its beaches offer plenty to do outdoors, too. Due to the size of the city, it is essential to rent a car to get around.

Cummer Museum of Art and Gardens

Key Sights

① **Cummer Museum of Art and Gardens** Play with digital paint on giant canvases, dance to create colorful patterns, and explore all forms of art at the Art Connections program in this museum.

② **Museum of Science and History (MOSH)** The KidSpace educational play area, a next-generation planetarium, and a schedule of thrilling shows make MOSH a huge draw for families.

③ **Jacksonville Landing** Shop at classy stores, dine in the international food court, and catch exciting events at this entertainment complex.

④ **Museum of Contemporary Art (MOCA)** Five galleries filled with modern and contemporary art, plus interactive fun at the ArtExplorium Loft await visitors at this impressive museum.

⑤ **EverBank Field** From major concerts, symphony performances, and outdoor festivals to NFL football with the Jacksonville Jaguars, this 76,000-seat facility hosts some of the biggest events in Jacksonville.

⑥ **Adventure Landing and Shipwreck Island Waterpark** There is lots to please kids at this theme park, including miniature golf, laser tag, go-karts, and a game arcade, as well as water rides in summer.

The Lowdown

🌐 **Map reference** 4 G3
Address Cummer Museum of Art and Gardens: 829 Riverside Ave, 32204; 904 356 6857; www.cummer.org. Museum of Science and History (MOSH): 1025 Museum Circle, 32207; 904 396 7062; www.themosh.org. Jacksonville Landing: 2 W Independent Dr, 32202; 904 353 1188; www.jacksonvillelanding.com. Museum of Contemporary Art (MOCA): Hemming Plaza, 333 N Laura St., 32202; 904 366 6911; www.mocajacksonville.unf.edu. EverBank Field: 300 A Philip Randolph Blvd, 32202;

904 633 6100; www.jaxevents.com/tickets. Adventure Landing: 1944 Beach Blvd, Jacksonville Beach, 32250; 904 246 4386; www.adventurelanding.com

🚗 **Bus** Jacksonville Transportation Authority (JTA) buses and shuttles serve the city and its beaches (www.jtafla.com). **Car** Rent a car from Jacksonville Airport.

ℹ️ **Visitor information** 208 N Laura St, Ste 102, 32202; 904 798 9111; www.visitjacksonville.com

🕐 **Open** Cummer Museum of Art and Gardens & Museum of Contemporary Art (MOCA):

closed Mon. EverBank Field: call 904 630 3900 for event timings or check website. All other sights are open daily.

💲 **Prices** Cummer Museum of Art and Gardens: $26–32; under 5s free. Museum of Science and History (MOSH): $40–46; under 3s free ($5 for all ages Fri). Jacksonville Landing: free. Museum of Contemporary Art (MOCA): $26–32; under 2s free; free for families on Sun. EverBank Field: ticket prices vary. Adventure Landing and Shipwreck Island Waterpark: attractions are individually priced. Waterpark

Lakeside picnic tables in Kathryn Abbey Hanna Park

Letting off steam

Go 15 miles (24 km) east to Atlantic Beach, where **Kathryn Abbey Hanna Park** (www.coj.net) offers swimming, surfing, biking, and a freshwater lake with a water playground for younger kids. Older kids can opt for canoes and kayaks.

Eat and drink

Picnic: under $25; Snacks: $25–50; Real meal: $50–80; Family treat: over $80 (based on a family of four)

PICNIC Publix at Riverside (2033 Riverside Ave, 32204; 904 381 8610; www.publix.com), a few minutes from downtown, has a good deli. Picnic in Memorial Park, just across Riverside Avenue.
SNACKS Cool Moose Cafe and Bistro (2708 Park St, 32204, 904 381 4242; www.coolmoosecafe.net), close to the attractions in downtown, has fresh cookies and muffins.
REAL MEAL Singleton's Seafood Shack (4728 Ocean St, Mayport, 32233; 904 246 4442) is a simple restaurant that serves tasty seafood dishes. It was well reviewed by The

New York Times and was featured on *Diners, Drive-Ins and Dives*.
FAMILY TREAT Cheesecake Factory (St. Johns Town Center™, 4663 River City Dr, 32246, www.stjohns towncenter.com) offers not just delectable cheesecakes, but also sandwiches, pizza, pasta, salads, and steaks.

Shopping

Drop in at **Peterbrooke Chocolatier** (2024 San Marco Blvd, 32207; 904 398 2488 www.peterbrooke.com) to pick up gourmet chocolates, and then take a tour of their production facility just down the street. The **St. Johns Town Center™**, a shopping and entertainment venue, houses many kids' apparel stores. Younger children will enjoy the kids' train and the koi pond.

Find out more

DIGITAL In 1864, a Union transport ship named the *Maple Leaf* was sunk by a Confederate torpedo in the St. Johns River, where it stayed until 1989. Take a look at what divers were able to bring up from the bottom more than 100 years later on www.themosh.org/curator.html.

Strolling the peaceful American Beach, Amelia Island State Park

Next stop...

BRIDGE TO THE ISLANDS
Broward Bridge, across the St. Johns River, is the gateway to **Amelia Island** (www.amelia island.com) and **Fernandina Beach** (see p166). This impressive bridge is more commonly known as the Dames Point Bridge by locals, and the "bowtie bridge" by kids.

(seasonal): $32.99 for guests 42 in (106 cm) and taller, $24.99 under 42 in (106 cm) tall; under 3s free

Cutting the line Most beaches and attractions are rarely crowded, except on summer weekends.

Age range 4 plus

Allow 2–3 days

Festivals Springing the Blues in Jacksonville Beach (Apr). Jacksonville Jazz Festival (May).

Good family value?
A good mix of inexpensive family-friendly attractions makes the city a great option to suit all budgets.

KIDS' CORNER

A river that flows north!

1 The St. Johns River is unusual because, like the Nile in Africa, it is one of the few rivers that flow south to north.
2 The river averages more than 2 miles (3 km) in width between Palatka and Jacksonville.
3 It drops only 30 ft (10 m)

 from its source to the sea, making it one of the laziest rivers in the world.

Sharks' teeth
You shouldn't expect to find an enormous tooth like you would see in a shop, though you might get lucky. Check the patches of small shells along the waterline for something tiny, black, and shiny.

REALLY THE BIGGEST?

Jacksonville is thought to be "the largest city in the US" in terms of square miles. But that's not really accurate – it's just the largest in the contiguous 48 states (the 48 that touch each other). Yakutat, in Alaska, is really the largest city, with 9,459 sq miles (15,223 sq km) of land area.

Saving sand dollars in the sandbank

The wide beaches of Jacksonville are scattered with more than 50 kinds of local shells that are fun to find and save. Look for lightning whelks, olives, angel wings, baby's ear moonsnails, scallops, and even a "Florida jewel box." The best time to find shells is at low tide, especially in late fall, after storms.

② Jacksonville Zoo and Gardens

Into the wild on a walking safari

Opened in 1914, Jacksonville Zoo started out with just one red deer. Today, it has grown into an award-winning regional zoo with more than 1,500 animals; among them are fierce-looking Komodo dragons, playful gorillas and bonobos, docile giraffes, high-spirited elephants in their massive pool, and delightful penguins. Extensive boardwalks with specially designed overlooks meander throughout this huge zoo, allowing visitors to experience a "walking safari."

Entry to the Range of the Jaguar exhibit

Key Features

The Lowdown

🌐 **Map reference** 4 G3
Address 370 Zoo Pkwy, Jacksonville, 32218; 904 757 4463; www.jacksonvillezoo.org

🚌 **Bus** Call Jacksonville Transportation Authority (JTA) Ride Request service (904 598 8724). **Car** Rent a car from Jacksonville. Free parking

🕐 **Open** 9am–5pm Mon–Fri (till 6pm Sat & Sun)

💲 **Prices** $55–70; under 3s free. The zoo charges additional fees for Stingray Bay ($2 per person), unlimited train rides ($4 per person), and unlimited carousel rides ($2 per person). Value Tickets include admission, Butterfly Hollow, Stingray Bay, and unlimited train and carousel rides ($83–106; under 3s free).

🧍 **Cutting the line** Buy tickets online and arrive early to avoid the crowds.

🔫 **Guided tours** The zoo offers many Behind the Scenes tours. Check website for details.

👫 **Age range** 2 plus

⏱ **Allow** 4–6 hours

♿ **Wheelchair access** Yes

☕ **Café** Several in the zoo (see p163)

🛍 **Shops** Many throughout the zoo (see p163)

🚻 **Restrooms** At the Main Camp Safari Lodge at the entrance

Good family value?

Exciting animals, carousel rides, and a train tour, along with affordable admission prices, make this zoo great for visitors of all ages.

Prices given are for a family of four

Entrance

① **Wild Florida** Florida's treasured wildlife is the focus of this exhibit. Check out more than two dozen species of reptiles and amphibians in the Reptile House.

② **River Valley Aviary** See a variety of birds, from Inca terns to colorful macaws, in this aviary. Also see the world's smallest deer and the largest freshwater fish.

③ **Stingray Bay** This interactive exhibit allows visitors to observe, touch, and feed stingrays.

④ **Play Park** Kids can cool off in the huge Splash Ground or find their way out of a hedge maze in this park. See penguins at close quarters in the Tuxedo Coast exhibit.

⑤ **Carousel and Zoo Train** The classic Wildlife Carousel with beautiful animal figures is a kid-pleaser. Don't miss a ride around the zoo on the Zoo Train.

⑥ **Asia and Australia** While the Komodo dragon exhibit steals the show at Monsoon Asia, kangaroos and wallabies delight visitors at the Australian Adventure exhibit.

⑦ **Range of the Jaguar** This award-winning jaguar exhibit also features a replica of a Mayan temple that is home to boa constrictors and bushmaster snakes.

⑧ **Africa Loop** Walk along an elevated boardwalk to view African animals, such as pelicans and zebras, in re-creations of their natural habitat. The African Reptile Building has cobras and mambas.

Kids feeding giraffes from the Giraffe Overlook, an elevated viewing area

Take cover
If it rains, head to one of the zoo's many indoor exhibits. The **Discovery Building**, in the Play Park area, runs excellent interactive educational programs for kids.

Eat and drink
Picnic: under $25; Snacks: $25–50; Real meal: $50–80; Family treat: over $80 (based on a family of four)

PICNIC Bring provisions from Jacksonville *(see p161)* for a picnic adjacent to the parking lot.
SNACKS Main Camp Café *(at the entrance),* a snack bar, serves popcorn, ice cream, and coffee.
REAL MEAL Palm Plaza Café *(in Range of the Jaguar)* has tacos, nachos, burritos, sandwiches, and salads on its Southwestern menu. The **Trout River Grille** *(near the Gardens at Trout River Plaza)* tempts with sandwiches, hot dogs, pretzels, and hamburgers.
FAMILY TREAT Junior's Seafood *(9349 N Main St, 32218; 904 751 9180),* a local favorite, is a spotlessly kept restaurant and grill, known for its superb food and efficient service. There are seafood dishes, burgers, pastas, and steaks on the menu.

Main Camp Café, a food kiosk in Main Camp Safari Lodge

Mombasa Gift Shop, one of the three gift shops in the zoo

Shopping
Drop in at **Mombasa Gift Shop** *(at Main Camp),* **Village Market** *(in Range of the Jaguar),* or **The Kids' Shop** *(near the train station)* to pick up plush toys, trinkets, apparel, puzzles, and other goodies.

Find out more
DIGITAL Visit *www.jacksonville zoo.org/things/kidzone* for fun games, coloring pages, and quirky animal trivia.

Next stop...
HUGUENOT MEMORIAL PARK
A horseshoe-shaped peninsula, the Huguenot Memorial Park *(10980 Heckscher Dr, 32226; 904 251 3335)* is popular with local families, surfers, and windsurfers. The park, 15 miles (24 km) east, is home to a variety of wildlife, and offers plenty of surfing, bird-watching, and windsurfing opportunities. Although the park gets crowded in summer, it can be an enjoyable outing in early spring or late fall. Be sure to check the tide tables *(www.srh.weather.gov/jax/tides.shtml)* – the shallow tidal pools are great for younger kids. Driving on the beach is allowed, but be warned – it is easy to get stuck in the sand.

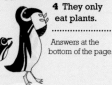

③ Timucuan Ecological and Historic Preserve

Marshes, highlands, and rivers galore

From highlands and rivers, to 40 miles (65 km) of Atlantic beaches, these state parks offers a chance to explore a range of natural habitats. Families can choose from many outdoor adventures such as fishing, canoeing, kayaking, surfing. Be sure to carry sunscreen, insect repellent, drinking water, and a picnic – the parks don't sell food or drink.

Aboard the St. Johns River Ferry from Jacksonville

Key Sights

① **Yellow Bluff Fort Historic State Park** Hike and picnic in this small peaceful park, a Civil War site that was used as an encampment by both Confederate and Union soldiers at different times.

② **Fort George Island Cultural State Park** Attractions here include the Ribault Club visitor center and the Kingsley Plantation (see p165) – the oldest plantation home in Florida.

③ **Little Talbot Island State Park** Noted for its stunning beach, the park offers campsites within walking distance of the ocean, complete with picnic pavilions and bathhouses.

④ **Pumpkin Hill Creek Preserve State Park** A vast area of uplands with miles of hiking and biking trails, this park also has great launch sites for kayaking and canoeing.

⑤ **Big Talbot Island State Park** With skeletal remains of oak trees scattered along its shore, Boneyard Beach is this park's best-known attraction.

⑥ **George Crady Bridge Fishing Pier** This mile-long pedestrian bridge across Nassau Sound is a favorite with North Florida anglers.

⑦ **Amelia Island State Park** Swim at a beautiful beach, hike through the coastal forest, fish from the shore, and kayak through creeks and marshes in this park.

Take cover

Head for the **Ribault Club** visitor center (www.nps.gov) to check out exhibits on the environment and culture of northeastern Florida.

Eat and drink

Picnic: under $25; Snacks: $25–50; Real meal: $50–80; Family treat: over $80 (based on a family of four)

PICNIC Marché Burette Deli (6800 First Coast Hwy, Amelia Island, 32034; 904 491 4834; www.

omnihotels.com) has deli items, sandwiches, and more. Picnic on the Amelia Island State Park beach.
SNACKS Long Island Outfitters (13030 Heckscher Dr, 32266; 904 251 0016; www.kayakamelia.com) sells beverages and healthy snacks.
REAL MEAL Sliders Seaside Grill (1998 S Fletcher Dr, 32034; 904 277 6652; www.slidersseaside.com) serves seafood dishes and tasty desserts. There is a playground and sandbox for kids, as well as a tiki bar and live music for grown-ups.

Play area for kids in the informal Sliders Seaside Grill

Prices given are for a family of four

The Lowdown

🌐 **Map reference** 4 H3
Address Yellow Bluff Fort: New Berlin Rd, 32226; 904 251 2320. Fort George Island: 11676 Palmetto Ave, 32226; 904 251 3537. Little Talbot Island, Big Talbot Island, Amelia Island & George Crady Bridge Fishing Pier: State Rd A1A/Heckscher Dr, 32226; 904 251 2320. Pumpkin Hill Creek Preserve: 13802 Pumpkin Hill Rd, 32226; 904 696 5980. Check www.floridastateparks.org for all parks.

🚗 **Car** Rent a car from Jacksonville International Airport.

🕐 **Open** Yellow Bluff Fort, Little Talbot Island, Big Talbot Island, Amelia Island & Pumpkin Hill Creek Preserve: 8am–sunset daily. Fort George Island: 8am–sunset daily. George Crady Bridge Fishing Pier: 24 hours daily

💲 **Prices** Yellow Bluff Fort, Fort George Island & Pumpkin Hill Creek Preserve: free. Little Talbot Island & Amelia Island: $5 per vehicle & $2 per pedestrian and cyclist. Big Talbot Island: $3 per vehicle. George Crady Bridge Fishing Pier: $2 per person (admission to Amelia Island includes pier access)

🚻 **Cutting the line** Parks are rarely crowded, except on holiday weekends, but book campsites and tours well in advance.

🔫 **Guided tours** Kelly Seahorse Ranch (904 491 5166) offers guided horseback-riding on the beach at Amelia Island. Kayak Amelia (904 251 0016) runs kayak, Segway, and canoe tours.

👫 **Age range** All ages for beaches; 5 plus for exhibits and tours

🏃 **Activities** Check websites for ranger programs.

⏱ **Allow** 1–4 hours at each park

♿ **Wheelchair access** Limited; call 850 245 2157

🚻 **Restrooms** At all parks, except Yellow Bluff Fort and Pumpkin Hill Creek Preserve

Good family value?
With a fantastic mix of outdoor activities, history, and culture, these state parks are a big draw for active families.

FAMILY TREAT Café 4750 (4750 Amelia Island Pkwy, 32034; 904 277 1100; www.ritzcarltonhotel.com), in the Ritz-Carlton on Amelia Island, offers a choice of indoor or terrace dining, and a menu with farm and coastal influences. Reserve ahead.

Shopping
Visit **Island Outfitters** (235 E Gulf Beach Dr, 32328; 850 927 2604; sgioutfitters.com) on St. George's Island for handcrafted necklaces, T-shirts, beach bags, and flip flops.

Next stop...
KINGSLEY PLANTATION Located on the northern tip of Fort George Island, this plantation (www.nps.gov/timu) was named for Zephaniah Kingsley, who owned four major plantations in the area. In 1814, he and his wife Anna Madgigine Jai made the island their main residence, and more than 100 slaves worked on the plantation. Walk the grounds to see the remains of slave cabins, the "Ma'am Anna" house, a barn, a kitchen house, and the main clapboard house.

The clapboard house surrounded by trees and lawns, Kingsley Plantation

KIDS' CORNER

Test your "bird brain"
See if you can spot the following birds at the park, using these descriptors:
1 Sandwich tern
These birds have shaggy black crests (crown on the head) and yellow-tipped black bills.
2 Laughing gull
Look out for long, red beaks and reddish-black to black legs.
3 Great blue heron
These herons have very hairy heads, chests and wings, and yellowish bills.

BLACK-MASKED BANDITS
If you're camping in northeastern Florida, a raccoon might want to steal your food. Just latching the cooler won't do. In one study, scientists found that it took fewer than ten tries for raccoons to figure out complex locks. Ask a park ranger for advice on keeping your food safe from raccoons.

Digging into the past
Native Americans lived on the Talbot Islands for thousands of years before Europeans arrived, and the area was the site of dozens of little settlements and hunting camps. More than 400 years ago, the Spanish mission San Juan del Puerto was established on Fort George Island, as well as smaller missions called *visitas* (visitors). Archaeologists' explorations indicate that one named "Sarabay" was on Big Talbot Island.

④ Fernandina Beach

Shrimps and small-town charm

Located on Amelia Island, with the Atlantic Ocean on one side and the Amelia River on the other, this quaint and quiet coastal town was the birthplace of the modern shrimping industry in the US. The historic business district, around Centre Street, is bordered by the docks, where visitors can watch the shrimp fleet return at sunset.

Old courthouse in the Historic District, Fernandina Beach

The Lowdown

- 🌐 **Map reference** 4 H2
- 🚗 **Car** Rent a car from Jacksonville International Airport.
- ℹ️ **Visitor information** 102 Centre St, 32034; 904 277 0717; www.fbfl.us
- 👫 **Cutting the line** Avoid visiting during holiday weekends.
- 📷 **Guided tours** For horse-drawn carriage rides, contact Amelia Island Carriages (904 556 2662).
- 👫 **Age range** 6 plus
- ⏱️ **Allow** 2 hours
- 🍽️ **Eat and drink** SNACKS Bright Mornings (105 S 3rd St, 32034; 904 491 1771; www.bright morningscafe.com), a local favorite, offers burgers, salads, and sandwiches. FAMILY TREAT Joe's Second Street Bistro (14 S 2nd St, 32034; 904 321 2558; www. joesbistro.com), an award-winning restaurant, serves salads, soups, and entrées.
- 🎪 **Festival** Isle of Eight Flags Shrimp Festival features pirate parades, exciting contests and music (May).

In the heart of Fernandina Beach, the 50-block Historic District is a neighborhood of gorgeous Victorian-era buildings. Listed in the National Register of Historic Places, the district is filled with shops and restaurants. Stroll the streets on a self-guided or museum-led tour, or take a trolley or a horse-drawn carriage, which kids are sure to enjoy.

Take cover

Visit the **Amelia Island Museum of History** (www.ameliamuseum.org) to learn about the history of Amelia Island. Housed in an old jail, this small museum's exhibits focus on the Timucuan Indians, the Civil War, railroads, and Spanish missions.

⑤ Fort Clinch State Park

Relive the Civil War

Named for Duncan Lamont Clinch, a general in the Seminole Wars (1816–58), Fort Clinch is a historic military site with a beach, trails, and campsites. Begun in 1847 to protect Fernandina Harbor, the fort was built right where the St. Marys River flows into the Atlantic Ocean.

The clean, quiet beach is a major draw for swimmers and sunbathers. Anglers frequent the beach to fish off the pier and the finger jetties, or to make the most of excellent surf fishing opportunities. Outdoor enthusiasts can walk the nature trails or bike the off-road trails.

However, for many families the prime attraction is the chance to see skilled re-enactors – or "living historians," as the park calls them – re-creating living conditions at the fort during the Civil War (1861–5). Watch them perform kitchen and

The Lowdown

- 🌐 **Map reference** 4 H2
- 🚗 **Address** 2601 Atlantic Ave, Fernandina Beach, 32034; 904 277 7274; www.floridastateparks. org/fortclinch
- 🚗 **Car** Rent a car from Fernandina Beach.
- 🕐 **Open** Park: 8am–sunset daily. Fort: 9am–5pm daily
- 💲 **Price** Park: $6 per vehicle; $2 per pedestrian or bicyclist. Fort: $2 per person
- 👫 **Cutting the line** The park is rarely crowded.
- 📷 **Guided tours** Guided nature walks at 10:30am on Saturdays, candlelight tours on Labor Day weekends, and daily Living History programs.
- 👫 **Age range** 4 plus
- 🏃 **Activities** Swimming, nature hikes, biking, fishing and camping
- ⏱️ **Allow** 2–4 hours
- ♿ **Wheelchair access** Yes
- 🍽️ **Eat and drink** PICNIC The Happy Tomato Courtyard Café and BBQ (7 S 3rd St, 32034; www.thehappy tomatocafe.com; closed Sat–Sun) is a good place to pick up tasty sandwiches and sides to enjoy near the marina. SNACKS The park store sells snacks and ice cream.
- 🚻 **Restrooms** At the foot of boardwalks, in the campgrounds, and on the fishing pier

laundry chores, and at times – to the delight of most kids – marching drills and artillery demonstrations.

Letting off steam

Amelia Island's beaches offer plenty of room to run about. Families can choose between the lively **Main Beach Park** (32 N Fletcher Ave, Fernandina Beach, 32034), with a beachfront playground and barbecue

Kids learning how to work a water pump at Fort Clinch State Park

A wild horse at the Dungeness Mansion in Cumberland Island National Seashore

grills, or the peaceful sands of **Peter's Point Beach Park** *(1974 S Fletcher Ave, Fernandina Beach, 32034).*

⑥ Cumberland Island National Seashore

In the lap of nature

Although Cumberland Island is just across the border, in Georgia, visitors to Fort Clinch can see its southern edge across Cumberland Sound. Unlike most barrier islands on the Atlantic, Cumberland is not home to golf courses and gated communities, but to pristine beaches, marshes, and bird and animal

species. Narrated sightseeing boats leave Fernandina daily. The ferry ride from St. Marys is fun; visitors may see dolphins leaping near the boat. The tranquil shell-strewn beach is a treat for collectors. Nature-lovers will love the hike trails through maritime forests, wetlands, and historic districts. Look out for herds of wild horses grazing among the ruins of Dungeness Mansion. The island also offers plenty of bird-watching opportunities.

Take cover
Parents might want to plan a visit to see the history exhibits in the **Ice House Museum** *(near the ferry dock; 912 882 4335)* to round off the outing – or during rough weather.

The Lowdown

🌐 **Map reference** 4 H2
Address Camden, Georgia; 912 882 4335; www.nps.gov/cuis

🚗 **Ferry** Ferries depart twice daily from St. Marys. Call ahead to book (912 882 4335). **Taxi** Rent a water taxi, a charter, or a private cruise from Amelia River Cruises & Charters *(1 N Front St, Fernandina Beach, 32034; 904 261 9972; www.ameliarivercruises.com)* or Lang's Charters *(304 Osborne St, St. Marys, 31558; 912 674 8062; www.langcharters.com).*

🕐 **Open** Park: daily. Visitor center: 8am–4:30pm daily

💲 **Price** Park: $10–20; under 16s free

🚹 **Cutting the line** Visit on weekdays or in off-season. Arrive early to beat crowds.

🎫 **Guided tours** Free hour-long tours twice daily, at 10am and 12:45pm

👫 **Age range** 6 plus; walking the long distances can be tiring for younger kids.

🧍 **Activities** The park runs a free kids' program at 2pm in summer. Kids' activity booklets are available at the Mainland Visitor Center.

🕐 **Allow** At least half a day

♿ **Wheelchair access** Yes

🍴 **Eat and drink** SNACKS Cedar Oak Café and Java Joe'z *(304 Osborne St, St Marys, 31558; 912 882 9555)* has muffins, sandwiches, and coffee. FAMILY TREAT Lang's Marina Restaurant *(307 W St. Marys St, St Marys, 31558; 912 882 4432; www.langcharters.com)* serves fresh seafood and has a kids' menu.

🚻 **Restrooms** At the visitor center in St. Marys, the ranger station near Cumberland Island dock, Sea Camp Campgrounds, and Plum Orchard

⑦ St. Augustine
A little bit of Spain

This remarkable city is home to living history museums and elaborate Spanish-style architecture. Its historic district includes 144 blocks, with a wealth of interesting sights, restaurants, and unique shops. Spanning the Matanzas River, the famous Bridge of Lions connects the city to Anastasia Island (*see p172*), which has a classic striped lighthouse and miles of white-sand beaches.

One of the marble lions on the Bridge of Lions

Key Sights

Oldest Wooden Schoolhouse
350 yards (320 m)

Plaza de la Constitución

KING STREET

CORDOVA STREET

SPANISH STREET

GRANADA STREET

CATHEDRAL PLACE

TREASURY STREET

ST GEORGE STREET

KING STREET

CHARLOTTE STREET

ARTILLERY LANE

AVENIDA MENENDEZ

AVILES STREET

Lightner Museum

Villa Zorayda Museum

Oldest House
700 yards (640 m)

Bridge of Lions

Oldest House The González-Alvarez House is the oldest home to survive from the city's Spanish Colonial period. The complex has two museums, an exhibition gallery, and an ornamental garden.

Plaza de la Constitución
Surrounded by historic buildings, this shady square has been a central part of the city's life – from treaty ceremonies to family picnics – for more than 400 years.

Villa Zorayda Museum Built in 1883, this building is a one-tenth scale replica of a portion of the Alhambra in Spain. Now a museum, it houses a superb collection of artifacts from the Middle East.

Oldest Wooden Schoolhouse
State-of-the-art Audio-Animatronic teachers and pupils re-create life as it was in this cedar and cypress school building more than 200 years ago.

Bridge of Lions During Florida's land boom in the 1920s – when the city had plenty of money – this historic landmark was built at an exorbitant cost, complete with the marble lions that guard it.

Letting off steam

The grounds of **Castillo de San Marcos** (*see p170*) offer lots of space to run around. Or visit the **Fort Matanzas National Monument**, a small island fort that guarded St. Augustine from the south, by taking a ferry from the Visitor Center.

Take cover

The eccentric Robert Ripley traveled the world looking for objects that were both weird and wonderful. After his death, his collection became the core of the **Ripley's Believe It or Not! Museum** (*19 San Marco Ave,*

Prices given are for a family of four

32084; 904 824 1606; www.ripleys. com/staugustine). It is a good place to while away an afternoon browsing through the astonishing displays.

Entrance to the bizarre Ripley's Believe It or Not! Museum

Eat and drink

Picnic: under $25; Snacks: $25–50; Real meal: $50–80; Family treat: over $80 (based on a family of four)

PICNIC Drake's Deli (*138 San Marco Ave, 32084; 904 814 3557; open Mon–Sat*) is a tiny eatery in St. Augustine that serves large sandwiches. Takeaway orders can be placed beforehand and picked up on the way.

SNACKS Hyppo (*48 Charlotte St, 32084; 904 217 7853; www.the hyppo.com*) offers gourmet popsicles with flavors such as "Elvis Presley," a mix of bananas, peanut butter, and honey, and tandoori pineapple.

The Lowdown

⊕ **Map reference** 6 F1
Address St. Augustine 32084.
Villa Zorayda Museum: 83 King
St; 904 829 9887; *www.villa
zorayda.com*. Oldest House:
14 St. Francis St; 904 824 2872;
*www.staugustinehistorical
society.org*. Oldest Wooden
Schoolhouse: 14 St. George St;
904 824 0192; *www.oldest
woodenschoolhouse.com*

🚗 **Car** Rent a car from Jacksonville
Airport. Parking is limited in
tourist areas.

ℹ **Visitor information** St. Augustine
& St. Johns County Visitor
Information Center, 10 Castillo
Dr W, 32084; 904 825 1000;
www.floridashistoriccoast.com

🕙 **Open** Villa Zorayda Museum:
10am–5pm Mon–Sat & 11am–
4pm Sun. Oldest House: 10am–
5pm daily. Oldest Wooden
Schoolhouse: 9am–4pm daily

💲 **Prices** Villa Zorayda Museum:
self-guided audio tours $20–30;
under 7s free. Oldest House:
$18 (family ticket). Oldest
Wooden Schoolhouse: $18–28;
under 5s free

🏴 **Guided tours** Old Town Trolley
Tours (*167 San Marco Ave,
32084; 904 829 3800; www.
trolleytours.com/st-augustine*)
offers tours of St. Augustine's
historic district. The Oldest
House runs free guided tours
every half hour 9:30am–4:30pm.
Villa Zorayda Museum offers
docent-led tours ($40–50; under
7s free) by reservation only. Call
904 829 9887 to book. Contact
St. Augustine Carriage (*www.
staugustinecarriage.com*) for
carriage tours.

👫 **Age range** 5 plus. The Villa
Zorayda Museum and Oldest
House will be of more interest
to kids 8 plus.

⏱ **Allow** A day

🎭 **Festivals** Rhythm and Ribs
Festival features live music,
barbecue, and kids' activities
(Apr). Nights of Lights celebrates
the holiday season with art
shows and parades (Nov–Jan).

Good family value?
A plethora of free, as well as paid,
attractions makes the city a great
place to spend a day.

**REAL MEAL Mango Mango's
Caribbean Grill and Bar** (*700 A1A
Beach Blvd, 32080; 904 461 1077*)
serves casual fare such as mahi
sliders and Caribbean island burgers
in a lively beach atmosphere.
FAMILY TREAT The Floridian (*72
Spanish St, 32084; www.thefloridian
staug.com*) offers creative Southern
dishes in a kid-friendly atmosphere.
The menu has vegetarian options.

Shopping
Most kids will enjoy browsing the
shops lining **St. George Street**,
where much of the merchandise on

sale is inexpensive but fun. Parents
will love the low-stress pedestrian
only atmosphere.

Next stop...
BLACK RAVEN PIRATE SHIP If the
kids have had enough architecture
and highbrow history for a while,
take them to the St. Augustine
Municipal Marina to see the Black
Raven Pirate Ship (*www.blackraven
adventures.com*). Climb aboard
the ship for a tour of the Matanzas
River. The adventure includes a
theatrical show with sword fights,
sea shanties, games, and more.

Shops lining St. George Street in the Historic District of St. Augustine

⑧ Lightner Museum/Ponce de León Hotel

The charm of bygone days

Commissioned by railroad tycoon Henry Flagler, *(see pp90–91)* these gorgeous Spanish Renaissance-style buildings were created as the ultimate luxury hotels. Flagler intended the **Ponce de León Hotel** to be "the world's finest hotel" of its time. Now a part of Flagler College, its splendid carvings and curved arches are worth a look.

The Hotel Alcazar – now the **Lightner Museum** – was not quite as luxurious as the Ponce, but it still had a three-story ballroom, tropical gardens, a courtyard for concerts, and spa facilities including Turkish baths and the nation's largest indoor swimming pool. The Lightner now displays an elegant collection of items from the 19th century, including cut glass, furniture, and paintings.

The splendid Victorian Music Room at the Lightner Museum, St. Augustine

The Lowdown

🌐 **Map reference** 6 F1
Address Ponce de León Hotel: in Flagler College, 74 King St, 32084; 904 829 6481; www. flagler.edu. Lightner Museum: 75 King St, 32084; 904 824 2874; www.lightnermuseum.org

🚗 **Car** Rent a car in St. Augustine.

🕐 **Open** Lightner Museum: 9am–5pm daily. Ponce de León Hotel: tours only

💲 **Price** Ponce de León Hotel: free, except for guided tours. Lightner Museum: $38–46; under 12s free

👪 **Cutting the line** Visit on a weekday morning.

Guided tours Tours of the Ponce de León Hotel from the college's main lobby at 10am & 2pm daily.

👫 **Age range** 8 plus

⏱ **Allow** An hour for the museum

♿ **Wheelchair access** At the Lightner Museum

🥄 **Eat and drink** SNACKS The Bunnery Bakery & Cafe (121 St George St, 32084; 904 829 6166; www.bunnerybakeryandcafe. com) offers fresh-baked treats and sandwiches. REAL MEAL Café Alcazar (25 Granada St, 32084; 904 825 9948; www.thealcazar cafe.com), an elegant lunch spot, is housed in the Alcazar Hotel's former swimming pool.

👫 **Restrooms** At both sights

Take cover

Children will love the **St. Augustine Pirate & Treasure Museum** (12 S Castilo Dr, 32084; 877 467 5863; www.thepiratemuseum.com), which has hundreds of fascinating artifacts, including the world's only known pirate treasure chest. Movie buffs can see Captain Jack Sparrow's sword from *The Black Pearl*. Kids can learn about the Golden Age of Piracy through interactive displays.

⑨ Castillo de San Marcos

Cannons and a castle

After the pirate Robert Searle attacked St. Augustine in 1668, the town's Spanish colonists decided they needed more protection, and in 1672 they began constructing the massive Castillo de San Marcos fort. Built of coquina rock quarried from just across the river on Anastasia Island, it took 23 years to build. The Castillo's design included a seawall

Cannon on the gun deck of Castillo de San Marcos, St. Augustine

The Lowdown

🌐 **Map reference** 6 F1
Address 11 South Castillo Dr, 32084; 904 829 6506 (ext. 227); www.nps.gov/casa

🚗 **Car** Rent a car in St. Augustine.

🕐 **Open** 8:45am–5:15pm daily

💲 **Price** $15– 30; under 15s free

👪 **Cutting the line** Early weekday mornings are quietest, but most re-enactments and cannon firings are on weekends.

Guided tours There are maps and brochures for self-guided tours.

👫 **Age range** 6 plus

👫 **Activities** Cannon firings, weapons demonstrations, short films, and ranger programs

⏱ **Allow** 1–2 hours

♿ **Wheelchair access** Yes, except for the upper gun deck

🥄 **Eat and drink** SNACKS Kilwin's (6 St. George St, 32084; 904 823 9226; www.kilwins.com) is a great stop for ice cream, fudge, and caramel apples. REAL MEAL Casa Maya (17 Hypolita St, 32084; 904 823 0787), in the historic district, is popular for its non-traditional, mostly organic menu. Hours vary; call ahead.

with floodgates that could be opened to fill the moat if an assault threatened. Often attacked, the fort was never taken by force, though it sometimes surrendered when faced with overwhelming odds. For much of its history, this oldest existing masonry fort in the US was used as a military prison.

There are lots of things to do here, such as exploring the gun deck and secret chamber, and

The sanctuary in the Cathedral Basilica of St. Augustine

watching re-enactments. Kids will enjoy the frequent cannon firings on weekends.

Take cover

If inclement weather threatens, head for the **Cathedral Basilica of St. Augustine** (*38 Cathedral Place, 32084; 904 824 2806; www.thefirstparish.org*). The historic cathedral was built around 1797, and it has a splendid bell tower.

⑩ Environmental Education Center

Marine encounters

A 10-minute drive north of St. Augustine is the Guana Tolomato Matanzas National Estuarine Research Reserve (GTM NERR), an environmental education center that is worlds away from the average handful of exhibits visitors might expect to find there. The $6.2-million center serves as a place for eco-educational activities for the GTM NERR, a water system that protects more than 109 sq miles (282 sq km) along northeastern Florida's coast.

The GTM center presents information about marine creatures in several interesting ways. Visitors can see small specimens in one of the three aquariums. Larger marine creatures are represented by full-scale models. The very largest – a North Atlantic right whale – hangs from the ceiling. There are also interpretive exhibits at the center, a high-tech theater that screens nature films, and an outdoor amphitheater.

The Lowdown

🌐 **Map reference** 6 F1
Address 505 Guana River Rd, S Ponte Vedra Beach, 32082; 904 823 4500; www.gtmnerr.org

🚗 **Car** Rent a car from St. Augustine.

🕐 **Open** Education Center: 9am–4pm daily. GTM trails and beach parking: 8am–sunset daily

💲 **Price** Parking $3 per car

👫 **Cutting the line** Early mornings and weekdays are best.

🚩 **Guided tours** For family programs or guided trail walks, call 904 823 4500. Ripple Effect Ecotours (*www.rippleeffect ecotours.com*) offers kayak and nature tours.

👫 **Age range** All ages

⏱ **Allow** 1–1½ hours

♿ **Wheelchair access** South parking lot accessible

🍴 **Eat and drink** PICNIC Publix Deli (*55 Ava Way, Vilano Beach, 32084; 904 827 1448; www.publix.com*) has ready-made food to go, and picnic supplies for lunch at the GTM picnic pavilion. REAL MEAL Barbara Jean's (*15 South Roscoe Blvd, Ponte Vedra Beach, 32082; 904 280 7522; www.barbarajeans.com*) is a hot spot for Southern cuisine. It includes a kids' menu.

👫 **Restrooms** In the Environmental Education Center

Natural exhibits in the Exhibit Hall of the Environmental Education Center

Letting off steam

Just east of the A1A are three walkovers that cross the dunes to an untouched stretch of beach, and on the west side are nature trails, boat launches, places to fish, and 10 miles (16 km) of hiking and biking trails.

⑪ Anastasia Island

A spooky lighthouse

The 165-ft (50-m) **St. Augustine Lighthouse** is definitely the high point of a visit to Anastasia Island, but there are many other attractions, too. At the northern tip is **Anastasia State Park**, whose 2.5 sq miles (6 sq km) include 4 miles (6 km) of beach with a surf break, a maritime hammock, a tidal salt marsh, and a sheltered lagoon favored by windsurfers. It is possible to fish, hike, or bike around the park, although most beachgoers come here to surf, sail, swim, or just enjoy lazing in the sun.

Energetic families can climb the 219 steps to the top of the lighthouse. Older kids and teens may be interested in a "Dark of the Moon" ghost tour – the lighthouse was featured on *Ghost Hunters*, a paranormal reality TV show. There is also an activity area for younger kids.

The Lowdown

🌐 **Map reference** 6 F1
🚗 **Address** Park: 300 Anastasia Park Rd, 32080; 904 461 2033; *www. floridastateparks.org.* Lighthouse: 81 Lighthouse Ave, 32080; 904 829 0745; *www.staugustine lighthouse.com*
🚗 **Car** Rent a car from St. Augustine.
🕐 **Open** Park: 8am–sunset daily. Lighthouse: 9am–6pm daily
💲 **Price** Park: $8 per vehicle. Lighthouse: $36–46
👪 **Cutting the line** Avoid midday and holiday weekends.
🔫 **Guided tours** RippleEffect EcoTours (904 347 1565; *www. rippleeffectecotours.com*) offers kayak/canoe tours. Call lighthouse for information on ghost tour.
👪 **Age range** All ages. For the lighthouse, kids must be taller than 44 in (112 cm), and able to climb alone.
🕐 **Allow** Park: 1–2 hours. Lighthouse: at least 1 hour
♿ **Wheelchair access** Yes
🍴 **Eat and drink** SNACKS Island Beach Shop and Grill *(in Anastasia State Park)* serves snacks and drinks. *REAL MEAL* O'steen's *(205 Anastasia Boulevard, 32080; 904 829 6974; closed Sun–Mon)* offers fried shrimp and scallops. Call ahead for opening hours.
🚻 **Restrooms** Park: at beaches and campgrounds. Lighthouse: near the gift shop

Fun at the beach in Anastasia State Park, Anastasia Island

Take cover

Head to the 299-seat **World Golf Hall of Fame's** IMAX® theater *(www.worldgolfimax.com)*, which has a 3-D digital projection system and the largest digital screen in the southeast. Or go 2 miles (3 km) west to **Whetstone Factory** *(139 King St, St. Augustine, 32084; 904 217 0275)* to learn the candymaker's secrets and do a little taste-testing along the way.

⑫ Marineland Dolphin Adventure

Steer a kayak on your own!

This attraction right on the Atlantic Ocean focuses on research on Atlantic bottlenose dolphins in human care as well as in the wild. It also offers educational programs for kids and adults alike.

Children will enjoy exploring the dolphins' natural habitat in the adjacent Matanzas River Estuary.

Visitors gather for an exhibit at Marineland Dolphin Adventure

The Lowdown

🌐 **Map reference** 6 F2
🚗 **Address** 9600 Oceanshore Blvd, 32080; 904 471 1111; *www.marineland.net*
🚗 **Car** Rent a car from St. Augustine.
🕐 **Open** 9am–4:30pm daily
💲 **Price** $35–45; dolphin programs range from $26 to $550
👪 **Age range** 3 plus
👪 **Activities** Several dolphin programs; call ahead for details.
🕐 **Allow** 1–2 hours
♿ **Wheelchair access** Yes
🍴 **Eat and drink** SNACKS A small concession stand *(on site)* serves snacks, hot dogs, and drinks. *REAL MEAL* Captain's BBQ *(5862 N Oceanshore Blvd, 32137; 386 597 2888; www.captainsbbq baittackle.com)* offers barbecued ribs, brisket, chicken and turkey, and a kids' menu.
🚻 **Restrooms** Near gift shop and main pool area

A Marineland partner here offers kayak tours that are guided by certified naturalists. The stable tandem- and triple-seat kayaks make the outing possible for complete beginners, and even for kids as young as 6. One can also go sailing with another partner that offers a more relaxed dolphin spotting experience, with informative Marineland educators on board. In addition, the center also organizes acrylic painting and photography workshops guided by an instructor that cater to art enthusiasts as well as professionals.

Take cover

If inclement weather threatens, visit the **Authentic Old Jail** (167 San Marco Ave, 32084) in St. Augustine. Costumed actors make the tour interesting and fun, if a bit spooky.

⑬ Washington Oaks Gardens State Park

For a fantastic day out

Roses in the ornamental gardens, Ice Age rocks on the beach – the two sides of Washington Oaks Gardens State Park couldn't be more different. Add to that the chance to see manatees hanging out in the river shallows – and this state park is definitely not a run-of-the-mill picnic stop. Saltwater anglers can fish from the rocky beach on the east side of A1A. The rocks make it a good place to hunt for sea glass that's been tumbled smooth. Budding anglers can try their hand at freshwater fishing from the seawall on the Matanzas River on the west side of A1A. In the cooler months, this is a good place to spot manatees. The park gardens are also attractive – developed in the 1930s, they include both native and exotic species. In early spring, visitors are greeted by an especially beautiful sight: colorful azaleas and camellias in full bloom.

Take cover

Skate and Shake Skating Center (386 672 8500), 25 miles (40 km) south in Ormond Beach, may be a bit of a drive, but it's a great way for kids to get lots of exercise even when it's pouring outside. Call ahead.

The 19th-century building housing the Authentic Old Jail, St. Augustine

The Lowdown

🌐 **Map reference** 6 F2

📍 **Address** 6400 N Palm Coast Blvd, Oceanshore, 32137; 386 446 6780; www.floridastate parks.org/washingtonoaks

🚗 **Car** Rent a car from St. Augustine.

🕐 **Open** 8am–sunset daily

💲 **Price** $5 per vehicle

🚻 **Cutting the line** The park is rarely crowded.

👫 **Age range** 4 plus

⏱ **Allow** 1–2 hours

♿ **Wheelchair access** Yes. Beach wheelchair with advance notice.

🍴 **Eat and drink** PICNIC Romano's Pizza on the Beach (4255 A1A S, 32080; 904 461 1111; closed Mon) has picnic supplies. REAL MEAL Matanzas Innlet Restaurant (8805 A1A South, 32080; 904 461 6824; www.matanzas.biz) offers boiled shrimp, steamer baskets, big burgers, and a water view.

🚻 **Restrooms** In the visitor center, picnic area, and on the beach

Manatee quiz

1 Manatees need to breathe air every 20 minutes. Is that true?
2 Are manatees
(a) herbivores (plant-eaters)
(b) carnivores (meat-eaters)
(c) omnivores (plant- as well as meat-eaters)?
3 Manatees are most closely related to:
a) elephants
b) cows
c) whales
4 Florida manatees can live for up to:
a) 10 years
b) 35 years
c) 60 years.

....

Answers at the bottom of the page.

More about manatees

Manatees are intelligent and can learn complex tasks. But they move slowly and don't hear the sounds of propeller-driven boats very well, so they're often injured or killed by boat strikes.

WHALE OR DOLPHIN?

Dolphins are one of the most playful mammals known to us, but they can also be a most ferocious predators. For example, the killer whale, or orca, is actually the largest dolphin in existence and can reach up to 30 feet in size!

Haunted lighthouse

Don't think ghosts exist? You might become a believer after a nighttime "Dark of the Moon" ghost tour of the St. Augustine Lighthouse. Visitors claim to have seen and heard the ghosts of two little girls from the 1800s, among others.

....

Answers: 1 Yes. 2 a. 3 a. 4 c.

Picturesque view of a gazebo on a pond in Washington Oaks Gardens State Park

Picnic under $25; **Snacks** $25–50; **Real meal** $50–80; **Family treat** over $80 (based on a family of four)

⑭ Daytona Beach
Fun on the run

Daytona Beach has been drawing adrenaline junkies since the early 1900s, when automobile-racing on the beach's firm sand pushed the boundaries of speed. Although the city is still popular with race fans, it has also become a favorite destination for millions of visitors each year, thanks to its beautiful beaches and great weather for outdoor activities.

The Southeast Museum of Photography

Key Sights

① **Daytona Lagoon** Although this amusement park is all about water rides from May to October, it also offers exciting year-round "dry attractions" such as laser tag, miniature golf, and go-karts.

② **Daytona Beach Boardwalk** Enjoy old-fashioned arcade games and rides, such as a Ferris wheel, Slingshot, and Hurricane, here. Check out the renovated pier and restaurant.

③ **Public beaches** Car-friendly sands and crowds of festive beachgoers have helped Daytona's 23 miles (37 km) of beaches gain a reputation as "The World's Most Famous Beach."

④ **Halifax Historical Museum** This museum features vintage toys and exhibits on Native American culture, along with beach racing. A 20-minute movie covers 130,000 years of local history.

Prices given are for a family of four

⑤ **Southeast Museum of Photography** This is the largest museum of its kind in the Southeast, with exhibits, lectures, and seminars, plus Family Photo Fun Days and photo workshops for kids.

⑥ **Daytona International Speedway** Young speed demons will like a tour of the legendary racetrack of the Daytona 500, one of the most famous NASCAR meets.

⑦ **Gamble Place** This Florida Cracker-style property preserves the Citrus-Packing House – the only one in Florida at its original location.

The Lowdown

🌐 **Map reference** 6 G3
Address Daytona Lagoon: 601 Earl St, 32114; www.daytonalagoon.com. Daytona Beach Boardwalk: 12 N Ocean Ave, 32118; www.daytonabeachboardwalk.com. Halifax Historical Museum: 252 S Beach St, 32114; www.halifaxhistorical.org. Southeast Museum of Photography: 1200 W International Speedway, 32114; www.smponline.org. Daytona International Speedway: 1801 W International Speedway Blvd, 32114; www.daytonainternationalspeedway.com. Gamble Place: 1819 Taylor Rd, Port Orange, 32127; www.moas.org

🚍 **Bus** Votran (www.votran.org) buses connect sights in the city.
Car Rent a car at Daytona Beach International Airport.

ℹ️ **Visitor information** Daytona Beach Area Convention & Visitors Bureau, 126 E Orange Ave, 32115; 386 255 0415; www.daytonabeach.com

🕐 **Open** Daytona Lagoon & Daytona Beach Boardwalk: hours vary by attraction and season; check websites. Public beaches: open 24 hours daily to pedestrians and bicyclists & sunrise–sunset to vehicles with driving passes. Halifax Historical Museum: 10:30am–4:30pm Tue–Fri & 10am–4pm Sat.

The redbrick gift shop next to the Ponce de Leon Inlet Lighthouse

Take cover

The modest **Marine Science Center** (www.marinesciencecenter.com), 11 miles (18 km) southeast of Daytona Beach in Ponce Inlet, has exhibits, aquariums, and guided beach walks.

Eat and drink

Picnic: under $25; Snacks: $25–50; Real meal: $50–80; Family treat: over $80 (based on a family of four)

PICNIC New York Style Bagel Deli and Restaurant *(3344 S Atlantic Ave, 32118; 386 760 0302)* offers deli items, salads, sandwiches, and bakery goods for a beachside picnic.
SNACKS Cow Licks *(2624 S Atlantic Ave, 32118; 386 761 1316)* is the place to chill, with home-made ice cream and Ms. Pac-Man games.
REAL MEAL Rossi's Diner *(2240 S Ridgewood Ave, 32119; 386 760 4564; www.rossisdiner.com)* is a favorite with locals, thanks to a huge menu, and desserts such as rice pudding and muffins.
FAMILY TREAT Don Vito's Italian Restaurant *(137 West International Speedway Blvd, 32114; 386 492 7935; www.donvitosrestaurant.com)* serves fine, but expensive, Italian fare. The kids' menu has spaghetti and meatballs. The desserts are a hit.

Shopping

Daytona's **Downtown Shopping District** has many antique stores, bookstores, and clothing shops.

Next stop...

PONCE DE LEON INLET LIGHTHOUSE AND MUSEUM
Go 10 miles (16 km) south to see the tallest lighthouse in Florida (www.ponceinlet.org), on the north bank of Ponce de Leon Inlet.

Southeast Museum of Photography: 11am–5pm Tue–Fri, 1–5pm Sat. Daytona International Speedway: event hours vary; tours from 10am–4pm daily. Gamble Place: 8am–5pm Wed–Sun

(S) Prices Daytona Lagoon & Daytona Beach Boardwalk: check websites for details; water park: $82–104. Public beaches: $10 to drive or park on beach (www.codb.us). Halifax Historical Museum: $12–22. Southeast Museum of Photography: free. Daytona International Speedway: for event and race prices, call 1 800 748 7467. Gamble Place: $6; under 5s free

Cutting the line VIP tours of the Daytona International Speedway can be booked ahead at $52 per person; call 877 306 7223.

Guided tours Take the 90-min ($66–72; under 5s free) or 30-min ($56–62; under 5s free) All Access Speedway Tour. Gamble House runs group tours by reservation.

Age range 4 plus

Allow At least half a day

Good family value?
Although lodgings can be relatively expensive in this city, the beach, and some sights, are free and many others are moderately priced.

⑮ Museum of Arts and Sciences (MOAS)

Not just another museum

Set in the lush Tuscawilla Preserve, this museum not only houses a superb collection of art, science, and history exhibits, but also allows kids to discover important scientific principles through hands-on exhibits, including the chance to design cars and test their designs by racing against competitors. The domed planetarium is another attraction here, with a Minolta MS-10 sky projector. The preserve also has an environmental education center, trails, and discovery stations.

Mold of the iconic
Coca-Cola contour bottle

Key Sights

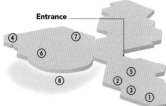

Entrance

④ ⑦
⑥
⑤
⑧ ② ①
③

① **"Sumar Special" Indy car** Housed in the Root Family Museum, the Sumar Special reached the amazing speed of 172 mph (276.5 km/h) in 1957. It was designed by Frank Kurtis and Chapman Root, whose company created the famous Coca-Cola contour bottle.

② **Coca-Cola** The mold of the original Coke bottle is part of Chapman Root's huge collection of historic Coca-Cola memorabilia on display in the Root Family Museum.

③ **Teddy bears** See more than 800 teddy bears, each depicting a different theme or historical period, in the Root Family Museum. Kids will love the large wedding party in full costume, with a bride, a groom, and even a ring bearer.

④ **Giant ground sloth** This 130,000-year-old 13-ft- (4-m-) tall skeleton of a giant sloth is a major draw in the Bouchelle Gallery of Changing Exhibitions.

⑤ **Planetarium** Located near the Root Family Museum, this facility hosts thrilling solar system-related shows using images from NASA space probes and 3-D special effects.

The Lowdown

🌐 **Map reference** 6 G3
Address 352 South Nova Rd, Daytona Beach, 32114; 386 255 0285; www.moas.org

🚗 **Car** Rent a car from Daytona Beach Airport. Free parking

🕐 **Open** 10am–5pm Mon–Sat & 11am–5pm Sun

💲 **Price** $40–50; under 6s free. General admission includes regular planetarium shows.

🎭 **Shows** The planetarium hosts laser rock concerts (tickets $5 for one show, $7 for two shows, or $9 for three shows) at 7pm, 8pm and 9pm on second Sat of each month. Limited seating. Tickets can be purchased at the main entrance or in advance. Call 386 255 0285 for information on specific shows.

🚶 **Cutting the line** Visit between 9am and 11am, when the museum is relatively uncrowded.

🏹 **Guided tours** The museum offers pre-scheduled tours.

👫 **Age range** 6 plus

👟 **Activities** The Klancke Environmental Education Complex in Tuscawilla Preserve has raised boardwalks and nature trails.

⏱ **Allow** 1–3 hours

♿ **Wheelchair access** Yes

🛍 **Shop** The small gift shop (by the main entrance) sells mostly art books, which grown-ups might like, as well as snacks.

🚻 **Restrooms** In each of the three wings: West Wing, North Wing, and the Root Family Museum

Good family value?

A wide range of educative and interactive exhibits make this museum a fun experience for the whole family.

⑥ **Charles and Linda Williams Children's Museum** Kids can race toy cars on the figure-eight track, and also explore numerous exciting hands-on science stations in this museum.

⑦ **Cuban Foundation Museum Collection** Former Cuban president Fulgencio Batista donated the core of the museum's famed Cuban art collection in the 1950s. It is considered to be the best collection outside Cuba.

⑧ **Sculpture Garden** This magical outdoor exhibition area is dotted with works by noted contemporary sculptors such as Ernest Shaw and Juan José Sicre.

Exploring a boardwalk trail through the lush Tuscawilla Preserve

Letting off steam

Burn off excess energy on the nature trails in the **Tuscawilla Preserve**, or take a turn in its **Sensory Garden**, which has herbs, native wildflowers, a butterfly and hummingbird garden, and a rock garden. The garden serves as the entry to the Klancke Environmental Education Complex.

Eat and drink

Picnic: under $25; Snacks: $25–50; Real meal: $50–80; Family treat: over $80 (based on a family of four)

PICNIC The Cracked Egg Diner *(3280 South Atlantic Ave, 32118; 386 788 6772; www.thecrackedegg diner.com)* is a great place to pick up subs, sandwiches, salads, and fried pickles. Picnic near the pool in the Sensory Garden.

SNACKS Dancing Avocado Kitchen *(110 South Beach St, 32114; 386 947 2022; closed Sun–Mon)* serves creative breakfast and lunch dishes

with many vegetarian selections. Reasonable prices and a smoothie and juice bar make this restaurant a good choice for snacks and meals.

REAL MEAL Steve's Famous Diner *(1584 S Nova Rd, 32114; 386 252 0101; stevesfamousdiner.biz)*, a popular place near the museum, offers superb fresh-baked breads. The wide-ranging menu has home-made soups, salads, and desserts.

FAMILY TREAT The Cellar *(220 Magnolia Ave, 32114; 386 258 0011; www.thecellarrestaurant.com; closed Mon)* is a major splurge for Italian cuisine, but the dishes created by chef Sam Maggio have ensured a loyal fan base. The restaurant also has an extensive wine list.

Find out more

DIGITAL Download the free MOAS iPhone app from *itunes.apple.com/us/app/moas/id391833573?mt=8* to stroll through the virtual galleries of the museum, get in-depth artist biographies, and check out exhibition and event schedules, as well as ticketing information.

Next stop...

DEVIL'S MILLHOPPER GEOLOGICAL STATE PARK Head 121 miles (195 km) northwest to the Devil's Millhopper Geological State Park *(see p181)* near Gainesville. A 120-ft (36.5-m) sinkhole, it is one of Florida's most unusual parks. Summer visitors who climb all the steps to the bottom of the sinkhole can experience cooler temperatures and views of diverse wildlife.

Boardwalk leading to the bottom of the sinkhole in Devil's Millhopper

KIDS' CORNER

Ice Age giants

Once upon a time, huge Ice Age mammals – some as big as a bus – lived in Florida, including these below:
1 The scimitar cat was the size of a lion, could run about 60 mph (96 km/h), and had razor-sharp teeth.
2 The dire wolf was much bigger and stronger than today's timber wolves, and hunted with up to 20 other wolves in a pack.
3 The giant terror bird, at 7 ft (2 m) tall, didn't actually fly – and was a carnivore (meat-eater).

HUNTING FOR BEARS

The museum's collection of teddies goes far beyond the "bear" essentials! As you explore this giant collection, try to discover the oldest, the newest, the prettiest, and the ugliest bears. Can you try sketching them?

Fossil find

In late 2011, a construction crew discovered some weird bones just down the road from the museum. The bones turned out to be from a 9-ft- (3-m-) tall mastodon, which weighed about 10,000 lbs (4,536 kg) and probably romped around Daytona about 50,000 to 100,000 years ago. Check the museum's website for more information.

Tubing in Blue Spring State Park, Ocala National Forest

⑯ Blue Spring State Park

Make a splash

When the summer's hottest days roll around, families love to take a refreshing plunge into Blue Spring, where they can swim, snorkel, canoe, kayak, or take a riverboat tour. Certified scuba divers can even dive here. With the onset of winter in mid-November, all water activities stop as Florida's manatees migrate here. The park is a designated Manatee Refuge, and children will delight in watching from the boardwalk as the manatees feed, frolic, and take care of their calves.

Take cover

Head northwest to the excellent **Appleton Museum of Art** (4333 E Silver Springs Blvd, Ocala, 34470; 352 291 4455; www.appleton museum.org). The museum's pre-Columbian and African collections are likely to keep kids enthralled for quite a while. The museum's gift shop, which offers art-inspired merchandise, is worth a visit.

⑰ Ocala National Forest

Tarzan's playground

The second-largest National Forest in the country, this 600 sq-mile (1,780-sq-km) jungle could take years to explore fully – from its sandy Big Scrub to the semitropical Juniper Springs. Among the many attractions for families, the Yearling Trail takes hikers to Pat's Island, the place where the family in the Pulitzer Prize-winning book *The*

A picturesque hiking trail running through Ocala National Forest

Yearling (1938) lived. Look out for the endangered Florida black bear on the Florida Black Bear Scenic Highway (State Road 19). Birding fans can spot bald eagles, ospreys, waterfowl, and owls. Several lakes draw bass anglers, and a full-facility marina rents boats. There are also campgrounds, horse trails, and springs popular for swimming, canoeing, and tubing.

Take cover

The dragsters and vintage cars at the **Don Garlits Museum of Drag Racing** (www.garlits.com), in Ocala, will fascinate kids and car buffs.

⑱ Ocala Thoroughbred Farm Country

Horsing around

Marion County, popularly known as "The Horse Capital of the World," is guaranteed to be a big hit with horse-crazy kids. Watch a polo match or a real rodeo, get a close

The Lowdown

🌐 **Map reference** 6 F4
Address 2100 W French Ave, Orange City, 32763; 386 775 3663; www.floridastateparks/bluespring

🚗 **Car** Rent a car from Orlando.

🕐 **Open** 8am–sunset daily

💲 **Price** $6 per vehicle; $2 per pedestrian and cyclist.

👫 **Cutting the line** Arrive early – on weekends, the park often closes by noon because of the crowds.

👫 **Age range** All ages

👫 **Activities** Observe manatees from the boardwalk during manatee season. Interpretive programs in the afternoon; call 386 775 3773. St. Johns River Cruises (386 917 0724) offers riverboat tours.

🕐 **Allow** 2–4 hours

♿ **Wheelchair access** Yes

🍴 **Eat and drink** SNACKS The snack bar (on site; 386 775 6888; www.myfloridamanatee.com) sells sandwiches, snacks, and drinks. REAL MEAL Texas Roadhouse (2518 Enterprise Rd, 32763; 386 532 7427; www.texasroadhouse.com) is a highly rated steakhouse with a great kids' menu.

👫 **Restrooms** Near the parking and picnic areas

The Lowdown

🌐 **Map reference** 6 E3
Address North of Orlando between the Ocklawaha and St. Johns Rivers; 352 625 2520; www.fs.usda.gov/ocala

🚗 **Car** Rent a car from Ocala.

ℹ️ **Visitor information** Ocklawaha: 3199 NE Hwy 315, Silver Springs, 34488. Salt Springs: 14100 N State Hwy 19, 32134; 352 685 3070. Pittman: 45621 State Rd 19, Altoona, 32702

🕐 **Open** 8am–8pm most sites

💲 **Price** Most sites $26–36

👫 **Cutting the line** Avoid weekends and holidays.

🧭 **Guided tours** Check www.ocala marion.com for tours by boat, horse, and all-terrain vehicle.

👫 **Age range** All ages

🕐 **Allow** Half a day

♿ **Wheelchair access** Limited

🍴 **Eat and drink** SNACKS Yomii Frozen Yogurt (2631 Enterprise Blvd, Orange City, 32763; 386 456 5080) offers a selection of self-serve toppings. REAL MEAL Laspada's Original (2200 N Volusia Ave, Orange City, 32763; www.laspadas.com) serves Philly cheese steaks and Italian hoagies.

👫 **Restrooms** At campgrounds

look at Thoroughbreds – including the famous Rohara Arabians and Young's Paso Finos – at one of the more than 600 Thoroughbred farms in the area, or explore the countryside on horseback at a ride-for-fun stable. Marion County boasts thousands of national and world champs, plus six Kentucky Derby winners.

Take cover
The Carriage Museum at **The Grand Oaks Resort** (thegrandoaks.com), in Weirsdale, has rides fit for royalty, but kids may like the life-size horse models as much as the vehicles.

The Lowdown

🌐 **Map reference** 5 D3

🚗 **Car** Rent a car from Ocala.

ℹ️ **Visitor information** 112 N Magnolia Ave, Ocala, 34475; 352 438 2801; www.ocalamarion.com

💲 **Price** Varies by tour and activity.

🚻 **Cutting the line** Choose weekdays when possible.

🚩 **Guided tours** Several tours, including by horse, motorbike, all-terrain vehicle, and canoe; check www.ocalamarion.com.

👫 **Age range** 4 plus

🏇 **Activities** Horse farm tours, horse-riding, and horse shows

⏱️ **Allow** 2–4 hours

♿ **Wheelchair access** Varies, call individual tours and attractions.

🍴 **Eat and drink** SNACKS Stella's Modern Pantry (20 SW Broadway St, 34471; 352 622 3663; closed Mon) gets kudos for desserts, but also offers sandwiches and flatbreads. REAL MEAL Royal Orchid Thai Cuisine (3131 SW College Rd 206, 34474; 352 237 4949) is a local favorite, thanks to an authentic menu and great service.

A room at the house in Marjorie Kinnan Rawlings Historic State Park

⑲ Marjorie Kinnan Rawlings Historic State Park
House of a literary genius

Although she was not a native Floridian, Marjorie Kinnan Rawlings' writings about this area and its people have made her one of the state's best-known authors. She came to live on this farmstead in search of a quiet place to write and fell in love with it, as most visitors do, too. Her books, especially *The Yearling*, which is a favorite among younger readers, help convey the realities of living close to the wilderness in harmony with nature. The park includes her home, furnished as it was when she lived here in the 1930s, a workers' home, a barn, a kitchen garden, and other outbuildings. The home's interior can be viewed only by guided tour.

Letting off steam
Kids can run around the house's extensive grounds to burn off excess energy.

The Lowdown

🌐 **Map reference** 5 D2
Address 18700 S County Rd 325, Cross Creek, 32640; 352 466 3672

🚗 **Car** Rent a car from Gainesville.

🕐 **Open** Park grounds: 9am–5pm daily

💲 **Price** Park admission: $3 per vehicle. House tours: $10–20; under 5s free

🚻 **Cutting the line** Winter is busy. Fri and Sun mornings are quietest.

🚩 **Guided tours** Hourly tours of house and property Oct–Jul: 10am–4pm Thu–Sun; call 352 466 3672.

👫 **Age range** 6 plus

⏱️ **Allow** 1–2 hours

♿ **Wheelchair access** Yes

🍴 **Eat and drink** REAL MEAL Blue Highway Pizzeria (204 NE Hwy 441, Micanopy, 32667; 352 466 0062) is a casual eatery where diners can customize their pizza. FAMILY TREAT The Yearling Restaurant (14531 E County Rd 325, Hawthorne, 32640; 352 466 3999; closed Mon–Wed) serves quail and frog legs, along with chicken, steak, and seafood.

🚻 **Restrooms** In the park, adjacent to the historic site

Picnic under $25; **Snacks** $25–50; **Real meal** $50–80; **Family treat** over $80 (based on a family of four)

⑳ Paynes Prairie Preserve State Park

Home on the range, where the deer and the buffalo roam

This 33-sq mile- (85-sq km-) preserve, 2 hours west of Daytona Beach, is home to deer, bison, wild horses, Florida Cracker cows, and alligators. It is not necessary to hike deep into the wilderness to see its wildlife – the park has multiple observation platforms, including a 50-ft (15-m) tower for a bird's-eye view. Remember to carry binoculars – 271 species of birds, from bald eagles to sandhill cranes, live here. There is plenty of human history here to explore, too. An audio-visual presentation at the visitor center tells the story of this wilderness, which goes back at least 12,000 years.

The Lowdown

🌐 **Map reference** 4 F6
Address 100 Savannah Blvd, Micanopy, 32667; 352 466 3397; www.floridastateparks.org

🚗 **Car** Rent a car from Gainesville.

🕐 **Open** 8am–sunset daily. Visitor center: 9am–4pm daily

💲 **Price** $6 per vehicle; $2 per pedestrian or cyclist

👫 **Cutting the line** Avoid weekends when the University of Florida football team plays at home. The park is less crowded May–Sep.

🚩 **Guided tours** Walk and talk programs run Nov–Apr on alternate Thu; call 352 466 4100 for reservations.

👫 **Age range** 4 plus

🕐 **Allow** 2 hours

♿ **Wheelchair access** Limited; call 850 245 2157.

🍴 **Eat and drink** SNACKS Coffee N Cream (201 Northeast 1st St, Micanopy, 32667; 352 466 1101; www.micanopycoffeeshop.com) offers coffee and other drinks, and home-made cookies. Or pick up sandwiches to take to Paynes Prairie. REAL MEAL Pearl Country Store (106A NE Hwy 441, Micanopy, 32667; 352 466 4025; www.pearlcountrystore.com) has barbecue and mac'n'cheese that customers swear by.

👫 **Restrooms** At the visitor center and Lake Wauberg campgrounds

Tree-lined drive in Paynes Prairie Preserve State Park, Gainesville

Take cover

Go to **Antique City Mall** (17020 SE County Rd 234, Micanopy, 32667; 352 466 1060) for Star Wars™ figures and cowboy collectibles.

㉑ Florida Museum of Natural History

Calling all "__ologists!"

For families with kids who love science – whether they want to grow up to be paleontologists, zoologists, or archaeologists – the University of Florida's Museum of Natural History in Gainesville is an astonishing treasure house of information and exhibits. One of America's top five natural history museums, it houses more than 30 million specimens in multiple disciplines. Exhibits at the Hall of Florida Fossils cover the last 65 million years in Florida, from the Eocene era (when the state was underwater) to the arrival of humans about 14,000 years ago. The McGuire Center, the largest research facility on the planet

The Lowdown

🌐 **Map reference** 4 F5
Address 3215 Hull Rd, Gainesville, 32611–2710; 352 846 2000; www.flmnh.ufl.edu

🚗 **Car** Rent a car in Gainesville.

🕐 **Open** 10am–5pm Mon–Sat & 1–5pm Sun

💲 **Price** Free. Butterfly Rainforest: $36–42. Under 3s free. Parking free on weekends and holidays

👫 **Cutting the line** The museum is not usually crowded.

🚩 **Guided tours** Hall of Florida Fossils tours at 11:30am & 2:45pm Sat, 2:45pm Sun

👫 **Age range** 4 plus

👫 **Activities** Live butterfly releases at 2pm, 3pm & 4pm Sat & Sun, weather permitting. Butterfly-friendly plant sale at 10am–5pm Mon–Sat & 1–5pm Sun

🕐 **Allow** 1–2 hours

♿ **Wheelchair access** Yes

🍴 **Eat and drink** REAL MEAL Satchel's Pizza (1800 NE 23rd Ave, 32609; 352 335 7272; www.satchelspizza. com; closed Sun & Mon) is known for its inventive pizzas. FAMILY TREAT Amelia's (235 S Main St, Suite 107, 32601; 352 373 1919; www. ameliasgainesville.com) serves fresh, home-style Italian food.

👫 **Restrooms** Near South Florida People and Environments exhibit, and off the Central Gallery

dedicated to the study of butterflies, includes a screened outdoor exhibit called the Butterfly Rainforest. This contains hundreds of butterflies from all over the world, living in a predator-free environment among waterfalls and tropical plants. On weekend afternoons, when the weather permits, visitors can view live butterfly releases.

Butterfly exhibit in the Florida Museum of Natural History, Gainesville

Steps leading to the bottom of the sinkhole in Devil's Milhopper Geological State Park

Water-Breathing Dragon Fountain in Kanapaha Botanical Gardens, Gainesville

Letting off steam

Head 4 miles (7 km) southwest to **Kanapaha Botanical Gardens** (www.kanapaha.org) to see the hummingbird garden, wildflower meadow, and "children's garden" featuring a treasure wall, a hedge maze, and a koi pond.

㉒ Devil's Millhopper Geological State Park

A sinking sensation

The Devil's Millhopper, in Gainesville, is a sinkhole that appeared when an underground cavern collapsed due to heat and humidity. The sinkhole created a miniature rain forest with many small springs whose streams flow down its sides. On a hot summer day, descending all 236 steps to the sinkhole's lowest point is rewarding for its noticeably cooler temperature. Remember to wear stout shoes if you are up for the

walk. Though younger kids may find it exhausting, the walk rewards the energetic ones with sightings of birds from the pinelands and suburbs.

Take cover

Travel 5 miles (8 km) south to check out the Asian wing and gardens of the first-rate **Harn Museum of Art** (SW 34th St, S Hull Rd, 32611; www.harn. ufl.edu). Kids may especially like the Ancient American collection with its Mayan and Aztec works.

The Lowdown

- **Map reference** 4 F5
  Address 4732 Millhoppper Rd, Gainesville, 32653; 352 955 2008; www.floridastateparks.org
- **Car** Rent a car in Gainesville.
- **Open** 9am–5pm Wed–Sun
- **Price** $4 per vehicle; $2 per pedestrian or cyclist
- **Cutting the line** Least crowded Wed–Thu from mid-afternoon on
- **Guided tours** Guided walk with ranger at 10am every Sat; call 386 462 7905
- **Age range** 4 plus
- **Activities** Hiking, picnicking, and wildlife viewing
- **Allow** 2 hours
- **Wheelchair access** Yes, limited
- **Eat and drink** PICNIC 43rd Street Deli (4401 NW 25th Place, Gainesville, 32606; 352 373 2927; www.43rdstreetdeli.com) is a convenient place to pick up sandwiches, sides, and salads for a picnic on the park's grounds. REAL MEAL Cedar River Seafood (5141 NW 43rd St, Gainesville, 32605; 352 371 4848; www. cedarriverseafoodlc.com) offers delicious, modestly-priced oysters, shrimp, and fried fish.
- **Restrooms** At the visitor center

Picnic under $25; **Snacks** $25–50; **Real meal** $50–80; **Family treat** over $80 (based on a family of four)

Where to Stay in the Northeast

This region offers a wide variety of accommodations, from award-winning resorts and luxurious hotels to campsites located in beautiful state parks within walking distance of the waves. Northeastern Florida offers plenty of both upscale and budget options to choose from.

AGENCY

Stockton Real Estate
www.stocktonrealestate.com
This local real estate company coordinates short-term rental of individual vacation homes and condos, from oceanfront to golf course locations in Jacksonville and its beaches, Ponte Vedra Beach, and St. Augustine.

Amelia Island   Map 4 H2

RESORTS

Omni Amelia Island Plantation Resort
6800 First Coast Hwy, 32034; 904 261 6161; www.omniameliaisland plantation.com
Spread over 2 sq miles (5 sq km), this resort has 150-plus guest rooms, plus a dazzling beach club and restaurants. Superb supervised kids' programs, along with games, dinner parties, and picnics are offered.
📶 🏖 ☕ 🚫 ❂ $$$

The Ritz-Carlton, Amelia Island
4750 Amelia Island Pkwy, 32034–5501; 904 277 1100; www.ritzcarlton ameliaisland.com
This oceanfront AAA four-diamond resort has luxurious guest rooms and public spaces. There is a beach, a spa, tennis courts, a fitness center, and stellar programs for kids and teenagers.
📶 🍽 🏖 ☕ ❂ $$$

SELF-CATERING

The Villas at Amelia Island Plantation
6800 First Coast Hwy, 32034; 904 261 6161; www.aipfl.com
This huge beach resort offers lodging in rooms, and one-, two-, and three-bedroom villas ideal for families. There's a private beach, golf, a spa, a fitness center, and restaurants.
🏖 🛏 ❂ 🚫 🍽 $$$

CAMPING

Little Talbot Island State Park
12157 Heckscher Dr, Jacksonville, 32226; 904 251 2320; www.florida stateparks.org/littletalbotisland
Located off A1A, this campground offers 40 campsites with water, electricity, and showers. Laundry facilities and bike rentals are available on site. Reserve ahead.
🛏 🚫 ⚲ $

Atlantic Beach   Map 4 H3

RESORT

One Ocean Resort & Spa
One Ocean Blvd, 32233; 904 249 7402; www.oneoceanresort.com
A small but beautiful resort hotel by the ocean, with airy rooms and suites equipped with flat-screen TVs and refrigerators. A personal docent will make reservations, and even enroll kids in the wide variety of programs available.
📶 🍽 🏖 ☕ ❂ $$–$$$

Daytona Beach   Map 6 G3

RESORTS

Perry's Ocean Edge Resort
2209 S Atlantic Ave, 32118; 386 255 0581 or 800 447 0002; www.perrysoceanedge.com
Most units in this property come with a full kitchen. The Kids' Beach Suites in the South Tower are a good option for families. There is an atrium pool that allows swimming year round, a fitness center, water aerobics, and bingo for kids.
📶 🍽 ☕ 🚫 ❂ 🛏 $

The Hilton Daytona Beach Oceanfront Resort
100 North Atlantic Ave, 32118; 386 254 8200; www.daytona hilton.com
Family suites and the D-Dawg's Kidszone, with arts and crafts, board games, and storytelling, make this oceanfront Hilton resort a great family option. Most of the resort's restaurants offer a kids' menu.
📶 🍽 🏖 🚫 ❂ $–$$

Wyndam Oceanwalk Resort
300 North Atlantic Ave, 32118; 386 323 4800; www.oceanwalk.com
Spacious one-, two-, and three-bedroom condos equipped with full kitchens, refrigerators, microwaves, and TVs. Amenities include pools with special play areas, a lazy river and water slide, a game room, and activities for kids.
📶 🍽 ☕ 🚫 ❂ 🛏 $$

Fernandina Beach   Map 4 H2

HOTEL

Amelia Hotel at the Beach
1997 South Fletcher Ave, 32034; 904 206 5200 or 877 263 5428; www.ameliahotel.com
Across the street from Fernandina's Main Beach, this family-owned hotel features rooms with king-size beds, microwaves, and

The King Terrace Suite at The Hilton Daytona Beach Oceanfront Resort

mini-refrigerators. Kids will love the fresh-baked cookies and milk in the afternoon. Bikes and beach gear can be rented next door. There is also complimentary hot breakfast for all guests.

🛜 🍴 P ⊗ ◑ $

CAMPING
Fort Clinch State Park
2601 Atlantic Ave, 32034; 904 277 7274 or 800 326 3521; www.florida stateparks.org/fortclinch
A fascinating fort and great freshwater and saltwater fishing draw visitors to this campground. Campers can choose between a beach and river location. Facilities include utility hook-ups, laundry, and an on-site store. Reserve well in advance.

🛏 ◑ ⚓ $

Gainesville   Map 4 F5

HOTEL
Hilton UF Conference Center
1714 SW 34th St, 32607; 1 352 371 3600; tinyurl.com/bm8oj4u
Located in the southwestern corner of the University of Florida (UF) campus, this hotel makes a superb base for visiting the UF museums and other sights. Rooms and suites are comfortably furnished. There is a fitness center, an outdoor pool, a sports bar, and gift shop on site.

🛜 🍽 🍴 ☕ ⊗ $$

Jacksonville   Map 4 G3

HOTELS
Hampton Inn Beach Boulevard/Mayo Clinic
13733 Beach Blvd, 32224; 904 223 0222; tinyurl.com/bo3jnlh
A 10-minute drive from the beach, this hotel is a great budget choice for its clean airy rooms and suites. There is an indoor heated pool, an on-site convenience store, and free hot breakfast.

🛜 🍽 🍴 P ⊗ $

Omni Jacksonville Hotel
245 Water St, 32202; 904 355 6664; www.omnihotels.com
Located in downtown Jacksonville, a block from riverfront restaurants and shops, this four-diamond Omni boasts a roof-top pool, an upscale restaurant, and kid-friendly services.

🛜 🍽 🍴 ☕ ⊗ $$

CAMPING
Kathryn Abbey Hanna Park
500 Wonderwood Dr, 32233; 904 249 4700; www.coj.net
Just north of Atlantic Beach, this popular park offers a full-facility campground, with tent and RV sites as well as cabins. A freshwater lake and great bike trails are added perks. Amenities include a general store, laundry, and showers. Reserve ahead.

🛏 P ◑ ⚓ $

Jacksonville Beach   Map 4 H3

HOTEL
Fairfield Inn & Suites Jacksonville Beach
1616 1st St N, 32250; 904 435 0100; tinyurl.com/82ahnvr
Steps away from the beach and local restaurants, this hotel offers suites suitable for larger families and is good for longer stays. Free breakfast.

🛜 🍴 P ⊗ $–$$

Cabin at the campsite in Blue Spring State Park, near Orange City

Ocala   Map 5 D3

HOTEL
Courtyard Ocala
3712 SW 38th Ave, 34474; 352 237 8000; tinyurl.com/7dvptlo
Rooms and suites in this renovated hotel have flat-screen TVs and mini-refrigerators. The on-site restaurant, The Bistro, serves healthy breakfast choices and many dinner options.

🛜 🍴 ☕ P ⊗ 🍽 $

Orange City   Map 6 F4

CAMPING
Blue Spring State Park
2100 W French Ave, 32763; 386 775 3663; www.floridastateparks.org
This winter home of manatees offers 51 campsites within walking distance of the spring, in addition to six

well-equipped cabins. The sites have water, electricity, picnic tables, and grills.

🛏 P ◑ ⚓ $

Ponte Vedra Beach   Map 4 H4

HOTEL
Sawgrass Marriott Golf Resort & Spa
1000 PGA Blvd, Ponte Vedra Beach, 32082; 904 285 7777; tinyurl.com/2qbqty
A top golf resort, this AAA three-diamond property is also terrific for a beach vacation, with a quick shuttle to the oceanfront club. The hotel offers high-quality kids' programs, a great spa, and an on-site restaurant.

🛜 🍽 ☕ ⊗ 🍴 $$

St. Augustine   Map 6 F1

HOTEL
Hilton St. Augustine Historic Bayfront
32 Avenida Menendez, 32084 904 829 2277; tinyurl.com/7od9wcd
Located in the historic district, this Hilton hotel makes a great base for exploring the nearby attractions. Rooms come with mini-refrigerators.

🛜 🍴 🍽 ☕ ⊗ $$$

BED & BREAKFAST
Bayfront Marin House Bed and Breakfast
142 Avenida Menendez, 32084– 5049; 904 824 4301; www.bayfront marinhouse.com
This B&B welcomes kids with family-friendly accommodations, private entrances, and a gorgeous bayfront location. Efficient service.

🎎 🛜 🍽 P $$–$$$

CAMPING
Anastasia State Park
1340 Florida A1A, 32080; 904 461 2033; www.floridastateparks.org
A short walk from the beach, the campsites include utility hook-ups, grills, fire rings, and picnic tables. The park has a store/restaurant that also rents beach and sports equipment.

🍴 🛏 P ◑ ⚓ $

Price Guide
The following price ranges are based on one night's accommodation in high season for a family of four, inclusive of service charges and additional taxes.
$ Under $150 **$$** $150–300 **$$$** over $300

Key to symbols *see back cover flap*

The Panhandle

The Panhandle has much to offer families besides miles of dazzling white beaches. This was where the Spanish first attempted to colonize Florida, and the region is rich in Spanish and Native American history. This northwest area, bordering the states of Georgia and Alabama, is also more Old South in spirit, with charm galore in cities such as Tallahassee and Pensacola, along with museums and aquariums for rainy days.

Highlights

Grayton Beach
The oldest town on the South Walton, the lanes here are paved with oyster shells and lined with historic cottages and modern beach homes (see p190).

Seaside
Admire pastel-colored cottages with picket fences in the town that was the film location for *The Truman Show* (see p190).

National Naval Aviation Museum
This museum, in Pensacola's Naval Air Station, traces aviation history with exhibits and hands-on training sessions (see pp196–7).

Gulf Islands National Seashore
Pick a spot to sunbathe on this 150-mile (240-km) paradise of pristine beach and dunes that can be accessed from Pensacola or Fort Walton (see p194).

Mission San Luis
A mission dating to the 1600s is brought to life by re-enacters at this site that was shared by the Spanish and the Apalachee Indians (see p200).

Wakulla Springs State Park
Take a riverboat tour or stand on the observation platform at this park, which has one of the world's deepest springs (see p202).

Left The Blue Angels flight demonstration team performing over Pensacola Beach
Above right Suwannee cooters sunning themselves on a log in Wakulla Springs State Park, Tallahassee

The Best of
The Panhandle

A driving tour is one of the best ways to sample the Panhandle's many fascinating facets. Families can choose between busy beach towns, serene villages, or cities that exude Southern charm. Tallahassee, the state capital, is steeped in history; Pensacola has a marvelous military museum; and Apalachicola offers the ambience of a traditional fishing town. The region's scenic state parks have pristine beaches, and are meccas for wildlife.

Outdoor action

The Panhandle's state parks contain unspoiled beaches and a rare feature – coastal dune lakes, 15 of which are found in the region. The lakes provide beautiful vistas, an abundance of bird life, and opportunities for canoeing or kayaking. **Lake Powell** (see p193), near Panama City, is the largest of the lakes, Western Lake in **Grayton Beach State Park** (see p190) is one of the loveliest, and **Topsail Hill Preserve State Park** (see p191), near Santa Rosa, boasts five scenic ponds. The state parks have miles of trails for hiking and biking. The Panhandle also has uncrowded beaches to escape to. **Shell Island** (see p193), reached by ferry from **St. Andrew's State Park** (see pp192–3) in Panama City, is pure bliss for shell collectors. **St. George Island State Park** (see p203), a barrier island near **Apalachicola** (see p203), has 9 miles (14 km) of tranquil beach and dunes, and the many miles of the **Gulf Islands National Seashore** (see p194) offer plenty of peace.

Historic highlights

This area provides many opportunities to see some of the best-preserved traces of Florida's first inhabitants. **Indian Temple Mound Museum** (see p191), in Fort Walton, marks what was once the center of one of the largest Native American communities. The mound, 17 ft (5 m) tall and 223 ft (68 m) long, is one of the biggest ever found. More Native American lore awaits at **Lake Jackson Mounds Archaeological State Park** (see p199) near **Tallahassee** (see pp198–9). A few miles away is

Below Spanish moss-draped trees shading the reflection pond in Eden Gardens State Park

the **Letchworth-Love Mounds Archaeological State Park** *(see p199)*, in Monticello, with the tallest recorded ceremonial mound.

Saluting the military

Two major military bases in the Panhandle are home to museums with great family appeal. The **National Naval Aviation Museum** *(see pp196–7)*, at Pensacola's Naval Air Station, has historic planes on display. In addition, there are flight simulators which offer visitors of all ages the thrill of experiencing air combat and stunt flying. For a slice of Pensacola's early military history, visit **Fort Barrancas** *(see p197)*, which dates from the Civil War, and **Fort Pickens** *(see p195)*, once a prison for Apache chief Geronimo. Located at Eglin Air Force base in Fort Walton is the **Air Force Armament Museum** *(see p192)*, with fighters, bombers, and spy planes.

Southern comfort

Visitors looking for Southern charm can head to **Tallahassee** and **Pensacola** *(see pp194–5)*, which show the influence of their southern neighbors. A city of rolling hills and canopy roads, **Tallahassee** has antebellum homes dating from its cotton and tobacco plantation days, such as **Goodwood Museum and Gardens** *(see p198)*, as well as the **Park Avenue Historic District** *(see p198)*, with parks and elegant pre-Civil War architecture. There is no mistaking the Southern sway in the accents and genteel tempo of **Pensacola**, as seen in the historic district's architectural styles, and in entertaining museums with unusual and educational exhibits.

The Panhandle

The Panhandle stretches for some 300 miles (483 km) across the northwest corner of the state, between the Gulf of Mexico and the southern states of Alabama and Georgia. Most families head straight for the beach resorts that extend in an arc between Pensacola and Panama City, but the less-explored interior – a hilly, pine-forested landscape unusual in Florida – also offers plenty of recreation. Though the region is large, excellent highways make it easy to navigate by car: I-10 links Tallahassee and Pensacola, and Highway 98 serves the beach towns.

A parrot at ZooWorld Zoological & Botanical Conservatory

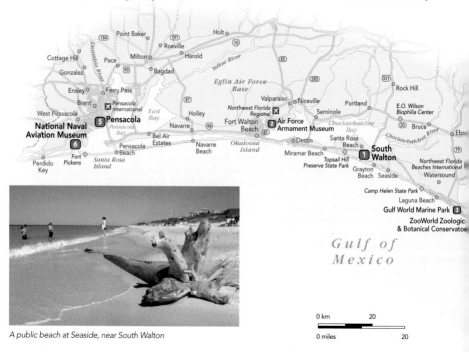

A public beach at Seaside, near South Walton

The Lowdown

🚗 **Getting there and around**
Air Fly to Pensacola International Airport (PNS) (www.flypensacola.com), Northwest Florida Beaches International Airport (ECP) (www.iflybeaches.com) in Panama City, Northwest Florida Regional Airport (VPS) (www.flyvps.com) in Fort Walton Beach, and Tallahassee Regional Airport (TLH) (www.talgov.com/airport). **Car** A rental car is essential to get around. Car rentals are available at all airports.

ℹ️ **Visitor information** See individual entries.

🛒 **Supermarkets** Publix (www.publix.com) is the premier supermarket throughout this region.
Markets Head to Palafox Market, in Pensacola (www.palafoxmarket.com), Tallahassee Downtown Market (www.downtownmarket.com), Tallahassee Farmers' Market, north of I-10 off US 319 (www.localharvest.org/tallahassee-farmers-market-M1165), Okaloosa County Farmers' Market (Apr–Sep) in Fort Walton Beach, or Seaside Farmers' Market in Santa Rosa Beach for fruit, meats, breads, books, art, and crafts. Most markets are open on Saturdays.

🎪 **Festivals** Panhandle Watermelon Festival, Chipley; 850 638 6013 (Jun). Blue Angels Air Show, National Naval Aviation Museum (Jul). Wausau Possum Festival; www.wausaupossumfestival.com (Aug). North Florida Fair, Tallahassee (Nov).

➕ **Pharmacies** Walgreens (www.walgreens.com) and CVS (www.cvs.com) are the two major pharmacies in the region.

🚻 **Restrooms** All major attractions, shopping malls, and gas stations have public restrooms.

Places of interest

At the water's edge in Wakulla Springs State Park, Tallahassee

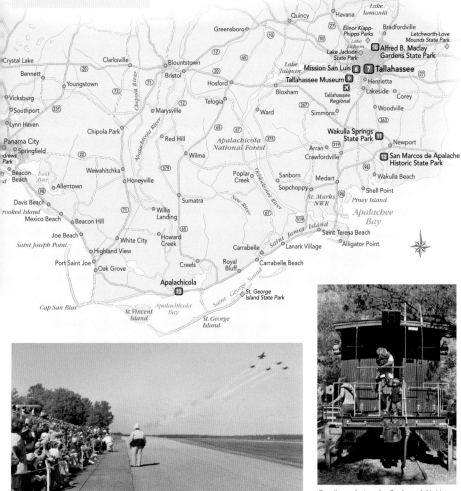

A Blue Angels Air Show in progress at the National Naval Aviation Museum, Pensacola

Family exploring the Seaboard Air Line caboose, Tallahassee Museum

① South Walton
Sparkling beaches and village charm

Lying between the high-rise buildings in Fort Walton and Panama City are 26 miles (42 km) of the finest beaches in Florida. The South Walton shoreline boasts sand that is almost pure quartz crystal, dazzling white to the eye, and soft underfoot. Lined with a string of low-rise, quiet villages, the beaches are great for families. Just under half of the region is preserved as state parks and forests, and opportunities for recreation are plentiful.

Grayton Beach, a charming beach town

Key Sights

① Baytowne Wharf This lively enclave along the shores of Choctawhatchee Bay has boutiques, eateries, and the Baytowne Wharf Adventure Zone with a climbing wall and a zip line for adventure-lovers.

② The Artists at Gulf Place This cooperative artists' colony and open-air market in Santa Rosa Beach is one of many colorful spots in South Walton where local art is featured.

③ Grayton Beach A laid-back town with narrow, oyster-shell-paved lanes, this is the oldest community on the shore. Here, weathered cottages blend with modern beach houses, shaded by pine and oaks.

④ Grayton Beach State Park Award-winning beaches, pine forest, and a nature trail through the dunes with views of scenic Western Lake make this park a special retreat.

⑤ Eden Gardens State Park The restored, antique-filled Wesley House, a typical Southern mansion of the 19th century, inspires visions of hoop skirts and Scarlett O'Hara in *Gone With the Wind*. Picnic along Tucker Bayou, and explore a nature trail and lush gardens shaded by moss-draped live oaks.

⑥ Seaside Developed in the 1980s, this planned village has quaint pastel-colored cottages, and lanes laced with sandy paths that lead to the beach, shops, and restaurants.

⑦ Timpoochee Trail Running the full length of Scenic Highway 30A, this superb 23-mile (37-km) bike path winds through the beach communities, along coastal dune lakes, and through picturesque scenery with views of the Gulf of Mexico.

⑧ Rosemary Beach Inspired by the Seaside model of a walkable village, this town has a mix of architecture, some with a New Orleans influence, and a wide village green.

The Lowdown

Map reference 1 D3
Address Baytowne Wharf: 9300 US Hwy 98 W, Destin, 32550; *www.baytownewharf. com*. The Artists at Gulf Place: 40 Town Loop Center, 32459; *www.artistsatgulfplace.com*. Grayton Beach State Park: 357 Main Park Rd, 32459; *floridastateparks.org*. Eden Gardens State Park:181 Eden Gardens Rd, 32459; *floridastateparks.org*

Car Rent a car from Northwest Florida Regional Airport.

Open Grayton Beach State Park & Eden Gardens State Park: 8am–sunset

Prices Grayton Beach State Park & Eden Gardens State Park: $5 per vehicle. Baytowne Wharf Adventure Zone: check *www.tinyurl.com/BWharfAdv.*

Activities Hiking, canoeing, and kayaking in the state parks.

Good family value?
South Walton combines beach fun and sightseeing for the whole family, with few expenses.

Prices given are for a family of four

View of the Gulf of Mexico from Deer Lake State Park, Santa Rosa Beach

Letting off steam

Deer Lake State Park (6350 E County Rd, 30-A, Santa Rosa Beach, 32459; 850 267 8300) and **Point Washington State Forest**, south of Freeport on I-98, have excellent hiking paths. For canoeing and kayaking, head to **Topsail Hill Preserve State Park** (7525 W Scenic Hwy 30-A, Santa Rosa Beach, 32459; 850 267 8330).

Eat and drink

Picnic: under $25; Snacks: $25–50; Real meal: $50–80; Family treat: over $80 (based on a family of four)

PICNIC Modica Market (109 Central Square, Seaside, 32459; 850 231 1214) offers fixings to enjoy a fine picnic at the Seaside beach.
SNACKS Pickles Beachside Grill (2236 Scenic Hwy 30-A, Seaside, 32459; 850 231 5686; www.sweet williamsltd.com) has hot dogs, chili cheese dogs, burgers, fried pickles, and funnel cakes.
REAL MEAL Bud & Alley's (2236 E County Rd, 30-A, Seaside; 850 231 5900; www.budandalleys.com) is a great spot for lunch on the deck with sandwiches and a pizza-pasta bar. There is also a kids' menu.
FAMILY TREAT Fish Out of Water (Watercolor Inn, off Scenic Hwy 30-A, Watercolor, 32459; 850 534 5050) serves up the area's best gourmet dinner fare – fresh seafood, chicken, and beef – in comfortable, informal settings with wonderful sea views.

Shopping

Big Mama's Hula Girl Gallery (303 E. Ruskin Pl, Seaside, 32459; 850 231 6201) is just one of the funky galleries that abound in South Walton's villages, with folk art that will delight all ages. Bargain-hunters can head to **Silver Sands**

Preium Outlets (10562 Emerald Coast Pkwy, 32550; 850 654 9771) for popular brands such as Esprit, Gap Kids, and OshKosh B'gosh.

Find out more

FILM The town of Seaside was the set for *The Truman Show*, a satirical comedy starring Jim Carrey, Ed Harris, and Laura Linney.

Take cover

Take a 15-mile (24-km) drive inland to the **E.O. Wilson Biophilia Center** (4956 State Hwy 20, 32439; 850 835 1824; www.eowilsoncenter.org) for nature dioramas, a working beehive, live turtles, snakes, and frogs, as well as films about nature.

Brightly colored interior of Pickles Beachside Grill, Seaside

Next stop...

INDIAN TEMPLE MOUND MUSEUM Located in Fort Walton, the Indian Temple Mound Museum (139 Miracle Strip Pkwy SE, Fort Walton Beach, 32548; 850 833 9595; www.fwb.org/museums) is on the site of a ceremonial and burial earthwork built by early Native Americans of the Mound Builder Culture, who lived between AD 800 and 1400. The museum has objects crafted from stone, bones, shell, and clay from this culture, as well as finds relating to the region's early explorers, and the later settlers.

KIDS' CORNER

Beach fun
Digging in the sand, playing in the waves, and building sand castles are some of the popular activities on the Panhandle's beaches. What else would you add to the list?

Suggestions at the bottom of the page.

TRIAL BY KITE
Around 300 years ago, judges in the US flew kites above people accused of crimes. They believed that the kite would dip down over a guilty person.

Taking off
South Walton's beaches are perfect for kite-flying. Probably the most famous kite-flyer in history was American politician Benjamin Franklin who, in 1752, flew a kite into a storm cloud to see if electricity would be conducted down its string. A key was attached near the bottom. The kite was struck by lightning and, when Franklin moved his hand toward the key, a spark jumped across and he felt shock, proving that lightning was electrical. Don't try this at home – it could be fatal!

Try: Kite-flying, frisbee-throwing, sunbathing, beach volleyball, surfing, swimming, and many more.

Inside the cockpit of an aircraft at the Air Force Armament Museum, Fort Walton

② Air Force Armament Museum

Take flight

This museum is located on the Eglin Air Force Base, home of the Air Armament Center (AAC), which is responsible for the development of air-delivered weapons. Start outside the building, where there is a lineup of over 20 military planes to inspect. These date from World War I to the present, and include the SR-71 Blackbird, the fastest plane ever built. It can fly at over 2,200 mph (3,520 km/h)! Inside the museum are four more vintage aircraft and an amazing collection of bombs, missiles, and rockets, as well as interactive displays including one that works the controls of a mock cockpit. Check out other fascinating exhibits, such as "bunker busters," bombs that can hit targets deep underground. There is also a 30-minute film that illustrates the AAC's history and accomplishments.

Letting off steam

Head 5 miles (8 km) south to **Okaloosa Island**, Fort Walton's beach community. This long strand stretching out to the neighboring town of Destin is accessed by bridges at each end. There is plenty of space on the beach for running around, and quiet picnic areas. The less crowded beaches are closer to Destin. Visit the **Gulfarium Marine Adventure Park** (*www.gulfarium.com*), a small

The Lowdown

🌐 **Map reference** 1 C3
Address 100 Museum Dr (State Rd 85), Eglin Air Force Base, 32542; 850 651 1808; *www.afarmamentmuseum.com*

🚗 **Car** From Fort Walton Beach

🕐 **Open** 9:30am–4:30pm Mon–Sat

💲 **Price** Free

👫 **Age range** 8 plus

⏱ **Allow** 2–3 hours

♿ **Wheelchair access** Yes

🍴 **Eat and drink** PICNIC Publix (*610 Eglin Pkwy NE, Fort Walton Beach, 32547; 850 862 6789; www.publix.com*), one of the Florida-wide supermarket chains, is well stocked with goodies for a picnic at Okaloosa Island. REAL MEAL IHOP (*348 SW Miracle Strip Pkwy, Fort Walton Beach, 32548; 850 243 9333; www.ihop.com*) serves pancakes day and night, along with omelets, sandwiches, and burgers. The kids' menu features a "Create a Face" pancake with strawberry eyes and a banana smile.

aquarium, and the diminutive but fun **Emerald Coast Science Center** (*www.ecscience.org*) nearby.

③ Gulf World Marine Park

Q & A sessions on sea life

An educational facility, this park is a contributor to the Gulf World Marine Institute that works to rescue and rehabilitate marine mammals before releasing them back into the wild. Activities include a delightful magic show that features spectacular illusions, comedy acts, special effects, and interactions with the audience. The aquarium's inhabitants include sharks, alligators, penguins, iguanas, and sea turtles. Watch the feeding sessions, as well as underwater scuba demonstrations, before heading for the stingrays that await visitors.

Letting off steam

Drive 9 miles (14 km) to **St. Andrews State Park** (*4607 State Park Lane, 32408; 850 233 5140; www.floridastateparks.org/standrews*), on a barrier island off of busy Panama

The Lowdown

🌐 **Map reference** 2 E3
Address 15412 Front Beach Rd, Panama City Beach, 32413; 850 234 5271; *www.gulfworldmarinepark.com*

🚗 **Car** From Fort Walton Beach

🕐 **Open** 9am–7pm in summer; 9:30am–4:30pm rest of the year

💲 **Price** $80–100; under 4s free

👫 **Activities** Kids aged 5 plus can sign up for the Swim with the Dolphins program. Check website for details.

👫 **Age range** All ages

⏱ **Allow** 3–4 hours

♿ **Wheelchair access** Yes

🍴 **Eat and drink** PICNIC Publix (*23026 Panama City Beach Pkwy, 32413; 850 233 4392; www.publix.com*) has all the ingredients for a fine picnic at the beach. REAL MEAL Schooners (*5121 Gulf Dr, Panama City Beach, 32408; 850 235 3555; www.schooners.com*), an informal eatery on the waterfront, has something for everyone. It serves salads, wings, burgers, grouper sandwiches, and fish tacos.

Great blue heron at St. Andrews State Park, Panama City

City Beach. The park's beach is relatively quiet, and offers opportunities for canoeing and kayaking, as well as two nature trails. Take the shuttle (850 233 0504) to **Shell Island** for a spot of beachcombing and a rock jetty that creates a shallow area in the water perfect for young kids

④ ZooWorld Zoological & Botanical Conservatory

A small animal kingdom

This little local zoo offers up-close views of over 250 animals in a tropical garden setting. Children can learn all about parrots, reptiles, and alligators at the live shows, and even pose for pictures with them. The petting zoo houses lots of farm animals for feeding, as well as a camel. A raised walkway allows for a special treat: feeding Sydney the giraffe. The zoo is especially recommended for younger children.

The historic Lodge in Camp Helen State Park

The Lowdown

- **Map reference** 2 E4
- **Address** 9008 Front Beach Rd, Panama City Beach, 32407; 850 233 1243; www.zooworldpcb.net
- **Car** From Fort Walton Beach
- **Open** 9:30am–5pm daily; last admission 4pm
- **Price** $48-62; under 4s free
- **Activities** The zoo organizes many educational animal shows; check website for schedule.
- **Age range** 3 plus
- **Allow** 3 hours
- **Eat and drink** SNACKS Mike's Café and Oyster Bar (17554 Front Beach Rd, Panama City Beach, 32413; 850 234 1942; www.mikes cafeandoysterbar.com) has a simple, diner-like decor and lunch choices such as seafood baskets, salads, and sandwiches to please grown-ups, as well as a bargain children's menu. FAMILY TREAT Captain Anderson's Restaurant (5551 N Lagoon Dr, Panama City Beach, 32408; 850 234 2225; www.captanderson.com; closed Sun) is a longtime local dinner favorite for steaks and the freshest of seafood. The restaurant claims to serve the "world's best seafood platter." Kids will find their own special menu.

Letting off steam

Go 14 miles (22 km) northwest to **Camp Helen State Park** (www. floridastateparks.org/camphelen), which is bordered by the Gulf of Mexico on three sides, and by Lake Powell, one of the largest coastal dune lakes in Florida. A private company resort from 1945 until 1984, the huge park offers lots of space for picnicking, as well as swimming, beachcombing, fishing, and hiking.

Wolf Show at the ZooWorld Zoological & Botanical Conservatory, Panama City Beach

Picnic under $25; **Snacks** $25–50; **Real meal** $50–80; **Family treat** over $80 (based on a family of four)

⑤ Pensacola
Beaches and the Blue Angels

A distinct Southern accent borrowed from the neighboring state of Alabama, and influences from a colorful past, give Pensacola a unique flavor. The Historic Pensacola Village, its oldest quarter, comprises 27 buildings and museums reflecting 450 years of history. Two of the city's best family attractions are the superb sands of the Gulf Islands National Seashore and tours of the National Naval Aviation Museum (*see pp196–7*), where the famous Blue Angels stunt flyers practice.

Costumed guides in the Historic Pensacola Village

Key Sights

Museum of Commerce This reconstruction of Pensacola's late 19th- and early 20th-century streetscape features a print workshop, and leather and harness shops.

Pensacola Children's Museum Its many imaginative exhibits and dress-up period clothing make this museum a great place to take younger kids.

Museum of Industry Exhibits depicting the industries that helped build the city – fishing, brick-making, lumber, and railroads – include a vintage fishing boat and a 1905 locomotive.

British Officer's Compound Built during the early years of the American Revolution, this compound's foundations are among the many finds that form Pensacola's Colonial Archaeological Trail.

Seville Square

Barkley House

GOVERNMENT ST
JEFFERSON ST
ZARRAGOSSA ST

Museum of Industry

Museum of Commerce

Pensacola Museum of Art Once a jail, this building now houses contemporary art, decorative glass, and African tribal art.

Seville Square The heart of Pensacola when the area was first settled by the Spanish, this square served as the parade ground for the Fort of Pensacola during British rule in the 1770s.

Barkley House Built in 1825, this is the oldest surviving example of a "high-house" in the city. Tours of the Historic Pensacola Village include a stop at the house, where visitors can learn about the Barkley family.

Letting off steam

The US 98, leading south to Pensacola Beach on Santa Rosa Island, passes through the community of Gulf Breeze, and the glorious **Gulf Islands National Seashore**. Go to the **Naval Live Oaks** area (*www.nps.gov*), on the US 98 east of Gulf Breeze, for miles of picturesque nature trails and swimming in Santa Rosa Sound. There is also a campground with a covered picnic pavilion, restrooms, and outdoor showers. Maps are available at the park's **Visitor Center** (*1801 Gulf Breeze Pkwy, 32561; 850 934 2600*).

Prices given are for a family of four

Enjoying a meal at the popular New Yorker Deli & Pizzeria

Eat and drink

Picnic: under $25; Snacks: $25–50; Real meal: $50–80; Family treat: over $80 (based on a family of four)

PICNIC New Yorker Deli & Pizzeria (*3001 E Cervantes St, 32503; 850 469 0029*) offers a variety of sandwiches for a picnic in Seville Square.
SNACKS Santino's Pizza (*Bruno's Shopping Center, 368 Gulf Breeze Pkwy, Gulf Breeze, 32561; 850 932 1211; www.santinospizza.net*) serves pizza, salads, and brownies.
REAL MEAL Dharma Blue (*300 S Alcaniz St, 32501; 850 433 1275*) is located in leafy Seville Square, and

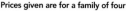

offers a wide-ranging menu, from sandwiches to paella. There is an appealing children's menu too. **FAMILY TREAT Fish House** (600 S Barracks St, 32502; 850 470 0003; www.goodgrits.com), on the bay, serves the freshest Gulf seafood, with Southern sides such as cheese grits, collard greens, and corn fritters.

Shopping
The **Quayside Art Gallery** (17 E Zarragossa St, 32502; www.quayside gallery.com) is southeastern Florida's largest cooperative artists' gallery. Go to the **Blue Moon Antique Mall** (3721 W Navy Blvd, 32507; 850 455 7377) for old postcards, toys, jewelry, vintage pottery, and glassware.

Find out more
DIGITAL Learn about Pensacola's history at www.visitpensacola.com/articles/pensacola-history. Visit uwf.edu/anthropology/research/colonial/trail to find out about the discoveries along the Colonial Archaeological Trail.

Next stop...
FORT PICKENS World War II gun emplacements are some of the military artifacts that come to life at Fort Pickens (www.npa.gov), 8 miles (13 km) southwest of Pensacola. Completed in 1834, it was the largest of four forts built to defend Pensacola Bay. National Park Service Rangers lead tours at 2pm daily.

KIDS' CORNER
Test your Pensacola IQ
1 The flags of five different countries have flown over Pensacola during its long history. Which country was the first, and which was the last?
2 Pensacola got its name from the Native American tribe that greeted the first Spanish explorers in 1559. What were they called?
3 Which city was the original capital of Florida?

Answers at the bottom of the page.

Miles of bliss
Along Florida's heavily built-up shoreline are some magical stretches of unspoiled beach, known as National Seashores, and preserved by the US government for public recreation. The Gulf Islands National Seashore (www.nps.gov/guis) offers superb boat rides, and campgrounds.

Outer walls of Fort Pickens, a massive brick fort at Gulf Islands National Seashore

The Lowdown

Map reference 1 A3
Address Pensacola 32502. Museum of Commerce: 201 E Zarragossa St; 850 595 1559. Pensacola Children's Museum: 115, E Zarragossa St; 850 595 1559. Museum of Industry: 120 E Church St; 850 595 5985. Pensacola Museum of Art: 407 South Jefferson St; 850 432 6247; www.pensacolamuseumof art.org. Barkley House: 10 S Florida Blanca St; 850 595 5993, call ahead; historicpensacola.org

Bus Escambia County Area Transit (ECAT) buses serve many areas, but the wait between buses can be an hour or more. It's best to rent a car.

Visitor information Pensacola Bay Area Convention and Visitors Bureau, 1401 E Gregory St, 32502; 800 874 1234; www.visitpensacola.com

Open Tickets for visiting the sights in the Historic Pensacola Village can be purchased at the Tivoli High House Gift Shop

(205 E Zarragossa St, 32502; 850 595 5993; 10am–4pm Tue–Sat).

Price Historic Pensacola Village: $28–32; under 4s free. An individual visit to the T. T. Wentworth, Jr. Florida State Museum is half price on Sun.

Guided tours The village runs 1–1½-hour tours at 11am, 1pm & 2:30pm, which include the Lavalle House, the 1871 Dorr House, the 1832 Old Christ Church & the 1890 Lear-Rocheblave House. Walking tours, at 2pm, cover Zarragossa Street and the Barkley House.

Age range 6 plus

Allow 1 day

Festival Blue Angels Air Shows (Jul & Nov)

Good family value?
Reasonably priced tickets, free museum visits and a walk through the historical district, all make Pensacola an exciting destination.

DID YOU KNOW...
In 1559, Pensacola became the first European settlement in the US. But it didn't last. A month later, a hurricane destroyed supplies, causing the Spanish to flee.

Living in the past
The homes in the Historic Pensacola Village depict how kids lived many years ago. If you had existed then, your family would have done the washing by hand, dipped candles for light, and made their own clothes. Which parts of your life today would you miss?

Answers: 1 Spain; USA. **2** Panzacola Indians. **3** Pensacola.

⑥ National Naval Aviation Museum
Spacecraft and fighter planes

Located at the Pensacola Naval Air Station, a training ground for the US Navy and Marine Corps, this museum traces the history of aviation with thrilling displays. Its amazing exhibits include over 150 restored aircraft and spacecraft, dating from the era of the earliest biplanes to the Space Age, and the Mercury and Apollo space capsules. Hands-on elements include the chance to sit at the controls of a jet trainer, while practice sessions by the Blue Angel stunt pilots add to the excitement.

A Blue Angel pilot signing autographs

Key Features

Upper Level Hall of Honor, Medal of Honor, Art Gallery, Flight Adventure Deck, MaxFlight Simulator, and Cockpit Trainers

Main Deck Level WWII–Korean Aircraft, Sunken Treasures, *USS Cabot* Flight Deck, Early Aircraft, Modern Aircraft, and Museum Store

Hangar Bay One Apollo Exhibit, Women in Naval Aviation, MiG-21 Cockpit

Entrance

① **MaxFlight Simulator** High-tech video and real motion simulate the feeling of being on a mission in a high-speed fighter plane.

② **Sunken Treasures** The two aircraft displayed here were used for training during World War II before they sank in Lake Michigan. They were recovered from the lake, remarkably well preserved by the cold water.

③ **Cockpit Trainers** Kids can climb into cockpits, including those of the A-4 Skyhawk and Corsair II, in this simulated flying experience.

④ **The IMAX® Theater** Four different features are shown daily on one of the largest IMAX® screens in the world. *The Magic of Flight* is a regular on the schedule.

⑤ **Blue Angels** Check out the display of four A-4 Skyhawks, used by the daredevil Blue Angels, suspended from the ceiling of a seven-story glass atrium.

⑥ **USS *Cabot* Flight Deck** See the replica of a flight deck, and the superstructure of a World War II aircraft carrier, complete with fighter planes.

⑦ **Space Capsule Display** Here, space exploration exhibits include a Skylab Command Module, a Mercury capsule, and a Moon Rover vehicle. Astronaut suits and memorabilia are also on display.

⑧ **Biplane** With one wing fixed above the other, biplanes were important early aircraft used in World War I. They are favorites in barnstorming air shows today.

⑨ **Hangar Bay One** On display are aircraft of the post-World War II era, including a Marine One presidential helicopter and a replica of the Apollo 17 lunar module. There is also a section on Coast Guard aircraft and prisoners of war.

The Lowdown

🌐 **Map reference** 1 A3 **Address** 1750 Radford Blvd, Suite C, Naval Air Station, 32508; 850 452 3604; www.navalaviationmuseum.org

🚌 **Bus** ECAT bus 57. **Car** Rent a car from Pensacola Gulf Coast Regional Airport.

🕐 **Open** 9am–5pm daily

💲 **Price** Free

🎫 **Cutting the line** Arrive early as seats fill up fast for the Blue Angels practice flights (Mar–Nov: see website for dates and times). Pilots often come out to shake hands and sign autographs.

🚶 **Guided tours** Daily 20-min trolley tours of 50 aircraft outdoors at 10 & 11am, 1 & 2pm. Self-guided tours can be downloaded from the museum's website.

👫 **Age range** 6 plus

🎨 **Activities** Flight Adventure Deck tour at 1pm, 2pm & 3pm Mon–Fri, in which trained volunteers introduce visitors to hands-on exhibits. Watch the practice flights, weather permitting.

⏱ **Allow** At least 4 hours

♿ **Wheelchair access** Yes

☕ **Café** Cubi Bar Café (see p197)

🚻 **Restrooms** On every level

Good family value? The free museum is entertaining and watching the Blue Angels is an unforgettable experience.

The kid-friendly Cubi Bar Café at the National Naval Aviation Museum

Letting off steam

If kids need a break, head 8 miles (13 km) west to the **Perdido Kids Park** *(3453 Nighthawk Lane, 32506)* on Perdido Key. An imaginative multilevel wooden play area, it includes climbing areas such as mock forts, a lighthouse, a pirate ship, and Blue Angels planes. There is also a special toddler area, designed for children aged 2 to 5.

Eat and drink

Picnic: under $25; Snacks: $25–50; Real meal: $50–80; Family treat: over $80 (based on a family of four)

PICNIC Winn-Dixie Market *(50 S Blue Angel Pkwy, 32506; 850 458 1375)* offers the makings of a picnic that can be enjoyed on the museum's lawn.
SNACKS Cubi Bar Café *(Main Deck Level)* serves nachos, hot dogs, sandwiches, and salads in a setting similar to the bar area of the famous Cubi Point Officers' Club. Kids love the Whirly Bird, a make-your-own peanut butter and jelly sandwich.
REAL MEAL The Burger Factory *(314 S Navy Blvd, 32507; 850 435 4155; www.theburgerfactory.net)* offers a wide range of burgers with home-made dressings and sauces.
FAMILY TREAT Jackson's Steak House *(400 S Palafox St, 32502; 850 469 9898; jacksons.goodgrits.com)*, in Pensacola's Historic District, serves prime steaks with prices to match. Children can order half portions.

Shopping

Everyone will enjoy the **Museum Shop**, which is well stocked with caps and T-shirts for all ages, kids' clothing from infant bodysuits to aviator

jackets, Blue Angels souvenirs, DVDs, flags, posters, and toys. The cute aviator bears wearing goggles, helmet, and scarf are irresistible.

Find out more

DIGITAL Learn about the exciting Blue Angels flight team and see a demo flight on *www.blueangels. navy.mil.* The museum website, *www.navalaviationmuseum.com,* has an electronic scrapbook with photos of important events in aviation history.

Entrance to the historic Fort Barrancas in Pensacola Bay

Next stop...

FORT BARRANCAS Located near the National Naval Aviation Museum, Fort Barrancas *(3182 Taylor Rd, 32508; 850 455 5167; www.nps.gov/guis/planyourvisit/ fort-barrancas-area.htm)* is a two-part fort worth exploring. Its strategic location on a bluff overlooking Pensacola Bay inspired three nations – Britain, Spain, and the US – to build forts here. The Visitor Center screens an informative film. The Spanish Water Battery is a gentle 500-ft (152-m) walk, while the over-look near the fort's entrance offers beautiful views of Pensacola Bay.

⑦ Tallahassee

Tons of Southern charm

Encircled by rolling hills and dotted with pine forests, this state capital has a rich Southern flavor. This former site of an Apalachee Indian settlement is now home to several historical museums. Located in the heart of the city, and spreading over several landscaped blocks, the Capitol Complex offers much to see and do for all ages. Pretty gardens, the nearby beaches, beautiful canopied roads, and a wide choice of dining venues are further lures to this city.

The canopied Meridian Road, Tallahassee

Key Sights

The Lowdown

🌐 **Map reference** 3 A3
Address Florida State University: 600 W College Ave, 32306; www.fsu.edu. Museum of Florida History: 500 South Bronough St, 32399; www.museumoffloridahistory.com. Florida Historic Capitol Museum: 400 South Monroe St, 32399; www.flhistoric capitol.gov. Goodwood Museum and Gardens: 1600 Miccosukee Rd, 32308; www. goodwoodmuseum.org

🚗 **Car** Rent a car from the Tallahassee Regional Airport. **Bus** Star Metro (talgov.com) buses cover much of the city.

ℹ️ **Visitor information** Tallahassee Visitor Information Center, 106 E Jefferson St, 32301; 800 628 2866; www.visittallahassee.com

🕐 **Open** Museum of Florida History and Florida Historic Capitol Museum: 9am–4:30pm Mon–Fri, 10am–4:30pm Sat & noon–4:30pm Sun. Goodwood Museum and Gardens: 10am–4pm Mon–Fri & 10am–2pm Sat

💲 **Prices** Museum of Florida History and Florida Historic Capitol Museum: free. Goodwood Museum and Gardens: $30–36; under 3s free

🚩 **Guided tours** Florida State Capitol's Welcome Center has self-guided tour brochures.

⏱️ **Allow** 2–3 days

🚻 **Restrooms** In the museums and public parks

Good family value?

Most attractions are free and the city offers a unique look at American history.

① **Florida State University** This university is noted for its highly regarded music and theater departments, which stage concerts and plays during the school year.

② **Museum of Florida History** Prehistoric mastodons, Native American exhibits, and a replica riverboat brings the state's past to life in this excellent museum.

③ **Florida State Capitol** Built in 1977, the tower behind the Historic Capitol houses art exhibits on the main floor. The 22nd floor observation deck offers views for miles around.

④ **Florida Historic Capitol Museum** See the house and senate chambers, the governor's suite, and the supreme court, all restored just as they were in the state's original columned capitol.

⑤ **Park Avenue Historic District** This central chain of green parks is lined with 27 homes that predate the Civil War. Built around 1830, the oldest one, The Columns, houses the James Madison Institute.

⑥ **Lake Ella** One of Tallahassee's many lakes, Lake Ella is centered by a spraying fountain and circled by a paved walking trail. The surrounding park has picnic tables and some quaint shops.

⑦ **Goodwood Museum and Gardens** Discover what life was like for kids in the South long ago in this 1834 plantation house, where much of the original art and furnishings have been restored.

Prices given are for a family of four

Dog Et Al, a populat spot for hot dogs in Tallahassee

Letting off steam

Tallahassee has excellent parks with wooded areas and lakes. **Tom Brown Park** (*1125 Easterwood Dr, 32312*) has tennis courts and nature trails. The **Elinor Klapp- Phipps Park** (*4000 N Meridian Rd, 32308*) offers 10 miles (16 km) of trails, including Bluebird and Butterfly trails.

Take cover

Visit the **Challenger Learning Center** (*200 S Duval St, 32301; 850 645 7827; www.challengertlh.com*), which features shows such as Hubble Space Telescope at its IMAX® Theater.

Eat and drink

Picnic: under $25; Snacks: $25–50; Real meal: $50–80; Family treat: over $80 (based on a family of four)

PICNIC Publix Super Market (*1700 N Monroe St, 32303; 850 222 1975; www.publix.com; 7am–11pm daily*) has ingredients for a picnic that can be savored with a view at Lake Ella.
SNACKS Dog Et Al (*1456 S Monroe St, 32301; 850 222 4099; 10am–6pm Mon–Sat*) serves great hot dogs with a variety of toppings.
REAL MEAL Red Elephant Pizza and Grill (*1872 Thomasville Rd, 32303; 850 222 7492; www. redelephantpizza.com; 11am–9pm daily*) has grilled sandwiches, salads, and pizza. It also has a kids' menu.
FAMILY TREAT Sage (*3534 Maclay Blvd S, 32312; 850 270 9396; www. sagetallahassee.com*) offers freshly-prepared dishes in an upscale but casual environment.

Shopping

Head for **Market Square** (*1415 Timberlane Rd, 32312; 850 906 2453*), where kids will like the toys

and the soda fountain treats at Lofty Pursuits. **Governor's Square Mall** (*1500 Apalachee Pkwy, 32301; 850 877 8106*) has stores such as Justice, for tweens, and Lids, a world of sports team caps.

Find out more

DIGITAL Learn about Florida's ancient Native American settlements and ceremonial mounds at *lostworlds. org/ancient_civilizations_florida*.

Pathway at Lake Jackson Mounds Archaeological State Park

Next stop...

MOUNDS OF HISTORY Head 6 miles (10 km) north to **Lake Jackson Mounds Archaeological State Park** to learn about Native American history. The site of an important ceremonial center, it has two remaining large mounds and one smaller mound. Visitors can hike the nature trails and picnic near the two large mounds. 22 miles (35 km) east is the **Letchworth-Love Mounds Archaeological State Park**, which has one of the largest surviving mounds in Florida. The mound is a truncated pyramid and rises over 42 ft (13 m). Visit *www.floridastateparks. org* for more details.

KIDS' CORNER

Capitol Museum quiz
1 What year did Tallahassee become the state capital?
2 The city's first mayor, Francis W. Eppes, had a famous grandfather. Who was he?
3 Florida State University is the oldest state school. What was the school called before it became a co-ed in 1947?

Answers at the bottom of the page.

Canopied roads
Tallahassee is known for its canopied roads, where moss-draped live oaks and other trees have grown so tall that their limbs meet to shade the roads beneath them.

CAPITAL FIGHTERS
Tallahassee was the only Southern capital east of the Mississippi River not captured by the Union during the Civil War. Most men were off serving in the Southern army, but when warned of a pending attack, local volunteers – old men and young boys – met the Union forces at Union Bridge and fought off three major attacks.

Where the four shall meet
In Colonial times, the only part of Florida that was settled was the north and there were just two major towns, St. Augustine and Pensacola. According to legend, a rider set out on horseback from each town and at the spot where they met, the capital city of Tallahassee grew up.

Answers: 1 1824. **2** Thomas Jefferson. **3** Florida State College for Women.

A cannon on display in the gardens at Mission San Luis

A re-enactor dressed as a blacksmith in Mission San Luis

⑧ Mission San Luis
Time travel back to the 1600s

Costumed interpreters bring to life a reconstruction of one of Florida's rarest sites: a 1600s mission that was shared by Spanish settlers and the native Apalachee Indians. This unusual cooperation worked because the Spanish needed labor and provisions while the Apalachee Indians wanted peace and prestige. The arrangement lasted until 1704,

The Lowdown

- 🌐 **Map reference** 3 A3
  Address 2100 West Tennessee St, 32304; 850 245 6406; www.missionsanluis.org
- 🚗 **Car** Rent a car from Tallahassee Regional Airport.
- 🕐 **Open** 10am–4pm Tue–Sun
- 💲 **Price** $12–14; under 6s free
- 👫 **Activities** Choose from musket firing demonstrations (11am–noon Sat), Historical Happenings presentations, Colonial crafts for children, archaeology lab tours, historic gardening tours, blacksmithing, and historical cooking classes. Check website for schedules.
- 👫 **Age range** 6 plus
- ⏱ **Allow** 2–3 hours
- 🍴 **Eat and drink** *PICNIC* Publix Super Market (800 Ocala Rd, 32304; 850 575 6997; www.publix.com) offers the makings for a lunch to be enjoyed at picnic tables in the Mission grounds. *REAL MEAL* Wells Brothers (1710 W Tharpe St, 32303; 850 942 6665; www.wellsbrothersbarandgrill.com) serves salads, sandwiches, burgers, and burritos.
- 🎉 **Festival** Winter Solstice Celebration, a festival of Native American culture (Dec)

when both groups fled from British invaders. See the enormous, five-story Indian Council House with its palm-thatched roof. It stands next to a Franciscan church that was constructed by the Apalachee Indians under Spanish supervision. The defensive fort, El Castillo de San Luis, has been re-created, and a Spanish home and working gardens portray everyday life in a community of 1,600 people. The excellent on-site museum traces the archaeological excavations of the area and displays artifacts found during the digs, such as tools and pottery.

Letting off steam

While the paths of the vast grounds provide plenty of scope for exercise, any excess energy can be expended on a nature trail in the wooded area behind the Spanish home. Pick up a brochure in the Visitor Center to identify some of the dozens of butterfly species that can be spotted here.

⑨ Tallahassee Museum
A farm, a plantation, and a zoo – in a museum

Popular with children, this sprawling, multifaceted museum can entertain for hours. Visit farm animals such as cows, sheep, goats, and pigs in the Big Bend Farm, an 1880s farm complete with reconstructed and restored buildings. The garden grows crops such as corn, cotton, and sugarcane. The museum also has a zoo that features Florida wildlife in natural habitats – there are black bears, a red wolf, a black

The Lowdown

- 🌐 **Map reference** 3 A3
  Address 3945 Museum Dr, 32310; 850 575 1636; www.tallahasseemuseum.org
- 🚗 **Car** Rent a car from Tallahassee Regional Airport.
- 🕐 **Open** 9am–5pm Mon–Sat, 11am–5pm Sun
- 💲 **Price** $33-42; under 3s free
- 👫 **Activities** The museum offers family and youth programs; check website for schedule.
- 👫 **Age range** All ages
- ⏱ **Allow** 4 hours
- ♿ **Wheelchair access** Yes
- 🍴 **Eat and drink** *PICNIC* Metro Deli (104 1/2 South Monroe, 32301; 850 224 6870; www.metrodelis.com) has a Metro Box Lunch that offers a choice of sandwiches or wraps, chips, a cookie and a drink. Enjoy it in the museum's spacious grounds. *REAL MEAL* The Trail Break Café (on site) has a variety of sandwiches and a "Bug Bites" children's meal which includes a toy, a drink, chips, and a choice of corn dog, chicken nuggets, grilled cheese, or a hot dog.
- 🎉 **Festival** Jazz and Blues Festival (late Mar)

A bobcat in the zoo within the Tallahassee Museum grounds

panther, bobcats, playful river otters, and a Florida alligator. Other attractions include a restored plantation that has an original home, a kitchen, and a slave cabin – a dwelling that tells of a time when slaves were brought from Africa against their will to work the fields on Southern plantations. Families can take a walk on the nature trail, head indoors to experience the hands-on exhibits in the Discovery Center, or discover underwater life in the Fleischmann Natural Science

An elegantly furnished room in Maclay House, Alfred B. Maclay Gardens State Park

building. The latter has two small freshwater aquariums and an observation window to watch birds feeding outside.

Letting off steam

The zoo's paths, and the many acres of grounds, provide plenty of opportunities for walking. If any energy is left, take advantage of the museum's wooded nature trail.

⑩ Alfred B. Maclay Gardens State Park

A floral wonderland

Alfred B. Maclay, a New York financier, and his wife Louise planned the gardens in the grounds of their winter home in 1923. This blooming oasis, with over 200 varieties of plants, is a vision in late winter and early spring, when camellias, dogwoods, and azaleas are in flower. The season lasts from January to April, with the beauty at its peak in March. Brick walkways and pine needle paths make for a serene stroll through landscapes that include a walled garden, ponds, fountains, and a lovely lake. Look for the narrow path leading to a secret garden. This secluded spot shelters small plants and has pretty wrought-iron benches that are perfect for a break. Lake Hall provides opportunities for swimming, fishing, canoeing, and kayaking, and two nature trails through the woods overlook the lake. Still furnished as it was when the owners were in residence, the Maclay House is open for visits from January through April.

Take cover

A short drive south is **Books-a-Million** *(3521 Thomasville Road, 32308; 850 893 3131; www.books amillion.com)*, a bookstore well stocked with choices to please all ages, from tots to teens, as well as a range of genres for adults. Be prepared to be wheedled into a purchase.

The Lowdown

🌐 **Map reference** 3 A3
Address 3540 Thomasville Rd, 32309; 850 487 4556; *www.florida stateparks.org/maclaygardens*

🚗 **Car** Rent a car from Tallahassee Regional Airport.

🕐 **Open** Gardens: 9am–5pm daily

💲 **Price** $15–18; under 2s free. $6 per vehicle for parking and additional fee Jan–Apr, when gardens are in bloom

🚩 **Guided tours** From Jan–Apr, guided tours are offered on most Sats and Suns. A *Gardens Walking Tour* brochure is available at the Ranger Station.

👫 **Age range** 5 plus

⏱ **Allow** 2–3 hours

🍴 **Eat and drink** PICNIC The Fresh Market *(1390 Village Square Blvd, Ste 4, 32312; 850 907 1392; www.thefreshmarket.com)* offers gourmet fixings for a picnic. Pavilions and grills along the Lake Hall shore provide the perfect setting for a picnic. REAL MEAL Red Elephant Pizza and Grill *(1872 Thomasville Rd, Suite A, 32303; 850 222 7492; www.redelephant pizza.com)* serves pizza, burgers, sandwiches, and desserts. It also has a kids' menu.

⑪ Wakulla Springs State Park

Gator-gazing, swims, and walks

A popular location for *Tarzan* movies in the past, Wakulla is home to one of the world's deepest natural springs. Spot alligators, turtles, and birds of all shapes and sizes on one of the park's daily ranger-led riverboat tours. An observation platform offers superb views of the springs, and a safe area has been set aside for swimming; the crystal-clear waters are also great for snorkeling. A 6-mile (10-km) hiking trail weaves through a hardwood forest of magnolia oak, beech, and hickory, as well as a longleaf pine forest. Be sure to decide in advance how far to walk, as this is not a loop trail. Built in Mediterranean style in the 1930s, the park's handsome Wakulla Springs Lodge is on the National Register of Historic Places.

Take cover

If it rains, head for the **Wakulla Springs Lodge** and enjoy a treat at the Soda Fountain.

Tour boats at the jetty in Wakulla Springs State Park

Entrance to the elegant Wakulla Springs Lodge, Wakulla Springs State Park

The Lowdown

- 🌐 **Map reference** 3 A4
  Address 465 Wakulla Park Dr, Wakulla Springs, 32327; 850 561 7276; www.floridastateparks.org/wakullasprings
- 🚗 **Car** Rent a car from Tallahassee.
- 🕐 **Open** 8am–sunset daily
- 💲 **Price** 6 per vehicle. Boat tours $21–26, under 3s free
- 🚩 **Guided tours** The park offers 40–60-min guided riverboat tours with plenty of wildlife viewing opportunities. Glass-bottom boat tours are also available.
- 👫 **Age range** 5 plus
- 🧍 **Activities** Swimming, biking, and hiking
- 🕐 **Allow** 3–4 hours
- 🍴 **Eat and drink** SNACKS The Soda Fountain (*Wakulla Springs Lodge; 850 421 2000; www.wakullaspringslodge.com*) boasts the world's longest marble counter top, and has milk shakes, sodas, hot dogs, and sandwiches. REAL MEAL The Ball Room Restaurant (*Wakulla Springs Lodge*) serves breakfast, lunch, and dinner. Navy Bean Soup and Southern fried chicken are among the specialties, and views from here are lovely.

⑫ San Marcos de Apalache Historic State Park

Biking, hiking, birds, and a historic fort

This state park is situated in the tiny historic fishing town of St. Marks on Apalachee Bay. The flags waving over the entrance mark a site fought over by Spanish, English, American, and Confederate forces. Though the first Spanish settlement was built in 1528, the original fort, now a National Historic Landmark, was built in 1679. The fort was later replaced by a stone fortress. A museum in the park exhibits pottery and tools unearthed near the original fort; and displays and a video reveal the site's colorful history.

Although a small town today, St. Marks was once a major port. Built in 1830 to bring cotton from Tallahassee plantations, the railroad is known today as the **Tallahassee-**

The Lowdown

- 🌐 **Map reference** 3 A4
  Address 148 Old Fort Rd, St. Marks, 32355; 850 925 6216; www.floridastateparks.org/sanmarcos
- 🚗 **Car** Rent a car from Tallahassee.
- ℹ️ **Visitor information** St. Marks Visitor Center, 15 Old Palmetto Path, St. Marks, 32355; 850 925 0400; www.cityofstmarks.com
- 🕐 **Open** 9am–5pm Thu–Mon
- 💲 **Price** Free. Museum: $8–12, under 5s free
- 🚩 **Guided tours** The park offers a self-guided trail winding through the historic ruins. Guided tours available with two weeks' notice.
- 👫 **Age range** 6 plus
- 🧍 **Activities** Families can hike trails and explore the fort ruins.
- 🕐 **Allow** 2 hours
- 🍴 **Eat and drink** PICNIC Bo Lynn's Grocery (*850 Port Leon Dr, 32355; 850 925 6156*) stocks provisions for a picnic in the state park or the refuge. REAL MEAL Riverside Café (*69 Riverside Dr, 32355; 850 925 5668*) is an informal eatery where the menu ranges from wings and burgers to full dinners. Grouper sandwiches are one of the favorites here.
- 🎪 **Festival** St. Marks Stone Crab Festival (mid-Oct)

St. Marks Historic Railroad Trail State Park, a paved 16-mile (26-km) trail for hikers and bikers ending at the St. Marks waterfront.

Letting off steam

Only the Everglades can boast more species of birds than the **St. Marks National Wildlife Refuge** (*www.fws.gov/saintmarks*), located 5 miles (3 km) southwest of the state park. The refuge has forests, swamps, marshes, and a saltwater estuary, which explains the huge variety of birds. It also has Florida's second-oldest lighthouse, built around 1830. The Visitor Center has road and trail maps, including part of the Florida National Scenic Trail.

⑬ Apalachicola
Oyster town

A major seaport when cotton was coming down from northern Florida's plantations, this quaint little town waned after the Civil War (1861–5). But it has a wonderfully walkable Historic District, with many beautifully restored homes and warehouses. Start with the walking tour map from the Information Center and take a look at the town's 50-plus pre-Civil War buildings, many of which house gift shops and restaurants. Today, the town relies on the sea for its livelihood, and is famous for its oysters. A variety of boat trips take visitors out into Apalachicola Bay.

Palm trees lining the path to the lighthouse, St. George Island State Park

Letting off steam
Located about 15 miles (24 km) east of Apalachicola on a barrier island, **St. George Island State Park** (*www.floridastateparks.org/stgeorge island*) boasts 9 miles (14 km) of pristine, dune-backed beach, with pavilions for picnics, as well as a lighthouse. The 2½-mile (4-km) trail to Gap Point meanders through a pine forest to Apalachicola Bay. The 1-mile (2-km) East Slough Trail offers boardwalks and resting benches.

Jetty at Apalachicola Bay, near the town of Apalachicola

The Lowdown

🌐 **Map reference** 2 G5

🚗 **Car** Rent a car from Tallahassee.

ℹ️ **Visitor information** 122 Commerce St, 32320; 850 653 9419; www.apalachicolabay.org

🎣 **Guided tours** Backwater Guide Service (*Scipio Creek Marina, 32320; 850 899 0063*) offers guided fishing and wildlife tours. Alternatively, learn how to tong and cull your own oysters on Captain Doug's oyster boat with Affordable Fishing (*604 Wilderness Rd, Eastpoint, 32320; 850 524 5985*)

👫 **Age range** All ages

🎯 **Activities** Kids will enjoy Grady Market (*76 Water St, 32320; 850 653 4099; www.apalachicolabay. com*) with its ships and maritime memorabilia. Browse through toys,

games, and souvenirs at Kids Port (*21 Ave C, 32320; 850 653 2899*). Stop at the John Gorrie Museum (*46 6th St, 32320; 850 653 9347*) to see the ice-making machine that Gorrie patented in 1851, marking the beginning of air conditioning.

⏱️ **Allow** A day

🍴 **Eat and drink** SNACKS Old Time Soda Fountain (*93 Market St, 32320; 850 653 2606*) has a vintage 1950s-style interior. The menu offers sandwiches, as well as sodas and ice cream. REAL MEAL Boss Oyster (*River Inn, 123 Water St, 32320; 850 653 9364*) is the place to try the town's specialty – it offers oysters in 17 different ways. Kids can go for seafood pizza.

🎪 **Festival** Florida Seafood Festival (early Nov)

Where to Stay in the Panhandle

From beach bungalows and condo resorts to city hotels, the Panhandle offers a wide range of accommodations. The numerous cottages and low-rise condos within walking distance of South Walton's beaches are especially appealing for families.

AGENCIES

Ocean Reef Vacation Rentals
www.oceanreefresorts.com
This agency offers lodging options across South Walton, including the villages of Seagrove, Grayton Beach, and Santa Rosa.

Rosemary Beach Rentals
www.rosemarybeach.com
This website has links to agencies with properties ranging in size from two to seven bedrooms.

Apalachicola Map 2 G5

HOTEL
Water Street Hotel & Marina
329 Water St, 32320; 850 653 3700;
www.waterstreethotel.com
A modern choice in a vintage town, this is a small all-suite hotel with a prime location by the water. Family suites have rooms with a queen bed, plus a small adjoining room with a bunk or full bed, as well as kitchens, balconies, and washer-dryers.

📶 🛏 P ⊘ $$

BED & BREAKFAST
Coombs House Inn
80 Sixth St, 32320; 888 244 8320;
www.coombshouseinn.com
Three elegant Victorian homes make up this charming 23-room inn. Some suites have kitchenettes and private verandas. Guests are treated to daily breakfast and afternoon tea, and wine on weekend evenings. Chairs, towels, and umbrellas are provided for excursions to St. George Island.

📶 🛏 P ⊘ $–$$

Pensacola Map 1 A3

HOTELS
Crowne Plaza-Pensacola Grand Hotel
200 E Gregory St, 32501; 850 433 3336; www.pensacolagrandhotel.com
The former 1912 L&N railroad passenger depot, furnished with antiques, is this hotel's old-fashioned lobby and restaurant, but its 15-story glass tower beyond is strictly modern. Many rooms offer views of the Historic Pensacola Village. There is a fitness center on site.

📶 🍴 P ⊘ $–$$

New World Inn
600 S Palafox St, 32501; 850 432 4111; www.newworldlanding.com
This 15-room boutique hotel, located in the Historic district, features a grand staircase and lofty rooms with attractive, traditional decor. Free Continental breakfast.

📶 🍴 P $$

MOTEL
Suburban Extended Stay Pensacola
3984 Barrancas Ave, 32507; 850 453 4140; www.choicehotels.com
A convenient option if visiting the Naval Aviation Museum, this motel is well equipped and provides free Internet access. Laundry facilities, barbecue grills, and a fitness room are available. Despite the name, extended stays are not required.

📶 🛏 P ⊘ $

BED & BREAKFAST
Lee House Bed & Breakfast
400 Bayfront Pkwy 32501; 850 912 8770; www.leehousepensacola.com
With its classic Southern columns and spacious public rooms, Lee House offers modern comforts. Several of the eight suites can accommodate four. Enjoy breakfast with views of Pensacola Bay and Seville Square on the expansive porches.

📶 P $$

Pensacola Beach Map 1 B3

RESORT
Portofino Island Resort and Spa
10 Portofino Dr, 32561; 877 484 3405; www.portofinoisland.com
This luxurious resort, situated on 8 miles (13 km) of pristine beach within the Gulf Islands National

A well-lit luxurious room in Sandestin Golf and Beach Resort, South Walton

Seashore, offers spacious two- and three-bedroom apartments equipped with washer-dryers. There are whirlpools, a spa, and special programs for kids and teens.

🛏 🍴 P ⊘ ⊘ $$$

MOTEL
Days Inn Pensacola Beachfront
Via De Luna Dr, 32561; 800 934 3301; www.daysinn.com
Located right on the beach, this basic motel offers rooms with microwaves, refrigerators, and coffee-makers. Amenities include laundry facilities, a pool, and free Continental breakfast.

📶 P ⊘ ⊘ $–$$

South Walton

RESORT
Sandestin Golf and Beach Resort Map 1 C3
9300 Emerald Coast Pkwy, Destin, 32550; 800 622 1038; www.sandestin.com
This excellent resort features a 7-mile (11-km) beach, tennis courts, a fitness center, and biking trails. Lodging options range from high rises to cottages in beach, bay, and golf communities. Baytowne Wharf, a pedestrian village within the resort, offers shops, dining, and fun activities including a zip line. The resort has programs for children and teens.

📶 🍴 🛏 P ⊘ $–$$$

CONDO RESORTS
The Inn at Gulf Place   Map 1 D3
95 Laura Hamilton Blvd, Santa Rosa Beach, 32548; 888 909 6807; www.gulfplacefl.com
Across the road from the beach, this small complex offers rooms that sleep four, or one-bedroom condos with full kitchens and balconies. There are tennis courts, a hot tub, and a washer-dryer on site.

⌂ ⇝ ⌂ P ❂ $–$$

Waterscape Condominiums
Map 1 D3
1110 Santa Rosa Boulevard, Ft. Walton Beach, 32548; 850 226 8700; www.wyndhamvacationrentals.com
These beachfront condos offer three swimming pools, a waterfall and a lazy river, along with barbecue grills and tables in the courtyard, and a children's playground.

⏿ ⇝ ⌂ P ❂ $–$$

WaterSound Resort   Map 1 D3
6652 E County Hwy 30A, Watersound, 32413; 800 413 2363; www.watersoundvacationrentals.com
A beach home community spread over an extensive area that includes the towering dunes along the Gulf of Mexico, this resort offers a beach club with a free-form pool and tennis courts. Lodgings vary from individual homes to condo units.

⏿ ⇝ ⌂ ❂ ◑ $–$$$

HOTEL
30-A Suites   Map 1 D3
6904 Hwy 30A West, Santa Rosa Beach, 32459; 850 499 5058; www.30asuites.com
Spacious and attractively furnished, this 15-suite boutique hotel offers rooms with walk-in closets and private balconies. Although the hotel is recommended for families

traveling with teens, younger kids are also welcome in its nearby two-bedroom condos.

⌂ ⇝ ⌂ $$

INN
Watercolor Inn   Map 1 D3
34 Goldenrod Circle, Santa Rosa Beach, 32459; 888 775 2545; www.watercolorresort.com
This luxurious 60-room inn near the Gulf of Mexico offers large rooms with king-size beds and queen sofa sleepers, a mini-refrigerator, and balconies with fabulous views. Bikes and kayaks are complimentary.

⌂ ⏿ P ❂ $$–$$$

CAMPING
Grayton Beach State Park   Map 1 D3
Off Scenic Hwy 30A, Grayton Beach, 32459; 800 326 3521 (reservations); www.floridastateparks.org
Famous for its beautiful beaches, this state park offers full camping facilities plus 30 modern two-bedroom cabins accommodating six. Cabins have central heating and cooling, kitchen, and an outdoor grill, as well as an initial set of linen and towels. Minimum two-night stay in cabins on weekends.

⇝ ⌂ ◑ $

Topsail Hill Preserve State Park   Map 1 D3
7525 W Scenic Hwy 30A, Santa Rosa Beach, 32459; 800 326 3521; www.floridastateparks.org
This scenic park offers ample choices from a fully equipped campground and tent sites to one-bedroom bungalows and

The scenic pool at Watercolor Inn, Santa Rosa Beach

two-bedroom cabins. Cabins have full kitchens. Guests can take a free tram to the beach.

⇝ ⌂ ❂ $

Tallahassee   Map 3 A3

HOTELS
Doubletree Hotel
101 S Adams St, 32301; 850 224 5000; www.doubletree.hilton.com/tallahasee
Located close to Florida State Capitol and the Capitol Museum, this full-service downtown hotel is a good choice for families. Rooms are comfortable, and cribs and high chairs are available. The on-site restaurant has a children's menu.

⌂ ⏿ ❂ P $–$$

Governor's Inn
209 South Adams St, 32301; 850 681 6855; www.thegovinn.com
Originally a livery stable, this boutique 41-room hotel near Florida State Capitol has rooms named for former Florida governors. The rooms are spacious, with two queen beds.

⌂ ⏿ ⇝ $$

Holiday Inn Express Tallahassee I-10 E
1653 Raymond Diehl Rd, 32308; 850 386 7500; www.cabotlodge thomsvilleroad.com
Executive rooms haveare equipped with a microwave and mini-refrigerator. Complimentary features include breakfast, daily newspaper, evening cocktails, and computers in the lobby.

⌂ P ❂ ⌂ $

Camped RVs in Topsail Hill Preserve State Park, Santa Rosa Beach

---

Price Guide
The following price ranges are based on one night's accommodation in high season for a family of four, inclusive of service charges and additional taxes.
$ Under $150 **$$** $150–300 **$$$** over $300

The Gulf Coast

Florida's Gulf Coast feels as if it could have been designed with families in mind. Alongside some of the state's best beaches, it has a major theme park and a spectacular aquarium, mermaids and manatees, and top museums for kids. Chic towns such as Tampa, St. Petersburg, and Sarasota offer world-class attractions and entertainment for adults. And there is still room for an abundance of unspoiled wild Florida.

The Gulf Coast

Highlights

The Ringling, Sarasota
See the elaborate estate on the bay created by circus legend John Ringling, and marvel at the world's largest miniature circus (see pp224–5).

The Dalí Museum, St. Petersburg
Discover this surreal museum, with unique art and architecture to fascinate all ages (see pp220–21).

Busch Gardens, Tampa
Ride on thrilling roller coasters, then say hello to hippos and lions, living as they would in the wild, at this exciting park (see pp214–15).

The Florida Aquarium
Go underwater without getting wet at the Coral Reef Gallery, a mammoth grotto where more than 2,300 fish are on the move (see p216).

Siesta Key
Take a walk on the beach that features on every list of "best in the US," and is known for its superb white sand (see p213).

Myakka River State Park
Explore these untouched lands that preserve Florida's lush natural landscape and diverse wildlife at its best (see p227).

Left Howard Bros. Circus model at the Tibbals Learning Center in The Ringling, Sarasota
Above right Giraffes and zebras in the Edge of Africa habitat at Busch Gardens, Tampa

The Best of
The Gulf Coast

The Gulf Coast is an area ripe for exploration. The cities clustered around Tampa Bay have distinct personalities and are famous for their winning combination of family attractions, wildlife, and abundant beaches. All these lie within a 100-mile (160-km) area and can easily be visited on a driving tour. With so much packed into a compact area, this beautiful part of the coast should not be missed.

Tale of three cities

Each of the three major cities in the Tampa Bay area has its own lures, and is less than an hour's drive from the others. **Tampa** (see pp214–19), the port and business hub of the region, is sometimes overlooked in favor of beach locations, but its riches include **Busch Gardens** (see pp214–15), with thrilling rides and animals, **The Florida Aquarium** (see p216), the Cuban flavor of **Ybor City** (see p218), major league sports, and the **Tampa Bay History Center** (see p217) with a special section for kids, and a choice of vibrant eateries downtown. **Sarasota** (see pp224–7) is an upscale community of about 60,000 people, with museums and performing arts venues that rival those of cities many times its size, plus some of the state's best beaches.

Left Water's Journey exhibit in the Glazer Children's Museum
Below An intricately carved circus wagon in The Ringling

Above *One of the many beautiful white-sand beaches along the Gulf Coast*

St. Petersburg *(see pp220–23)* is more serene, with a beautiful boulevard by the sea and the world-famous **The Dalí Museum** *(see pp220–21)*, as well as **St. Pete Beach** *(see p212)*, a distinct area about 10 miles (16 km) from downtown.

Wet and wild

Ever seen a manatee up close or "mermaids" doing acrobatics underwater? Drive from **Tampa** to see manatees drawn to the warm waters in winter and get even closer to these marine mammals in a floating observatory at the **Homosassa Springs Wildlife State Park** *(see p219)*. Costumed "mermaids" have been performing their antics to applauding crowds at **Weeki Wachee Springs State Park** *(see p215)* since 1947. **The Florida Aquarium** has daily dolphin cruises to view some of the 500 wild dolphins that live in Tampa Bay and Swim with the Fishes, an in-water reef experience, offers guests aged 6 plus a watery adventure indoors in the aquarium's replica coral reef.

The circus is in town

The excitement of Sarasota's old days comes to life at the Tibbals Learning Center in **The Ringling** *(see p224–5)*, which boasts the biggest model circus in the world. See this amazing handmade replica of the Ringling Bros. and Barnum & Bailey circus in its heyday, with its eight main tents, including a big top with three rings and four stages full of tiny model clowns, aerialists, and showgirls. Other exhibits focus on the most exciting circus acts, acrobats, aerialists, animals, and clowns. Try

out circus skills, such as walking a tightrope (safely close to the ground). Younger kids who are being taught circus arts show off their skills at the **PAL Sailor Circus** *(see p37)* in late December.

Treats for tots

Finding attractions for younger children away from the beach can be a challenge, but not on the Gulf Coast. Younger kids will enjoy the friendly **ZooTampa at Lowry Park** *(see p216)* in **Tampa**. With some 2,000 animals, there is plenty to see here, and lots of chances for close-up encounters. Another kids' favorite is the **Sarasota Jungle Gardens** *(see p225)*, with cool, shady paths, a Kiddie Jungle with a playground, as well as delightful shows such as parrots on roller skates. Tampa's **Glazer Children's Museum** *(see p218)* features fun experiences including flying a mock airplane or cooking as a chef. The **Great Explorations Children's Museum** *(see p223)* in **St. Petersburg** has crafts programs even for toddlers, along with plenty of attractions for older kids.

Right *Manatee at Homosassa Springs Wildlife State Park, one of the best places for viewing these fascinating marine mammals*

The Gulf Coast

This region stretches for hundreds of sandy miles along the western border of Florida, with a host of exciting stops along the way. From beaches and manatee-watching to circus tricks, roller coasters, animal parks, and one of Florida's most famous theme parks, the Gulf Coast has loads to keep families entertained. The cities welcome with aquariums and kid-friendly museums to intrigue all ages. Excellent roads make it easy to tour it all by car.

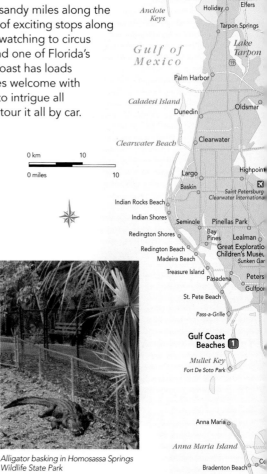

Homosassa Springs State Park 47 miles (76km)

Holiday
Elfers
Anclote Keys
Tarpon Springs
Gulf of Mexico
Lake Tarpon
Palm Harbor
Caladesi Island
Oldsmar
Dunedin
Clearwater Beach
Clearwater
Largo
Highpoint
Baskin
Saint Petersburg
Clearwater International
Indian Rocks Beach
Indian Shores
Seminole
Pinellas Park
Redington Shores
Bay Pines
Lealman
Redington Beach
Great Exploratio
Children's Museu
Madeira Beach
Sunken Gar
Treasure Island
Peters
Pasadena
Gulfpor
St. Pete Beach
Pass-a-Grille

Gulf Coast Beaches ■

Mullet Key
Fort De Soto Park

Anna Maria
Anna Maria Island
Bradenton Beach

Longboat Key
Longboat

Circus exhibits in the Ringling, Sarasota

Places of interest

■ **THE GULF COAST**

Alligator basking in Homosassa Springs Wildlife State Park

Kids splashing in the waves on Venice Beach, south of Sarasota

0 km   10
0 miles   10

A thrilling floorless roller coaster at Busch Gardens, Tampa

The Lowdown

Getting there and around
Air Fly to Tampa (*www.tampa airport.com*) or Sarasota (*www. srq-airport.com*) airports. Tampa has a comprehensive local bus service, as well as a trolley by day connecting downtown attractions, and a streetcar running from the city center to Ybor City.
Bus Tampa, St. Petersburg and Clearwater have Greyhound bus connections from other major cities in Florida. **Trolley** Sarasota, Bradenton, and Clearwater have a trolley service from town to the beach. Clearwater's Jolley Trolley (*clearwaterjolleytrolley.com*) links beaches from Clearwater south to St. Petersburg, and also runs north to Tarpon Springs on weekends. This is a convenient mode of transport. Check the website for schedules and routes.
Car A car is by far the best way to get around.

Visitor information See individual entries. Consider the Tampa Bay CityPASS, which saves more than half on admission to ZooTampa at Lowry Park, Busch Gardens Tampa, The Florida Aquarium, The Clearwater Aquarium, and Museum of Science & Industry and more.

Supermarkets Publix (*www. publix.com*) is the premier supermarket here, with outlets throughout the region.
Markets St. Petersburg Saturday Morning Farmers' Market, First Ave South and First St, on the waterfront, 33701; 727 455 4921; *www.saturdaymorningmarket. com*; Oct–May: 9am–1pm. Tampa Downtown Farmers' Market, 200 and 300 blocks on Twiggs St; *www.tampa downtownmarket.com*; Oct– May: 10am–2pm Sun. Ybor City Saturday Market, Centennial Park, 8th Ave and 19th St, 33605; 813 241 2442; *www.ybormarket. com*; 9am–3pm Sat year-round. Sarasota Farmers' Market, corner of State and Lemon Streets; 941 225 9256; *www.sarasota farmersmarket.org*; 7am–noon Sat year-round. Downtown Clearwater Farmers' Market, Station Square Park, 500 and 600 blocks of Cleveland St; 727 461 7674; 9am–2pm daily

Festivals Gasparilla Pirate Festival, Tampa: lavish costumed parades; *www.gasparillapirate fest.com* (late-Jan). Florida Strawberry Festival, Plant City; *www.flstrawberryfestival.com* (late-Feb–mid-Mar). Dunedin Highland Games, Dunedin (Apr). Medieval Fair, Sarasota; *sarasotamedievalfair.com* (Nov)

Pharmacies Walgreens (*www.walgreens.com*) and CVS (*www.cvs.com*) are the two major pharmacies in the region; some of their city branches are open 24 hours.

Restrooms All major attractions, shopping malls, and gas stations have public restrooms.

① Gulf Coast Beaches
Soft sands and warm sunshine

For many visitors, the Gulf Coast's fabulous barrier beaches are the biggest attractions; reached via causeway bridges, they encompass some 35 miles (56 km) of soft sand, lapped by the gentle waves of the Gulf of Mexico. Clearwater Beach and St. Pete Beach, lined with hotels, are convenient for families. At Sarasota, most development has been kept away from the beachfront. Several islands off the coast offer unspoiled sands ideal for beachcombers.

Surf kayaking at Turtle Beach, Siesta Key

Key Sights

③ **St. Pete Beach** This beach stretches for 7 miles (11 km) and is ideal for strolling. Lined with hotels, it is popular with families, and has excellent watersports.

① **Caladesi Island** Accessible only by boat, the island has a state park and an uncrowded beach ideal for playing.

④ **Pass-a-grille** This public beach at the quieter end of St. Pete Beach offers great sunset views. Bring quarters for parking.

⑤ **Fort De Soto Park** There are three sugar-sand beaches and a nature preserve with trails here (see p223).

⑥ **Anna Maria Island** Located at the quiet northern end of Bradenton, this island has picturesque beaches and a laid-back feel.

⑦ **Bradenton Beach** This small island appeals to families with its beaches as well as the quaint town, with its historic pier, and a variety of shops, restaurants, and lodging.

② **Clearwater Beach** Favored by active beachgoers, this resort beach has volleyball courts and watersports concessions. Sunset brings a nightly celebration with music and street performances.

⑧ **Longboat Key** This is an upscale resort island with lovely beaches and golf courses, but limited public access.

The Lowdown

🌐 **Map reference** 7 A1–3 and 7 B3–4

🚗 **Car** Rent a car from a rental agency at one of the airports to get around the region conveniently.

ℹ️ **Visitor information** Caladesi Island: 727 469 5918; www.florida stateparks.org/caladesiisland. Clearwater Beach: 727 464 7200; www.visitstpeteclearwater.com. St. Pete Beach: 727 464 7200;

www.visitstpeteclearwater.com. Pass-a-grille: 727 403 6136; www.visitpassagrille.com. Fort de Soto Park: 727 552 1862; www.pinellascounty.org/park. Anna Maria Island: 941 778 1541 www.annamariaisland chamber.org. Bradenton Beach: 941 778 1005; www.cityof bradentonbeach.com. Longboat Key and Lido Key: 941 383 2466; www.longboatkeychamber.com/ visitor. Siesta Key: 941 349 3800;

www.siestakeychamber.com. Venice Beach: 941 486 2626; www.venicegov.com

💲 **Prices** Caladesi Island: $6 per boat; $42–56 ferry. Fort De Soto Park and Pass-a-grille: $5 parking

👫 **Age range** All ages

🤸 **Activities** Various watersports – snorkeling, canoeing, and kayaking – can be enjoyed at beaches such as Caladesi Island, St. Pete Beach, Lido Key, and

⑨ Lido Key This barrier island offers spacious beaches in three sections – dunes and trails to the north; resorts in the center; and a handsome shaded beachfront park to the south.

⑩ Siesta Key Justly popular, this small island is famous for its dazzling white-quartz sand that stays cool even on the hottest days.

⑪ Venice Beach A bounty of sharks' teeth lures sharp-eyed beachcombers to this beach.

KIDS' CORNER

Sand craft
To make a fine sandy souvenir, pack up some sand and shells in a plastic container with a lid to take home from the beach. Spread glue on cardboard and cover it with sand, then glue shells in a pattern you like. Or make a border on a plain wooden frame for a picture or a mirror. Try to find enough scallop shells of the same size, since they look great as borders.

Bucket race
Here's a silly beach game to play with friends and family. Set up two buckets away from the water's edge and see who can fill the bucket first by carrying water from the sea using only their hands.

WHAT IS A SEA SHELL?
The shells you see were home to sea creatures who have moved on. Some of the prettiest are scallop shells. Others may have held sea snails, crabs, or mussels. Caladesi Island State Park is a good place to look for shells on the Gulf Coast.

Sandy facts
A beach is made up of super-tiny, loose specks of rock that gather at the shore and are carried onto the land by waves or ocean currents. Strong waves carry the sand farther inland and pile it into dunes. Underwater coral reefs are one source of sand. The finest white sand, found on beaches like Siesta Key, is made of pure quartz crystal that has washed down from mountains far away then been carried to the sea by rivers.

Siesta Key. There is fishing at Fort De Soto Park and on Anna Maria Island, while Venice Beach is perfect for beachcombing and coral reef diving.

⏱ **Allow** 1–3 days

Good family value?
The Gulf Coast beaches and islands offer a range of sporting and leisure options for the whole family at a reasonable price.

Map labels:

Palm Harbor
Caladesi Island ①
Dunedin (19)
Clearwater ②
Clearwater Beach
Largo   Highpoint
Baskin
Indian Rocks Beach
Indian Shores
Seminole   Pinellas Park
Redington Shores
Bay Pines   Lealman
Madeira Beach (19)
Treasure Island   Pasadena   Saint Petersburg
Gulfport
St. Pete Beach ③
Pass-a-grille ④
Mullet Key ⑤
Fort De Soto Park
Tampa Bay (275)
Anna Maria   Memphis
Anna Maria Island ⑥   Palmetto
Bradenton (64)
Bradenton Beach ⑦ Cortez
South Bradenton   West Samoset
Longboat Key ⑧   (70)
(41)
Gulf of Mexico
Sarasota
Lido Key ⑨
South Sarasota
Siesta Key ⑩   (72)
Vamo   (75)
Osprey (41)
Casey Key
Laurel
Nokomis
Venice
Venice Beach ⑪   Venice Gardens
South Venice   (41)

0 km   10
0 miles   10

② Busch Gardens, Tampa Bay
Rocking roller coasters and roaring animals

This granddaddy of Florida theme parks still thrills with its daring roller coasters, African safari, water adventures, and lively musical shows. The grounds are divided into themed locations, such as the Congo and Egypt – each featuring animals native to those regions; the Serengeti Plain is home to rhinos, giraffes, and more. Even the most adventurous will be challenged aboard the scream-inducing roller coasters, and little ones can enjoy their own special kingdom.

Flamingos in Busch Gardens, Tampa

Key Features

① **Falcon's Fury** Standing at 335 ft (102 m), this exhilarating ride is the tallest freestanding drop tower in North America. Riders can briefly enjoy the view from the top, before heading face-down at 60 mph (97 km/h).

② **Edge of Africa** This walking safari experience on the southern edge of the Serengeti Plain offers sightings of hippos, lions, hyenas, lemurs, and other exotic African animals in naturalistic habitats.

Entrance

④ **Sesame Street Safari of Fun** Aimed at pre-schoolers, this features rides and shows starring Sesame Street favorites.

⑤ **Serengeti Railway** Take this train for a relaxing ride through all the major areas in the park.

⑥ **Turn It Up!** This entertainment on ice, in the lavish Moroccan Palace Theater, features lavish costumes and world-class ice skaters..

⑦ **Cheetah Run** Get a close-up view of the world's fastest animals from these floor-to-ceiling, glass-paneled viewing areas.

⑧ **Cobra's Curse** The park's most recent coaster, the wildly spinning ride, featuring a vertical lift, is built around the legend of a snake king in ancient Egypt.

③ **Cheetah Hunt** Designed for speed, this roller coaster climbs more than 10 stories above the African landscape before plunging 130 ft (40 m) into an underground trench. It set a park record for distance with 4,429 ft (1,350 m) of track.

Prices given are for a family of four

The Lowdown

🌐 **Map reference** 7 B1
Address 10165 N McKinley Dr, Tampa, 33612; 888 800 5447; seaworldparks.com/en/busch gardens-tampa

🚍 **Bus** Hartline bus 18 (hartline.org) from downtown to Busch Blvd. Shuttle Express available from Orlando to Busch Gardens

🕐 **Open** 10am–6pm Mon–Fri & 9am–7:30pm Sat–Sun. Hours may vary with season; check website.

💲 **Price** $250–320; under 3s free. Save on selected tickets when buying online.

👫 **Cutting the line** The Quick Queue pass ($20–40 per person; prices vary with season) gives access to the head of the line on each ride. Book tickets online to avoid waiting lines at the entrance and get a discount. Ride lines are shortest near park opening and closing times.

🚩 **Guided tours** Insider tours with keepers, as well as Safari tours

👫 **Age range** 3 plus. Stop by Guest Relations to pick up kids' wristbands with space

Letting off steam

With climbing nets, bridges, crawl tubes, and a multilevel maze, **Treetop Trails** (on site), a three-story play area in the Jungala area, gives kids plenty of exercise. If any energy remains, head for **Adventure Island** (www.adventureisland.com), a tropical-themed water park across the street. This features Vanish Point, a 70-ft (17-m) drop slide, Wahoo Run, a river raft ride, and twisting spirals on the Aruba Tuba run.

Eat and drink

Picnic: under $25; Snacks: $25–50; Real meal: $50–80; Family treat: over $80 (based on a family of four)

PICNIC Garden Gate Café (in the Bird Gardens area) serves pizza, flatbreads and more on the lakeside patio overlooking the Bird Gardens.
SNACKS Zagora Café (in the Morocco Village area) offers burgers, fajita wraps and sandwiches.
REAL MEAL Zambia Smokehouse (in the Stanleyville area) has barbecued chicken and ribs, and mac and cheese.

Fried fish served with french fries at a local Tampa café

to write a contact number in case children get separated.
Allow At least a day
Wheelchair access Yes
Café Eateries throughout the park (outside food not allowed)
Restrooms In every section of the park, except Serengeti Plain

Good family value?
Although Busch Gardens is quite expensive, it offers a full day's entertainment that may well be the highlight of a trip to the Gulf Coast.

FAMILY TREAT Dragon Fire Grill & Pub (in the Pantopia area) offers families an international menu in a market-style restaurant, with adult beverages as well as a children's menu.

Plush toys for sale at a store in the Moroccan Village area

Shopping

Throughout the park, shops tempt with attractive souvenirs. Find legions of plush animals at the **Sahara Trading Company** (in the Morocco area). Sesame Street favorites are the lure at **Abby Cadabby's Treasure Hut** (in Safari of Fun) and both teens and parents like the apparel, souvenirs, and jewelry found at the **Painted Camel Bazaar** (in Pantopia). **Caravan Crossing** (in the Nairobi Village area) stocks beach towels, backpacks, and T-shirts.

Find out more

DIGITAL Explore the real Serengeti Plain of Africa at www.serengeti.org. Go to www.eyewitnesstohistory.com/tut.htm to find out about the amazing discovery of King Tut's tomb in Egypt. Learn how to make a mini-coaster at home on pbskids.org/zoom/activities/sci/rollercoaster.html.

Next stop...

WEEKI WACHEE SPRINGS STATE PARK About 40 miles (64 km) north of Busch Gardens, the Weeki Wachee Springs (6131 Commercial Way, Weeki Wachee, 34606; 352 592 5656; weekiwachee.com) is where mermaids await. They aren't real mermaids, of course, but families have been enjoying the acrobatic antics of costumed swimmers since 1947. The arena is a natural spring so deep that the bottom has never been found. Seats are built into the limestone sides of the spring.

A diver amid reefs and exotic fish at The Florida Aquarium, Tampa

③ The Florida Aquarium

Fishy fun – from sharks to sea horses

Florida's largest aquarium is a great outing for all ages. In the Coral Reef Gallery, get a close-up view of a colossal and colorful underwater world that is usually only seen by deep-sea divers. Discover Florida's freshwater creatures, such as otters, alligators, and snakes, in the Wetlands exhibit, while the Ocean Commotion has predators including sharks, a giant Pacific octopus, and a lionfish. Children will love the sea horse exhibit, which shows off these adorable creatures that come in a surprising number of varieties. At the touch tank in the lobby, kids can pet a starfish and feel other sea creatures.

Letting off steam

If children get restless, head to **The Splash Pad**, an extensive outdoor water adventure zone in The Florida Aquarium. With a rain-forest theme, the area features dump buckets, spray zones, and a designated water play area for toddlers, plus dry areas to climb and play in.

④ ZooTampa at Lowry Park

Walk with a wallaby, feed a giraffe

This major zoo, with 2,000 animals on 56 lush acres (23 ha), is fun for all ages, but is especially recommended for younger kids. It allows close-up encounters, including those with stingrays and giraffes, a petting zoo, and a special viewing area for watching manatees underwater. The zoo's Manatee Hospital offers care for injured, sick, and orphaned wild manatees. Animals are divided into seven sections that include Asia Domain, Safari Africa, and Florida Wildlife Center. The zoo also has the Tasmanian Tiger Family Coaster, and the gentle Roaring Springs Ride.

The Lowdown

- **Map reference** 7 B1
- **Address** 701 Channelside Dr, Tampa, 33602; 813 273 4000; www.flaquarium.org
- **Trolley** TECO (tecolinestreetcar. org) Line Streetcar Route 8
- **Open** 9am–5pm daily
- **Price** $96–100
- **Cutting the line** Book tickets online and get discounts.
- **Guided tours** Behind the Scenes and Feeding tours, as well as a dolphin-spotting cruise, are offered for an additional fee.
- **Age range** 2 plus
- **Activities** Shows begin every few minutes and feature coral reef divers, otters at play, stingray feedings, and a Penguin Promenade. Check the daily schedule in the lobby.
- **Allow** At least 4 hours
- **Eat and drink** SNACKS Café Ray (on site) offers sandwiches, wraps, paninis, and salads. It also has a kids' menu. REAL MEAL Splitsville (615 Channelside Dr, 33602; 813 514 2695; www.splitsvillelanes. com) is an entertaining eatery set in a bowling alley, which has everything from burgers to sushi.

The Lowdown

- **Map reference** 7 B1
- **Address** 1101 West Sligh Ave, Tampa, 33604; 813 935 8552; www.zootampa.org
- **Bus** Hartline buses 41 and 45 stop at the zoo.
- **Open** 9:30am–5pm daily
- **Price** $96–120; under 2s free (including rides and the Expedition Africa Guided Safari). Stroller rentals $9.63 single, $11.77 double
- **Cutting the line** Lines can be long in early afternoon and on weekends.
- **Guided tours** Go for safari tram rides through the Safari Africa exhibit.
- **Age range** 2 plus
- **Activities** The zoo offers animal feedings, animal keeper talks, and birds of prey shows.
- **Allow** At least 4 hours
- **Eat and drink** SNACKS Garden Grille (on site) sells burgers, grilled cheese sandwiches, salads and kids' favorites in air-conditioned comfort. REAL MEAL La Pequeña Colombia (6312 N Armenia Ave, 33604; 813 876 8338) is an unassuming family-owned and family friendly restaurant that offers authentic Latin food.

A white tiger lounging in the Asian Gardens habitat area in ZooTampa at Lowry Park

Tampa Bay History Center located on the riverfront in downtown Tampa

Letting off steam

The zoo's Aussie-themed **Wallaroo Station** offers kids a chance to work off energy with slides, tunnels, and ladders. It includes a cooling water play area, and kids can also splash around in the waters of the Manatee Fountain near the entrance.

Kids splashing in the water play area in Wallaroo Station, ZooTampa

⑤ Tampa Bay History Center

Explore 12,000 years of Tampa's past

Founded in 1989, this 60,000 square-foot facility on Tampa's Riverfront was opened in 2009. The kid-friendly History Center includes three floors of permanent and temporary exhibition galleries focusing on 12,000 years of Florida's history. From the First People exhibit, to that on European Exploration, the museum helps children trace the changes in life and culture in Florida. The Treasure Seekers exhibition includes a life-size replica of a pirate ship, examples of navigational tools, a choose-your-own-adventure-style interactive story, and treasure recovered from

Florida's waters. Cattlemen, soldiers, farmers and orange growers. The map library contains more than 8,000 maps, charts and other documents dating back more than 500 years. It also runs many programmes for families and children, along with contests and craft activities.

Letting off steam

The nearby Museum of Science and Industry's outdoor **Backwoods Forest Preserve** offers plenty of room to work off excess energy, and its multilevel **Sky Trail® Ropes Course** is designed with challenges for all ages.

The Lowdown

- 🌐 **Map reference** 7 B1
- **Address** 801 Old Water St, Tampa, 33602; 813 228 0097; www.tampabayhistorycenter.org
- 🚌 **Bus** Hartline bus 5 from downtown
- 🕐 **Open** 10am–5pm daily
- 💲 **Price** $41-52; under 7s free
- 🧍 **Cutting the line** Book tickets online or by phone.
- 👫 **Age range** 5 plus
- 🧍 **Activities** The museum offers kids the chance to jump in the saddle with the cattle ranchers, play with tiny Tampa trains, or dress up like a pioneer in the Cracker cabin.
- ⏱ **Allow** At least 4 hours
- 🍴 **Eat and drink** SNACKS The Corner Cafe & Deli (100 Ashley Dr S #220, 33602; 813 273 9711; closed Sat, Sun) Good breakfast and lunch spot on the river. REAL MEAL Columbia Cafe (on site) offers Spanish- and Cuban-inspired dishes in a waterfront setting

---

Picnic under $25; **Snacks** $25–50; **Real meal** $50–80; **Family treat** over $80 (based on a family of four)

Facade of the yellow-brick building housing the Ybor City Museum State Park, Tampa

⑥ Ybor City

Cuban flavor in a cloud of cigar smoke

This Tampa neighborhood is named for Don Vicente Martinez Ybor, whose cigar-making business opened here in 1886, spawning the most vibrant Cuban community in the US. Head to the **Ybor City Museum State Park**, housed in a historic bakery, to find out more about Ybor City's history, and to see how workers lived. Stroll along 7th Avenue, where the old architecture remains, along with the many cafés and shops that have opened more recently. The Saturday morning market in Centennial Park draws crowds for its farm-fresh produce, Cuban coffee, arts and crafts, and live music.

Letting off steam

If kids need a break, pop over to the **Tampa Riverwalk**, running from Florida Aquarium north past Glazer Children's Museum to Armature Works, a newly opened food hall. It is more easily accessed and protected from automotive traffic. Along the way, it meets 3 city parks with playgrounds, play fountains (Curtis Hixon Waterfront Park) and a splash pad (Water Works Park).

The Lowdown

- **Map reference** 7 B1
  Address Ybor City Museum State Park: 1818 E 9th Ave, Tampa, 33605; 813 247 6323; floridastateparks.org/yborcity/
- **Trolley** TECO line streetcar from downtown Tampa to Ybor City
- ℹ **Visitor information** The Visitor Information Center, Centro Ybor, 1600 East 8th Ave, Tampa, 33605; 813 241 8838; www.ybor.org
- **Open** Ybor City Museum State Park: 9am–5pm Wed–Sun
- **Price** Ybor City Museum State Park: $16; under 5s free
- **Guided tours** Self-guided audio walking tours of the neighborhood are available from the museum.
- **Age range** 8 plus
- **Activities** The museum runs guided tours of a Casita – a cigar worker's house – on the hour 11am–3pm Wed–Sun.
- **Allow** 2 hours
- **Eat and drink** SNACKS La Tropicana Café *(1822 E 7th Ave, 33605; 813 247 4040)* is a favorite for authentic Cuban sandwiches, snacks, and other treats. *FAMILY TREAT* Columbia Restaurant *(2117 E 7th Ave, 33605; 813 248 4961)* is Florida's oldest restaurant and well worth a splurge for fine Cuban/Spanish cuisine and flamenco entertainment.

⑦ Glazer Children's Museum

Big fun for small kids

This Tampa museum offers young children the chance to learn through discovery and play in mock settings – from a firehouse and a vet's office to a bank. Flying an airplane, shopping for groceries, and serving as a waiter are some of the experiences that kids will enjoy. In Tug Boat Tots, children aged 3 and under can explore a boat, play

The Lowdown

- **Map reference** 7 B1
  Address 110 W Gasparilla Plaza, Tampa, 33602; 813 443 3861; www.glazermuseum.org
- **Bus** Hartline buses 30 and 70
- **Open** 10am–5pm Mon–Fri, 10am–6pm Sat & 1pm–6pm Sun
- **Price** $50–60
- **Cutting the line** Advance tickets can be ordered online, but there is rarely a queue.
- **Age range** 3 plus
- **Activities** Special programs are scheduled frequently; check website for details.
- **Allow** 2–4 hours
- **Wheelchair access** Yes
- **Eat and drink** SNACKS Subway *(on site)* offers wholesome 6-inch- and 12-inch-long sandwiches with drinks, snacks, and cookies. *REAL MEAL* Eddie & Sams *(203 E Twiggs St, 33602; 813 229 8500)* offers authentic New York-style pizza, served by the slice or by the pie, alongside tasty pastas, sandwiches, and gelato.

Budding architects in the Design + Build area in Glazer Children's Museum, Tampa

at fishing, and listen to stories. The museum also features water play, as well as various arts and crafts activities.

Letting off steam

The Glazer Museum is located in **Curtis Hixon Waterfront Park** *(600 N Ashley Dr, 33602)*, which offers a playground and a scenic paved waterside path. The playground has a unique feature – an interactive NEOS 360 Ring, which combines video games with aerobic exercises.

Sculpture of a manatee by Silas Beach, Homosassa Springs Wildlife State Park

⑧ Manatee Viewing Center

Florida's favorite mammal, close up

The Florida manatee is a swimming mammal and an endangered species whose closest relative is the elephant. It has a huge, seal-like body, flippers, and a flat tail, and can weigh as much as 1,000 lb (450 kg) and grow as long as 10 ft (3 m). These gentle creatures need warmth and, in cooler months, they flock to the warm water generated at the Tampa Electric Company's Big Bend Power Station. They can be seen close up from the viewing platform at the Manatee Viewing Center, which is situated within the power station. Manatees are also drawn year-round to the warm springs at **Homosassa Springs Wildlife State Park** (*4150 S Suncoast Blvd, Homosassa, 34446, 352 628 5343; www.floridastateparks.org/*

homosassasprings), located 87 miles (140 km) from Tampa. Here, manatees can be seen from the park's underwater observatory. The park is also home to bears, alligators, otters, deer, flamingos, and a 50-year-old, 6,000-pound hippopotamus.

Letting off steam

The viewing center's **Tidal Walk** to the Tampa Bay Estuary works off energy and also offers a chance to see native coastal plants and birds. At the end of the walkway is another view of manatees swimming – in the plant's discharge canal.

The Lowdown

🌐 **Map reference** 7 B2
Address 6990 Dickman Rd, Apollo Beach, 33572; 813 228 4289; www.tampaelectric.com/manatee

🚗 **Car** Rent a car from Tampa Airport. Parking is available.

🕐 **Open** Nov 1–Apr 15: 10am–5pm daily

💲 **Price** Free

👫 **Age range** All ages

Activities There is lots of fun stuff for kids on www.tampaelectric.com/manatee/funstuff/webcam2.

⏱ **Allow** 1 hour

🍽 **Eat and drink** SNACKS San Remo Pizza Restaurant (*6426 N US 41, 33572; 813 645 9742*) is a pleasant, family-run spot serving calzone. REAL MEAL Circles Waterfront Dining (*1212 Apollo Beach Blvd, 33572, 813 641 3275; closed Sun*) provides great views along with a varied menu and plenty of choices for children.

KIDS' CORNER

Watch out for....

When you visit Ybor City, head for:
1 The Visitor Information Center. The Centro Ybor at 1600 East 8th Avenue is housed in the world's largest cigar box, along with the Ybor City Museum.
2 José Martí Park. Located on the corner of 8th Avenue and 13th Street, this park honors José Martí, who fought for Cuba's independence from Spain. The Pedroso family bought the land and donated it to what is now the independent Republic of Cuba as a memorial to Martí. So, technically, you are standing on Cuban soil.

FAMOUS CIGAR SMOKERS

Though smoking isn't good for you, a lot of famous people have been photographed smoking cigars. They include past US presidents Bill Clinton and John F. Kennedy, Britain's former prime minister Winston Churchill, and Cuba's former president, Fidel Castro.

Massive manatees

To get enough nourishment for their mammoth bodies, manatees spend 6 to 8 hours a day feeding. How much do you think you would weigh if you ate for that long? Full-grown manatees can eat 100 lb (45 kg) to 150 lb (68 kg) of food per day – and they are vegetarians. They only eat green things growing in the ocean. Would you like that many vegetables in your diet?

Flamingos in the water at Homosassa Springs Wildlife State Park

Picnic under $25; **Snacks** $25–50; **Real meal** $50–80; **Family treat** over $80 (based on a family of four)

⑨ The Dalí Museum, St. Petersburg
The Surreal world of Salvador Dalí

The whimsical creations of Spanish artist Salvador Dalí, with his use of optical illusions and dreamlike canvases, intrigue all ages. Brought to St. Petersburg in 1982 by businessman A. Reynolds Morse and his wife, Eleanor, this is the biggest collection of Dalí's works outside Spain. The 2,140 pieces are housed in a concrete building wrapped in a fantastic geodesic "wave."

Aerial view of the spectacular Dalí Museum and Avant-Garden

Key Features

■ **Third Floor** Permanent collection, and a special exhibitions gallery

■ **Second Floor** Business, research, and meeting rooms

■ **First Floor** Theater, gift shop, and café

① **West Entrance** The austere west facade of the museum gives no hint of the surprises inside. The entry through a dim, grotto-like space leads to a light-flooded three-story atrium.

② **East facade**
The undulating windows on the museum's east facade are made of 1,062 triangular glass panes, of which no two are alike. They infuse the interior with light and offer visitors a unique view of St. Petersburg's waterfront.

③ **Helical staircase** The staircase spirals toward the skylight, leading visitors to the galleries on the third floor. While a permanent gallery holds the paintings, another gallery has Dalí's sculptures and films.

④ **The Discovery of America by Christopher Columbus** This painting, over 5 ft (1.5 m) tall, is one of eight "masterworks" in the collection. Each painting has its own gallery for best viewing.

⑤ **Avant-Garden** The museum's waterside garden is a wonder, with boulder outcrops, eerie tropical plantings, a "golden rectangle" with multicolor paving, and a labyrinth. Some of the curved benches are draped with melting clocks.

⑥ **The Disintegration of Persistence of Memory** With its melting watches, this is one of Dalí's most famous paintings.

⑦ **The Hallucinogenic Toreador** Painted in the years 1969–70, this is one of Dalí's dreamlike paintings, employing optical illusions that are especially engaging to young viewers.

Prices given are for a family of four

The Lowdown

🌐 **Map reference** 7 A2
Address 1 Dalí Blvd, St. Petersburg, 33701; 727 823 3767; www.thedali.org

🚗 **Trolley** The Downtown Looper trolley line ($0.50 per person; under 5s free) has a stop at the museum.

🕐 **Open** 10am–5:30pm Mon–Sat (till 8pm Thu)

💲 **Price** $75–84; under 5s free ($10 for ages 6–12 & $17 for ages 13–17)

👫 **Cutting the line** Order tickets online to avoid queuing. Use the online coupon to save on adult admission.

🪧 **Guided tours** The museum runs daily tours on the half hour at 10:30am–3:30pm, as well as at 5:30pm and 6:30pm Thu. Tours run at 12:30pm–3:30pm Sun.

👫 **Age range** 5 plus

🧒 **Activities** Dilly Dally with Dalí children's programs are held on some Sat. There are arts and crafts at 11:45am–4:30pm on Sat and storytelling at 11:15am & 3:30pm Thu.

⏱ **Allow** 2–3 hours

♿ **Wheelchair access** Yes

🍽 **Café** Café Gala (on site) serves soups, salads, and tapas.

🛍 **Shop** On the first floor (see p221)

🚻 **Restrooms** On the first and third floors

Good family value?
The Dalí introduces kids to Surrealist art. Although expensive for a family visit, the museum is a memorable experience.

Wide variety of apparel and bags in the wonderful Dalí Museum Store

Letting off steam
The **Albert Whitted Park**, near the museum and adjacent to a small city-owned airport, offers an aviation-themed playground, and a "control tower" to watch airplanes taking off.

Eat and drink
Picnic: under $25; Snacks: $25–50; Real meal: $50–80; Family treat: over $80 (based on a family of four)

PICNIC Mazzaros Italian Market (2909 22nd Ave N, 33713; 727 321 2400; www.mazzarosmarket.com) has wonderful fixings for a picnic to be enjoyed in a park by Tampa Bay.
SNACKS Hangar Restaurant & Flight Lounge (540 1st St SE, 33701; 727 823 7767; www.thehangarst pete.com), in Albert Whitted Airport, offers sandwiches and snacks to go.

Outdoor seating at The Moon Under Water, St. Petersburg

REAL MEAL The Moon Under Water (332 Beach Dr NE, 33701; 727 896 6160; www.themoonunder water.com) serves pub grub such as fish and chips, plus Indian food. There is also a kids' menu.
FAMILY TREAT Red Mesa Cantina (128 3rd St S, 33701; 727 896 8226; www.redmesacantina.com) serves great tacos and burritos in an uncon-ventional, Mexican ambiance with both indoor and outdoor seating.

Shopping
The **Dalí Museum Store** stocks merchandise inspired by Dalí imagery. There is home ware, trendy Art to Wear in the form of jewelry, scarves, fashion apparel, and totes – and more. Kids will like the puzzles and books on optical illusions.

Find out more
DIGITAL Check out academickids. com/encyclopedia/index.php/ Surrealism for a good introduction to Surrealism.

Next stop...
CRYSTAL RIVER ARCHAEOLOGICAL STATE PARK A 2-hour drive north of St. Petersburg, this National Historic Landmark (www.floridastateparks.org/crystal riverarchaeological) is one of the best places to see glimpses of the lives of ancient Native Americans in Florida. Once an important ceremonial center for burying the dead and conducting trade, this huge site has six burial mounds, temple platform mounds, and a midden, which is a mound containing shells, bones, and other relics dating as far back as 1,600 years.

Burial mounds in Crystal River Archaeological State Park

The Tampa skyline viewed from Bayshore Drive

⑩ Bayshore Drive

Culture on the water

The Dali Museum *(see pp220–21)* anchors one end of St. Petersburg's extensive system of handsome waterfront parks, which stretch for some 23 blocks on Bayshore Drive beside Tampa Bay. A short walk away, **The Mahaffey Theater** – Duke Energy Center for the Arts hosts eminent international and national artists, Broadway shows, childrens theater, and musical performances that vary from classical to pop and rock. For soccer fanatics, the **Al Lang Stadium**, home to the renowned Tampa Bay Rowdies, is located next door. At the northern end of Bayshore Drive, the restored Renaissance Vinoy Resort is worth a stop to see photo displays of what life was like here in the posh 1920s.**Vinoy Park** is great for a stroll, with its view of the

sailboats on the bay. A popular space for concerts and outdoor music, the park comes alive over the weekends.

Letting off steam

Energetic kids will find plenty of room to run on the park paths that stretch the length of **Bayshore Drive**. They are the perfect place for a bike ride, too. Visit the nearby **Demen's Landing Park** *(1st St, 33701)*, with a playground and nice spots for a picnic. The park also offers open lawns for frisbees, a game of catch, or kite-flying. Walk over to the **South Straub Park** *(1st Ave N, 33701)*, which has a rock sculpture that kids love to climb.

⑪ Museum of Fine Arts

Small museum, great artists

Housed in a handsome building overlooking Tampa Bay, this museum is located in the center of the bayside park system. While introducing kids to fine art can be difficult if the museum is big and overwhelming, this museum is small enough to suit short attention spans. It contains a world-class collection of works by many great artists – Cézanne, Monet, Gauguin, Renoir, Rodin, and O'Keeffe, to name but a few. Other galleries display ancient Greek and Roman pottery and ceramics, and Asian religious and decorative objects, as well as Egyptian, African, pre-Columbian, and Native American art. The photography collection is one of the finest in the Southeast. The museum also has a sculpture

The Lowdown

🌐 **Map reference** 7 A2

Address 255 Beach Dr NE, St. Petersburg, 33701; 727 896 2667; *www.fine-arts.org*

🚐 **Trolley** The St. Pete trolley

🕐 **Open** 10am–5pm Mon–Sat, till 8pm Thu & noon–5pm Sun

💲 **Price** $10–17; under 7s free

👉 **Guided tours** The museum runs docent-led tours at 11am, 2pm Tue–Sat, and 2pm Sun.

👫 **Age range** 7 plus

🖌 **Activities** There are children's programs every third Saturday of the month.

⏱ **Allow** 2 hours

🍴 **Eat and drink** SNACKS MFA Café *(on site; 727 822 1032; closed Mon)*, an airy space in the museum, offers a nice selection of sandwiches and salads. FAMILY TREAT Parkshore Grill *(300 Beach Dr NE, 33701; 727 896 9463; www.parkshore grill.com)* has outdoor seating overlooking the Vinoy Yacht Basin. It also has a handsome dining room, with an open kitchen. The varied American menu ranges from crab cakes to steaks. There is also a well-priced kids' menu.

View of the stately building housing the Museum of Fine Arts, St. Petersburg

garden, a Steuben glass gallery, and special exhibitions. A video screen at the entrance informs visitors of daily child-friendly activities, such as special family tours (11am Sat), treasure hunts, and the chance to create an artwork inspired by works in the museum. The museum café offers waterfront dining with a view of the downtown skyline.

Letting off steam

Run around in the bayside park around the museum, or take a trip 12 miles (19 km) southwest to the **Fort De Soto Park**

The Lowdown

🌐 **Map reference** 7 A2

Address The Mahaffey Theater: 400 1st St S, St. Petersburg, 33701; 727 893 7832; *www.themahaffey.com*

🚐 **Trolley** The St. Pete trolley ($2, under 5s free) runs along Bayfront Drive to Mahaffey.

🕐 **Open** The Pier: 10am–8pm Mon–Thu, 10am–9pm Fri–Sat, & 11am–7pm Sun

💲 **Price** varies according to venue.

👫 **Age range** All ages

🖌 **Activities** Walking, jogging, and attending theatrical events.

⏱ **Allow** 2–4 hours

Prices given are for a family of four

(www.fort desoto.com). A great day's getaway, this is a county park of five interconnected islands with beautiful beaches and a cool historic fort to explore. The islands are home to mangroves, wetlands, and palm hammocks, as well as numerous species of birds. Fishing piers, hiking trails, and canoe, kayak, and bike rentals provide plenty of activities. There are restrooms, a food concession, and outdoor showers to wash away beach sand.

Picturesque view of the Fort De Soto Park

⑫ Great Explorations Children's Museum

Create a robot, run a pizzeria

Kids take charge here, in little re-creations of grown-up domains such as a pizza parlor, a fire engine house, a veterinary office, and a supermarket. There is a pretend orange grove where they can pick, pack, and ship oranges, plus turn them into orange juice. A treehouse built for climbing, a lab for making moving robots, and the chance to create animation using a digital video recorder are among the favorite activities in this museum.

Letting off steam
Go to the **Sunken Gardens** (1825 4th St N, 33702; 727 551 3102; www.stpete.org/sunken), adjacent to the museum. This long-established attraction has paved paths to stretch young legs, cascading waterfalls, and some 50,000 exotic plants and flowers from around the world.

The Lowdown

🌐 **Map reference** 7 A2

📍 **Address** 1925 4th St N, St. Petersburg, 33704; 727 821 8992; www.greatexplorations.org

🚌 **Bus** PSTA (www.psta.net) city bus 4 stops near the museum. Check website for routes.

🕐 **Open** 10am–4:30pm Mon–Sat & noon–4:30pm Sun

💲 **Price** $40–50

🚻 **Age range** 2 plus

🚹 **Activities** The museum hosts many special Saturday programs. Check the current schedule on the website.

⏱ **Allow** 2 hours

☕ **Eat and drink** SNACKS Panera Bread (1908 4th St N, 33701; 727 895 5441) stocks delicious breads that make fine sandwiches. The desserts are tasty. REAL MEAL Fourth Street Shrimp Store (1006 4th Ave N, 33701; 727 822 0325; www.theshrimpstore.com) is set in a former service station and has a funky ambience. Great seafood, and a children's menu too.

Meandering path through lush greenery at the Sunken Gardens, St. Petersburg

Picnic under $25; **Snacks** $25–50; **Real meal** $50–80; **Family treat** over $80 (based on a family of four)

⑬ The Ringling, Sarasota
The greatest show on Earth!

Built in 1925, the art museum holding multimillionaire circus owner John Ringling's famous art collection is just one part of his vast estate beside Sarasota Bay. Ringling's original collection of 600 paintings has grown to over 2,000 objects, including Asian and contemporary art. Peppered with gardens, the estate boasts America's only authentic 18th-century European theater, as well as the exquisite Ringling home and two museums filled with circus nostalgia and fun.

Circus Poster in the Ringling Museum of Art

Key Features

④ Ringling Museum of Art Now the State Art Museum of Florida, this houses priceless Old Master paintings. Look out for Rubens' *Gathering of the Manna* – it is hard to say whether the figure of Moses has rays of light or horns coming from his head.

① Cà' d'Zan The Ringlings' restored Venetian-style palazzo, completed in 1926, has a bathtub carved from a huge single block of marble. Look up at the ballroom's ceiling – it has a painting by children's book illustrator Willy Pogany, showing dancing couples from all over the world.

② Circus Museum Established after Ringling's death, this documents the rich history of the circus, and also features colossal parade wagons, sequined costumes, and Ringling's private rail car.

③ Historic Asolo Theater This restored theater serves as the venue for film screenings and concerts. Built in Italy in 1798, it was moved to the Ringling estate in the 1940s.

⑤ Courtyard of the Museum of Art Find casts of original antiquities and Renaissance sculptures, including the towering *David* by Michelangelo, along with two replicas of Roman fountains. The *Fountain of the Tortoises* is a favorite with kids.

Entrance

⑥ Tibbals Learning Center Kids can walk a safe tightrope, fire a miniature cannon, dress up as a circus clown, and try to fit into a midget car here. The handmade miniature Howard Bros. Circus model fills an entire room, with eight tents and 152 wagons, and is very detailed, right down to the smallest dishes in the mess tent.

The Lowdown

🌐 **Map reference** 7 B3

🏠 **Address** 5401 Bay Shore Rd, Sarasota, 34243; 941 359 5700; *www.ringling.org*

🚌 **Bus** Sarasota County Area Transit (SCAT) bus 99 arrives hourly from downtown (*www.scgov.net/scat*).

🕐 **Open** 10am–5pm daily & till 8pm Thu (museums only)

💲 **Price** $55–60. Free entry to the Ringling Museum of Art on Mon.

Cutting the line Call 941 358 3180 for advance ticketing

information and 941 360 7399 to book tickets for the Historic Asolo Theater.

🚩 **Guided tours** Hourly docent-led tours of the Ringling Museum of Art and the Circus Museum. The first floor of Cà' d'Zan can be visited on guided tours only.

👫 **Age range** 6 plus; the Cà' d'Zan is not recommended for younger kids due to its narrow walkways.

Activities Check website for information on shows at the Historic Asolo Theater.

⏱ **Allow** At least half a day

♿ **Wheelchair access** Yes

☕ **Café** Banyan Café, opposite the Circus Museum, serves hot dogs and chicken fingers.

🛍 **Shop** In the Visitors Pavilion (see p225)

🚻 **Restrooms** In every building

Good family value?
Kids will enjoy the Museum's attractions, especially the Circus Museum, though it is expensive.

Sculptures and blooming rose beds in Mable's Rose Garden

Letting off steam

The vast grounds of the Ringling estate have many paths for working off excess energy and beautiful gardens to admire. John Ringling's wife, Mable, was an avid gardener and her **Rose Garden**, patterned after an Italian circular design, is one of the estate's prettiest spots. When the 1,200 rose bushes are in bloom, the scents are delightful. Kids will have fun finding **Mable's Secret Garden**, the **Dwarf Garden**, and the estate's **Millennium Tree Trail**.

Blue Dolphin Café in the historic St. Armands Circle, Sarasota

Eat and drink

Picnic: under $25; Snacks: $25–50; Real meal: $50–80; Family treat: over $80 (based on a family of four)

PICNIC Publix *(1044 N Tamiami Trail, 34236; 941 366 3270)* has picnic fixings and snacks to enjoy at the outdoor tables in the grounds near the Rose Garden.
SNACKS St. Armands Circle, the shopping area developed by John Ringling on Lido Key, has many good choices. **Venezia** *(373 St. Armands Circle, 34236; 941 388 1400; venezia-1966.com)* serves tasty pizza.
REAL MEAL Blue Dolphin Café *(470 John Ringling Blvd, 34236; 941 388 3566; bluedolphincafe. com)*, an informal diner, offers a kids' menu for breakfast and lunch.

FAMILY TREAT Café L'Europe *(431 St. Armands Circle, 34236; 941 388 4415; www.cafeleurope. net)* is a traditional French favorite for a special night out. The kids' menu has salads, chicken fingers, and Key lime pie.

Shopping

The **Museum Store** delights kids with souvenirs such as juggling balls, clown noses, and puzzles of museum sites. Grown-ups will find scarves with Venetian themes from Cà' d'Zan, interesting jewelry, and home accessories. **St. Armands Circle** is lined with dozens of shops of all kinds, plus conveniently located ice-cream parlors for a break.

Find out more

DIGITAL See *www.ringling.com* to learn more about the history of the Ringling circus, the best circus acts, animal care, and other interesting topics. Discover what it takes to be a clown at *www.allaboutclowns.com*.

Next stop...

SARASOTA JUNGLE GARDENS
One mile (2 km) south of the Ringling, the Sarasota Jungle Gardens *(www.sarasota junglegardens.com)* have been pleasing families since the 1940s. Trails run through 10 acres (4 ha) of lush tropical vegetation and a "kiddie jungle" with an imaginative playground. Grown-ups and kids will like feeding the flamingos. Kids can enjoy shows that feature alligators, snakes, birds of prey, and tropical birds – interacting with these exotic animals is a favorite.

KIDS' CORNER

Test your circus IQ...
1 Can you name three props you would need to look like a clown?
2 The biggest miniature circus in the world was made by one man, Howard Tibbals. How long do you think it took him? How many figures are in the circus?

3 Circus people have their own lingo: can you guess what a Joey is? And a funambulist?

Answers at the bottom of the page.

BIG CLOWN, MIDGET CAR
One of the clowns featured in the Circus Museum is Lou Jacobs, who had a midget car. The car was 2 ft (60 cm) wide by 3 ft (90 cm) long, and Lou was over 6 ft (2 m) tall. But he managed to fold himself inside the car and drive it into the center ring, amazing everyone when he popped out.

Going for Baroque
John Ringling's favorite artists, including Peter Paul Rubens, created elaborate paintings in the style known as Baroque. Popular in Europe from the early 17th to the mid-18th century Baroque paintings were dramatic, grand in scale, and at times exaggerated in detail. Housed in the Ringling Museum of Art, Rubens' *Eucharist* series is a famous example. Can you make a drawing in Baroque style?

Answers: 1 A red nose, big shoes, and a funny wig. **2** 50 years; over 1,300 figures. **3** Clown; tightrope walker.

⑭ The Aquarium at Mote Marine Laboratory

Close encounters of the marine kind

From seeing shark habitats, a dolphin lagoon, and a 23-ft (7-m) giant squid to getting up close with sea turtles and manatees and feeling a stingray's velvety back in a touch pool, The Aquarium at Mote Marine Laboratory, has it all. Attached to a major marine research facility, The Aquarium showcases the Lab's work and includes exhibits that feature real scientific studies on coral reefs and with other species. The chance to see exhibits where sea horses are hatched and raised, or learn how injured sea creatures are healed and returned to the wild at Mote's Dolphin & Whale Hospital and the Sea Turtle Rehabilitation Center, are exceptional opportunities that make a visit to this aquarium unique.

Letting off steam

A large swath of parkland with great views bordering Sarasota Bay, the **Ken Thompson Park** (*1700 Ken Thompson Pkwy, 34236*), nearby, has swings for kids, a fishing pier, and lots of green lawn for games and picnics.

Children observing tropical fish at The Aquarium at Mote Marine Laboratory

The Lowdown

- 🌐 **Map reference** 7 A3
- **Address** 1600 Ken Thompson Pkwy, Sarasota, 34236; 941 388 4441; www.mote.org
- 🚗 **Car** Rent a car from Sarasota Airport.
- 🕐 **Open** 10am–5pm daily
- 💲 **Price** $50–66; under 3s free
- 🔫 **Guided tours** The 90-minute Morning Rounds tour allows up to three guests aged 10 plus to get an up-close look at feeding and care of the animals.
- 👫 **Age range** All ages
- 👫 **Activities** Feed seahorses at the Seahorse Conservation Lab. Check website for current schedule of family programs. The aquarium also offers Eco-Boat tours of Sarasota Bay.
- ⏱ **Allow** 3 hours
- ♿ **Wheelchair access** Yes
- 🛍 **Shop** The gift shop sells toys, plush birds, T-shirts, and puzzles.
- 🍴 **Eat and drink** SNACKS Deep Sea Diner (*on site*) is fine for snacks or a light lunch. REAL MEAL The Old Salty Dog (*1601 Ken Thompson Pkwy, 34236; 941 388 4311*), nearby, is one of Sarasota's best family choices, with an informal menu and an outdoor deck for watching the boats go by.

The Lowdown

- 🌐 **Map reference** 7 B3
- **Address** 811 South Palm Ave, Sarasota, 34236; 941 366 5731; www.selby.org
- 🚌 **Bus** SCAT bus 17 on Tamiami Trail (US 41) stops nearby.
- 🕐 **Open** 10am–5pm daily
- 💲 **Price** $65–80; under 4s free
- 👫 **Age range** 5 plus
- 👫 **Activities** Little Sprouts is a fun interactive program for pre-schoolers, with stories and games.
- ⏱ **Allow** 2 hours
- 🍴 **Eat and drink** SNACKS Selby House Cafe (*on site*) serves snacks, sandwiches, and desserts. REAL MEAL Hillview Grill (*1920 Hillview St, 34239; 941 346 6989; closed Sun*) offers a varied Italian and Mediterranean menu, including pastas, sandwiches and salads.

⑮ Marie Selby Botanical Gardens

Orchids, fish, and an enchanted garden

The more than 6,000 orchids are the showstoppers, but not the only lures, at this beautiful world of exotic plants. While known for its epiphytes – plants such as orchids that grow on other plants – the gardens also include bamboo and banyan groves, hibiscus, ferns, tropical fruits, cactus, native Florida plants, a mangrove forest, and eight plant-filled greenhouses. Kids are welcomed here and encouraged to wander the paths and run on the great lawn. Check out the weird plants that live on trees, feed the fish in the koi pond, and conduct a plant hunt, which can be printed out from the website, with one of the children's guides.

A short drive 1 mile (2 km) north is the **Sarasota Children's Garden** (*www.sarasotachildrens garden.com*), a magical world where a tunnel leads to a space filled with whimsical sculptures of friendly dragons and octopuses, a pirate ship with rigging to be climbed, a maze to be explored, a tree fort, and a fairy garden for tea parties.

Take cover

If raindrops fall, the Kids' Corner in the **Historic Selby House** on site is the perfect shelter. This interactive space is filled with plant-themed books, puzzles, activities, and crafts. A volunteer is often on hand to help.

Kids' Corner in the Historic Selby House in the Marie Selby Botanical Gardens

A girl learning to walk on a tightrope at the Circus Arts Conservatory

⑯ The Circus Arts Conservatory

Circus by kids – for kids

The Sailor Circus Academy, America's oldest youth circus, is a key element of The Circus Arts Conservatory, a performing arts educational organization. What started in 1949 as a high-school gymnastics class has grown into a spectacular training program for youngsters aged 8–18. In a fun atmosphere, students learn circus skills, but also the importance of discipline, self-confidence, and a commitment to achievement. The students' annual performances are a major attraction in Southwest Florida.

Letting off steam

There are lots of activities at **Bayfront Park**, and families can happily while away an afternoon. Alternatively, for a wilderness experience just 9 miles (14 km) southeast of Sarasota, head for **Myakka River State Park** (*www. myakkariver.org*). Here, the wild and scenic Myakka River flows through miles of untouched wetlands, prairies, and woodlands. Admire its beauty from a canopy walkway high above the ground, a boardwalk across Upper Myakka Lake, a tram tour through the backcountry, airboat tours, or on hiking trails, and watch out for wildlife such as alligators and armadillos.

The Lowdown

🌐 **Map reference** 7 B3

Address 2075 Bahia Vista Street, Sarasota, 34239; 941 355 9335; *www.circusarts.org*

🚌 **Bus** SCAT bus 11 stops on Bahia Vista and runs hourly from downtown.

🕐 **Open** For performances; times vary, check website.

💲 **Price** $42–52 for circus; circus arts classes charge a fee.

👫 **Age range** 5 plus

🤸 **Activities** A wide variety of demonstrations of circus arts and classes are available. Check website for schedule.

⏱ **Allow** 2–3 hours

♿ **Wheelchair access** Yes

🍴 **Eat and drink** PICNIC Morton's Gourmet Market (*1924 S Osprey Ave, 34239; 941 955 9856*) stocks goodies for picnics that can be enjoyed in Bayfront Park. **REAL MEAL** Mattison's City Grille (*1 Lemon St at Main St, 34236; 941 330 0440; closed Sun*) has outdoor seating on Sarasota's pleasant Main Street and a menu offering everything from pizza to steak.

The pristine landscape of Myakka River State Park

Picnic under $25; **Snacks** $25–50; **Real meal** $50–80; **Family treat** over $80 (based on a family of four)

Where to Stay on the Gulf Coast

A major draw for families, the Gulf Coast offers everything from campsites and budget motels to luxurious condos. Numerous all-suite properties afford extra space and even modest lodgings usually offer air-conditioning and swimming pools – welcome features in the warm climate.

AGENCIES

Find Vacation Rentals
www.findvacationrentals.com/florida.html
This website provides condo listings throughout the state, including the Gulf Coast.

Florida Vacation Connection
3720 Gulf of Mexico Dr, Longboat Key, 34228; 877 702 9980; flavacationconnection.com
Use this reservation service for vacation rentals, ranging from beachfront resorts to condos, on Longboat Key and Lido Key, Sarasota's choice beach locations.

Bradenton Beach Map 7 A3

HOTEL
Bridgewalk, a Landmark Resort
100 Bridge St, 34217; 941 779 2545; www.silverresorts.com
Bradenton's historic Bridge Street is charming, and this well-appointed property is right across the road from the beach. The hotel has suites and apartments with kitchens, with shops and restaurants next door. The free Bradenton trolley takes guests to the town and other Gulf Coast beaches.
🛢️🏨🖥️ $$

St. Pete Beach Map 7 A2

HOTELS
Plaza Beach Hotel
4506 Gulf Blvd, 33706; 800 257 8998; www.plazabeachresorts.com
For families who want to be on the beach, this small, low-key resort of just 39 suites is right on the sands. The good-size suites come with full kitchens. Besides the pool, kids will find mini-golf, shuffleboard, and other games here. Beach cabanas and beachside BBQ grills are free, as is the Wi-Fi service.
🔚🏖️🏨🖥️🌀 $–$$

Don CeSar Hotel
3400 Gulf Blvd, 33706; 727 360 1881; www.loewshotels.com/en/Don-CeSar-Hotel
A luxury landmark since it opened in 1928, this cotton-candy pink palace by the sea is hard to miss. The building is well maintained and enjoys a beachfront location.
🔚🍽️🏨🖥️🌀 $$$

St. Petersburg Map 7 A2

RESORT
The Vinoy Renaissance
501 5th Ave NE, 33701; 727 894 1000; www.marriott.com
This beautifully restored historic hotel blends the grandeur of the past with modern conveniences, including a lavish pool, tennis, golf and spa, and a highly regarded restaurant. It overlooks Tampa Bay and makes a good base for visiting nearby sights.
🔚🍽️🏨🖥️ $$$

INNS & SUITES
Hampton Inn & Suites St. Petersburg
80 Beach Dr NE, 33701; 727 892 9900; hamptoninn3.hilton.com
This renovated property offers good-size rooms with refrigerators, microwaves, and DVD players. There is a laundry facility, as well as free Wi-Fi and hot breakfasts. Guests can check email at the business kiosk.
🔚🖥️ $$

BED & BREAKFAST

Dickens House Bed and Breakfast
335 8th Ave Northeast, 33701; 727 822 8622; www.dickenshouse.com
Bed and breakfast fans, with kids aged 9 plus, will love this warm 1912 Craftsman-style home. It serves sumptuous breakfasts and is located two blocks from the waterfront parks. Amenities include refrigerators in rooms and a computer for guests.
🔚 P $–$$

CAMPING

Fort De Soto Park
3500 Pinellas Bayway S, Tierra Verde, 33715; 727 582 2267; www.pinellascounty.org/park
This beautiful park, 12 miles (19 km) southwest of St. Petersburg, offers tent camping just steps from the beach and full-service RV hook-ups. There are fishing piers, hiking trails, and canoe, kayak, and bike rentals, as well as a fort to explore.
P🌀🥾 $

Sarasota Map 7 B3

HOTELS
Siesta Key Banyan Tree Resort and Vacation Rentals Map 7 B4
378 Canal Rd, Siesta Key, 34242; 941 346 0651; siestakeybanyanresort.com
Studio apartments and one-, two-, and three-bedroom condos are available by the week here. All units

Don CeSar Hotel, a renowned beachfront luxury hotel

Camping near the water at Fort De Soto Park

have full kitchens. The award-winning Siesta Key Beach and Siesta Key Village are within walking distance.

🐾 🛏 ☉ $–$$

Lido Beach Resort
700 Ben Franklin Dr, 34236; 941 388 2161; www.lidobeachresort.com
This resort offers the choice of a tower with spacious condo suites or a low-rise hotel. Even basic hotel rooms have kitchenettes with microwaves and refrigerators. Check website for discounts.

🔊 🛏 🛏 ☉ ☉ $$–$$$

Ritz-Carlton Hotel
1111 Ritz-Carlton Dr, 34236; 941 309 2000; www.ritzcarlton.com
The most elegant accommodation in Sarasota welcomes kids with board games at the concierge desk, assorted games at the pool, and a children's menu. Shuttles take guests to a private club on Lido Beach with counselor-supervised kids' programs.

🔊 🍽 🛏 ☉ ☉ $$–$$$

INN & SUITES
La Quinta Inn & Suites
1803 N Tamiami Trail, 34234; 941 366 5128; www.lq.com
A well-kept motel within an easy drive of the Ringling Museum or the beach, La Quinta has rooms with mini-refrigerators and comfy beds. Free Internet access and Continental breakfast are offered.

🔊 P ☉ $

Regency Inn and Suites
4200 N Tamiami Trail, 34234; 941 355 7616; www.regencyinnandsuites sarasota.com
This budget motel offers 14 rooms with refrigerators and microwaves, and 20 one-bedroom suites with full-size kitchens. Its location on the main highway is convenient for visiting the city's best attractions.

🔊 🛏 ☉ $

Holiday Inn Lido Beach
233 Ben Franklin Dr, 34236; 941 388 5555; www.ihg.com
This property boasts an unmatched location, sitting directly across the road from Lido Beach. Amenities include an indoor fitness center. The enclosed-rooftop dining room offers fabulous views, and kids eat for free.

🔊 🍽 🛏 ☉ $$

CAMPING
Myakka River State Park Cabins and Camping   Map 7 B4
13208 State Rd 72, 34241; 941 361 6511; www.floridastateparks.org/park/Myakka-River
Stay near the city but in the heart of unspoiled nature in these five rustic log cabins lodging up to six people. Amenities include linen and blankets, kitchen utensils, and microwaves.

🐾 🛏 ☉ 🚲 $

Tampa   Map 7 B1

HOTELS
Hampton Inn-International Airport/Westshore
4817 W Laurel St, 33607; 813 287 0778; www.hamptoninn.hilton.com
Among the hotels clustered near Tampa Airport, where expressway connections make it easy to reach downtown, the Hampton Inn is one of the best. The spacious rooms are equipped with refrigerators and microwaves. Free breakfast.

🔊 🛏 ☉ $

Wingate By Wyndham
3751 E Fowler Ave, 33612; 813 867 2878; www.wingatehotels.com
This hotel is a good base for visiting Busch Gardens, and offers a free daily shuttle to the park. Rooms have refrigerators and microwaves, and the full breakfast buffet and Wi-Fi are free. The outdoor pool and indoor hot tub are refreshing after a day out in the theme park.

🔊 P ☉ $

Embassy Suites Tampa Airport/Westshore
555 N Westshore Blvd; 813 875 1555; www.embassysuites.com
This all-suite property stands out for families, as it provides a full living room with sofa bed and the privacy of a separate bedroom, plus two

TVs. Rooms have refrigerators and microwaves. The cooked-to-order breakfast and nightly cocktails are free.

🔥 🔊 🛏 🐾 ☉ $$

Embassy Suites Tampa Downtown Convention Center
513 South Florida Ave, 33602; 813 769 8300; www.embassysuites.com
This excellent family choice has the added plus of a downtown location served by the TECO trolley, making it easy to get to The Florida Aquarium or the Glazer's Children's Museum.

🔊 🛏 🐾 ☉ $$

Westin Tampa Harbour Island
725 S Harbour Island Blvd, 33602; 813 229 5000; www.westintampa waterside.com
On a private island but just a footbridge away from downtown, the luxurious Westin has spacious rooms with oversize windows, many of which overlook Tampa Bay.

🔊 🍽 P ☉ $$$

Westin Tampa Harbour Island, a luxury waterfront hotel in downtown Tampa

CAMPING
Hillsborough River State Park   Map 7 B1
15402 US 301 N, Thonotosassa, 33592; 813 987 6771; www.stateparks.com
This state park on the river 12 miles (19 km) north of Tampa has a 108-site campground for tents and RVs. Most sites have electricity and all have water. Fishing, hiking, and bike trails.

☉ ☉ 🚲 $

Price Guide
The following price ranges are based on one night's accommodation in high season for a family of four, inclusive of service charges and additional taxes.

$ Under $150 **$$** $150–300 **$$$** over $300

The Lower Gulf Coast, Everglades, and Keys

Florida's southernmost tip offers an irresistible package for families interested in history, culture, watersports, and nature. Lying close to the Caribbean islands, the Keys also share some of the former's characteristics. The Everglades are the culmination of the state's wilds, and have a Native American heritage. In the Fort Myers-Naples area, the barrier islands boast some of the state's best beaches, while Naples is famous for arts and golf.

The Lower Gulf Coast, Everglades, and Keys

Highlights

Sanibel Island
Collect shells at this famous island and enjoy its safe beaches, family resorts, and great museums *(see p238)*.

Edison and Ford Winter Estates
Stimulate inventive young minds at the homes, gardens, and laboratories of two of America's greatest geniuses *(see p236)*.

Everglades National Park
Hike, bike, kayak, and boat around this mysterious land of mangrove forest, forgotten islands, wetlands, and a river of grass that teems with rare wildlife *(see pp242–3)*.

John Pennekamp Coral Reef State Park
Visit this undersea park to see brilliantly colored coral reefs by snorkel or aboard a glass-bottom boat *(see p251)*.

Key West
Head to this legendary island town to experience its eccentricity and unique spirit *(see pp246–7)*.

Fort Myers River District
Take in local history and culture in downtown Fort Myers, which has historic buildings, museums, galleries, and monthly street parties *(see p236)*.

Left *Signboards at the entrance to Robbie's Marina, Islamorada*
Above right *Wooden boardwalk winding through the swamp forest, Fakahatchee Strand State Preserve*

The Best of The Lower Gulf Coast, Everglades, and Keys

The great outdoors, history, and culture make this region a well-rounded destination with plenty for everyone. Families can get their fill of sunny beaches, warm seawaters, and watersports such as fishing, boating, jet-skiing, kayaking, and paddleboarding during their stay in this area. Massive national and state parks, as well as wildlife preserves, provide opportunities to hike, bike, and get close to nature.

In and on the water

Flanked by the Atlantic Ocean, Florida Bay, and the Gulf of Mexico, this area demands getting wet – or at least wetting a line. **Key Largo** *(see pp250–51)* is a good place to initiate kids into the wonderful world of underwater sightseeing. Ease them into it with a glass-bottom boat tour at **John Pennekamp Coral Reef State Park** *(see p251)*. When they are ready to jump in, try the snorkeling tours offered by the park, or sign up with one of the numerous operators in town. Fishing in the Atlantic can get rough, so begin gently with a backwater Everglades fishing excursion from **Flamingo Visitor Center** *(see p242)* or in **Everglades City** *(see p245)*. Head to Sanibel Island for an educational sea-life cruise into **J. N. "Ding" Darling National Wildlife Refuge** *(see p239)*.

Right Christ of the Deep, *John Pennekamp Coral Reef State Park* **Below** *Anhinga and alligator, Everglades National Park*

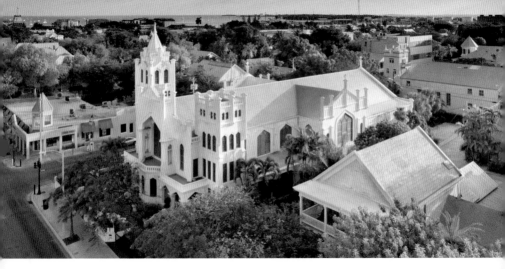

Above Aerial view of Duval Street, a famous shopping and dining hub in the heart of Old Town in Key West

Wildlife-watching

Alligator sightings are practically guaranteed at **Royal Palm Visitor Center** *(see p242)*, to the east of **Everglades National Park** *(see pp242–3)*, and at **Shark Valley Visitor Center** *(see p242)*, in the west, while white-tailed deer and raccoons also make occasional appearances. At **Flamingo Visitor Center**, saltwater crocodiles often sun themselves on the boat ramp. Bird-watchers should be able to tick off dozens of bird species from their "life list" of sightings in the **Everglades National Park** and **Big Cypress National Preserve** *(see pp244–5)*. Other birding hot spots include **Tigertail Beach** on **Marco Island** *(see p241)*, and **Corkscrew Swamp Sanctuary** *(see p240)*, north of **Naples** *(see p240)*.

Rambling around the Keys

With five to seven days to spend in the Florida Keys, start with a trolley tour in **Key West** *(see pp246–7)*. Spend the remainder of the day

walking around the Old Town and exploring the **Key West Aquarium** *(see p246)* and the **Eco-Discovery Center** *(see p246)* before hitting the beach at **Fort Zachary Taylor Historic State Park** *(see p246)*. However, don't miss sunset at Mallory Square. Heading north, families can bike or kayak into **National Key Deer Refuge** on **Big Pine Key** *(see p248)*, then factor in some quality beach or snorkeling time at **Bahia Honda State Park** *(see p248)*. **Marathon** *(see p249)* merits a day of exploration: go to **Crane Point** in the morning and either **Pigeon Key** or **Sombrero Beach** in the afternoon. Devote the remaining days to kayaking and snorkeling in **Islamorada** and **Key Largo** *(see p250)*.

History hot spots

Local history runs deep throughout the region. One of Florida's oldest commercial ports, **Key West** holds the most treasures in its Old Town. **Pigeon Key** has the historic remains of the operation to build a railroad to Key West. The **Museum of the Everglades** *(see p243)* tells the story of the building of Tamiami Trail through the Everglades' wetlands and swamps. The **Marco Island Historical Museum** *(see p241)* focuses on the island's past as an ancient Calusa Indian capital. The **Edison and Ford Winter Estates**, in **Fort Myers** *(see pp236–7)*, shed light on the lives of the two scientists who vacationed there. The **Southwest Florida Museum of History** *(see p236)* explores the area's fishing, cattle-ranching, and baseball heritages.

Left Cyclists heading towards Pigeon Key on the historic Seven-Mile Bridge

The Lower Gulf Coast, Everglades, and Keys

Florida tapers off to its narrowest and flattest at its southern tip. While barrier islands rim the shoreline along the Gulf Coast, sandy beaches, mangrove estuaries, saltwater marshes, and the shallow Florida Bay make up the unique Everglades. Farther south |are the Florida Keys, a string of islands that rest on a bed of coral and limestone from ancient reefs. The Tamiami Trail (Highway 41) passes through the Everglades, connecting Tampa to Miami. Interstate 75, often called "Alligator Alley", is a faster route, linking Fort Lauderdale to Fort Myers and Naples.

Informative displays in the Bailey-Matthews Shell Museum, Sanibel Island

The Lowdown

🚗 **Getting there and around**
Air Southwest Florida International Airport (RSW), in Fort Myers, serves most of the major and low-fare airlines from destinations in and outside Florida. A couple of carriers fly small planes between Fort Myers and Key West. Several taxi companies service the airport and provide transportation throughout the region. Naples and Key West have small airports with a limited service. Most visitors to Key West fly into Miami International Airport (MIA) and drive to the Keys. **Car** Several rental car agencies are based at RSW. Note that all cars, including rentals, need a transponder device to use for the toll road from Miami to the Keys. Check www.sunpass.com/rentalcar for details.

ℹ️ **Visitor information** See individual entries.

🍽 **Supermarkets** Publix (www.publix.com) is the major chain here with outlets throughout this region. There is also Winn-Dixie, which is slightly more affordable.

Markets Different communities host farmers' markets on various days, sometimes only in the winter or spring season. Contact tourist offices for details.

🎊 **Festivals** Edison Festival of Light, Fort Myers: junior parade with floats and street performers; www.edisonfestival.org (Feb). Conch Republic Independence Celebration, Key West; www.keywestchamber.org (Apr)

🕐 **Opening hours** Some facilities in the Everglades area close in summer and the fall. Many restaurants in the Everglades and Keys close for a month in the fall.

➕ **Pharmacies** Walgreens (www.walgreens.com) pharmacies in Fort Myers and Naples stay open 24 hours. However, in the Keys, CVS (www.cvs.com) and Walgreens do not stay open all night. Be sure to stock up on medical supplies before visiting the Everglades and Keys.

🚻 **Restrooms** All major attractions, fast-food restaurants, shopping malls, supermarkets, and gas stations have public restrooms.

Breathtaking view of Long Pine Key Lake, Everglades National Park

Places of interest

SIGHTS

1 Fort Myers
2 Sanibel and Captiva Islands
3 Upper Islands
4 J. N. "Ding" Darling National Wildlife Refuge
5 Corkscrew Swamp Sanctuary
6 Naples
7 Marco Island
8 Everglades National Park
9 Biscayne National Park
10 Miccosukee Indian Village
11 Big Cypress National Preserve
12 Everglades City
13 Key West
14 Big Pine Key
15 Bahia Honda State Park
16 Marathon
17 Islamorada
18 Key Largo
19 John Pennekamp Coral Reef State Park

The Busy Beehives exhibit in the Imaginarium Science Center, Fort Myers

Feeding tarpons at Robbie's Marina, Islamorada

① Fort Myers
Sunny skies and island beaches

Born out of the Seminole Wars that drove Native Americans into the Everglades, Fort Myers grew slowly along the Caloosahatchee River. In 1885, Thomas Edison saw bamboo growing here, and, hoping to use it as filament for his new invention, the light bulb, he built a winter home, putting Fort Myers on the map. Today, the Historic Downtown District draws visitors to its museums, theaters, shops, and restaurants. A trolley service links Fort Myers' main sights.

Pirate manatee at Manatee Park

Key Sights

⑤ **Naples Botanical Garden** Walk among several beautiful tropical and subtropical gardens and a nature preserve spread over 170 acres (69 ha). Kids will love the interactive Children's Garden, complete with colorful butterflies, a tree-house, and a Hidden Garden.

④ **Cape Coral** Enjoy a day of fun at the Sunsplash Family Waterpark and Greenwell's Bat-a-Ball and Family Fun Park, located in this town across the river from Fort Myers.

⑥ **Manatee Park** In winter, watch snout-faced manatees in the warm waters of this park from the observation decks, or kayak among them for a whole new experience.

① **Edison and Ford Winter Estates** Edison built two homes and a lab on the river and his friend Henry Ford of Ford Motors later moved in next door. Tour a museum, botanical gardens, and the homes.

② **IMAG History & Science Center** Children can see and touch marine life, observe gears and pumps at work, and learn about nano-technology.

③ **Centennial Park** Families can stroll and picnic at this large community park on the banks of the Caloosahatchee River, also the site for the Thursday Farmer's Market.

⑦ **Calusa Nature Center and Planetarium** Meet fascinating creatures from southwest Florida, then head to the planetarium to view the heavens.

The Lowdown

🌐 **Map reference** 7 C5
Address Edison and Ford Winter Estates: 2350 McGregor Blvd, 33901; edisonfordwinterestates.org. Centennial Park: 2000 W First St, Fort Myers, 33901; www.cityftmyers.com. IMAG History & Science Center: 2000 Cranford Ave, 33916; www.theimag.org. Naples Botanical Garden: 4820 Bayshore Dr, Naples, 34112; www.naplesgarden.org. Manatee Park: 10901 State Rd 80, Palm Beach Blvd, 33905; www.leegov.com/parks. Calusa Nature Center and Planetarium: 3450 Ortiz Ave, 33905; calusanature.org

🚌 **Bus** LeeTran buses (www.leegov.com/leetran) to most sights

ℹ️ **Visitor information** Lee County Visitor & Convention Bureau, 2201 2nd St, 6th floor, 33901; www.fortmyers-sanibel.com

🕑 **Open** Edison and Ford Winter Estates: 9am–5:30pm. IMAG History & Science Center: 10am–5pm Tue–Sat; noon to 5pm Sun. Naples Botanical Garden: 8am–2pm daily. Manatee Park: 8am–sunset. Calusa Nature Center and Planetarium: 10am–4pm Mon–Sat, 11am–4pm Sun

💲 **Prices** Edison and Ford Winter Estates: $62–100; under 6s free. Calusa Nature Center and Planetarium: $25–30; under 3s free. IMAG History & Science Center: $38–48; under 3s free. Naples Botanical Garden: $40–50; under 4s free. Manatee Park: free

🚶 **Cutting the line** Arrive early, as parking lots fill up quickly.

🚩 **Guided tours** Admission to the Edison & Ford Winter Estates is by guided or self-guided audio tour. There is also an extensive Behind the Scenes tour.

Prices given are for a family of four

Letting off steam

Get some fresh air and play time at **Centennial Park** *(2000 W 1st St; 239 321 7530)*, which overlooks the Caloosahatchee River in the River District. A fishing pier, picnic tables, and lots of benches overlooking the river give the park an old-world charm.

Uncommon Friends *by D.J. Wilkins in Centennial Park*

Eat and drink

Picnic: under $25; Snacks: $25–50; Real meal: $50–80; Family treat: over $80 (based on a family of four)

PICNIC Publix Delis *(13401 Summerlin Rd, 33919; 239 481 2242; www.publix.com)* has great subs, salads, and chicken wings. Picnic at **Lakes Regional Park** *(7330 Gladiolus Dr, 33908; www.leegov. com/parks)*, a 20-minute drive on the highway, where kids can ride a mini-train, or cool off in the fountain. **SNACKS Rene's** *(7050 Winkler Rd, 33919; 239 489 0833)* offers some of the best sandwiches and salads in town. In addition, there are

👫 **Age range** 2 plus for most sights in the area; 6 plus for Edison and Ford Winter Estates

🏃 **Activities** Edison and Ford Young Inventors family tours at 11am on Sat

⏱ **Allow** 3 days or more

👫 **Restrooms** In all the sights

Good family value?

Fort Myers Beach is known for its affordable accommodations and restaurants. Cape Coral, too, offers good value for families who don't mind a drive to the beach.

soups, pitas, and croissants on the menu. Do try their great carrot cake. **REAL MEAL The Edison** *(3583 McGregor Blvd, 33901; 239 936 9349; www.edisonrestaurantfort myers.com)* is perfect before or after visiting Edison's digs. There are soups, pizza, pasta, and seafood. Kids eat free on Mondays. **FAMILY TREAT Bayfront Bistro** *(4761 Estero Blvd, 33931; 239 463 3663; www.bayfrontbistro.com)* offers seafood quesadillas, fish tacos, and fish sandwiches. Sit on the porch overlooking the marina for the view.

Shopping

Look for bargains at flea markets in Fort Myers, such as Fleamasters *(4135 Dr. M. L. King Jr Blvd; 239 334 7001; www.fleamall.com)*. Downtown's **Franklin Shops** *(2200 1st St; 239 333 3130; www.the franklinshops.com)* have everything from apparel and jewelry to fine art within a historic building.

Find out more

DIGITAL Visit the Young Inventors page at www.edisonfordwinter estates.org and find coloring sheets and a detective game to play. **FILM** The movie *Hoot* (2006), based on the book of the same name, is set in a fictional town based on Cape Coral and its burrowing owl population. Much of the filming was done in this area.

Relaxing at tranquil Bowditch Point Park, Fort Myers Beach

Next stop…

FORT MYERS BEACH Take a LeeTran bus 16 miles (26 km) southwest to Fort Myers Beach, a favorite with families. Visit its Lynn Hall Memorial Park beach, which has a cool playground, a fishing pier, and a pedestrian mall. Hit Bowditch Point Park for a quieter, more natural beach experience.

② Sanibel and Captiva Islands

Shell-bent and water-bound

These two barrier islands, attached by a short bridge, boast a reputation for shelling, and also for wildlife and watersports. The islands have given rise to the expressions Sanibel Stoop and Captiva Crouch, which refer to the posture shell-seekers habitually assume while hunting on the shell-blanketed beaches.

A causeway from the mainland brings visitors to Sanibel Island, more than half of which is a protected wildlife refuge. The **Sanibel Historical Museum and Village** exhibits historic island homes and buildings. At Sanibel's **Lighthouse Beach**, there is lots to do – from fishing off the pier to exploring the historic lighthouse and the nature trails. Along the island's "conservation corridor,"

Vacationers at one of Sanibel Island's beautiful beaches

nature-lovers can learn how the **Clinic for the Rehabilitation of Wildlife (CROW)** administers to sick and orphaned animals. Visit a butterfly house, climb an observation tower for fine views, and hike trails at the **Sanibel-Captiva Conservation Foundation (SCCF)**.

Farther north, Captiva Island has an off-the-beaten-path vibe. Rent a boat or kayak at one of the marinas to fish, or to explore the upper islands *(see below)*. Charter and tour boats customize tours for shelling, fishing, and dolphin-watching.

The Lowdown

🌐 **Map reference** 7 C6

📍 **Address** Sanibel Historical Museum and Village: 950 Dunlop Rd, 33957; *www.sanibelmuseum. org.* Lighthouse Beach: East end of Periwinkle Way, 33931; 239 472 3700. CROW: 3883 Sanibel-Captiva Rd, 33957; *www.crow clinic.org.* SCCF: 3333 Sanibel-Captiva Rd, 33957; *www.sccf.org*

🚗 **Car** Rent a car from Fort Myers.

ℹ️ **Visitor information** Sanibel Island & Captiva Island Chamber of Commerce, 1159 Causeway Rd, 33957; 239 472 1080; *www.sanibel-captiva.org*

🕐 **Open** Sanibel Historical Museum and Village: 10am–1pm Tue–Sat. SCCF: 8:30am–4pm Mon–Fri (Jun–Sep: till 3pm; Dec–Apr: Mon–Sat)

💲 **Prices** Sanibel Historical Museum and Village: $20. SCCF: $10; under 18s free. CROW: $14–28; under 13s free

🚻 **Cutting the line** Sanibel's sights are not usually crowded, except when school groups visit them.

🚶 **Guided tours** SCCF runs guided nature and beach walks and butterfly house tours seasonally.

⏱️ **Allow** At least a day

🍵 **Eat and drink** SNACKS Over Easy Café *(630 Tarpon Bay Rd, Sanibel Island, 33957; 239 472 2625; www.overeasycafesanibel.com)* offers giant cinnamon rolls, egg skillets, and sandwiches. REAL MEAL Jerry's Foods Family Restaurant *(1700 Periwinkle Way, 33957; www.jerrysfoods.com)* serves a range of cuisines all day.

Kids learning about shells at the Bailey-Matthews Shell Museum, Sanibel Island

Take cover

Head for Sanibel's **Bailey-Matthews Shell Museum** *(3075 Sanibel-Captiva Rd, 33957; www.shellmuseum.org),* to identify beach findings and admire seashells, or take part in shell-scavenger hunts.

③ Upper Islands

Adrift from the mainland

North of Captiva Island are a set of islands with no bridges to the mainland, and no means of access other than by boat. Closest to Captiva, North Captiva Island broke

The Lowdown

🌐 **Map reference** 7 C5

📍 **Address** Cayo Costa State Park: Cayo Costa, 33922; 941 964 0375; *www.floridastateparks.org*

🚤 **Boat** Water taxi from Jensen's Marina *(www.gocaptiva.com)* on Captiva Island to the Upper Islands. Captiva Cruises *(www. captivacruises.com)* does lunch excursions to Cabbage Key.

ℹ️ **Visitor information** Sanibel Island & Captiva Island Chamber of Commerce, 1159 Causeway Rd, Sanibel Island, 33957; 239 472 1080; *www.sanibel-captiva.org*

🕐 **Open** Cayo Costa State Park: 8am–sunset daily

💲 **Price** Cayo Costa State Park: $8

🚻 **Cutting the line** Avoid Cabbage Key when the Captiva Cruises lunch excursion is on the island.

🚹🚺 **Age range** 3 plus

⏱️ **Allow** Half a day or more

🍴 **Eat and drink** REAL MEAL Barnacle's Waterfront Dining *(North Captiva, 33924; 239 472 1200)* is famous for its black beans and rice. REAL MEAL Cabbage Key Inn *(Cabbage Key, 33922; 239 283 2278; www.cabbagekey.com)* is where diners write their family name on a dollar bill and tape it to the wall before digging into burgers, grilled cheese sandwiches, and seafood.

off from its parent island during a hurricane in the 1920s. Private and vacation rental homes, a grassy airstrip, and a club occupy the quiet, 5-mile- (8-km-) long island, along with superb beaches and restaurants. Walk or rent a golf cart to get around the island.

Farther north, Cayo Costa Island is mostly occupied by the **Cayo Costa State Park**, where visitors can swim, collect shells, hike, and camp or rent cabins. Look out for the pioneer cemetery along one of several nature trails.

Between Cayo Costa and the mainland, Cabbage Key has no beaches, but its rustic 1920s Cabbage Key Inn is a great attraction for the island-hopping lunch crowd. Have a bite to eat, and then walk it off along a short nature trail. Visitors can also spend the night at the inn, or in one of its cottages.

Letting off steam

Head to the uninhabited **Picnic Island**, near Sanibel Island, for a picnic on its beach park. Be sure to bring along essential supplies. Banana Bay Tour Company (www. bananabaytourcompany.com) runs half-day tours to the island from Fort Myers Beach.

Boating off a beach at Cayo Costa State Park

④ J. N. "Ding" Darling National Wildlife Refuge

Into the wild

Named for Jay Norwood, a Pulitzer-Prize-winning American cartoonist, and covering more than half of Sanibel Island, "Ding" gives the island its reputation among wildlife-lovers, especially birders. It counts about 230 species of birds among its resident and migrating populations, including the bald eagle, the roseate spoonbill, and the mangrove cuckoo.

At its main campus along Sanibel-Captiva Road, the refuge has an Education Center, a 4-mile (6-km) Wildlife Drive through wetlands, an observation tower, and several trails. Nearby, Bailey Tract protects a different freshwater habitat, which alligators and nocturnal bobcats frequent.

Horseshoe crab in J. N. "Ding" Darling National Wildlife Refuge, Sanibel Island

Take cover

The **"Ding" Darling Education Center** in the refuge has various interactive exhibits. Check out the eBird computer, habitat vignettes, a Kids' Corner, and the nature store with games, books, and toys.

The Lowdown

🌐 **Map reference** 7 C6
Address 1 Wildlife Dr, Sanibel Island, 33957; 239 472 1100; www.fws.gov/dingdarling

🚗 **Car** Rent a car from Fort Myers.

ℹ **Visitor information** Sanibel Island & Captiva Island Chamber of Commerce, 1159 Causeway Rd, 33957; 239 472 1080; www.sanibel-captiva.org

🕗 **Open** 7am–sunset Sat–Thu

💲 **Price** $5 per vehicle; $1 per cyclist or pedestrian

🚶 **Guided tours** For a narrated tour of Wildlife Drive, hop aboard the refuge tram (239 472 1351). The Sealife Nature Tour at Tarpon Bay Recreation Area (www.tarponbay explorers.com), located south of the refuge, includes a touch tank presentation.

👫 **Age range** 3 plus

🖊 **Activities** Download activity and coloring books from the website. For information on Junior Manager activities, check at the refuge visitor center. At the Tarpon Bay Recreation Area, kayak, nature and sea life, and sunset boat tours take visitors into the area's preserved rookeries, or along a mangrove estuary trail.

⏱ **Allow** At least half a day

🍴 **Eat and drink** SNACKS Lazy Flamingo (6520-C Pine Ave, 33957; 239 472 5353; www.lazy flamingo.com) offers reasonably priced sandwiches and seafood. **REAL MEAL** Doc Ford's Sanibel (975 Rabbit Rd, 33957; 239 472 8311; www.docfordssanibel.com) tempts with family favorites such as fish fingers and beach bread.

Picnic under $25; Snacks $25–50; Real meal $50–80; Family treat over $80 (based on a family of four)

⑤ Corkscrew Swamp Sanctuary

A big bird's nest and age-old trees

Some 20 miles (32 km) inland lies a whole different brand of water wonderland – the swamp. The Corkscrew Swamp Sanctuary is the regional headquarters of the Great Florida Birding Trail, and here nature-lovers can wander a 2-mile (4-km) boardwalk to explore a rich habitat where alligators, bobcats, black bears, and white-tailed deer cavort. Perhaps the sanctuary's most important creature, however, is the wood stork. These big white-and-black birds come to nest in the 500-year-old bald cypress trees. The towering trees, with their protruding "knees," constitute the species' largest old-growth stand in the country. The wood stork is only one of the 200 or so species that visit the sanctuary – others include wading birds, songbirds, raptors, the tricolored heron, and the fabulous painted bunting.

Black-crowned night heron in the Corkscrew Swamp Sanctuary

Take cover

After exploring the Corkscrew trail, visit the **Blair Audubon Center** *(on site)* and learn about the sanctuary's ecology. Kids will love the Swamp Theater, which re-creates a day in the swamp with sound and light, and the cool nature store.

⑥ Naples

A little Italy, Florida-style

The hardy pioneers who settled south of Florida's west coast compared the area's beaches and waterways to those of Italy, and so they named their settlement Naples-on-the-Gulf. Today, the city's architecture and cuisine have an Italian flavor.

Once a rough-and-tumble Indian trading post, Naples has evolved into a haven for vacationers seeking golf, shopping, and fine dining. The heart of downtown, known as Old Naples, has two fashionable streets – Fifth Avenue South and Third Street South. Most of the town's superb restaurants are located here. Near Third Street South, the Naples Pier stretches into the Gulf of Mexico from the beach's soft white sands.

Northeast of the downtown area, the **Children's Museum of Naples** is located in North Collier Regional Park, also home to the **Sun-n-Fun Lagoon** water park. In the museum, kids can drive a facsimile of the Naples Trolley, climb up to a tree house, walk into a seashell, and chill out in an igloo.

With the Everglades at its back door, Naples sees plenty of wildlife. However, the easiest way to spot animals – local and from as far away as Madagascar – is to head to **Naples Zoo**. Special animal shows, giraffe hand-feeding, and a boat excursion to Primate Island add adventure to a visit.

The Lowdown

🌐 **Map reference** 9 D1

📍 **Address** 375 Sanctuary Rd, 34120; 239 348 9151; *corkscrew.audubon.org*

🚗 **Car** Rent a car from Fort Myers.

ℹ️ **Visitor information** Greater Naples Marco Everglades Convention & Visitors Bureau, 2660 N Horseshoe Blvd, 34104; *www.paradisecoast.com*

🕐 **Open** 7am–5:30pm daily (last adm 1 hour before closing)

💲 **Price** $36; under 6s free

👫 **Cutting the line** Call ahead to see if any school or youth groups will be visiting that day.

🔫 **Guided tours** The education staff leads tours early morning, at sunset, and at night in season. Check website for dates and timings.

👫 **Age range** 5 plus

⏱️ **Allow** 2 hours

🍽️ **Eat and drink** PICNIC Publix *(12900 Trade Way Four, Bonita Springs, 34135; 239 992 2159; www.publix.com)* sells a range of salads, sandwiches, and drinks. There is a picnic area across the parking lot.

The Lowdown

🌐 **Map reference** 9 C1

📍 **Address** Children's Museum of Naples: 15080 Livingston Rd, 34109; *www.cmon.org*. Sun-n-Fun Lagoon: 15000 Livingston Rd, 34109; *www.napleswaterpark.com*. Naples Zoo: 1590 Goodlette-Frank Rd, 34102; *www.napleszoo.com*

🚗 **Car** Rent a car from Fort Myers.

ℹ️ **Visitor information** Greater Naples Marco Everglades Convention & Visitors Bureau, 2660 N Horseshoe Blvd, 34104; 800 688 3600; *www.paradisecoast.com*

🕐 **Open** Children's Museum of Naples: 10am–5pm Mon, Tue & Thu–Sat, 11am–4pm Sun. Sun-n-Fun Lagoon: hours vary, check website for timings. Naples Zoo: 9am–5pm daily

💲 **Prices** Children's Museum of Naples: $40; under 1s free. Sun-n-Fun Lagoon: $38–52; under 4s free. Naples Zoo: $70–80; under 3s free

🔫 **Guided tours** The Naples Trolley *(www.naplestrolleytours.com)* runs tours of the town from Old Naples north to Vanderbilt Beach.

⏱️ **Allow** A day

🍽️ **Eat and drink** SNACKS Aurelio's Is Pizza *(590 N Tamiami Trail, 34102; 239 403 8882; www.aureliosofnaples.com)* offers tasty pizza, pasta, and sandwiches. REAL MEAL Dock at Crayton Cove *(845 12th Ave S, 34102; 239 263 9940; www.dockcraytoncove.com)* is an old fishhouse-style place on the water with a kids' menu.

Ring-tailed lemur, one of the many animals that can be seen at Naples Zoo

Letting off steam

Head north of Naples to **Delnor-Wiggins Pass State Park** *(11135 Gulf Shore Dr N, 34108; 239 597 6196; www.floridastateparks.org/delnor-wiggins)* on Vanderbilt Beach.

Vanderbilt Beach, a popular white-sand beach in Naples

Families can soak up the sun, climb the observation tower, fish in the pass, kayak, and, in summer, follow a ranger on a sea turtle walk.

⑦ Marco Island
Indians, fishermen, and one cool cat

The jumping-off point for Ten Thousand Islands, a maze of protected islands to the south, Marco Island prides itself on its fishing and boating. Rent or charter a boat from one of the island's marinas and get out on the water. At its east end, the fishing town of Goodland retains the salty character of old-time fishing communities.

The Calusa Indians fished these waters for 1,500 years, until they were wiped out by European invaders. They built one center of their kingdom on Marco Island, as revealed by archaeological excavations in 1895. One important find, a carved wood effigy known as the Key Marco Cat, now resides in the Smithsonian Institution in Washington D.C. Families can drive over the top of one 58-ft (18-m) ancient shell mound and follow trails along another at the **Otter Mound Preserve**.

Two public beach accesses welcome visitors to Marco's wide beaches. **Tigertail Beach** has playgrounds and a sheltered lagoon that draws lots of birds, especially in winter.

Take cover
Go to the **Marco Island Historical Museum** (180 S Heathwood Dr, 34145; 239 642 1440; www.themihs. org), which was built to look like a

Calusa Indian village on the outside. The museum has displays that tell the local history. Replicas of the Key Marco Cat can be seen and purchased in the museum's store.

The Lowdown

🌐 **Map reference** 9 D2
Address Otter Mound Preserve: 1831 Addison Ct, 34145; 239 252 2961; www.colliercountyfl. gov. Tigertail Beach: 430 Hernando Dr, 34145; 239 252 4000; www.collierparks.com

🚗 **Car** Rent a car from Naples.

ℹ **Visitor information** Greater Naples Marco Everglades Convention & Visitors Bureau, 2660 N Horseshoe Blvd, 34104; www.paradisecoast.com

🕙 **Open** Otter Mound Preserve: daily. Tigertail Beach: 8am–sunset

💲 **Price** Otter Mound Preserve: free

🚻 **Cutting the line** Arrive early as Tigertail Beach's parking lot fills quickly in season, and on weekends.

🚩 **Guided tours** Check the website of the Conservancy of Southwest Florida (www.conservancy.org) for tours.

👫 **Age range** All ages

🕐 **Allow** A day

🥤 **Eat and drink** SNACKS Tigertail Beach Cafe (490 Hernando Dr, 34145; 239 389 8414; www. tigertailbeach.net) has casual window service with burgers, hot dogs, fish and chips. There is outdoor seating at picnic tables with umbrella shades.
REAL MEAL Snook Inn (1215 Bald Eagle Dr, 34145; 239 394 3313; www.snookinn.com) overlooks the Marco River outside, under a thatched tiki roof; inside an aquarium and salad bar dominate. The menu offers seafood and meat dishes.

⑧ Everglades National Park
Florida's land down under

Displaced Native Americans and outlaws were among the first to settle in this forbidding land riddled with swamps at the very bottom of Florida. Later came slick developers who wanted to drain the precious wetland in favor of building. Luckily, Marjory Douglas Stoneman stepped up in the 1940s to make sure that this special territory would forever be protected as the Everglades National Park. Today, the park safeguards 2,200 sq miles (3,540 sq km), and more than 1,000 species of fish, birds, reptiles, amphibians, and mammals.

View from the observation tower

Key Sights

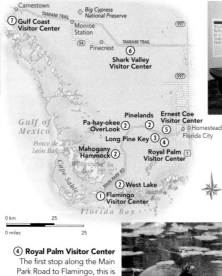

① **Flamingo Visitor Center** See the exhibits and pick up maps for exploring trails and waterways. Clean up efforts after Hurricane Irma are ongoing. The center also has a campground on Florida Bay.

② **Trails along the drive to Flamingo** The 38-mile (60-km) Main Park Road passes four major trailheads for short hikes: Pinelands Trail, Pa-hay-okee Overlook, Mahogany Hammock Trail, and West Lake.

③ **Long Pine Key** Arguably the prettiest spot in the Everglades, this area's forest of pine trees is perfect for picnicking, or an overnight stay in the well-kept campground.

④ **Royal Palm Visitor Center** The first stop along the Main Park Road to Flamingo, this is one of the best places to spot wildlife. The popular Anhinga and Gumbo Limbo trails begin here.

⑤ **Ernest Coe Visitor Center/ Main Entrance** This center lies outside the park gates and its interactive exhibits make a good introduction to the park.

⑥ **Shark Valley Entrance/ Visitor Center** Hike, bike, or take the tram tour from here around the 15-mile (24-km) loop trail. Climb the observation tower for fine views.

⑦ **Gulf Coast Entrance/ Visitor Center** A temporary station stands here after the storm in 2017 at this west coast gateway in the historic fishing town of Everglades City.

Letting off steam
Head to the **Historic Homestead Town Hall Museum** (41 N Krome Ave, Homestead, 33030; 305 242 4463), which contains a captivating selection of historical films and photos about the Everglades. There is also an American La France fire truck from 1925.

Eat and drink
Picnic: under $25; Snacks: $25–50; Real meal: $50–80; Family treat: over $80 (based on a family of four)

PICNIC Robert Is Here Fruit Stand (19200 SW 344th St, Homestead, 33034; 305 246 1592; www.robert here fruit stand.com)

Prices given are for a family of four

ishere.com) offers fruit smoothies and snacks. Picnic in the grounds near the free petting farm and splash pool.
SNACKS Buttonwood Café (Flamingo Visitor Center; 239 695 3101; tinyurl.com/7d5bjne)

Fresh produce for sale at the Robert Is Here Fruit Stand, Homestead

operates in the winter–spring season. It has hot dogs, burgers, steaks, and a kids' menu. It also cooks guests' fish catches for a nominal charge.
REAL MEAL Island Cafe (305 Collier Ave, Everglades City, 34139; 239 695 0003) with its mounted animals and crazy memorabilia keeps all the families entertained. The service is impeccable and their fried gator or frog legs are a must try.
FAMILY TREAT Capri Restaurant (935 N Krome Ave, Florida City, 33034; 305 247 1542; www.dine capri.com) offers a menu that covers everything from sandwiches and entrée salads to pizza and pasta.

The Lowdown

🌐 **Map reference** 9 F4
Address Flamingo Visitor Center: 38 miles (61 km) past entrance on Main Park Rd; 239 695 2945. Royal Palm Visitor Center: 2 miles (3 km) past entrance on Royal Palm Rd; 305 242 7237. Ernest Coe Visitor Center: 40001 State Rd 9336, Homestead, 33034; 305 242 7700. Shark Valley Visitor Center: 36000 SW 8th St, Miami, 33194; 305 221 8776. Gulf Coast Visitor Center: 815 Oyster Bar Lane, Everglades City, 34139; 239 695 3311

🚗 **Car** Rent a car from Homestead for the Main Entrance; Miami airport for Shark Valley Entrance; and Naples airport for the Gulf Coast Entrance.

🕐 **Open** Everglades National Park & trails: daily. Flamingo Visitor Center: mid-Nov–mid-Apr: 8am–4:30pm daily; all day in summer. Royal Palm Visitor Center: 8am–4:15pm daily. Ernest Coe Visitor Center: mid-Apr–mid-Dec: 9am–5pm daily; rest of the year 8am–5pm daily. Shark Valley Visitor Center: 9am–5pm daily. Gulf Coast Visitor Center: mid-Nov–mid-Apr: 8am–4:30pm daily (from 9am rest of the year)

💲 **Prices** Everglades National Park (Ernest Coe & Shark Valley Entrance): $25 per

vehicle; $8 per pedestrian or cyclist, under 17s free; no fee at Gulf Coast Entrance

👫 **Cutting the line** The Everglades' two seasons are dry (winter) and wet (summer). Low risk of flooding and fewer mosquitoes make winter the most popular time to visit. Be sure to carry bug repellent, especially in the wet season.

🚌 **Guided tours** Go for a 2-hour tram tour at Shark Valley (www. sharkvalleytramtours.com). Boat tours depart from the Flamingo marina and Gulf Coast entrance; Check website for tours, call for schedule and prices.

👫 **Age range** 6 plus

🧒 **Activities** Download the Junior Ranger Book at www.nps.gov/ever/forkids/beajuniorranger.htm, or ask for it at the visitor centers.

⏱ **Allow** At least 2 days

☕ **Café** Buttonwood Café in the Flamingo Visitor Center (see p242)

🚻 **Restrooms** In all visitor centers and campgrounds

Good family value?
The Everglades offers year-round outdoor fun, with amazing wildlife to see and great trails to explore. The prices suit all budgets.

Shopping
Drop in to the **Gift Shop** (at most visitor centers) and support conservation efforts. Choose from rubber snakes, plush birds, wildlife puzzles, books, and T-shirts.

Find out more
DIGITAL Check out the kids' pages on www.nps.gov/ever/forkids/learning-about-the-everglades.htm.

Take cover
The **Museum of the Everglades** (www.colliermuseums.com), in Everglades City, focuses on the huge feat of blazing a road through the swampy Everglades, and on the region's Calusa Indian and fishing heritage.

Next stop...
WILDER WILDERNESS Head 73 miles (117 km) northwest to explore the **Rookery Bay National Estuarine Research Reserve** (www.rookerybay. org), an unspoiled mangrove estuary. The learning center here has a huge aquarium and interactive exhibits about the park's history. The **Ten Thousand Islands National Wildlife Refuge** (www.fws.gov) offers fishing and a chance to observe wildlife.

Mangroves in Rookery Bay National Reserve

KIDS' CORNER

Croc or gator?
How can you tell a crocodile from an alligator? Luckily, you don't have to get too close to distinguish one from the other!
1 The American alligator has dark skin and a wide snout for cracking turtle shells.
2 A croc is lighter in color than a gator, with a narrower, pointier snout and a flatter profile in the water.
3 When a gator closes its mouth, the teeth in its top jaw are the only ones visible. When a croc closes its mouth, you can see its distinctive overbite: the teeth of both jaws are visible.

HOW DO YOU SPELL "EVERGLADES"?
Write out Everglades National Park, leaving spaces between the letters. For each letter in the park's name, think of something you saw or learned about that starts with that letter. Write them down, until you've used up all 22 letters with no repeated words.

Collecting birds
Serious birders keep what they call a life list – a record of every species of bird they have seen in the wilds during their lifetime. The Everglades, with 366 species, is the best place to start your Florida life list.
With the help of a ranger, see how many birds you can spot. Print the Florida bird list at fl.audubon.org/PDFs/birds_checklist.pdf, and check off all the birds you saw.

⑨ Biscayne National Park

Water, water, everywhere

This vast, mostly underwater refuge encompasses the third-longest stretch of coral reef in the world. Geographically, the park kicks off the Florida Keys, and, for outdoor enthusiasts, it has it all – boating, kayaking, snorkeling, scuba diving, hiking, camping, and also a slice of history dating back to the Tequesta Indians. However, it takes some effort to enjoy what's best about the park, namely what's under and out on the water. Biscayne's two main islands – Boca Chita and Elliott Key – are accessible only by boat, but worth the trip to learn about some quirky elements of local history, hike trails, go fishing, and camp overnight.

Take cover

Overlooking the marina at Biscayne National Park, the **Dante Fascell Visitor Center** (*9700 SW 328th St, Homestead, 33033; 305 230 1144; www.nps.gov/bisc*) houses artistic exhibits representing the park's

Palmetto dolls and beadwork for sale in the Miccosukee Indian Village

different maritime habitats. In the auditorium, rotating exhibits show the Biscayne-related art of local painters.

⑩ Miccosukee Indian Village

Going native

The Miccosukee Indian tribe has lived at the edge of the Everglades on a narrow strip of land since the Seminole Wars chased them from their homeland, Tallahassee, in the 1800s. Today, visitors can experience their way of life and learn about their beliefs at this village. Guided and self-guided tours of the superb museum and its grounds explore the history of the Miccosukee and their thatched huts, or *chickee*, with elevated floors. Members of the tribe give daring alligator presentations and demonstrate native crafts all day.

Letting off steam

Hop aboard an airboat tour from the Miccosukee Village to visit a Native American clan camp. A former tribal chief takes visitors out on a cultural experience with **Buffalo Tiger's Airboat Tours** (*www.buffalotigers airboattours.com*).

⑪ Big Cypress National Preserve

Bald cypresses, furry critters, and feathered friends

The US government legislated the creation of Big Cypress to put an end to logging operations that were depleting the forest of its tall, beautiful, bald cypress trees. The preserve provides a number of options for adventure enthusiasts. Begin at the **Oasis Visitor Center** or **Big Cypress Swamp Welcome Center**. The Oasis' boardwalk is a great place to see gators swimming down below. Walk the boardwalk at the Big Cypress and listen to the manatees blow as they surface for a breath of air. Pick up a map at either center and rent a kayak

Young visitors at the Big Cypress Swamp Welcome Center

The Lowdown

🌐 **Map reference** 10 H3
📍 **Address** 9700 SW 328th St, Homestead, 33033

🚗 **Car** Rent a car from Homestead. The park provides boats to the main islands (305 230 1100).

ℹ️ **Visitor information** Tropical Everglades Visitor Center, 160 US Hwy 1, Florida City, 33034; 305 245 9180; www.tropical everglades.com

🕐 **Open** Visitor center: 9am–5pm daily (Nov–Apr: 10am–5pm daily); grounds: 7am–5:30pm daily

💲 **Price** Free

🚩 **Guided tours** The park conducts snorkeling, scuba, and glass-bottom boat tours Jan–Apr. Rangers run programs during the same season.

👫 **Age range** 5 plus

🏃 **Activities** Pick up a Junior Ranger activity booklet at the visitor center.

⏱️ **Allow** 1–2 days

🍴 **Eat and drink** PICNIC The visitor center (on site; 305 230 1100) sells cold sandwiches, snacks, and beverages. REAL MEAL Cracker Barrel Old Country Store (155 N. Krome City, Florida City, 33034; 305 248 2033; www.crackerbarrel. com) an American chain serving an array of country dishes.

The Lowdown

🌐 **Map reference** 10 F3
📍 **Address** MM 70, Tamiami Trail, Miami, 33194; 1 877 242 6464; www.miccosukee.com/ indian-village

🚗 **Car** Rent a car from Miami airport.

ℹ️ **Visitor information** Tropical Everglades Visitor Center, 160 US 1, Florida City, 33034; 305 245 9180; www.tropicaleverglades.com

🕐 **Open** 9am–5pm daily

💲 **Price** $36–48; under 6s free

🚩 **Guided tours** Museum and airboat tours run all day.

👫 **Age range** 5 plus

⏱️ **Allow** Half a day

🍴 **Eat and drink** SNACKS Everglades Gator Park (24050 SW 8th St, Miami 33194; 305 559 2255; www.gatorpark.com) offers local delicacies such as gator tail, gator sausage, and catfish sandwiches. REAL MEAL Empeeke AAweeke (on site; 305 894 2374) serves frog legs, pumpkin bread, and other Native American dishes, as well as burgers and salads.

The Lowdown

🌐 **Map reference** 10 E2
Address Ochopee 34141.
Big Cypress National Preserve:
33100 Tamiami Trail E; 239 695
2000; www.nps.gov/bicy. Big
Cypress Swamp Welcome Center:
33000 Tamiami Trail E; 239 695
4758. Oasis Visitor Center: 52105
Tamiami Trail E; 239 695 1201

🚗 **Car** Rent a car from Naples.

ℹ️ **Visitor information** Greater
Naples Marco Everglades
Convention & Visitors Bureau,
2800 N Horseshoe Blvd, Naples,
34104; 239 252 2384; www.
paradisecoast.com

🕐 **Open** Oasis Visitor Center & Big
Cypress Swamp Welcome Center:
9am–4:30pm daily

💲 **Price** Free

🚩 **Guided tours** Free ranger-led
tours in winter and spring.

👫 **Age range** 6 plus

👪 **Activities** Ask for a Junior Ranger
activity booklet at either center.

⏱️ **Allow** Half a day to a full day

🍴 **Eat and drink** SNACKS Coopertown
(22700 SW 8th St, Miami; 305 226
6048; www.coopertownairboats.
com) sells sandwiches and frog
legs. REAL MEAL Joanie's Blue Crab
Café (39395 Hwy 41, 34141; 239
695 2682; joaniesbluecrabcafe.
com) serves Everglades cuisine.

Bald cypress trees in Fakahatchee
Strand State Preserve

(www.wootenseverglades.com),
6 miles (9 km) to the northeast, where
a gator pond and animal exhibits,
as well as shows, supplement tours.

Take cover
Across a causeway from Everglades
City, Chokoloskee Island is home
to the **Historic Smallwood Store
& Museum** (www.smallwoodstore.
com), an old Indian trading post on
the bay that still holds some vintage
products and historic exhibits.

The Lowdown

🌐 **Map reference** 10 E2
Address Fakahatchee Strand
State Preserve: 137 Coastline Dr,
Copeland, 34137; www.florida
stateparks.org. Collier-Seminole
State Park: 20200 Tamiami Trail E,
Naples, 34114; www.floridastate
parks.org. Wooten's Airboat Tours:
32330 Tamiami Trail E, Ochopee,
34141; wootensairboats.com

🚗 **Car** Rent a car from Miami airport.

ℹ️ **Visitor information** Visitors
Bureau, 2800 N Horseshoe Blvd,
Naples, 34104; 239 252 2384;
www.paradisecoast.com

🕐 **Open** Fakahatchee Strand State
Preserve, Collier-Seminole Park
& Wooten's Airboat Tours: daily

💲 **Price** Fakahatchee Preserve: $3 per
vehicle, $2 per pedestrian. Collier-
Seminole Park: $5 per vehicle

🚩 **Guided tours** Seasonal tours at
Fakahatchee and Collier-Seminole.

🍴 **Eat and drink** SNACKS City Seafood
(702 Begonia St, Everglades City,
34139; 239 695 4700) serves half
portions for kids. REAL MEAL The
Rod & Gun Club (200 Riverside
Dr, Everglades City, 34139; 239
695 2101) has fried gator. Try
the chocolate peanut butter pie.

in Everglades City to paddle trails, or
hike on part of the statewide Florida
Trail. In the dry season, following one
of the scenic drives is a good idea.

Take cover
Visit the **Big Cypress Swamp
Welcome Center** to learn about
Florida's wildlife and watersheds,
using games and hands-on devices.

⑫ Everglades City
Gateway to the Gulf Coast

Located at the western entrance to
the Everglades National Park, this
sleepy little town offers opportunities
for fishing, kayaking, and airboat
rides. Nearby, there are attractions
that introduce families to the
Everglades' unique plant and animal
life. The **Fakahatchee Strand State
Preserve**, 5 miles (8 km) north of
town, is known for its wild orchids.
Located 15 miles (24 km) to the
northwest, the **Collier-Seminole
State Park** is the place for biking,
hiking, and camping. From here,
head for **Wooten's Airboat Tours**

⑬ Key West

Pirates, shipwrecks, and treasure

Ever seen a six-toed cat or a man riding a bike with an iguana on his shoulder? Both sights are likely in Key West, the most popular destination in the Florida Keys. The Old Town, the city's downtown core, is known for its party vibe. Nonetheless, a wealth of attractions and a history dating back to 19th-century pirates makes it a huge draw for families. It lies at the end of a necklace of keys (small islands) where wildlife encounters, beaches, parks, and watersports fill mellow days.

Entrance to Mallory Square

Key Sights

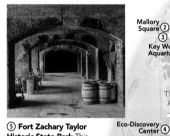

① **Historic Seaport at Key West Bight** This restored neighborhood and its Harborwalk form the earthy heart of Old Town, filled with activity, shopping, dining, and watersports charters.

② **Mallory Square** Celebrate sunset every night at this cruise ship dock, with musicians and magicians, and conch fritter and margarita vendors.

③ **Key West Aquarium** Built in 1934, this was the world's first open-air aquarium, though it is now mostly enclosed. Take a tour to watch the guides feed sharks, stingrays, and sea turtles.

④ **Eco-Discovery Center** This attraction shows off the Keys' natural treasures – their valuable coral reef and ecosystems. Kids will like the walk-through model of an underwater ocean lab.

⑤ **Fort Zachary Taylor Historic State Park** This Civil War-era fort sits on prime beachfront. Follow a fort tour with a dip and a nature hike.

⑥ **Key West Lighthouse Museum** Climb the 88 steps to the top of the 92-ft (28-m) tower built here in 1844, for fine views. Go to the adjacent lighthouse-keeper's home, where historic exhibits tell the story of the keepers.

⑦ **Ernest Hemingway Home and Museum** Find about 50 six-toed cats snoozing around this house, where famous novelist Ernest Hemingway lived and wrote from 1931 to 1942.

⑧ **Key West Butterfly and Nature Conservatory** Walk into a glass bubble that encases more than 40 species of butterflies, plus birds, waterfalls, and lush vegetation. The gift shop is also a must-visit.

The Lowdown

🌐 **Map reference** 9 D6
Address Key West 33040.
Historic Seaport at Key West Bight: off Front St; www.keywest seaport.com. Mallory Square: 40 Wall St; www.mallorysquare.com. Key West Aquarium: 1 Whitehead St; www.keywestaquarium.com. Eco-Discovery Center: 35 E Quay Rd; floridakeys.noaa.gov/eco_ discovery.html. Fort Zachary Taylor Historic State Park: 601 Howard English Way; www. floridastateparks.org/fort taylor. Ernest Hemingway Home and Museum: 907 Whitehead St;

www.hemingwayhome.com. Key West Lighthouse Museum: 938 Whitehead St; www.kwahs.org. Key West Butterfly and Nature Conservatory: 1316 Duval St; www.keywestbutterfly.com

🚗 **Bus** From Marathon (www.kw transit.com). **Car** Park at 300 Grinnell St, and take a hop-on hop-off trolley tour. **Ferry** From Fort Myers (seakeywestexpress.com)

ℹ **Visitor information** Greater Key West Chamber of Commerce, 510 Greene St, 33040; 305 294 2587; www.keywestchamber.org

🕑 **Open** Most sights are open daily; check websites for timings.

💲 **Prices** Key West Aquarium: $50–64. Eco-Discovery Center: free. Fort Zachary Taylor Historic State Park: $6 per vehicle, $2 per pedestrian. Ernest Hemingway Home and Museum: $38–52; cash only. Key West Lighthouse Museum: $30–40. Key West Butterfly and Nature Conservatory: $41–8. Most sights are free for under 6s.

👥 **Cutting the line** The sights are busiest during the spring break,

Posing for photos at the marker denoting the Southernmost Point

Letting off steam

After visiting the Hemingway Home and the lighthouse across the street, walk to the **Southernmost Point** *(South St, 33040)*. Taking photos at the US's most southerly mainland spot is *de rigueur*. While grown-ups read the historic markers, kids can run along the waterfront plaza.

Eat and drink

Picnic: under $25; Snacks: $25–50; Real meal: $50–80; Family treat: over $80 (based on a family of four)

PICNIC Cuban Coffee Queen *(5 Key Lime Square, 33040; 305 294 7787; www.cubancoffeequeen.com)* offers breakfast sandwiches and smoothies, popular among the locals. The grown-ups can enjoy excellent Cuban coffee.
SNACKS B.O.'s Fish Wagon *(801 Caroline St, 33040; 305 294 9272; www.bosfishwagon.com)* serves up a true taste of Key West in a funky setting at the Historic Seaport. Grouper sandwiches with Key lime sauce are the specialty.

Fantasy Fest (Oct), and when cruise ships are in port.

🍴 **Guided tours** Check *www.conch train.com* and *www.cityview trolleys.com* for details.

👫 **Age range** 5 plus

⏲ **Allow** 3–5 days

👫 **Restrooms** In most sights

Good family value?
Online discounts make Key West's sights affordable. At the beaches, the only charge is for parking.

REAL MEAL Croissants de France *(816 Duval St, 33040; 305 294 2624; www.croissants defrance.com)* offers baked goodies and sweet and savory crêpes. The less adventurous can order a *croque monsieur* (grilled ham and cheese sandwich).
FAMILY TREAT Latitudes *(245 Front St, 33040; 305 292 5394; www.sunsetkeycottages.com)* serves fish tacos, burgers, and other kid-pleasers. Its outdoor dining room overlooks the Gulf of Mexico. A meal here means taking the free ferry ride to Sunset Key to reach the restaurant.

Shopping

Walk along Duval Street, in the Old Town, where merchandise ranges from tacky T-shirts to fine art glass. **Cayo Hueso y Habana** *(410 Wall St, Mallory Square, 33040; 305 293 7260)* is part-museum part-mall, with souvenirs such as rooster mementos and hand-rolled cigars.

Seaplanes on the beach at Dry Tortugas National Park

Next stop...

DRY TORTUGAS NATIONAL PARK
Board the *Yankee Freedom II* fast ferry *(www.drytortugas.com)* for a day trip to the Dry Tortugas National Park *(www.nps.gov/drto)*, located 68 miles (109 km) west of Key West. The Dry Tortugas comprise seven reef islands, of which Garden Key is the most visited. The islands are a treat for bird-watchers, especially between March and October. Besides awesome coral reefs, families can explore the 19th-century **Fort Jefferson** *(www.fortjefferson.com)*, the largest brick fortification in the US.

⑭ Big Pine Key

Home of the Key deer

Just over the bridge from downtown Key West, there is a distinct change of pace as the Overseas Highway takes visitors to a slower, more relaxed part of Florida.

Look out for Mile Markers, the small green rectangular signs that mark the miles and give directions in the Keys. Around about MM 32, signs caution drivers to slow down to protect the endangered Key deer population of Big Pine Key. The best place to spot these undersized deer, fewer than 800 of which remain, is the **National Key Deer Refuge** at No Name Key. While in the refuge, visit the Blue Hole, an old quarry filled with water that is home to one resident alligator, as well as other wildlife, and then hike the easy trails.

Big Pine Key is also known for fishing and kayaking. Paddling trails lead into refuge waters that look like a maze of mangrove islands. Follow a tour to avoid getting lost.

The Lowdown

- 🌐 **Map reference** 10 E6
  Address National Key Deer Refuge: 179 Key Deer Blvd, 33043; 305 872 0774; www.fws. gov/nationalkeydeer
- 🚌 **Bus** Key West Transit (www.kw transit.com) runs buses from Key West to Marathon daily.
- ℹ️ **Visitor information** Lower Keys Chamber of Commerce, 31020 Overseas Hwy (MM 31), Big Pine Key, 33043; 800 872 3210; www.lowerkeyschamber.com
- 🕐 **Open** National Key Deer Refuge: sunrise–sunset daily
- 💲 **Price** National Key Deer Refuge: free
- 🚩 **Guided tours** Guided walks take place Dec–Mar. Visitors can even download a bird list from the website. Big Pine Key Kayaking Adventures (www.keyskayaktours. com) takes tours into the refuge.
- 🚻 **Age range** 5 plus
- ⏱️ **Allow** Half a day for the refuge, a full day if kayaking
- 🍴 **Eat and drink** SNACKS No Name Pub (N. Watson Blvd, 33043; 305 872 9115; www.nonamepub.com) has a full menu of favorites, including pizza. REAL MEAL Hogfish Bar & Grill (6810 Front St, Stock Island, 33040; 305 293 4041; www.hogfishbar.com) offers fresh seafood. Try the hog snapper.

Take cover
Head for the small **visitor center** at the **National Key Deer Refuge**, located within the Big Pine Key Shopping Plaza. It has indoor displays that help visitors discover the local habitat and wildlife.

An alligator in the Blue Hole, a flooded limestone quarry in Big Pine Key

⑮ Bahia Honda State Park

Great beaches and a really long bridge

Often seen on America's best beaches lists, Bahia Honda's white sands, turquoise waters, multihued coral reefs, and well-stocked marina make it great for families. Swimming and snorkeling are the most popular activities, but the marina also rents kayaks. It is possible to explore the offshore reef on a snorkeling cruise that the marina offers twice a day. Rangers lead hikes and host talks year-round; consider hiking the beautiful Silver Palm Nature Trail.

At the south end of Bahia Honda an abandoned railroad bridge can be seen. This railroad bridge is now disused but was considered an engineering marvel when it was completed in 1912 and is listed on the National Register of Historic Places. It runs parallel to the famous Seven Mile Bridge that is a few miles north of Bahia Honda and it is possible to walk or bike and fish from some portions of the bridge near Marathon.

Take cover
The park's **Sand and Sea Nature Center** introduces visitors to local sea life, with exhibits as well as an aquarium. Learn about the park's six different habitats, play games, watch one of 30 nature videos, and guess what is in the Mystery Boxes.

The Lowdown

- 🌐 **Map reference** 10 E6
  Address 36850 Overseas Hwy (MM 37), 33043; 305 872 2353; www.bahiahondapark.com
- 🚌 **Bus** Key West Transit runs buses from Key West to the park's entrance daily.
- ℹ️ **Visitor information** Lower Keys Chamber of Commerce, 31020 Overseas Highway (MM 31), Big Pine Key, 33043; 800 872 3210; www.lowerkeyschamber.com
- 🕐 **Open** 8am–sunset daily
- 💲 **Price** $8 per vehicle, $2 per pedestrian
- 🚻 **Cutting the line** Arrive early in spring and summer, to avoid long lines at the park entrance.
- 🚻 **Age range** 2 plus
- 🚶 **Activities** Ranger-led Beach Walks at 9am on Wednesdays
- ⏱️ **Allow** At least half a day
- 🍴 **Eat and drink** SNACKS The park concession stand (305 872 3210) sells hot dogs, sandwiches, and nachos. REAL MEAL Head south to Big Pine Key or north to Marathon for restaurants.

Old Bahia Honda Bridge, seen at sunset from Bahia Honda State Park

Prices given are for a family of four

The Dolphin Research Center, Grassy Key, home to both dolphins and sea lions

⑯ Marathon

Dolphins and pirates

Outside of Key West, the town of Marathon, set on 13 islands, holds most of the Keys' historic and natural attractions.

An important type of Keys sea life can be seen on the mend at the aptly named **Turtle Hospital**. In summer, the possibility of seeing sea turtle hatchlings adds further excitement for children, in addition to visiting and feeding the mammoth adults.

Another site, **Crane Point** combines nature and history in extensive waterfront woods. There is a natural history museum, a pirate dress-up ship for kids, the Wild Bird Center, a historic home, and nature trails here.

The town of Marathon was named for the breakneck speed at which the railroad was built. Below the Seven-Mile Bridge, **Pigeon Key** was once home to the construction workers. Visitors can board a ferry *(305 743 5999)* at Marathon's southern end to tour the old village and its fascinating railroad museum.

The preserved village of Pigeon Key beside the Seven-Mile Bridge

Letting off steam

Head south to **Sombrero Beach** *(2150 Sombrero Beach Rd, MM 50; 305 743 0033)*, which offers plenty of room to play, as well as barbecue grills, picnic tables, and a playground.

The Lowdown

🌐 **Map reference** 10 E6
Address Marathon 33050. Dolphin Research Center: 58901 Overseas Hwy (MM 59); *www.dolphins.org*. Dolphin Connection: 61 Hawks Cay Blvd (MM 61) at Hawks Cay Resort; *www.dolphinconnection.com*. Turtle Hospital: 2396 Overseas Hwy (MM 48.5); *www.turtlehospital.org*. Crane Point: 5550 Overseas Hwy (MM 50.5); *www.cranepoint.net*. Pigeon Key: 1 Knights Key Blvd (MM 45); *www.pigeonkey.net*

🚌 **Bus** Key West Transit runs buses from Key West to Marathon daily.

ℹ️ **Visitor information** Greater Marathon Chamber of Commerce, 12222 Overseas Hwy (MM 53.5); *www.floridakeysmarathon.com*

🕙 **Open** Dolphin Research Center: 9:30am–4pm daily. Dolphin Connection: call 1 888 251 3674 to reserve. Turtle Hospital: 9am–6pm daily (educational center). Crane Point: 9am–5pm Mon–Sat, noon–5pm Sun. Pigeon Key: 9:30am–4pm daily

💲 **Prices** Dolphin Research Center: $102–112; under 4s free. Dolphin Connection: prices differ with programs; check website. Turtle Hospital: $66–88; under 4s free. Crane Point: $46–52; under 5s free

👫 **Age range** 4 plus

⏱️ **Allow** At least a day

🍴 **Eat and drink** SNACKS Herbie's *(6350 Overseas Hwy MM 50.5; 305 743 6373)* serves seafood and cheeseburgers. REAL MEAL Keys Fisheries Market *(3502 Gulfview Ave, 33050; www.keysfisheries.com)* has fresh seafood.

Picnic under $25; **Snacks** $25–50; **Real meal** $50–80; **Family treat** over $80 (based on a family of four)

Kayak Shack at Robbie's Marina selling a variety of merchandise, Islamorada

(17) Islamorada

Fighting fish, hungry tarpon, and the tree of life

Known as the sport-fishing capital of the world, Islamorada is a 20-mile (32-km) strip of seven separate islands. A good place to start exploring Islamorada's rich sea world is **Robbie's Marina**, located at the southern end of the chain of keys. Buy a bucket of bait to feed the powerful tarpon at the dock, shop the crafts booths, and sign up for a boat ride to the **Indian Key State Park** and **Lignumvitae Key Botanical State Park**. Alternatively, rent a kayak from Robbie's Marina and paddle out to Indian Key State Park. Be sure to bring along snorkeling equipment.

Visit the **History of Diving Museum** to discover more about underwater exploration. The museum has exhibits on sunken treasure, the filming of *20,000 Leagues Under the Sea*, and early diving gear.

Letting off steam

For young kids who are not yet comfortable swimming in the sea, the pool at **Founder's Park** *(87000 Overseas Hwy, MM 87)* is a good option. The park also has a beach, a skate park, and a tennis court.

(18) Key Largo

Underwater capital of the world

One of the most popular destinations for snorkeling in the world, Key Largo is famous for its namesake movie *Key Largo* (1948) starring Humphrey Bogart , although no actual filming took place here. Today you can see the original steamboat that starred in *The African Queen* (1952) at the marina, next to the Holiday Inn at MM 100 – it does cruise tours. There is also a glass-bottom boat here, the *Key Largo Princess* (*www.keylargo princess.com*), which offers tours of the region's legendary coral reefs.

Created in 1990, the **Florida Keys National Marine Sanctuary** protects 2,900 sq nautical miles (9,947 sq km) of waters surrounding the Florida Keys and more than 6,000 marine species. Just step into the water to reach the sanctuary, or explore the colorful world of coral and fish by snorkeling or scuba diving. Charters also take visitors under water to see the submerged 9-ft (3-m) statue, *Christ of the Deep*. Alternatively, the dolphin encounter operation in Key Largo, **Dolphins Plus**, offers educational and interactive programs, as well as sea lion swims.

The Lowdown

- 🌐 **Map reference** 10 G5
  Address Key Largo 33037. Florida Keys National Marine Sanctuary: *floridakeys.noaa.gov*. Dolphins Plus: Oceanside, 31 Corrine Pl (MM 99), 33037; *1 866 860 7946; www. dolphinsplus.com*

- 🚗 **Car** Rent a car from Key West or Miami.

- ℹ️ **Visitor information** Key Largo Chamber of Commerce, 106000 Overseas Hwy (MM 106); *305 451 1414; www.keylargochamber.org*

- 🕐 **Open** Dolphins Plus: reserve ahead. Florida Keys National Marine Sanctuary: 24 hours daily

- 💲 **Prices** Florida Keys National Marine Sanctuary: free. Dolphins Plus: $79–210 per swimmer

- 👫 **Age range** 5 plus

- ⏱️ **Allow** A day

- 🍴 **Eat and drink** SNACKS Mrs. Mac's Kitchen (*99336 Overseas Hwy, MM 99.4; 305 451 3722; www. mrsmacskitchen.com*) offers comfort food, all-you-can-eat specials and beverages. **REAL MEAL** Fish House (*102401 Overseas Hwy, MM 102.4; 305 451 4665; www.fishhouse. com*) serves fresh seafood in a classic Keys setting and has a kids' menu.

The Lowdown

- 🌐 **Map reference** 10 G5
  Address Islamorada 33036. Robbie's Marina: 77522 Overseas Hwy (MM 77.5); *www.robbies.com*. Indian Key State Park: 77200 Overseas Hwy; *www.floridastateparks. org*. Lignumvitae Key Botanical State Park: *www.floridastate parks.org*. History of Diving Museum: 82990 Overseas Hwy (MM 83); *www.diving museum.org*.

- 🚗 **Car** Rent a car from Key West.

- ℹ️ **Visitor information** Islamorada Chamber of Commerce (MM 83.2); *www.islamoradachamber.com*

- 🕐 **Open** Robbie's Marina & Lignumvitae Key Botanical State Park: 9am–5pm Thu–Mon. Indian Key State Park: 8am–sunset daily. History of Diving Museum: 10am–5pm daily. Theater of the Sea: 10am–5pm daily

- 💲 **Prices** Indian Key or Lignumvitae Botanical State Park: $10. History of Diving Museum: $30–36; under 5s free. Theater of the Sea: $95–118; under 3s free

- 🚣 **Guided tours** Florida Keys Kayak (*www.kayakthefloridakeys.com*) offers a 2-hour kayak back-country tour and sunset tour.

- 👫 **Age range** 7 plus for kayaking and diving

- ⏱️ **Allow** A day

- 🍴 **Eat and drink** SNACKS Hungry Tarpon (*77522 Overseas Hwy, MM 77.5; 305 664 0535; hungrytarpon.com*) has pancakes, sandwiches, and a kids' menu. **REAL MEAL** Morada Bay Beach Café (*81600 Overseas Hwy, MM 81; moradabay.com*) offers full meals.

Prices given are for a family of four

Colorful corals in Key Largo, with the Christ of the Deep in the background

Take cover

If inclement weather threatens, head to **Shellworld** *(97600 Overseas Hwy MM 101.9; 305 852 8245)*, for merchandise such as specimen shells, plush toys, and Key Lime products.

⑲ John Pennekamp Coral Reef State Park

Nature meets history

The first undersea park in the US, the John Pennekamp Coral Reef State Park is located close to the Florida Keys National Marine Sanctuary. The visitor center has a massive reef aquarium, and the park's concessions provide diving, snorkeling, and glass-bottom boat excursions, and rent out equipment. Snorkelers off Cannon Beach can see the ruins of a Spanish ship just 100 ft (30 m) from shore. Families can rent kayaks, canoes, and powerboats, or hike the short trails and then picnic at one of the two beaches in the park. Pretty,

palm-fringed Far Beach is ideal for a relaxing day spent sunbathing or splashing around in the water.

Take cover

Besides the 30,000-gallon (113,562-liter) aquarium, the park's visitor center houses six other aquaria that display the local sea fauna. Listen to rangers at the center explain how they are re-growing damaged coral. The center's theater screens videos about the park, and natural history exhibits interpret the different habitats of corals.

The Lowdown

🌐 **Map reference** 10 G4

Address Overseas Hwy (MM 102.5); *www.florida stateparks.org*

🚗 **Car** Rent a car from Key West or Miami.

ℹ️ **Visitor information** Key Largo Chamber of Commerce, 106000 Overseas Hwy (MM 106); *305 451 1414; www.keylargochamber.org*

🕐 **Open** Park: 8am–sunset. Visitor Center: 8am–5pm

💲 **Price** $8 per vehicle, $2 per pedestrian

👥 **Cutting the line** Arrive early in the day to avoid long queues.

🎯 **Guided tours** The 2½-hour snorkeling tours start at 9am, 10:30am, noon, 1:30pm & 3pm daily; equipment rental extra. The 2½-hour glass-bottom boat tours begin at 9:15am, 12:15pm & 3:15pm daily.

👫 **Age range** All ages

⏱️ **Allow** Half a day to a full day

🍴 **Eat and drink** SNACKS A food counter and snack bar *(on site)* serves breakfast and lunch. REAL MEAL Sundowners *(103900 Overseas Hwy; MM 104; 305 451 4502; sundownerskeylargo.com)* serves fresh seafood, salads, sandwiches, steaks, and beverages.

Far Beach, a scenic strip of sand in John Pennekamp Coral Reef State Park

Picnic under $25; **Snacks** $25–50; **Real meal** $50–80; **Family treat** over $80 (based on a family of four)

Where to Stay in the Lower Gulf Coast, Everglades, and Keys

From waterfront campgrounds and chain hotels to vacation homes and grand resorts, this region has it all. While Key West is renowned for its B&Bs, camping is part of the Everglades experience. For exploring the Everglades and the Keys, staying at a chain hotel in Homestead or Florida City is the best option.

AGENCIES
Island Visitors Center
www.sanibel-captiva.org
This agency lists a variety of vacation rentals for visitors, such as condos, cottages, and luxury homes.

Rent Key West
www.rentkeywest.com
This website offers weekly and monthly rentals, from historic downtown bungalows to waterside homes with their own pool.

A bedroom at Port of the Islands Everglades Adventure Resort

Everglades National Park
Map 10 F3
SELF-CATERING
Port of the Islands Everglades Adventure Resort
25000 Tamiami Trail E, Naples, 34114; 239 394 3005; poiresort.com
Located near the Gulf Coast entrance to the Everglades National Park, this pleasant place packages adventure excursions with lodgings. It is the resort nearest to the national park.
꩜ ꕤ P ✪ $$

CAMPING
Big Cypress National Preserve Campgrounds
Tamiami Trail; 239 695 1201; www.nps.gov/bicy
These four free, quite basic campgrounds, and two fee-paying parks with RV lodging,

are located off the Tamiami Trail. The campgrounds have no showers or restrooms, and sites are available on a first-come, first-served basis. Some sites are inaccessible in summer due to flooding.
꩜ P $

Flamingo Campground
Flamingo; 305 242 7700 (park) and 877 444 6777 (reservations); www.nps.gov/ever
This campground sits on the shores of Florida Bay, and more than 60 of the sites offer great bay views. Most of the sites are drive-in, but some are walk-in. Close to the marina, the campground affords easy access to paddlecraft rentals and boating tours.
☕ ✪ $

Fort Myers
Map 7 C5
RESORT
Sanibel Harbour Marriott
17260 Harbour Pointe Dr, 33908; 239 466 4000; www.marriott.com
An award-winning destination resort just east of the Sanibel Causeway, this is known for its full complement of facilities and kids' programs. Choose from rooms and one-bedroom suites. Families can also book boating excursions. A shuttle bus takes guests to Sanibel Island.
꩜ IOI P ✪ $$$

Fort Myers Beach
Map 7 C6
RESORT
Outrigger Beach Resort
6200 Estero Blvd, 33931; 239 463 3131 or 800 657 5659; www.outriggerfmb.com
At the southern end of the island, this resort offers a peaceful respite from the party atmosphere around the rest of Fort Myers Beach. It

offers simple accommodations with an old Florida feel. Some of the rooms come with kitchens. The wide stretch of white sands, a lively pool deck, and a tiki bar area add to the family-holiday air.
꩜ IOI P ✪ ✿ $$

Key Largo
Map 10 G5
RESORT
Hilton Key Largo Resort
97000 Overseas Hwy (MM 97), 33037; 305 852 5553 or 888 871 3437; www.keylargoresort.com
With its lovely private beach, 12.5 acres (5 ha) of tropical hardwoods, and two pools, this full-service resort is good for families. It feels safer than some of the other resorts because it is set back from the main road.
꩜ ⚇ IOI P ✪ $$$

CAMPING
John Pennekamp Coral Reef State Park
Map 10 G4
102601 Overseas Hwy (MM 102.5), 33037; 305 451 1202 (park); www.floridastateparks.org/pennekamp
RV and tent sites are tucked into this park's shady grounds, out of the way of day visitors. A variety of activities sure to keep the kids happily occupied are available here, with beaches

An RV parked at John Pennekamp Coral Reef State Park

and glass-bottom boat tours, plus woods to explore. Call well in advance for reservations.

🎣 🌙 P 🛶   **$**

Key West
Map 9 D6

RESORTS
Hyatt Key West Resort
601 Front St, 33040; 305 809 1234; keywest.centric.hyatt.com
Near the Historic Seaport, the Hyatt has its own small beach, lots of options for watersports, and a spa. Close enough to all the action in the Old Town, yet away from its noise and crowds.

🐟 🍴 P ⊘   **$$$**

Ocean Key Resort
Zero Duval St, 33040; 305 296 7701, 800 328 9815; www.oceankey.com
Families who love being in the thick of the action will enjoy this full-service resort's location next to Mallory Square. Enjoy hanging out at its pool and Sunset Deck restaurant. Ask for a suite with a sleeper sofa or adjoining rooms.

🍴 🛎 🅱 P ⊘   **$$$**

BED & BREAKFAST
Ambrosia Key West
615, 618, 622 Fleming St, 33040; 305 985 1078; www. ambrosiakeywest.com
One of the few B&Bs in Key West that welcome kids, this one spreads down a city block with rooms, town houses, suites, and a cottage. Some pets are also allowed.

🎣 🐟 P ⊘   **$$$**

Island City House Hotel
411 William St, 33040; 305 294 5702; www.islandcityhouse.com
Another family-friendly B&B, this property's suites occupy a former cigar factory complex. There are resident cats for the kids to play with.

🎣 🐟 P ⊘   **$$$**

Marathon/Big Pine Key
Map 10 E6

RESORTS
Gulf View Waterfront Resort
58743 Overseas Hwy (MM 58.5), Marathon, 33050; 305 289 1414 or 877 289 0111; www.gulfview waterfrontresort.com
Not far from the Dolphin Research Center, this resort offers discount vouchers to the sealife-encounter

The artificial lagoon at Hawks Cay Resort

attraction, and also has its own small menagerie of critters. Rooms are simple, but families will spend most time on the beach, in the pool, or paddling in the Gulf.

🎣 🐟 P ⊘   **$$**

Hawks Cay Resort
Hawks Cay Blvd (MM 61), Duck Key, 33050; 305 743 7000 or 888 395 5539; www.hawkscay.com
Something of its own little village, this resort caters to families with its on-site Dolphin Connection interaction operation, a kids' club with a fun pirate ship-themed pool and games, supervised programs, and watersports concessions at the marina.

🐟 🍴 P ⊘   **$$**

CAMPING
Bahia Honda State Park
36850 Overseas Hwy, Big Pine Key, 33043; 305 872 2353 (park) or 800 326 3521 (reservations); www. floridastateparks.org/bahiahonda
Choose from waterfront cabins or RV and tent campsites close to the most beautiful beaches in the Keys. Guests have access to the park's additional facilities: snorkeling, beaches, nature trails, and educational programs. Reserve well in advance.

🎣 🏕 P 🌙   **$–$$**

Naples
Map 9 C1

HOTEL
Naples Beach Hotel
851 Gulf Shore Blvd N, 34102; 239 261 2222 or 800 237 7600; www.naplesbeachhotel.com
Naples' first hotel, and one of its most popular with families, this place is loaded with family-friendly

features. Kids will love the pool, beach, and Kids' Club; grown-ups will like the fine spa and 18-hole golf course. The hotel offers several dining options, including a pool bar and grill where all gather for sunset.

🐟 🍴 P ⊘ 🌙   **$$$**

Sanibel and Captiva Islands
Map 7 C6

RESORT
South Seas Island Resort
5400 Plantation Rd, Captiva Island, 33924; 239 472 5111 or 800 965 7772; www.southseas.com
One of Florida's first and largest gated destination resorts, this offers accommodations ranging from guestrooms to rental homes. It also has a mini-waterpark, lots of beaches, nine holes of golf, top-rated kids' programs, and a nature center.

🐟 🍴 🛎 ⊘ 🌙   **$$$**

HOTEL
Gulf Breeze Cottages & Motel
1081 Shell Basket Lane, Sanibel Island, 33957; 239 472 1626 or 800 388 2842; www.gbreeze.com
Cozy and family-friendly, this hotel's cottages and duplexes sit right on the beach, and the owners provide beach toys. There is a fairy-tale quality to its gingerbread detailing and lush gardens.

🛎 🏕 P 🌙   **$$$**

Price Guide
The following price ranges are based on one night's accommodation in high season for a family of four, inclusive of service charges and additional taxes.

$ Under $150 **$$** $150–300 **$$$** over $300

An aerial view of Miami's skyscrapers at sunset, seen from the air

Florida
MAPS

Florida Maps

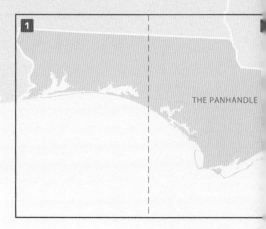

THE PANHANDLE

1

KEY TO MAPS 11–16

▪	Major sight	▭▭	Railroad line
▪	Place of interest	▭▭	Metromover line
▫	Other building	▫	Beach
🚉	Train station		
Ⓜ	Metromover station		
ℹ	Visitor information		
🛝	Playground	**Maps 11–16**	
🚓	Police station	0 km — 2	
⋯	Pedestrian street	0 miles — 2	

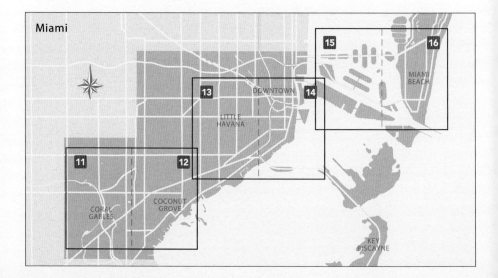

Miami

15 16

MIAMI BEACH

13 DOWNTOWN 14

LITTLE HAVANA

11 12

CORAL GABLES COCONUT GROVE

KEY BISCAYNE

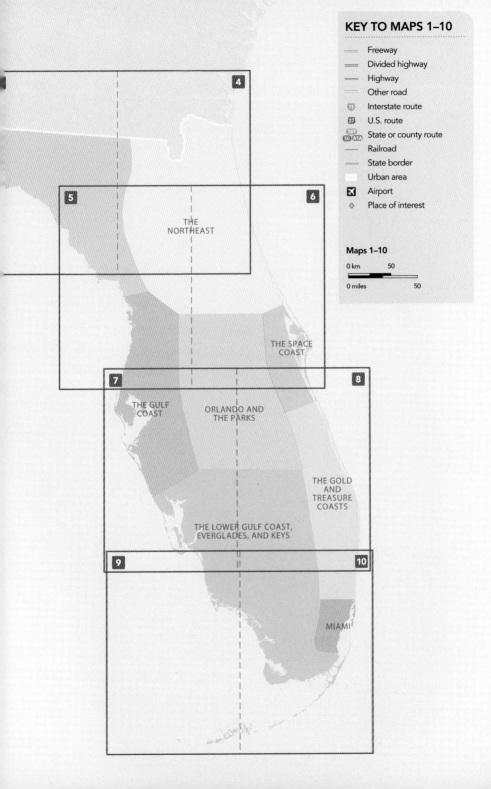

KEY TO MAPS 1–10

	Freeway
	Divided highway
	Highway
	Other road
75	Interstate route
27	U.S. route
589 50 A1A	State or county route
	Railroad
	State border
	Urban area
✈	Airport
◇	Place of interest

Maps 1–10

0 km   50

0 miles   50

4

5   THE
            NORTHEAST   6

THE SPACE
COAST

7   THE GULF   ORLANDO AND
            COAST   THE PARKS   8

THE GOLD
AND
TREASURE
COASTS

THE LOWER GULF COAST,
EVERGLADES, AND KEYS

9   10

MIAMI

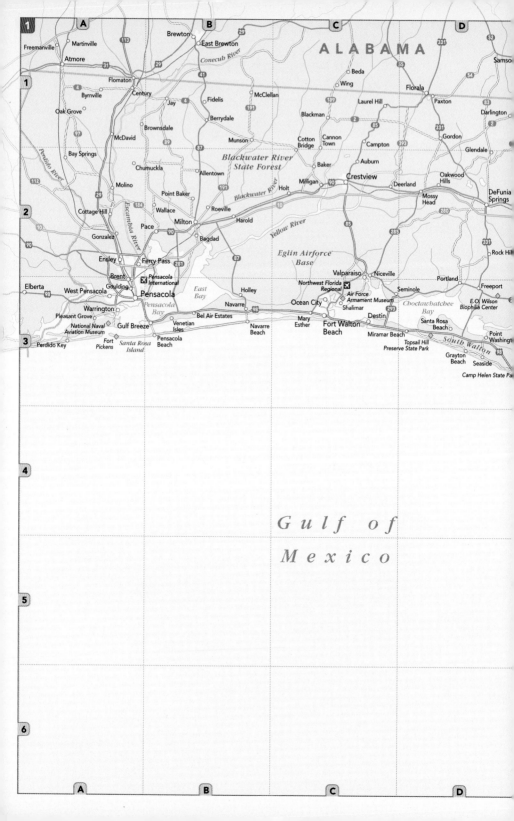

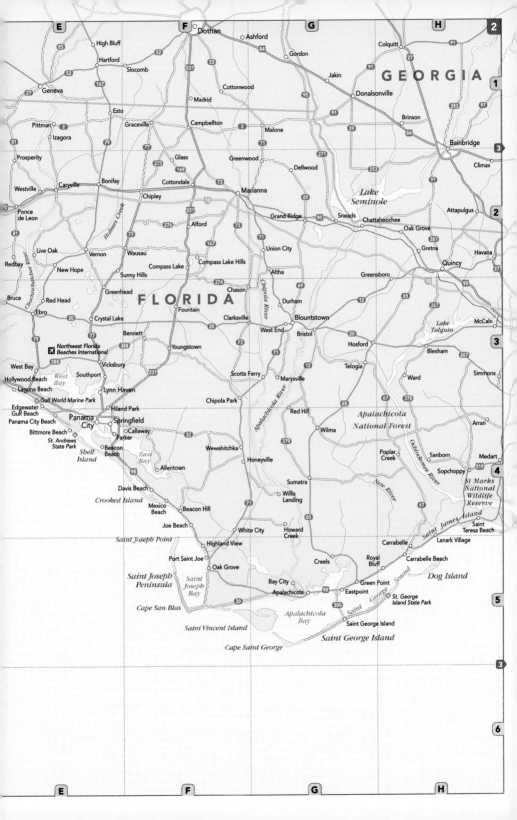

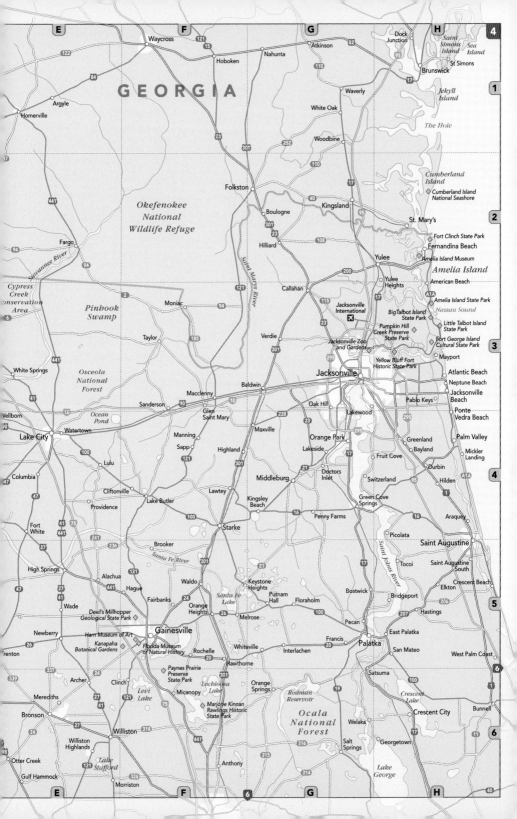

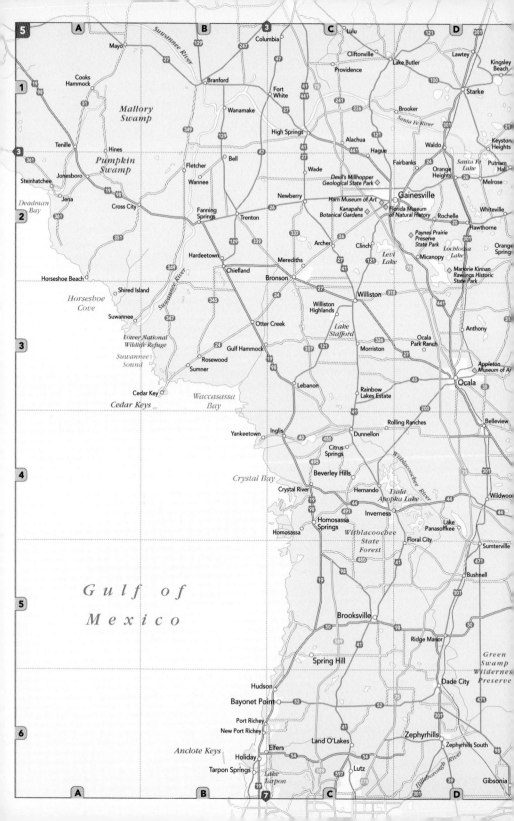

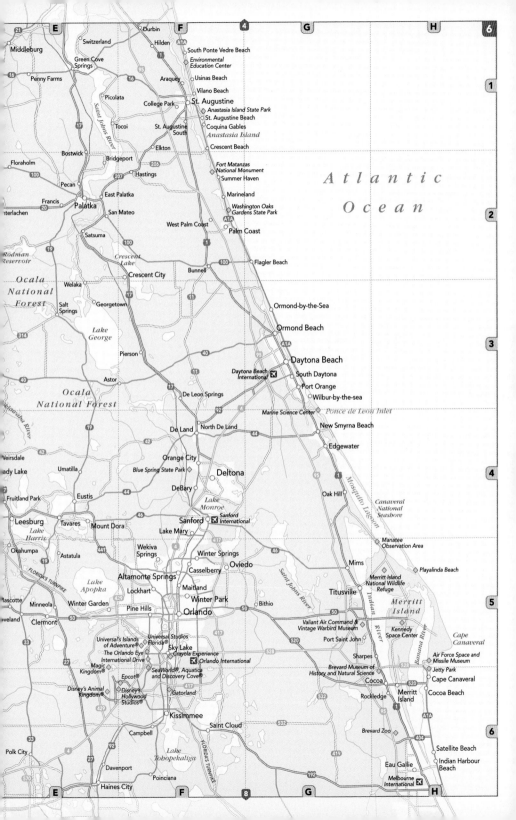

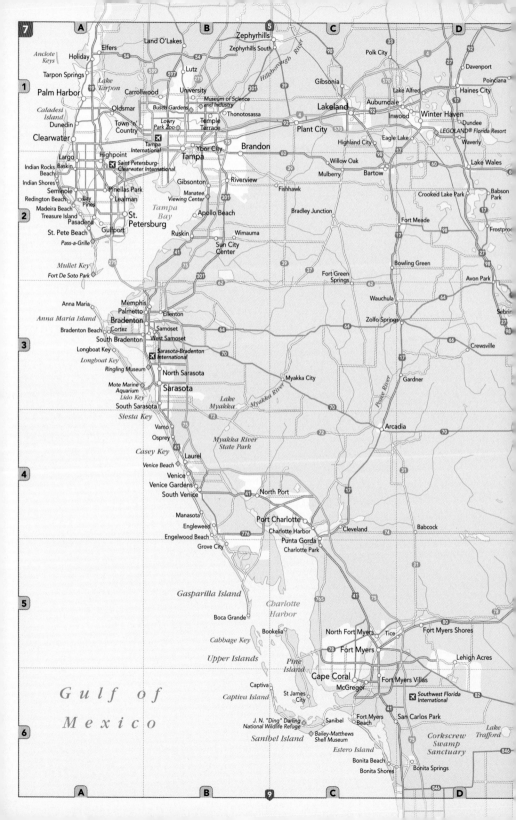

A t l a n t i c

O c e a n

E **F** **6** **G** **H** **8**

Saint Cloud
Lake
Tohopekaliga
Brevard Zoo
Satellite Beach
Indian Harbour Beach
Eau Gallie
Melbourne
International
Melbourne
1
West
Melbourne
Melbourne Beach
Palm Bay

FLORIDA'S TURNPIKE
Micco
Sebastian

Lake
Kissimmee
Fellsmere
Wabasso
2
Lake
Weohyakapka
Blue Cypress
Lake
Gifford
Indian Lake
Estates
Yeehaw
Junction
Vero Beach

Kissimmee River
Lakewood Park
Fort Pierce
Inlet State Park
St Lucie
3
Lake
Istokpoga
Fort Pierce
Fort Pierce South
White City
Hutchinson Island
Lake June
in Winter
Lake Placid
Cypress
Quarters
Port Saint Lucie
Jensen Beach
Lake
Placid
Okeechobee
Stuart
Saint Lucie Inlet
Port Salerno
Hobe Sound
National Wildlife Refuge
4
Brighton Seminole
Indian Reservation
Indiantown
St Lucie Canal
Hobe Sound
Palmdale
Port Mayaca
Jonathan Dickinson
State Park
Jupiter Island
Blowing
Rocks Preserve
Lake
Okeechobee
Jupiter
Juno Beach
North Palm Beach
John D.
MacArthur Beach
State Park
Moore Haven
Pahokee
Palm Beach Gardens
Riviera Beach
Caloosahatchee River
Lake
Hicpochee
Clewiston
West Palm
Beach
Flagler
Museum
5
La Belle
Lion Country
Safari
Palm Beach
International
Palm Beach
Palm Beach Zoo
Belle Glade
Wellington
Palm
Springs
Lake Worth
South Bay
Belle Glade Camp
Lantana
Graham
Sun
Valley
Boynton
Beach
Marsh
Delray Beach
Kings Point
Morikami Museum
and Japanese Gardens
6
Immokalee
Mission Bay
Red Reef Park
Boca del Mar
Boca Raton
Deerfield Beach
Coral Springs

E **F** **10** **G** **H**

Big Cypress Seminole
Indian Reservation

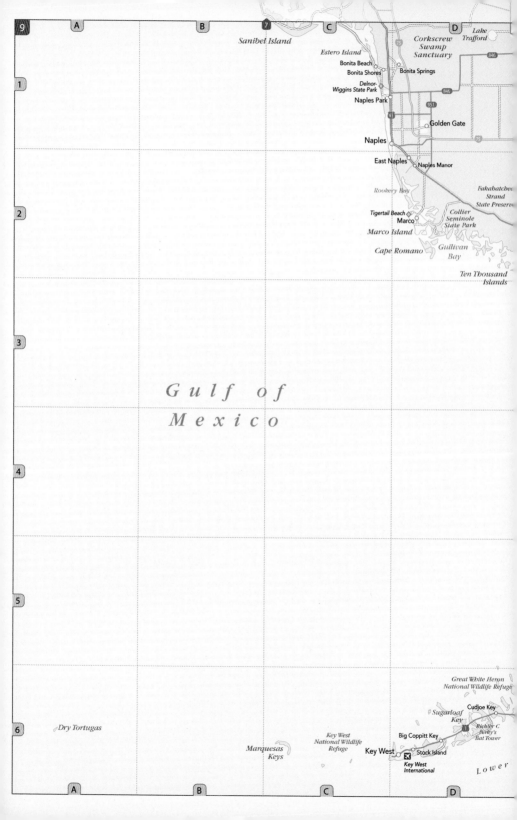

9

A   B   C   D

Sanibel Island

Corkscrew
Swamp
Sanctuary

Lake
Trafford

Estero Island

Bonita Beach
Bonita Shores   Bonita Springs

Delnor-
Wiggins State Park

1

Naples Park

Golden Gate

Naples

East Naples   Naples Manor

*Fakahatchee
Strand
State Preserve*

Rookery Bay

Tigertail Beach   Collier
Marco   Seminole
               State Park
Marco Island

2

Cape Romano   *Gullivan
                Bay*

*Ten Thousand
Islands*

3

G u l f   o f

M e x i c o

4

5

*Great White Heron
National Wildlife Refuge*

*Sugarloaf
Key*   Cudjoe Key

*Richter C.
Perky's
Bat Tower*

Key West
National Wildlife
Refuge   Big Coppitt Key

6   *Dry Tortugas*

*Marquesas
Keys*   Key West   Stock Island

Key West
International   *L o w e r*

A   B   C   D

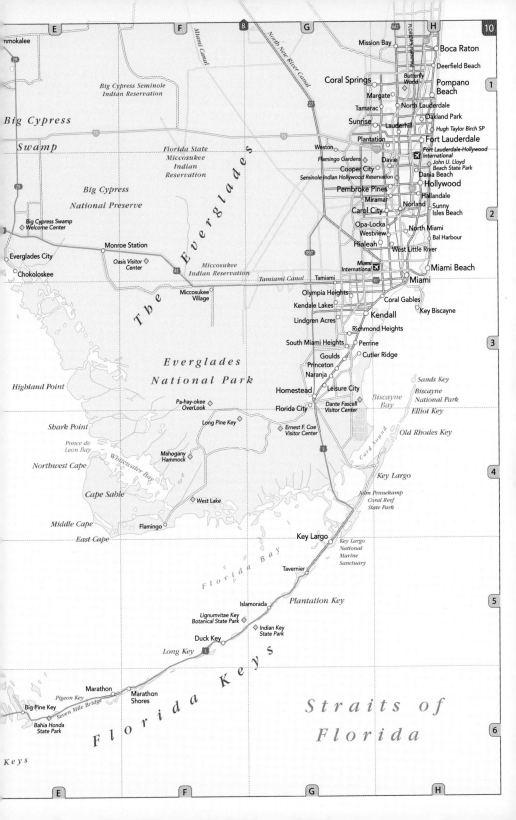

Selected Florida Town Index

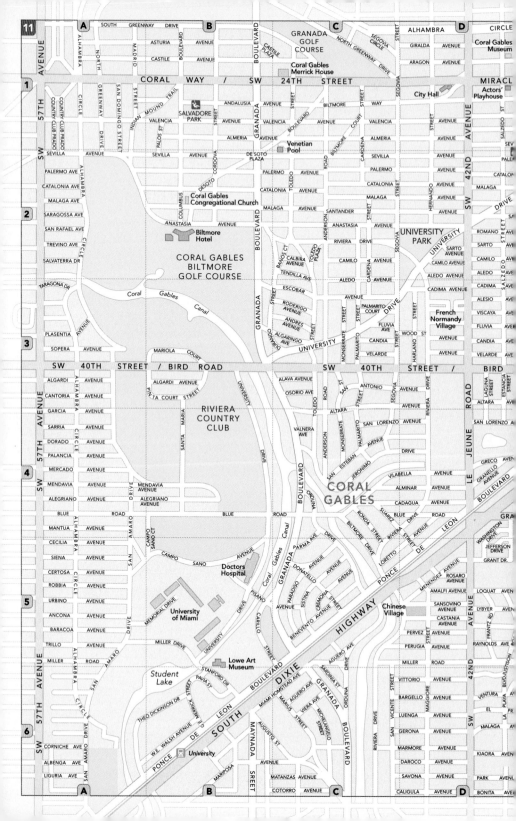

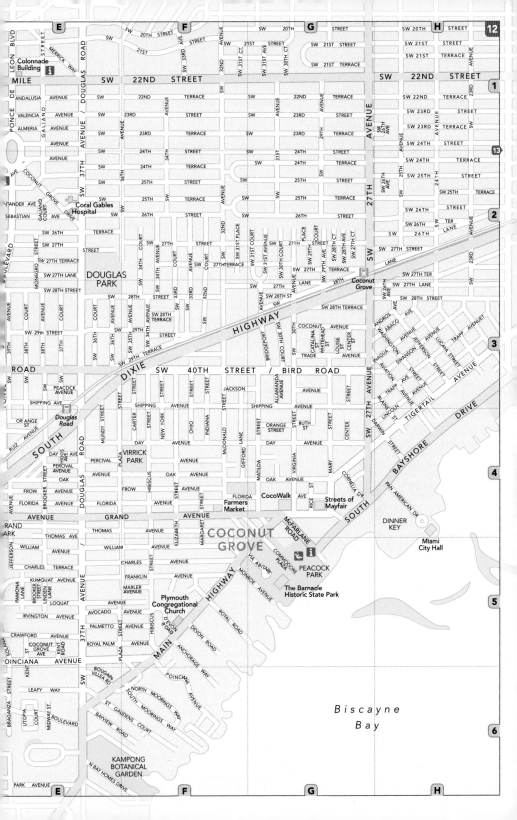

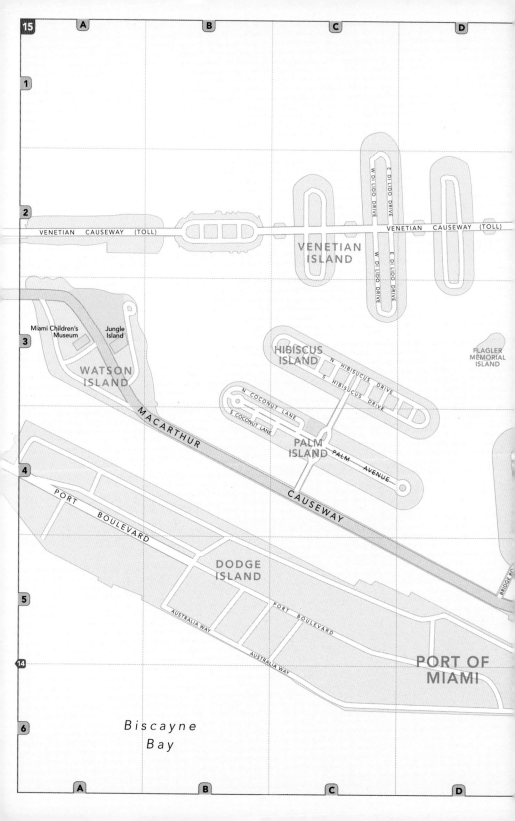

A   B   C   D

1

2

VENETIAN CAUSEWAY (TOLL)   VENETIAN CAUSEWAY (TOLL)

W DI LIDO DRIVE

E DI LIDO DRIVE

VENETIAN
ISLAND

W DI LIDO DRIVE

E DI LIDO DRIVE

3

Miami Children's
Museum

Jungle
Island

WATSON
ISLAND

HIBISCUS
ISLAND

N HIBISUCUS DRIVE

S HIBISUCUS DRIVE

FLAGLER
MEMORIAL
ISLAND

MACARTHUR

N COCONUT LANE

S COCONUT LANE

PALM
ISLAND   PALM   AVENUE

4

PORT   BOULEVARD

CAUSEWAY

DODGE
ISLAND

AUSTRALIA WAY

PORT   BOULEVARD

5

BRIDGE RD

14

PORT OF
MIAMI

AUSTRALIA WAY

6

Biscayne
Bay

A   B   C   D

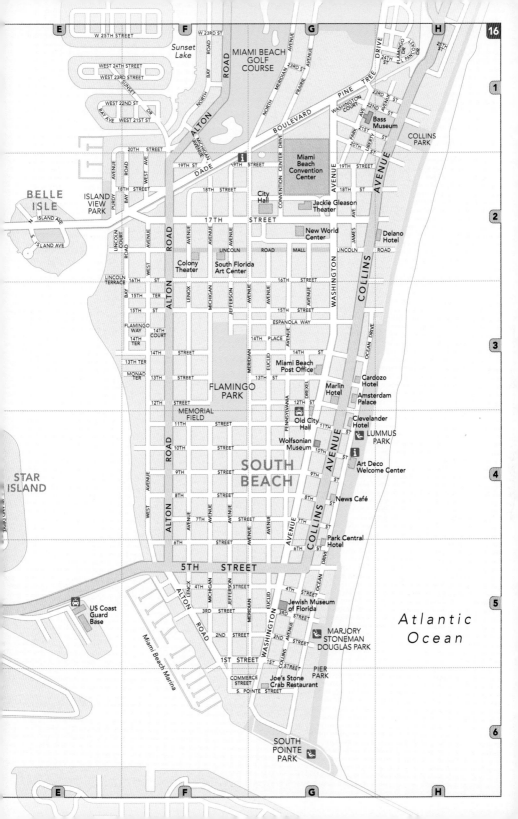

Miami Street Index

Index

Page numbers in **bold** type refer to main entries.

Acknowledgments

Dorling Kindersley would like to thank the following people whose help and assistance contributed to the preparation of this book.

Main Contributors

Eleanor Berman is a widely published writer for magazines and newspapers and the author of 14 travel guides. Her books include two other guides for Dorling Kindersley, *Top 10 New York City* and the *Eyewitness Travel Guide: New York City*, which won a Thomas Cook award for best guidebook. She also contributed to *DK Family Guide: New York City* and *Family Guide: Washington, DC*.

Joseph Hayes moves between New York, Italy, Scotland, and his home in Orlando, while writing about travel, food, and art for print and online publications across the world. He is the restaurant critic for *Orlando Magazine* and has worked with DK Eyewitness Travel since 2003. He is also a playwright and a jazz event producer, whose work has been produced in New York, California, Florida, and the United Kingdom. Hayes worked for many years in the publishing field in New York before moving to central Florida to take up writing as a full-time career.

Stephen Keeling has been traveling to Florida since 1991, and covering the state for various travel guides since 2008. He worked as a financial journalist and editor in Asia for seven years before writing his first travel book. Since then he has written for *The Independent*, *The Daily Telegraph*, and various travel publications. He has authored an award-winning family guide to Tuscany and Umbria, and has researched travel guides to Puerto Rico, New England, Mexico, and Canada. Stephen lives in New York City.

Chelle Koster Walton, a travel writer, has written and contributed to 10 guidebooks – two of which won Lowell Thomas Awards – and articles for magazines such as *FamilyFun*, *Caribbean Travel + Life*, *National Geographic Traveler*, *Arthur Frommer's Budget Travel*, *Endless Vacation*, *The New York Post*, and other print and electronic media. She is the co-founder of *www.guidebookwriters.com* and is a member of the Society of American Travel Writers.

Sharon Weightman Hoffmann is a freelance writer and editor based in Atlantic Beach, Florida. Although her primary work is in journalism and marketing, she also provides emerging authors with a range of "book doctor" services. Her first non-fiction book is a biography of blues musician Blind Blake, forthcoming from Blues Images.

Additional Contributor

Jennifer Greenhill-Taylor

Editorial Consultant

Fay Franklin

Additional Photography

Max Alexander; Dave King; Pearson Education: Gideon Carpenter; Rough Guides: Demetrio Carrasco, Angus Oborn, Anthony Pidgeon; Steven Greaves; Steven Greaves / Dolphin Research Center, Grassy Key, Florida, www.dolphins.org; Stephen Whitehorn; Linda Whitwam; Peter Wilson.

Design and Editorial

PUBLISHER Vivien Antwi

LIST MANAGER Christine Stroyan

SENIOR DESIGN MANAGER Mabel Chan

SENIOR CARTOGRAPHIC EDITOR Casper Morris

SENIOR EDITOR Georgina Palffy

JACKET DESIGN Shahid Mahmood, Nicole Newman, Tracy Smith

ICON DESIGN Claire-Louise Armitt

SENIOR DTP EDITOR Jason Little

PICTURE RESEARCH Ellen Root, Marta Bescos

PRODUCTION CONTROLLER Kerry Howie

READER Debra Wolter

FACT CHECKER Melinda S. Koster

PROOFREADER Lucilla Watson

INDEXER Hilary Bird

Revisions Team

Avanika, Subhadeep Biswas Bharti Karakoti, Shikha Kulkarni, Priyanka Kumar, Rahul Kumar, Gaurav Nagpal, Todd Obolsky, Bandana Paul, Lucy Richards, Christine Stroyan, Avantika Sukhia, Sylvia Tombesi-Walton, Catherine Waring, Ajay Verma, Nikhil Verma

With thanks to Douglas Amrine for his help in developing this series.

Special Assistance

Dorling Kindersley would like to thank the following for their assistance:

Kathy White at The Dalí Museum; David Carson at The Flagler Museum; Julian Ashmore & Martha J. Robinson at Florida Department of Environmental Protection; Kerry Falwell at Glazer Children's Museum; John Kennedy at Kennedy Space Center; Jacqueline Luzunaris at LEGOLAND® Florida Resort; Rene Bell Adams at The

Museum of Arts and Sciences; Kristi Ballinger Taylor at Museum of Science & History; Mark Schaub at Orlando Science Center; Brittany Tollerton Baron at Universal Orlando® Resort; Holly Blount at Vizcaya Museum and Gardens.

Photography Permissions

DORLING KINDERSLEY would like to thank all the museums, galleries, churches and other sights that allowed us to photograph at their establishments:

Actors' Playhouse at the Miracle Theatre; Air Force Armament Museum; Al's Coffee Shop; The Bailey-Matthews Shell Museum; The Barefoot Cafe; The Bass Museum of Art; Busch Gardens Tampa Bay & Adventure Island; Cummer Museum of Art & Gardens; The Florida Museum of Natural History; IGFA Fishing Hall of Fame and Museum; Imaginarium: Science Center; Indian River Citrus Museum; Jacksonville Zoo and Gardens; The John and Mable Ringling Museum of Art; The Lightner Museum; Museum of Science & History; National Naval Aviation Museum; Orlando Science Center; Wet 'n Wild®; Walt Disney World® Resort.

Works of art have been reproduced with the kind permission of the following copyright holders:

Pink Snail © Cracking Art Group 62br; *Daniyyel* © Boaz Vaadia 66br; *Sword Dance* © Kent Ulberg 83cl; *Trial Scene* © 94tr; *Water-Breathing Dragon Fountain* © Patrick McGee 181cl; *The Indian Heritage Tableau* © Cooley artists Bradley Cooley and Bradley Cooley Jr. 186cl; *The Hallucinogenic Toreador* © Salvador Dalí, Fundació Gala-Salvador Dalí, DACS, 2012 220bl; *Uncommon Friends* © D. J. Wilkins 237cl.

Picture Credits

a = above; b = below/bottom; c = centre;
f = far; l = left; r = right; t = top.

The publisher would like to thank the following for their kind permission to reproduce their photographs:

123RF.COM: Michael Ransburg 145tl.

ALAMY IMAGES: AAA Photostock 40cl; Ange 222tl; Jerry Ballard 154-155, 173tc; Ron Buskirk 29bl, 34bl; Chris A Crumley 232cr; Ian Dagnall 125tc; Greg Davis 137tc; Danita Delimont 141cr; Disney Magic 114cla; Findlay 35bl, 124bl; Furlong Photography 23bl; Susan Gottberg 167tl; Jeff Greenberg 26br, 28br, 29br, 32bc, 46cl, 225tl; Eric James 23br; Andre Jenny 227tl; JHP Attractions 211tr; JTB Media Creation, Inc. 1c; Klaus Lang 222cr; Judie Long 168cr; Dennis MacDonald 27br, 171tl; Rod McLean 233t; North Wind Picture Archives 39cl; Michael Patrick O'Neill 77bl; Philipus 27bl; Peter Ravallo 28bl; RosalreneBetancourt 9 83tl; James Schwabel 21bl, 22bl, 173bl; Jack Sullivan 44-5; Tom & Therisa Stack 12br; Frank Tozier 187bl; Gregory Wrona 103t; The

Palm Beach Post / Bill Ingram 20br; Joel Zatz 172bc; Zuma Wire Service 25br; 220bl.

THE BILTMORE HOTEL: 31bc, 72br.

BIRCH PATIO MOTEL: 98c.

THE BREAKERS PALM BEACH: 99bl.

BUSCH GARDENS TAMPA BAY & ADVENTURE ISLAND: 214cb, 215ca.

BUTTERFLY WORLD: 79tr, 85tl.

COASTAL AND AQUATIC MANAGED AREAS: 171cb.

COLUMBIA RESTAURANT: 32bl.

CORBIS: Bettmann 40tr; Stephen Frink 19clb; NewSport / Walter G Arce 17br; Patrick Ward 16bc.

CRAYOLA EXPERIENCE: 125bl.

THE DALÍ MUSEUM, ST. PETERSBURG: Dana Hoff 220tr, 220cl, 220clb, 220cb; Rixon Photography 34br, 221tl.

DORAL GOLF RESORT & SPA MIAMI: 19t.

DORLING KINDERSLEY: Courtesy of Coral Gables Venetian Pool, Florida / Peter Wilson 52clb.

DREAMSTIME.COM: Avion58 / Craig Sims 219bl; Aguina 114crb; Apexgs 251tl; Cheryl Casey 184-5; Christian De Grandmaison 68c; Diver721 198cl; Dominishka 63tc; Drlunatik 213tc; Fotomak 22br; Giovanni Gagliardi 254-255; Geraldmarella 212cra; Giprico9 4br, 126br; Alex Gorodnitchev 212cl; Gynane 25bl; Jcmeyer72 197c; Wangkun Jia 114tr; Lisa Kelly 192bc; Kmiragaya 64cla; Littleny 24bl; Luckynick 240tc; Michael Ludwig 19bl; Heikki Mäkikallio 47br; Gilles Malo 56bc; Nadezda Murmakova 236ca; Mpwood 185cr; Passion4nature 240crb; Sborisov 47t; Typhoonski 68cr; Wilsilver77 195cl, 245tc; Michael Wood 21clb.

FLAGLER MUSEUM: 74-5, 90tr, 90cr, 90crb, 91cl, 91cb.

FLORIDA DEPARTMENT OF ENVIRONMENTAL PROTECTION: 19cla, 30bl, 73c, 97bl, 164clb, 177bl, 183c, 193cl, 199c, 205bl, 209br, 239cl, 243bc, 252br; Thelma Proctor 18cra.

FLORIDA KEYS NEWSROOM: 14-15bc, 15br.

FLORIDA STATE FAIR: 17bl.

FLORIDAYS RESORT ORLANDO: 136bl.

FLYING HIGH CIRCUS: 36br.

FORT DE SOTO PARK: 229tl.

FOTOLIA: se7enimage 42-43.

GETTY IMAGES: Encyclopaedia Britannica / UIG 38cr; John Coletti 141t; Lonely Planet Images / Stephen Saks 194cr; Photographer's Choice / Mitchell Funk 13bl; George Rose 229cr McClatchy-Tribune / Miami Herald 133bl.

GLAZER CHILDREN'S MUSEUM: 208cl, 218cr.
GREATER FORT WALTON BEACH CHAMBER OF COMMERCE: 14bl.
GREYHOUND LINES, INC.: 23bl.

HAWKS CAY RESORT: 30-31bc, 253tr.

HILTON HOTELS & RESORTS: 31br, 182br.

INTERNATIONAL PALMS RESORT: 152tc.

INTERNATIONAL POLO CLUB PALM BEACH: 89cl.

ISTOCKPHOTO.COM: no_limit_pictures 124tr.

JACKSONVILLE ZOO AND GARDENS: 163c, 163bl.

THE JOHNNY ROCKETS GROUP, INC: 33bc.

KATHRYN ABBEY HANNA PARK: 161tl.

KENNEDY SPACE CENTER: 138-139, 140b, 144tr, 144clb, 144crb, 144bc, 145cl, 145c, 145clb, 145bc, 146tr, 146cl, 146cr.

LEGOLAND® FLORIDA RESORT: Chip Litherland 132tr, 133c, 134tl, 134clb; Merlin Entertainments Group 132cl, 132cr, 134cr, 135cr.

LOEWS® DON CESAR HOTEL: 228br.

MASTERFILE: Alberto Biscaro 8-9.

MIAMI CITY BALLET: Alexander Iziliaev 37br.

MID-AMERICA FESTIVALS: 14bc.

MOON UNDER WATER: 221cl.

MORIKAMI MUSEUM AND JAPANESE GARDENS: 87tl.

MURDER MYSTERY DINNER TRAIN: 37bl.

MUSEUM OF ARTS AND SCIENCES: 176tr, 176cl, 176cr, 176crb, 177tl.

NAVAL AVIATION MUSEUM FOUNDATION: 196clb.

OLD SALTY DOG CORP: 32-33bc.

ORLANDO SCIENCE CENTER: Frank Weber 128cl, 128cra; 129cl, 129c.
ORLANDO SHAKESPEARE THEATER: 36bl.

PIZZA AL FRESCO: 88bc.

PORT D'HIVER BED & BREAKFAST: 153bl.

EARL QUENZEL: 16bl.

SAILOR CIRCUS ACADEMY: 227tl.

SANDESTIN GOLF AND BEACH RESORT: 204cl.

SEAWORLD® PARKS & ENTERTAINMENT: 11cra; 122cl, 122cr, 122cra, 123c, 123bl.

SEMINOLE HARD ROCK HOTEL AND CASINO: Costea Photography Inc. 83bc.

SLIDERS SEASIDE GRILL: 164br.

SUNSTREAM HOTELS & RESORTS: 252cl.

SUPERSTOCK: Joe Fox 144cl.

© 2012 UNIVERSAL ORLANDO® RESORT. ALL RIGHTS RESERVED: 118ca, 118c, 119tc, 119c, 120tr, 120cl, 120cra, 120cr, 120bc, 121tl, 121c; Harry Potter characters, names and related indicia are trademarks of and © Warner Bros. Entertainment Inc. Harry Potter Publishing Rights © JKR 118cl.

VIZCAYA MUSEUM AND GARDENS: 60crb, 61c; Bill Sumner 60clb.

WATERSOUNDVACATIONRENTALS.COM: 205tr.

Cover images: Front: 4CORNERS: Reinhard Schmid tr; ALAMY IMAGES: Songquan Deng b; nagelestock.com tl; CORBIS: Annie Griffiths Belt tc; Back: ALAMY IMAGES: Travelshots.com / Peter Phipp tl; DORLING KINDERSLEY: Steven Greaves tc; SUPERSTOCK: F1 ONLINE tr; Spine: DORLING KINDERSLEY: Steven Greaves t.

All other images © Dorling Kindersley.
For further information see: www.dkimages.com.

SPECIAL EDITIONS OF DK TRAVEL GUIDES

DK Travel Guides can be purchased in bulk quantities at discounted prices for use in promotions or as premiums.

We are also able to offer special editions and personalized jackets, corporate imprints, and excerpts from all of our books, tailored specifically to meet your own needs.

To find out more, please contact:
(in the United States) **specialsales@dk.com**

(in the UK) **travelguides@uk.dk.com**

(in Canada) **specialmarkets@dk.com**

(in Australia) **penguincorporatesales@ penguinrandomhouse.com.au**